THE LABELLING OF DEVIANCE

the labelling of deviance

evaluating a perspective

Edited by

Walter R. Gove

Vanderbilt University

SAGE Publications

Halsted Press Division
JOHN WILEY & SONS
New York—London—Sydney—Toronto

Distributed by Halsted Press, a Division of
John Wiley & Sons, Inc., New York

Printed in the United States of America

Library of Congress Cataloging in Publication Data

Vanderbilt Sociology Conference, 3d, Vanderbilt University, 1974.
The labelling of deviance.

1. Deviant Behavior–Congresses. I. Gove, Walter R. II. Title.
HM291.V33 1974 301.6'2 75-14102
ISBN 0-470-31930-5

FIRST PRINTING

CONTENTS

PREFACE

For more than a decade, the labelling perspective has provided the most popular way of explaining stabilized deviant behavior. In spite of its popularity, this perspective has received very little empirical scrutiny. This book (and the conference from which it springs) were planned to fill this basic gap in the literature by making a careful evaluation of the empirical evidence bearing on the perspective in the eight areas of deviant behavior to which the perspective has been most commonly applied. In short, the aim is to give an overall evaluation of the labelling explanation of deviant behavior.

The book starts with an overview of the labelling perspective which reviews the theoretical statements of proponents of the perspective and blocks out the issues to be evaluated. This is followed by chapters evaluating the perspective in the areas of alcoholism, physical disability, mental illness, mental retardation, adult crime, juvenile delinquency, drug use, and sexual deviance. The book concludes with two extended comments by proponents of the labelling perspective, and a brief summation.

–W.R.G.

THE VANDERBILT SERIES OF SOCIOLOGY CONFERENCES

This book presents the proceedings of the third Vanderbilt Sociology Conference, which was held October 28-29, 1974, at Vanderbilt University, Nashville, Tennessee. This conference was made possible by grants to the Department of Sociology and Anthropology of Vanderbilt University from the Shell Foundation and from the National Institute of Mental Health (grant 5-T01-MH08941-10).

The first conference produced *Power in Organizations,* edited by Mayer N. Zald and published by the Vanderbilt University Press in 1970. The second conference produced *Racial Tensions and National Identity,* edited by Ernest Q. Campbell and published by the Vanderbilt University Press in 1972. The fourth conference, entitled "The Production of Culture," is being organized by Richard Peterson and will be held at Vanderbilt University in November 1975.

Chapter 1

THE LABELLING PERSPECTIVE: AN OVERVIEW

WALTER R. GOVE

In 1938, Tannenbaum published a statement that was to become a landmark of what is now known as either the societal reaction or the labelling perspective. Tannenbaum (1938: 19-20) wrote:

> The process of making the criminal is a process of tagging, defining, identifying, segregating, describing, emphasizing, making conscious and self-conscious; it becomes a way of stimulating, suggesting, emphasizing, and evoking the very traits that are complained of.
>
> The person becomes the thing he is described as being. Nor does it seem to matter whether the valuation is made by those who would punish or by those who would reform. In either case the emphasis is upon the conduct that is disapproved of. The parents or the policeman, the older brother or the court, the probation officer or the juvenile institution, insofar as they rest on the thing complained of, rest upon a false ground. Their very enthusiasm defeats their aim. The harder they work to reform the evil, the greater the evil grows under their hands. The persistent suggestion, with whatever good intentions, works mischief, because it leads to bring out the bad behavior it would suppress. The way out is through a refusal to dramatize the evil. The less said about it the better.

The next major development in the labelling perspective is found in Lemert's book *Social Pathology*, published in 1951, which outlined the

AUTHOR'S NOTE: I would like to thank Dan Bednarz, Antonina Gove, Lisa Heinrich, and Donna Wood for their comments on an earlier draft of this paper.

perspective in considerable detail. Probably the next development was Garfinkel's (1956) discussion of status degradation ceremonies. These works were followed in the early sixties by the now classic statements of Becker (1963), Erikson (1962), Goffman (1961), Kitsuse (1962), and Kitsuse and Cicourel (1963). Since then there has been a flood of work expanding, modifying, and restating the perspective (e.g., see Lemert, 1967; Matza, 1969; Scheff, 1966, 1974, 1975; Becker, 1973, Schur, 1969, 1971, 1973, 1974; Prus, 1975; Rubington and Weinberg, 1968; Thorsell and Klemke, 1972; Roman and Trice, 1969, 1971; Trice and Roman, 1970; Orcutt, 1973; Lorber, 1966; Freidson, 1965; Bustamante, 1972; Rotenberg, 1974; Scott, 1972; Gusfield, 1967; Lofland, 1969; Downes and Rock, 1971; Bordua, 1967; Gibbons and Jones, 1971; Horan and Austin, 1974; Hartjen, 1974; Kitsuse, 1972; Quinney, 1970; DeLamater, 1968; Antonio, 1973). Let me start by summarizing the perspective as best I can.

One of the most fundamental distinctions made by the labelling theorists is between primary deviance, which may cause someone to be labelled as a deviant, and secondary deviance, which is the behavior produced by being placed in a deviant role. Regarding primary and secondary deviance, Lemert (1967: 17) says:

> Primary deviation is assumed to arise in a wide variety of social, cultural, and psychological contexts, and at best has only marginal implication for the psychic structure of the individual; it does not lead to symbolic reorganization at the level of self-regarding attitudes and social roles. Secondary deviation is deviant behavior or social roles based upon it, which becomes a means of defense, attack or adaptation to the overt and covert problems created by the societal reaction to primary deviation.

The labelling theorists do not appear to attach significance to an act of primary deviance except insofar as others react toward the commission of the act. To them, deviance is not a quality of an act, but instead is produced in the interaction between a person who commits an act and those who respond to it (Becker, 1963: 14). As Erikson (1962: 11) says:

> Deviance is not a property *inherent in* certain forms of behavior; it is a property *conferred upon* these forms by the audiences which directly or indirectly witness them. The critical variable in the study of deviance, then, is the social audience rather than the individual actor, since it is the audience which eventually determines whether or not any episode of behavior or any class of episodes is labelled deviant.

Similarly Becker (1963: 9) states:

> Social groups create deviance by making rules whose infractions constitute deviance, and by applying those rules to particular people and labelling them as outsiders. From this point of view, deviance is not a quality of the act a person commits, but rather a consequency of the application by others of rules and sanctions to an 'offender'. The deviant is one to whom the label has successfully been applied; deviant behavior is behavior that people so label.

Becker goes on to emphasize the distinction between rule-breaking and deviance, noting that many persons who commit rule-breaking acts do not receive a deviant label, while others who have committed no rule-breaking act may, by mistake, be labelled deviant.

Persons do not usually commit acts that would place them in a deviant status without some reason. Although the societal reaction theorists have not been particularly concerned with explaining acts of primary deviance, they have provided a number of explanations of why a person might commit such acts. (1) A person may belong to a minority group or subculture whose values and ways of behaving may lead to violations of the rules of the dominant group. (2) He or she may have conflicting responsibilities, and the adequate performance of one role may produce violations in a second role. (3) He or she may violate rules for personal gain, usually with the expectation that (s)he won't be caught. (4) He or she may be simply unaware of the rules and violate them unintentionally. Primary deviance is thus attributed to inconsistencies in the social structure, to hedonistic variables, or to ignorance, while psychological characteristics such as personality or psychiatric disorders are ignored.[1]

What concern the societal reaction theorists have with an individual's personal and social attributes is focused on how these attributes affect the way others respond to an act of primary deviance. Thus, they are not concerned with whether a particular societal attribute is related to the likelihood that an individual will commit a deviant act but with whether that societal attribute facilitates or impedes that individual's ability to avoid the imposition of a deviant label. In general, it is their formulation that those on the margin of society, particularly those who have little power and few resources, are those who are least able to resist a deviant label and are therefore most likely to be channeled into a deviant role.

According to this approach, the most crucial step in the development of a stable pattern of deviant behavior is usually the experience of being caught and publicly labelled deviant. Whether or not this happens to a person "depends not so much on what he does as on what other people do" (Becker, 1963:31). Erikson (1962:311), writing about the public labelling process, states:

> The community's decision to bring deviant sanctions against the individual . . . is a sharp rite of transition at once moving him out of his normal position in society and transferring him into a distinctive deviant role. The ceremonies which accomplish this change of status, ordinarily, have three related phases. They provide a formal confrontation between the deviant suspect and representatives of his community (as in the criminal trial or psychiatric case conference); they announce some judgment about the nature of his deviancy (a verdict or diagnosis for example), and they perform an act of social placement, assigning him to a special role (like that of a prisoner or patient) which redefines his position in society.

Erikson (1962: 311) goes on to state: "An important feature of these ceremonies in our culture is that they are almost irreversible."[2] Why might this be the case? According to the labelling theorists, the status of deviant is a master status which overrides all other statuses in determining how others will act toward one (Becker, 1963: 33). Once a person is stigmatized by being labelled a deviant, a self-fulfilling prophecy is initiated, with others perceiving and responding to the person as a deviant (Becker, 1963: 34; Erikson, 1962: 311). Furthermore, once persons are publicly processed as deviants, they are typically forced into a deviant group (often by being placed in an institution). As Becker notes (1963: 38), such groups have one thing in common—their deviance. They have a common fate, they face the same problems and, because of this, they develop a deviant subculture. This subculture combines a perspective on the world with a set of routine activities. According to Becker (1963: 38), "Membership in such a group solidifies a deviant identity" and leads to rationalization of their position.

Once labelling has occurred, it is extremely difficult for the person to break out of the deviant status. As Lemert (1967: 55) states. "Once deviance becomes a way of life, the personal issue often becomes the cost of making a change rather than the higher status to be gained through rehabilitation or reform. Such costs are calculated in terms of the time, energy and distress seen as necessary for change." The deviant has learned to perform deviant activities with a minimum of trouble (Becker, 1963: 39). He or she has already failed in the normal world, suggesting to him- or herself and others an inability to make it even when things are relatively normal; now (s)he faces the world as a stigmatized person. If he or she is in an institution, such as a mental hospital or prison, to become a candidate for reinstatement in society (s)he must, as Lemert (1967: 45) notes, give allegiance to an often anomalous self-conception and view of the world. Denial of the organizational ideology may lead to the judgment that the deviant is "unreformed" or still "sick." Even in the community, the deviant presumably will face an audience which anticipates the worst and which will take steps to protect itself which will make it difficult for a person to succeed. Furthermore, in the community, (s)he may be on a form of probation which forces him or her to live by extremely rigorous rules, the violations of which are grounds for reinstitutionalization.

In summary, the labelling theorists have focused on the societal attributes of those who react and those who are reacted against in order to explain why certain persons and not others are labelled as deviant. They argue that once a person has been labelled a deviant—and particularly if that person has passed through a degradation ceremony and been forced to become a member of a deviant group—the person has experienced a profound and frequently irreversible socialization process. He or she has not only acquired an inferior status, but has also developed a deviant world view and the knowledge and skills that go with it. And perhaps equally important, he or she has developed a deviant self-image based upon the image of him- or herself received through the actions of others.

Since the mid-sixties, the labelling perspective has been the subject of a number of critical evaluations and comments (e.g., Gibbs, 1966, 1972; Lemert, 1972, 1974; Manning, 1973; Warren and Johnson, 1972; Gove, 1970; Hagan, 1972, 1973, 1974; Liazos, 1972; Davis, 1972; Ward, 1971; Fletcher and Reynolds, 1967; Schervish, 1973; Hirschi, 1973; Mankoff, 1971; Thio, 1973; Akers, 1968; Gouldner, 1968). However, with only a few exceptions (particularly Gove, 1970, Hagan, 1972, 1973; Tittle, 1975), these evaluations have not involved a careful sifting of the empirical evidence bearing on the adequacy of the societal reaction formulation. The main purpose of the papers presented in this book is to fill this basic gap in the literature. I anticipate that these evaluations will not only clarify the strengths and weaknesses of the labelling explanation of deviant behavior but will also provide a basis for integrating the labelling perspective with other modes of explanation.

TWO BASIC QUESTIONS

One of the most difficult tasks in attempting to evaluate the empirical support for the labelling perspective is the fact that its proponents have not developed a systematic theory. This is probably due to the fact that the labelling perspective is rooted in the symbolic interaction tradition which has been much more concerned with developing insight and sensitizing concepts than with developing sets of testable propositions. I will attempt to develop some testable propositions from the labelling perspective. The reader, of course, should be aware that these propositions are developed out of my interpretation of the perspective and that not everyone will agree that I have captured the perspective correctly.

Before turning to the propositions, two comments are in order. First, in attempting to evaluate the evidence bearing on the labelling perspective, the issue should not be whether there is *any* evidence supporting the labelling perspective, for I think we can all agree that there is at least some supportive evidence. Similarly, the question should not be whether there is *any* evidence supporting alternative explanations of the behavior in question, for I think we can also agree that there are other processes involved besides those described by the labelling theorists. Instead, the issue should be the importance of the labelling explanation *relative to* other explanations. At the crudest level, then, the issue is which explanation is the most powerful, i.e., which accounts for the most variance. Hopefully, we will be able to move beyond this either/or form of evaluation and specify with more precision the predictive power of the various perspectives and how they interact. We should be aware, however, that although some labelling theorists, such as Scheff (1974: 445), agree that the weighing of the relative importance of the societal reaction explanation vis-à-vis its competitors is an extremely relevant question, this type of quantitative question lies outside the labelling tradition (e.g., see Back, 1975), and it has been held that it is not a particularly appropriate strategy (e.g., Schur, 1971: 155, 1974: 11). It is my position, however, that if a perspective which presumes to explain a particular phenomenon cannot be operationalized and tested, then that perspective does not provide a sociologically valid explanation of that phenomenon.

Second, it is extremely important to understand that the processes described by the labelling theorists have a particular thrust or direction. Thus, the labelling perspective specifies who is likely to be channelled into a deviant role, and this channelling process is viewed in a negative light. As Akers (1968: 463) puts it, "One sometimes gets the impression from reading this literature that people go about minding their own business and then 'wham'—bad society comes along and slaps them with a stigmatized label. Forced into the role of a deviant the individual has little choice but to be deviant."

As indicated by Becker (1963, 1967), Lofland (1969), Lemert (1951: 394-97), Sagarin (1975), Rubington and Weinberg (1971), and Gibbs (1962), the labelling theorists side with the underdog, and they apparently equate the underdog with those on the margin of society who, because of their societal attributes, are ill-equipped to prevent the imposition of a deviant label. Thus, the labelling perspective provides an explanation why those on the margin—for example, the poor and the black—are particularly likely to be labelled deviant. Furthermore, their explanation differs radically from the more traditional sociological explanations (e.g., Merton, 1957), which have attributed the higher rates of deviant behavior among marginal groups to characteristics of the social structure which increase the likelihood that persons in such groups will commit deviant acts.

In evaluating the labelling perspective, we should be aware that virtually all explanations of the development of deviant behavior involve a consideration of contingencies. Thus, the discovery that there are consequences to particular acts is consistent with most explanations and should not, by itself, be used as support for the labelling perspective. To constitute supporting evidence for the labelling perspective, the contingencies in question must work against those on the margin of society, and the imposition of a deviant label must work to promote the development of a deviant career. A finding that those who have the most power and the greatest number of resources were, controlling for level of deviant behavior, more likely to be labelled deviant would not be consistent with the labelling perspective. Similarly, the discovery that, controlling for level of deviant behavior, those who were labelled by society as deviant were, over their lifetimes, less likely to either commit deviant acts or occupy a deviant role would also be evidence against the labelling perspective.[3]

Labelling as a Dependent Variable

In discussing societal reactions, it is useful to distinguish between labelling as a dependent and as an independent variable (e.g., Orcutt, 1973). We will first treat it as a dependent variable, which means we are concerned with explaining why certain people come to be labelled deviant and others do not.

The traditional view is that a person is labelled deviant primarily because he or she either acts in a deviant manner or has characteristics that mark him or her deviant. For example, a person is labelled a criminal because of the commission of criminal acts; he or she is labelled mentally ill because he or she *is* mentally ill and behaves accordingly; or he or she is labelled physically disabled because he or she *has* a physical disability.

The societal reaction view is that a person is labelled as a deviant primarily as a consequence of societal characteristics—particularly, the power or resources of the individual, the social distance between the labeler and the labelee, the tolerance level in the community, and the visibility of the individual's deviant behavior (e.g., Scheff, 1966: 100). The attribute which has received by far the most attention in the literature is the resources and power of the individual, and it is argued that persons with few resources and little power are the ones most likely to have a deviant label imposed upon them. Similarly, it is assumed that the greater the social distance between the labeler and the potential labelee, the greater the likelihood the person will be labelled deviant. However, there is the implicit assumption that this relationship holds only if the potential labelee is of lower status than the labeler, and, in fact, it is assumed that if the status of the potential labelee is higher, that person will have a better-than-average chance of avoiding the deviant label.

If there is a low tolerance level in the community (or sub-community, or group), it is assumed that a person is more likely to be labelled deviant than if there is a high degree of tolerance. The question of tolerance level does not, per se, involve a question of status or power, but given the labelling theorists' explicit focus on the underdog, implicit in their analysis is the premise that the tolerance level for those on the margin of society will be lower than for those who are well integrated into society (e.g., see Roman and Trice, 1971). From a labelling point of view, the question of visibility does not concern itself with the degree of deviant behavior but with the extent a given amount of deviant behavior is visible. Thus they are concerned with whether a person, because of his role, is more likely to be visible and thus more likely to be labelled a deviant. For example, a black man in a white neighborhood may be more visible and more likely to be questioned about a crime than a black man in a black neighborhood. Again there is the implicit assumption that the deviant acts of those on the margin of society are more visible than the acts of those who are well integrated and rewarded by the system.

For some deviant behaviors, it is not clear that the posited relationships hold even when we don't control for other relevant variables. Thus for some forms of deviant behavior it has not been established that persons who are labelled as deviant differ from those who are not labelled on relevant behavioral, personality, and physical characteristics. Similarly, it may not always be clear that power differences, social distance, tolerance levels, and visibility are related to entering a deviant status. Furthermore, even if individual characteristics or societal attributes are related to a deviant label, it needs to be established that they are related in the predicted direction. Once it has been established that the predicted relationships hold, we must turn to the strength of the relationship when other relevant variables are controlled for. Thus we must look at (a) the relationship between the degree of actual individual deviance and the label of deviance, controlling for the relevant societal attributes and (b) the relationship between relevant societal attributes and the label of deviance controlling for the level of actual individual deviance. In Table 1.1, I have presented a fourfold illustration of the relation-

TABLE 1.1
INFORMATION NEEDED TO EVALUATE THE SOCIETAL REACTION AND TRADITIONAL PERSPECTIVES

		Societal Marginality	
		High	Low
Actual Individual Deviance	High	percent labelled deviant Cell 1	percent labelled deviant Cell 2
	Low	percent labelled deviant Cell 3	percent labelled deviant Cell 4

ships that need to be considered. In treating the societal attributes, I have focused exclusively on the marginality of the person, in part because such marginality is relatively easy to measure, but primarily because the degree of marginality both captures the direction of the relationship predicted by the societal reaction theorists and highlights the fact that they are trying to explain why those on the margins of society, the underdogs, have the highest rates of perceived deviance. In looking at the table, we should realize that the degree of actual individual deviance and the degree of social marginality may be conceived of as continuous variables, as occasionally may be the case with a label of deviance.

A few comments on the interpretation of the table may be in order. Let us take five hypothetical cases, beginning with the case where all four cells have relatively comparable rates of labelled deviance. This would provide strong negative evidence for both the societal reaction and traditional perspectives. Second, let us take the case where cells 1 and 2 both have high rates of labelled deviant behavior and cells 3 and 4 have low rates. This would provide strong evidence for the traditional perspective and negative evidence for the labelling perspective. In this case, if cell 1 had a somewhat higher rate than cell 2, it would indicate that, although actual individual deviance is a necessary condition for labelling, among those who are actually deviant, the societal marginality is related to labelling in the manner predicted by the labelling perspective. Conversely, if cell 2 had a higher rate of labelled deviants than cell 1, this would indicate that, although societal attributes do make a difference, the relationship is in the opposite direction from that predicted by labelling theorists. Third, let us take the case where cells 1 and 3 have high rates of labelled deviance, and cells 2 and 4 have low rates. This would provide strong evidence for the labelling perspective and negative evidence for the traditional perspective. In this case, if cell 1 had a somewhat higher rate than cell 3, it would indicate that, although societal marginality was a necessary condition for being labelled a deviant, among the marginals actual deviance did make a difference in who was labelled. Fourth, let us take the case where cell 1 had the high rate of labelled deviants and all the other cells had low rates. This would indicate that both actual individual deviance and societal marginality were necessary for labelling to occur and that neither variable was sufficient. Finally, let us take the case where cell 1 had the highest rate of labelled deviance, cells 2 and 3 moderate rates, and cell 4 a very low rate (the most likely case). It would indicate that the processes pointing to the labelling and traditional perspectives make a difference, that neither is necessary or sufficient, and that the two processes interact. In this case, the comparison of cells 2 and 3 would give some indication of the relative importance of the two processes when they were taken by themselves. The differences between cell 2 and cell 1, and cell 3 and cell 1 would give an indication of the relative importance of the interaction of the two processes.

Labelling as an Independent Variable

The traditional perspective is that if someone is seriously deviant in behavior or condition, affixing a deviant label to that person and treating him or her accordingly will have certain positive consequences. First, with at least certain types of deviance, treating the individual as a deviant will tend to isolate him or her and thus prevent corruption of other members of society. Second, with regard to behaviors which persons may find personally rewarding, such as crime or drug use, the manifestation of deviant labels and the concomitant sanctions may deter others who are potential deviants. Third, the traditional view is that if people are seriously deviating from the norm, setting them apart and responding to their deviance will often have long-range positive consequences for these individuals. For example, it can be argued that punishing someone for a criminal act may channel him or her out of a lifetime career in crime, that giving psychiatric treatment to someone who is mentally ill will help return him or her to normal roles, and that training the disabled individual may enable him or her to function in a relatively normal manner. The labelling perspective is primarily concerned with the transformation of the person's identity, role, and behavior. Thus, in evaluating the labelling perspective we will only be concerned with the third point–namely, the short- and long-range consequences for the individual of being reacted to as a deviant. We should remember, however, that even if the consequences for the individual are unfavorable (i.e., that the labelling theorists are right), there may be other reasons for treating the individual as deviant.

In contrast to the traditional formulation, the labelling theorists argue that reacting to persons as if they were deviants is the major cause of deviant identities and life styles. It is assumed that, without a societal reaction, most deviant behavior would be transitory. In contrast, if the individual is reacted to as a deviant, it is assumed that the deviant status will become more or less permanent. It is argued that deviant status will act as a master status, which will determine how others will act toward him or her across the range of social interaction. It is argued that (s)he will be cut off from interaction with normals and channelled into contact with similar deviants. Furthermore, as was noted above, it is presumed that once this happens it becomes very difficult for the individual to return to a normal status.

In short, when labelling is treated as an independent variable, the critical question becomes whether or not the societal reaction increases or decreases the amount of that individual's deviant behavior. To properly evaluate this question, we should be concerned with the person's behavior over his or her lifetime.

The two questions covered in this section are probably the two key questions that need to be answered in evaluating the labelling perspective. There are, however, a number of subsidiary questions, the answers to which would significantly increase our understanding of societal reactions and their consequences.

SUBSIDIARY QUESTIONS

One question is when and how deviant labels become affixed to the individual and whether these labels may be changed. Many labelling theorists have focused on official reactions (such as court hearings, being admitted to psychiatric treatment, etc.) as the process which affixes the deviant label to the individual. According to this view, the individual deviant status is generally not established until there has been an official reaction. However, with many forms of deviant behavior—for example, with some types of crime, sexual deviance, and possibly drug use—it would appear that many persons have established a deviant pattern of behavior that persists for a prolonged period in the absence of an official societal reaction and possibly even in the absence of an informal reaction. Such cases, assuming they exist, would seem to run counter to the labelling mode of explanation, and it would certainly appear that their frequent occurrence would require a substantial modification of the labelling perspective. Assuming such cases do exist, we need to know what role an official does play in the labelling process. Does it simply reaffirm an already established status, or does it tend to relabel the person's deviance—for example, changing the label from obnoxious and intolerable to sick or disabled and in need of help (Gove, 1975; Haber and Smith, 1971; Trice and Roman, 1970)?

Another issue that needs to be considered is the role played by the individual in acquiring a deviant identity. For example, with a number of behaviors, the individual often appears to play a very active role in acquiring a formal deviant identity. Thus, in the area of mental illness, persons often appear to be the oncs who initiate their own psychiatric care. Societal reaction theorists have generally ignored such a phenomenon and, when they do attempt to explain it, they generally attribute the individual's labelling of himself to his acceptance of a deviant stereotype. This tactic enables the labelling theorists to ignore the fact that many people appear to initiate entrance into the deviant role because they find their condition very debilitating and painful. The tendency of the labelling theorists to ignore the apparent contribution of the individual to the establishment and modification of a deviant identity is particularly puzzling in light of the fact that the perspective has very strong ties to the symbolic interaction school, which has focused very heavily on the contribution that the individual makes to his or her own identity and behavior. At any rate, the degree to which the individual shapes and modifies the societal reaction towards him or her needs further investigation.

Much of the argument of the labelling theorists rests on the assumption that deviance acts as a master status that activates a general exclusionary reaction. This assumption needs further investigation. For example, when someone is believed to be a homosexual, we need to know the extent to which this belief shapes the reactions of others and the extent to which those are guided by other considerations. It is possible that if one has close ties to a perceived deviant–for example, if he or she is a member of the family–the consequence of believing (s)he is a deviant is overshadowed by other status considerations. Thus, it is possible that the deviant stereotype activates an exclusionary reaction only when dealing with a relative stranger. Conversely, it is also possible that when dealing with a stranger, others may not be particularly concerned about what he or she does, and only when others are closely involved with people do they care enough to take meaningful action. As noted earlier, societal reaction theory has generally sided with the first view–namely, that societal reactions tend to occur when there is a considerable social distance between the actor and the reactor.

A related but generally ignored question is the intent of a societal reaction. Orcutt (1973), on the basis of small group research, has made a distinction between inclusive societal reactions and exclusive societal reactions. Orcutt (1973: 260) defines inclusive reactions as "those attempts at social control which are premised on the assumption that the rule-breaker is and will continue to be an ordinary member of the group (relationship, community). This form of reaction attempts to control the rule-infractions by bringing the present or future behavior of the rule-breaker into conformity with the rules of the group without excluding him from it." He goes on to indicate that, in the small group literature, inclusive reactions are characterized by a high intensity of interaction, a low to moderate degree of attitudinal hostility, and a high degree of interactional hostility. Orcutt (1973: 260-261) defines exclusive reactions as "those attempts at social control which operate to reject the rule-breaker from the group and revoke his privileges as an ordinary member. In short, exclusive reactions treat the rule breaker as an outsider." He then indicates that in the small group literature exclusive reactions are characterized by a lack of intensity in interaction, a high degree of attitudinal hostility and a low level of interactional hostility.

The societal reaction theorists have assumed that when members of society label a person as deviant and/or funnel him or her into the societal mechanism set up to deal with deviant behavior, these members are manifesting an exclusionary reaction. However, this may not always be the case. For example, when others channel a person into psychiatric treatment or take action to stop drug addiction, they may be trying to help the person and may see the action as necessary if the person is to remain a member of their group. If the reaction is inclusionary, at least in intent, then, from the point of view of the reactors, the reintegration of those now labelled deviant would be much easier than the labelling theorists have suggested. Thus, it would appear important to determine whether a particular reaction was inclusionary or exclusionary in intent. To some extent, this might be determined by looking at attitudinal and at interactional hostility. The type of reaction may be reflected by who initiated the reaction. An act may tend to be an inclusionary reaction if it is initiated by someone who has close ties to the person and an exclusionary reaction if it is initiated by someone who is relatively distant from the person.

A final issue with which we might be concerned is how a person can leave a deviant status and return to a normal status. In general, the labelling theorists have treated such a return as very difficult and have ignored the processes which might bring it about.[4] However, it is obviously the case that, with at least some forms of deviant behavior, persons often do shift back to normal roles. There are two questions involved here. The first deals with what has caused the person to stop behaving in a deviant manner. The cessation of deviant behavior might be directly related to maturational processes or it might reflect motivational issues where, for example, the individual may simply decide that being a deviant is too painful–a manifestation of the deterrent effect of a societal reaction. Alternatively, the shift back to a normal state may be greatly facilitated by positive aspects of a societal reaction such as might be associated with treatment or training. Almost without exception, the labelling theorists have ignored the possibility of positive aspects of societal reaction, and these need to be given considerably more attention.

The second question has to do with the shift in labels from deviant to normal. We simply do not know much about what produces such a shift. Does it simply require the nonperformance of deviant acts or does it require an overly conformist adoption of normal roles? Of particular relevance to the labelling perspective is the extent to which the person's societal characteristics, such as race or education, determine the ease with which he or she can shift into a normal role. Presumably, there is a transition period when the person's status is in question, and we need to know more about how long such periods last and what determines their length. Similarly, we need to know if the shift to normalcy tends to be marked by formal or informal transition points. For example, does the termination of psychiatric treatment, the ending of probation, or possibly the graduation from a training program play a major role in the reacquisition of a normal identity? The labelling theorists (e.g., Lemert, 1967) have argued that, during the transition period, the person will be on a form of probation, which requires that he abide by rules that are much more stringent than those encountered by "normal" members of society. However, it is at least plausible that during the transition period others will be especially considerate and supportive. Perhaps during the transition period there is a peculiar combination of a heightened sensitivity and reaction to subtle cues of deviance combined with a tendency to be unusually helpful and supportive.

NOTES

1. For the exception to this otherwise apparently uniform trend, see Lemert (1967: 55-59).

2. Becker (1963: 37) notes that in the situation where a person is apprehended for the first time, the act of apprehension does not necessarily lead to secondary deviance if the person is still in a position to choose alternative lines of action. Similarly, Lemert (1967: 42) indicates that the importance of degradation rituals is not in their drama but in their consequences and that "for stigmatization to establish a total deviant identity it must be disseminated throughout the society."

3. Thus, according to my formulation, Schur (1974: 19) is incorrect when he takes as evidence for the societal reaction perspective the finding that there are positive consequences associated with being labelled mentally ill.

4. For an important exception to this trend, see Lofland (1969: 209-224).

REFERENCES

Akers, Ronald L.

1968 "Problems in the sociology of deviance: social definitions and behavior." Social Forces 46 (June): 455-465.

Antonio, Robert

1973 "On ignoring the subtle dimensions of labeling: the case of mental disorder." Unpublished manuscript.

Back, Kurt

1975 "Mental Health," in Jay Demerath, Otto Larson and Karl Schuessler (eds.) Social Policy and Sociology. New York: Academic Press.

Becker, Howard S.

1963 Outsiders: Studies in the Sociology of Deviance. New York: Free Press.

1967 "Whose side are we on?" Social Problems 14 (Winter): 239-247.

1973 "Labelling theory reconsidered." Pp. 177-208 in Howard Becker (ed.) Outsiders. New York: Free Press.

Bordua, David

1967 "Recent trends: deviant behavior and social control." Annals of the American Academy of Political and Social Science 374 (January): 149-163.

Bustamante, Jorge

1972 "The 'wetback' as deviant: an application of labelling theory." American Journal of Sociology 77 (January): 706-718.

Davis, Nanette

1972 "Labeling theory in deviance research: a critique and reconsideration." Sociological Quarterly 13 (Fall): 447-474.

DeLamater, John

1968 "On the nature of deviance." Social Forces 46 (June): 445-455.

Downes, David and Paul Rock

1971 "Social reaction to deviance and its effects on crime and criminal careers." British Journal of Sociology 22 (December): 351-364.

Erikson, Kai T.

1962 "Notes on the sociology of deviance." Social Problems 9 (Spring): 307-314.

Fletcher, C. Richard and Larry Reynolds

1967 "Residual deviance, labelling, and the mentally sick role: a critical review of concepts." Sociological Focus 1 (Winter): 33-37.

Freidson, Eliot

1965 "Disability as social deviance." Pp. 71-99 in Marvin Sussman (ed.) Sociology and Rehabilitation. Washington, D.C.: American Sociological Association.

Garfinkel, H.

1956 "Conditions of successful degradation ceremonies." American Journal of Sociology 61 (March): 420-424.

Gibbons, Don and Joseph Jones

1971 "Some critical notes on current definitions of deviance." Pacific Sociological Review 14 (January): 20-37.

Gibbs, Jack

1962 "Rates of mental hospitalization: a study of societal reaction to deviant behavior." American Sociological Review 27 (December): 782-792.

1966 "Conceptions of deviant behavior: the old and the new." Pacific Sociological Review 9 (Spring): 9-14.

1972 "Issues in defining deviant behavior." Pp. 39-68 in Robert Scott and Jack Douglas (eds.) Theoretical Perspectives on Deviance. New York: Basic Books.

Goffman, Erving

1961 Asylums. Garden City, N.Y.: Doubleday Anchor.

Gouldner, Alvin

1968 "The sociologist as partisan: sociology and the welfare state." American Sociologist 3 (May): 103-116.

Gove, W. R.

1970 "Societal reaction as an explanation of mental illness: an evaluation." American Sociological Review 35 (October): 873-884.

Gove, W. R.

1975 "Societal reaction theory and disability" to appear in Gary Albrecht (ed.) Socialization and Disability. University of Pittsburgh Press.

Gusfield, J.

1967 "Moral passage: the symbolic progress in public designations of deviance." Social Problems 15 (Fall): 175-188.

Haber, Lawrence and Richard Smith

1971 "Disability and deviance: normative adaptations of role behavior." American Socialization Review 36 (February): 87-97.

Hagan, John

1972 "Cognitive assumptions in the explanation of opiate addiction." Presented at the meeting of the Pacific Sociological Association, Portland, April.

1973 "Labelling and deviance: a case study in the 'sociology' of the interesting." Social Problems 20 (Spring): 447-458.

1974 "Conceptual deficiencies in an interactionist's perspective on 'deviance.'" Criminology 11 (November): 383-404.

Hartjen, Clayton

1974 Crime and Criminalization. New York: Praeger.

Hirschi, Travis

1973 "Procedural rules and the study of deviant behavior." Social Problems 21 (Fall): 159-173.

Horan, Patrick and Patricia Austin

1974 "The social bases of welfare stigma." Social Problems 21 (June): 648-657.

Kitsuse, J. I.

1962 "Societal reaction to deviant behavior: problems of theory and method." Social Problems 9 (Winter): 247-257.

1972 "Deviance, deviant behavior and deviants: some conceptual problems." In William Filstead (ed.) An Introduction to Deviance: Readings in the Process of Making Deviants. Chicago: Markham.

Kitsuse, J. I. and A. V. Cicourel

1963 "A note on the uses of official statistics." Social Problems 11 (Fall): 131-139.

Lemert, Edwin M.

1951 Social Pathology. New York: McGraw-Hill.

1967 Human Deviance, Social Problems, and Social Control. Englewood Cliffs, N.J.: Prentice-Hall.

1972 "Social problems and the sociology of deviance." Pp. 3-25 in Edwin Lemert (ed.) Human Deviance, Social Problems and Social Control. Englewood Cliffs, N.J.: Prentice-Hall.

1974 "Beyond Mead: the societal reaction to deviance." Social Problems 21 (April): 457-468.

Liazos, Alexander
1972 "The poverty of the sociology of deviance: nuts, sluts, and perverts." Social Problems 20 (Summer): 103-120.

Lofland, John
1969 Deviance and Identity. Englewood Cliffs, N.J.: Prentice-Hall.

Lorber, Judith
1966 "Deviance as performance: the case of illness." Social Problems 14 (Winter): 302-310.

Mankoff, Milton
1971 "Societal reaction and career deviance: a critical analysis." Sociological Quarterly 12 (Spring): 204-218.

Manning, Peter
1973 "On deviance." Contemporary Sociology 2 (November 2): 123-128.

Matza, David
1969 Becoming Deviant. Englewood Cliffs, N.J.: Prentice-Hall.

Merton, Robert
1957 Social Theory and Social Structure. Glencoe, Ill.: Free Press.

Orcutt, James
1973 "Societal reaction and the response to deviation in small groups." Social Forces 52 (December): 259-267.

Prus, Robert
1975 "Labelling theory: a reconceptualization and a propositional statement on typing." Sociological Focus 8 (January): 79-96.

Quinney, Richard
1970 The Social Reality of Crime. Boston: Little, Brown.

Roman, Paul and Harrison Trice
1969 "The self reaction: a neglected dimension of labeling theory." Presented at the meeting of the American Sociological Association, San Francisco, August.
1971 "Normalization: a neglected complement to labelling theory." Presented at the meeting of the American Sociological Association, Denver, August.

Rotenberg, Mordechai
1974 "Self-labelling: a missing link in the societal reaction theory of deviance." Sociological Review 22 (August): 335-354.

Rubington, Earl and Martin Weinberg
1968 Deviance: The Interactionist Perspective. New York: Macmillan.
1971 "Labeling." Pp. 163-171 in Earl Rubington and Martin Weinberg (eds.) The Study of Social Problems. New York: Oxford University Press.

Sagarin, Edward
1975 Deviants and Deviance: An Introduction to the Study of Disvalued People and Behavior. New York: Praeger.

Scheff, Thomas J.
1966 Being Mentally Ill: A Sociological Theory. Chicago: Aldine.
1974 "The labelling theory of mental illness." American Sociological Review 39 (June): 442-452.
1975 "Reply to Chauncey and Gove." American Sociological Review 40 (April).

Schervish, Paul
1973 "The labeling perspective: its bias and potential in the study of political deviance." American Sociologist 8 (May): 47-57.

Schur, Edwin M.
1969 "Reactions to deviance: a critical assessment." American Journal of Sociology 75 (November): 309-322.

1971 Labeling Deviant Behavior. New York: Harper & Row.

1973 "Deviance and disorganization: persisting problems and emerging emphases." Presented at the meeting of the American Sociological Association, August.

1974 "The concept of secondary deviation: its theoretical significance and empirical elusiveness." Unpublished manuscript.

Scott, Robert

1972 "A proposed framework for analyzing deviance as a property of social order." Pp. 9-35 in Robert Scott and Jack Douglas (eds.) Theoretical Perspectives on Deviance. New York: Basic Books.

Tannenbaum, Frank

1938 Crime and the Community. Boston: Ginn.

Thio, Alex

1973 "Class bias in the sociology of deviance." American Sociologist 8 (February): 1-12.

Thorsell, B. A. and L. W. Klemke

1972 "The labeling process: reinforcement and deterrent." Law and Society Review 6: 393-403.

Tittle, Charles

1975 "Deterrents or labeling." Social Forces 53 (March): 399-410.

Trice, Harrison and Paul Roman

1970 "Delabeling, relabeling and Alcoholics Anonymous." Social Problems 17 (Spring): 538-546.

Ward, R. H.

1971 "The labeling theory: a critical analysis." Criminology 9 (August-November): 206-290.

Warren, Carol and John Johnson

1972 "A critique of labeling theory from the phenomenological perspective." Pp. 62-92 in Robert Scott and Jack Douglas (eds.) Theoretical Perspectives on Deviance. New York: Basic Books.

Chapter 2

ALCOHOLISM AND LABELLING THEORY

LEE N. ROBINS

As Tittle points out in Chapter 6, it is difficult either to support or refute labelling theory by appeal to empirical data because the theory has not been put into refutable form by its proponents. Nor can we soon expect them to do so or agree with others' attempts to do so, since the proponents of labelling theory tend to be just those sociologists most suspicious of the validity of "hard" data. They could scarcely feel otherwise, because the essential point made by labelling theory is that so-called "objective" records (i.e., data created by police or hospitals) are *not* objective representations of the behaviors they purport to refer to. Their contention is that even information collected by interview is distorted, since after having been labelled by official agencies, the labelled individual reinterprets his or her prelabelling behavioral history as deviant and acts in accordance with the label thereafter. In short, labelling theorists believe that deviance in a society is largely the product of attempts to measure or record it. Like Archimedes, who realized he would have to stand outside the earth if he were to move it, the sociologist accepting labelling theory has nowhere to stand from which he or she can observe the "natural" rates against which the size of the distortion in official rates and rates based on interviews can be measured, to estimate the impact of labelling.

I do not really believe that the attempt to test labelling theory empirically is that hopeless. At any rate, we shall try to see whether what is known about

AUTHOR'S NOTE: This work was supported by Research Grants DA 01120, MH-18864, AA-00209, RSA 36,598, and Contract HSM-42-72-75.

alcoholism is consistent with what labelling theory would suggest. If it is not, our doubts about labelling theory will be increased. If results are consistent with what labelling theory would lead us to expect, its plausibility will be increased, although its correctness will still not be demonstrated.

My own research experience has led me to have much more confidence in empirical data than have labelling theorists. Distortions undoubtedly do occur, perhaps as a result of labelling and certainly as a result of biases in likelihood of detection and recording as well as of measurement error. I have nevertheless been greatly impressed with the sturdiness of findings in the field of deviance, no matter what the bias of the investigator, how careless the methodology, what were the indices used, or how varied the social setting in which the research was done. Studies of predictors of deviant behavior have produced consistent results for forty years (from Healey and Bronner, 1926 to Wolfgang, 1972), in various countries (Sweden, the United States, Norway, Germany, Australia, and England, for example), and by authors with very different etiological theories and methods. Results compiled by social workers, criminologists, psychologists, educators, sociologists, psychiatrists—both Freudian and anti-Freudian—have agreed, whether their empirical data base was vital statistics, police records, school records, interviews, or anonymous questionnaires.

Both the predictors and their relative importance appear reasonably consistent from study to study. The best predictor of any specific later deviant act seems always to be early deviant behavior, and the specific *nature* of that earlier deviant behavior seems uniformly to be rather unimportant. Being a late adolescent or young adult male and having parents with a history of deviance—again, the specific nature of that deviance is not important—are the next best predictors of later deviance. Family history continues to be a potent predictor even when the child does not live with the affected parent. Social group memberships predict deviance, too, but they follow as a poor third. Being urban, poor, and/or undereducated, and in ethnic groups of low social status (black in the United States, Irish in the United Kingdom) are strong predictors only if family history and the person's own prior behavior are not held constant—for the latter variables tend to be highly correlated with social group membership.

These well-replicated findings have made me suspect that labelling theory is either incorrect or at least not a powerful explanatory theory for the continuation of deviance for several reasons:

(1) Since the social and personal predictors of deviance are as clear-cut when unlabelled behavior (covert illegal behavior, for instance) is

studied as when labelled behavior is studied (as long as some estimate of frequency or severity is used for the unlabelled behavior to parallel the fact that arrests and other official labels almost always occur after repeated occasions of deviance), labelling is clearly not a *necessary* intervening variable between social and personal history and later deviance.

(2) Labelling would not seem to have the irreversible effects on later behavior claimed for it. All common forms of deviance (drug use, theft, drinking, sexual promiscuity, fighting) seem to drop off with age, whether or not they have been labelled and whether or not their being labelled eventuated in intervention in the form of treatment or punishment. This dropping off of deviance with aging argues against labelling theory, because the number of times one has been labelled in a lifetime can only increase, not decrease, over time. If deviant labels produce enduring increases in the labelled behavior, one would expect increasing liabilities to deviance with age as the experiences of being labelled accumulate, instead of the actual self-limited period of risk for deviance, terminating for most people in middle age.

(3) Labelling theory argues that labels encourage the very behavior specified in the label. That is, one steals because one is labelled a thief; one acts "crazy" because one is designated psychotic. But in fact, labels for one kind of deviance frequently prognosticate different types of deviance as well or better than they do the continuation of the same type. Young girls caught stealing are less likely to be adult thieves than they are to be adult suicide attempters, sexually promiscuous, or alcoholic (Robins, 1966). Since these particular associations between childhood and adult behaviors are not generally known, it is unlikely that labelling a girl thief would give her the self-image of a suicide attempters. To attribute the powerful carryover between childhood deviance of one type and adult deviance of very different types to the effects of labelling, the symbolic meaning of the label would have to be a very general one indeed: "You're bad and that means you will continue to be bad in any way that becomes fashionable later." How else can labelling theory explain that young men expelled from school in the rural South, who had never thought of using heroin before they were sent to Vietnam in the Army, had a high risk of getting addicted to heroin if they experimented with it there (Robins, 1974)?

(4) The fact that the importance of the parents' deviance as a predictor was undiminished when the child did not live with or know about his or her parents means the parents' influence must be something *other* than the label which being their child provided. Indeed, the evidence

for genetic or perinatal factors in schizophrenia, crime, and alcoholism may be more substantial at this moment than is evidence not only for labelling theory but for any type of social causation.

These consistent findings with respect to predictors of deviance do not negate a possible effect of labelling in addition, but they do suggest that labelling is not the sole explanation, and perhaps not a very important one.

This brief overview of generalizations from empirical studies of predictors of deviance indicates why I did not anticipate finding very compelling evidence for labelling theory as an explanation for the intractability of alcoholism. There is, after all, a large body of research on alcoholism that shows its predictors follow much the same patterns that I have outlined above for deviance in general. Alcoholism, like other forms of deviance, is better predicted by early antisocial behavior of a nonspecific type than by any social characteristic (Cahalan and Room, 1974). It is largely confined to males in late adolescence and early adulthood (Cahalan, 1970: 42), although medical complications appear late in its course. It runs in families, and recent research has shown that biological parents appear potent influences even when the child is given up for adoption at an early age (Goodwin et al., 1973, 1974). The social correlates of alcoholism are being poor, male, undereducated, and in low-status ethnic groups (black, Indian, Spanish-American) (Cahalan, 1970), although in addition there appears a special vulnerability among Irish and perhaps Scandinavian and other groups of north European origin. These correlates are found equally reliably in official statistics of hospitals (Zax et al., 1967; Rosenblatt et al., 1971) and police (Zax et al., 1964), in area surveys that include "unlabelled" problem drinkers, and in randomly collected blood alcohol levels that cannot reflect either official labelling or self-labelling (Wechsler et al., 1970).

It is not surprising that patterns for deviance in general also hold for alcoholism, since alcoholics have elevated rates of every common form of socially disapproved behavior (fighting, poor work history, theft, marital instability, geographical mobility). Conversely, histories of problem drinking can be elicited from large portions of individuals who come to public attention for each of these forms of deviance.

Thus, any difficulties with labelling theory that apply to other forms of antisocial behavior apply equally well to alcoholism. In addition, there are some further findings specific to alcoholism that increase our doubts that labelling theory is a powerful explanation for the maintenance of problem drinking:

(1) The most common labeller of the alcoholic is a member of his own

family. Studies of social problems associated with heavy drinking (Cahalan and Room, 1974; Robins et al., 1968) consistently show that family complaint is the most common problem associated with drinking and that it tends to occur before problem drinking is detected by employers, police, or doctors. The risk of being labelled a problem drinker seems proportional to the social distance between the labeller and the alcoholic, decreasing from family to friends and neighbors, to employer, to police, to doctor. While labelling theory does not clearly indicate who is to be the first labeller if there are multiple stages in the labelling process, the prototypic examples are the delinquent, first labelled by the judge; and the psychotic, first labelled by the psychiatrist. The first labeller of the problem drinker is not such an outside authority whose right to label may be relatively exempt from challenge, but is rather someone who shares the alcoholic's own view of drinking and of his own behavior, and whose opinion is based on no special expertise. Thus, the power of the first label to modify future behavior and to change the drinker's self-image might be expected to be considerably less than the power of a label such as "delinquent" or "psychotic."

(2) There is typically a long delay between the onset of heavy drinking and the first application of a label, even by close relatives. In a recently completed study of 219 men aged 46 to 64, selected from patients in an acute psychiatric hospital, a medical clinic, job applicants to a casual labor office, and enrollees in a union-sponsored health maintenance organization, we found 78 who had regularly drunk more than a fifth of whiskey a day, almost all of whom had been labeled as alcoholics at some point in their lives (Robins and West, n.d.). Asking the age at which they first became heavy drinkers (defined as seven or more drinks at least one evening per week) and the age at which a member of their families first complained about their drinking yielded a median interval between the two of over eleven years. Apparently families do not typically rush to stigmatize their members as heavy drinkers. And, more importantly for questioning labelling theory, excessive drinking seems to persist for many years without benefit of the experience of having been labelled. The labelling theorists argue that occasional deviance will disappear spontaneously if it is not entrenched by labelling. Drinking heavily seems to provide sufficient reinforcement of its own so that this is not the case.

(3) There is bountiful evidence that, rather than being overeager to label, official agencies aid and abet the denial of alcoholism. Careful questioning of patients on medical wards (Barchha et al., 1968) shows very high rates of problem drinking, particularly among young and middle-aged males. Hospitalization of men this age should be expected to raise their doctors' suspicions

about their drinking histories, because they are not yet in the age range when nondrinkers are likely to develop serious medical problems. Yet there is rarely a mention of their drinking habits in the medical record. Alcoholism was also found to be a frequently missed diagnosis among emergency room patients unless they fulfilled the stereotype of the "Bowery bum" or had no medical or surgical problem that could serve as an alternative diagnosis (Blane et al., 1963). Death certificates grossly underreport alcoholism as a cause of death (Nicoll and Bellows, 1934; Puffer and Griffith, 1967), even when doctors admit in interview that they knew it to be the cause. Doctors explain that they avoid recording the deceased's alcoholism to spare the family embarrassment. Even police records fail to note how frequently men engaged in assault or breaking and entering are intoxicated, although interviews with these men show that they themselves often attribute their arrests to their drunkenness (Robins et al., 1968). The failure of doctors and police to recognize and report alcoholism probably grows out of conflicts in their own beliefs as to whether alcoholism is a disease or a characterological failing. Mulford and Miller (1961) found that doctors as well as the general public often hold both viewpoints simultaneously, leading to remarkably inconsistent and conflicting answers to a set of related questions. For instance, they state that alcoholism is a disease, but when given a case history of an alcoholic, reject the idea that the man described to them is sick; or if they do call him "sick," when asked where he should go to get help, they do not recommend medical care. Because doctors share the view that alcoholism is a disgrace, they avoid labelling "respectable" people. Judges, on the other hand, may be reluctant to use the label because it might excuse the crime on psychiatric grounds.

When there is so much denial of alcoholism in persons with long histories of excessive drinking, it is not clear how to interpret the fact that some groups do indeed have a greater likelihood of being labelled alcoholics than others. As we noted, the unemployed emergency room patient is more likely to be so diagnosed than is an equally addicted man with a job. Labelling theory would argue that the powerless, unemployed individual is more subject to premature labelling–i.e., to labelling on the basis of only occasional or sporadic problems. Another plausible interpretation is that neither the weak nor the powerful are prematurely labelled, and that the powerful are able to defer appropriate labelling even longer than the less powerful. Thus, in the case of alcoholism, the finding of differences between groups in their likelihood to be labelled might be evidence for a theory of the denial and normalization of deviance rather than for labelling theory.

(4) Frequent and heavy use of alcohol produces a physiological addiction that makes the heavy use of alcohol self-perpetuating. After physiological

addiction occurs, motivation to continue drinking becomes independent of any social factors or attitudes that may have explained the original excessive drinking. Evidence for this comes from animal experimentation (Ellis and Pick, 1971; Essig and Lam, 1971; Freund, 1971) which shows that all animals can, like man, develop alcohol dependence, as indicated by life-threatening withdrawal symptoms when the daily dose of alcohol is abruptly terminated, and from demonstrations of the development of tolerance in animals and human beings, which accounts for alcoholic's ability to behave normally after ingesting amounts of alcohol that would make a nontolerant individual comatose. Thus it is difficult to argue, as labelling theory does, that labelling accounts for maintenance of the deviant behavior. While labelling could conceivably play a role in perpetuating heavy drinking long enough to produce initial addiction, once physiological addiction takes place heavy drinking will tend to continue whether or not the individual has been labelled.

(5) When labelling of alcoholics is carried out by doctors, treatment is usually recommended. According to the medical view, treatment should reduce subsequent heavy drinking, while according to labelling theory, identification as an alcoholic should tend to increase it. Actually, evidence for the effectiveness of treatment is modest (Pokorny et al., 1968), but on the other hand, there are no studies showing an *increase* in the risk of drinking heavily as a result of referral for treatment. Alcoholics Anonymous, which is generally believed, despite a lack of well-controlled studies, to have a higher success rate than most alternative treatments, actively tries to persuade its members to internalize the label of "alcoholic," to announce that label publicly, and to view it as permanent. They teach that alcoholism is an inborn "allergy" to alcohol from which no recovery is possible, so that while drinking may be arrested, the condition exists to the grave. Thus, the alcoholic is never cured, but, by total abstinence and that alone, he can be spared the social and medical consequences of his disease. (Incidentally, there is no evidence for *this* theory and some evidence against it. A fair number of ex-alcoholics do return to moderate social drinking [Pattison et al., 1968].) Whether the "allergy" theory is right or wrong, if Alcoholics Anonymous does have as good or better a success rate than other therapies, their instruction to internalize the alcoholic label must not increase the danger of perpetuating heavy drinking.

A very small study of labelled and unlabelled untreated problem drinkers (Kendell and Staton, 1966) suggests that whether an alcoholic is labelled or unlabelled makes no difference in his outcome. The seven men they regarded as not alcoholic despite their appearance at an alcohol treatment center had outcomes at follow-up as poor as the untreated men they labelled as alcoholic—one had committed suicide and three had serious social problems as a result of drinking.

(6) The label of alcoholism applies to persons who drink heavily only if they have social or medical problems as a result. Indeed, heavy drinking without problems is something for a man to be proud of in a considerable segment of our society, although it is a necessary precursor of alcoholism. Labelling theory argues that membership in powerless social categories increases the risk of being labelled as deviant. Certainly powerless groups (lower-class, disadvantaged ethnic groups) are more frequently labelled alcoholic. However, when we restrict the population of interest to those at risk of alcoholism because they are heavy drinkers, we find that the poor and ethnic minorities have no more alcoholism than others (Robins et al., 1962; Cahalan and Room, 1974). In other words, the association between social characteristics and alcoholism seems to depend largely on the fact that there are disproportionate numbers of *nonlabelled* heavy drinkers with these characteristics. *Among* heavy drinkers, it is early deviance, not social characteristics, that predicts alcoholism. This same finding also appears to hold for heroin addiction. In our follow-up of Vietnam veterans (Robins, 1974), demographic variables predicted drug experimentation, but did not predict which soldiers who experimented with drugs would become addicted to them. On the other hand, a history of prior deviance did predict addiction, once exposed. These data suggest that a more appropriate version of labelling theory might be that a prior label as deviant for any reason increases the risk of being relabelled as a deviant of a different type.

(7) Labelling theory argues that once an individual is labelled, the label becomes a permanent identification which resists removal even when the behavior ends. Whether labelling theory is correct or incorrect, one would expect some delay in the reversal of labels after the cessation of problem drinking, since the prudent observer would require sufficient elapsed time to demonstrate that the former alcoholic can really drink moderately again. Labelling theory seems to claim that the delay is unreasonably long. However, in a recent study referred to above (Robins and West, n.d.), families that had previously objected to the drinking of men who had at some point drunk more than a fifth a day usually no longer felt that their drinking was a problem if the men had not been heavy drinkers in the past year. Seventeen of the seventy-eight formerly extremely heavy drinkers whose families had complained reported that they had not done any heavy drinking in the current year. Of these only three (seventeen percent) said the family still thought that they drank too much. Among those who had continued to drink heavily, seventy-five percent reported the family continued to object. Thus,

the label of excessive drinker does seem to be reversible in response to a termination of excessive drinking. Labelling by family members seems to be at least as susceptible to reversal as is "scientific" diagnosis by doctors, who usually insist on a three-year remission before they consider an alcoholic probably cured.

(8) There is one aspect of the labelling hypothesis of alcoholism with respect to which we have been able to muster no empirical evidence: that the label becomes a "master label"–i.e., that it colors the responses to a man in areas in which his drinking is irrelevant. How would one test this proposition for alcoholism? One could imagine doing so and proving the existence of a master label with respect to homosexuality, since sexual behavior affects only a circumscribed part of an individual's life. The male homosexual's life as public citizen, employee, son, and brother may be quite within normal limits. When a homosexual is deprived of his political freedom or his right to employment, clearly the label has affected how he is treated in irrelevant areas and must be interpreted as a "master label." But what areas of a male alcoholic's life are similarly segregated from his drinking? Drinking affects mood, participation in voluntary organizations, interpersonal relationships, work performance, health, ability to talk, walk, and make love. Without being able to delineate roles to which alcoholism is clearly irrelevant, it is impossible to support or negate the hypothesis that alcoholism becomes a master label.

In sum, we do have evidence that the process of labelling in alcoholism is rather different from that imagined by the labelling hypothesis. The alcoholic is likely to be first labelled by a member of his own social circle, not by some official. And even that label occurs only after many years of showing behavior that warrants the label of alcoholism, thus suggesting that labelling is seldom premature. In fact, the alcoholic's liability to premature labelling seems rather less than the likelihood that his identity as an alcoholic will be denied long after evidence for problem behavior is clearly available. His deviant behavior appears to be self-sustaining over many years, even when unlabelled, in part because it produces physical dependence. While we do not know for certain whether labelling improves or decreases the chances of recovery, evidence would seem to indicate that internalization of the label may actually help to improve the chances rather than lowering them. At any rate, there certainly is no evidence that being labelled an alcoholic encourages excessive drinking. Nor is there evidence that the label of alcoholic is irreversible when improvement in drinking behavior does take place, as it frequently does in middle age.

This picture of the course of alcoholism seems far from the model envisioned by the labelling theorists. Indeed, alcoholics seem a much less likely group to support such a hypothesis than do other types of deviants. Why does the public not rush to label the alcoholic as it does the homosexual, for instance? We may speculate that the reason that some types of deviance fail to fit the labelling model lies in the fact that they represent behavior that is not disjunctive with normative behavior, but is only an exaggeration of that behavior. In our society, drinking is not only accepted, but to a certain extent rewarded. This is particularly true for young males, who seem to be the group most likely to drink heavily. Thus, the difference between an alcoholic and a "normal" heavy drinker is quantitative, not qualitative, depending on the frequency of intoxication and the degree to which that intoxication interferes with role performance. Because there is no sharp breaking point, a decision that the limits of social drinking have been crossed tends to be deferred until the criteria have been met beyond any doubt.

Are there other forms of deviance that are exaggerations of acceptable behavior and to which this same pattern of deferral rather than premature labelling apply? It might be fruitful to consider religious fanaticism and obesity as possible examples. Both are excesses of behavior that is sometimes accepted when used moderately. The deferral of judgment when differences are quantitative rather than qualitative might also help to explain our "softness" on white-collar crime, which often seems to be only an extension of sharp business practices.

In contrast, society rushes to stigmatize deviance seen as qualitatively different from normal behavior. Male homosexuality is a good example here. Because all sexually tinged contacts between males are taboo, the mildest of "passes" is sufficient to bring about a label of homosexual, even in the absence of evidence of genital contact. Once labeled, the victim may be forced into homosexuality because others will not accept him, thus fulfilling the prediction of labelling theory. And, until very recently, the label of homosexual was extraordinarily hard to lose, and certainly became a master label in the sense that it was treated as relevant in many areas in which it really was not. If the critical issue is the perception of deviance as qualitatively rather than quantitatively different from normal behavior, we might expect to find labelling theory more nearly supported for alcoholism in abstinence cultures than in urban America. Where abstinence is required, there is no continuum between approved drinking and alcoholism. In such cultures, there may be a tendency to label a man as alcoholic the first time he is found drunk, and that label might "drive him to drink" if "nice" people will no longer associate with him. At least there is some supporting evidence for this view: In the Bible Belt and among students from abstinent subcultures there are many abstainers and some problem drinkers, but relatively few moderate drinkers (Cahalan and Room, 1974; Globetti, 1967; Skolnick, 1958), a situation which could occur if labelling forced moderate

drinkers into excessive drinking. (I personally hold what I consider a more parsimonious view of the reason for this pattern: when drinking is proscribed, everyone who can abstain does, leaving the drinking portion of the population to the problem drinkers.)

This paper has examined empirical evidence that alcoholism might fit the model suggested by labelling theory and found that model wanting. It has suggested one criterion that deviant behavior might need to comply with if the model is to fit the data: that the behavior in question be seen as qualitatively different from normative behavior. This is not to suggest that labelling theory is an appropriate model for all deviance that is seen as qualitatively different. As the other members of this group pursue its appropriateness for various kinds of deviance, they may still find that the labelling theory falls short for these as well. But at least when the deviant behavior is alcoholism and there is a continuum of accepted drinking behavior, societal reaction seems more characteristically denial than premature labelling.

REFERENCES

Bailey, M. B., P. W. Haberman, and H. Alksne
1965 "The epidemiology of alcoholism in an urban residential area." Quarterly Journal of Studies on Alcohol 26, 1: 19-40.

Barchha, R., M. A. Stewart, and S. B. Guze
1968 "The prevalence of alcoholism among general hospital ward patients." American Journal of Psychiatry 125, 5: 681-684.

Blane, H. T., W. F. Overton, Jr., and M. E. Chafetz
1963 "Social factors in the diagnosis of alcoholism: 1. Characteristics of the patient." Quarterly Journal of Studies on Alcohol 24, 4: 640-663.

Calahan, D.
1970 Problem Drinkers. San Francisco: Jossey-Bass

--- and R. Room
1974 Problem Drinking Among American Men. Monograph of the Rutgers Center of Alcohol Studies, New Brunswick, New Jersey.

Ellis, F. W. and J. R. Pick
1971 "Ethanol intoxication and dependence in Rhesus monkeys." In N. K. Mello and J. H. Mendelson (eds.) Recent Advances in Studies in Alcoholism. Publication (HSM) 71-9045. Washington, D.C.: Government Printing Office.

Essig, C. F. and R. C. Lam
1971 "The alcohol abstinence syndrome in dogs and its treatment with phenobarbital." In N. K. Mello and J. H. Mendelson (eds.) Recent Advances in Studies in Alcoholism. Publication (HSM) 71-9045. Washington, D.C.: Government Printing Office.

Freund, G.
1971 "Alcohol, barbiturate, and bromide withdrawal in mice." In N. K. Mello and J. H. Mendelson (eds.) Recent Advances in Studies of Alcoholism. Publication (HSM) 71-9045. Washington, D.C.: Government Printing Office.

Globetti, G.
1967 "A comparative study of white and Negro teenage drinking in two Mississippi counties." Phylon 28: 131-138.

Goodwin, D. W., F. Schulsinger, L. Hermansen, S. B. Guze, and G. Winokur
1973 "Alcohol problems in adoptees raised apart from alcoholic biological parents." Archives of General Psychiatry 28: 238-243.

Goodwin, D. W., F. Schulsinger, N. Moller, et al.
1974 "Drinking problems in adopted and nonadopted sons of alcoholics." Archives of General Psychiatry 31 (August): 164-169.

Healy, W. and A. F. Bronner
1926 Delinquents and Criminals: Their Making and Unmaking. New York: Macmillan.

Kendall, R. E. and M. C. Staton
1966 "The fate of untreated alcoholics." Quarterly Journal of Studies on Alcohol 27, 1: 30-41.

Mulford, H. A. and D. E. Miller
1961 "Public definitions of the alcoholic." Quarterly Journal of Studies on Alcohol 22, 2: 312-320.

Nicoll, M. Jr. and M. T. Bellows
1934 "Effect of a confidential inquiry on the recorded mortality from syphilis and alcoholism." American Journal of Public Health 24, 8: 813-820.

Pattison, E. M., E. B. Headley, G. C. Gleser, and L. A. Gottschalk
1968 "Abstinence and normal drinking." Quarterly Journal of Studies on Alcohol 29, 3: 610-633.

Pokorny, A. D., B. A. Miller, and S. E. Cleveland
1968 "Response to treatment of alcoholism: a follow-up study." Quarterly Journal of Studies on Alcohol 29: 364-381.

Puffer, R. and G. W. Griffith
1967 "Patterns of urban mortality." Pan American Health Organization Scientific Publication 151, September.

Robins, L. N.
1966 Deviant Children Grown Up. Baltimore: Williams & Wilkins. (Reprinted in 1974 by Robert E. Krieger, Huntington, New York.)
1974 "The Vietnam drug user returns." Special Action Office Monograph, Series A, Number 2, May.

——— and P. A. West
n.d. "Correlates of suicidal behavior and ideas in middle-aged black and white men." Unpublished manuscript.

Robins, L. N., W. M. Bates, and P. O'Neal
1962 "Adult drinking patterns of former problem children." In D. J. Pittman and C. R. Snyder (eds.) Society, Culture and Drinking Patterns. New York: John Wiley.

Robins, L. N., G. E. Murphy, and M. B. Breckenridge
1968 "Drinking behavior in young urban Negro men." Quarterly Journal of Studies on Alcohol 29, 3: 657-684.

Rosenblatt, S. M., M. M. Gross, M. Broman, E. Lewis, and B. Malenowski
1971 "Patients admitted for treatment of alcohol withdrawal syndromes: an epidemiological study." Quarterly Journal of Studies on Alcohol 32 (March): 104-115.

Skolnick, J. H.
1958 "Religious affiliation and drinking behavior." Quarterly Journal of Studies on Alcohol 19, 3: 452-470.
Wechsler, H., H. W. Demone, Jr., D. Thum, and E. H. Kasey
1970 "Religious-ethnic differences in alcohol consumption." Journal of Health and Social Behavior 11 (March): 21-29.
Wolfgang, M. E., R. M. Figlio, and T. Sellin
1972 Delinquency in a Birth Cohort. Chicago: University of Chicago Press.
Zax, M., E. A. Gardner, and W. T. Hart
1964 "Public intoxication in Rochester: a survey of individuals charged during 1961." Quarterly Journal of Studies on Alcohol 25, 4: 669-678.
1967 "A survey of the prevalence of alcoholism in Monroe County, New York, 1961." Quarterly Journal of Studies on Alcohol 28, 2: 316-327.

Chapter 3

LABELLING AND MENTAL ILLNESS: A CRITIQUE

WALTER R. GOVE

Virtually all labelling theorists seem to hold that their perspective is a powerful explanatory tool when applied to mental illness. This conviction would appear to be an outgrowth of the fact that while no one seems to know exactly what mental illness is, there are a number of obvious societal contingencies involved in entering the role of the mentally ill, and the role itself is held to be both debilitating and highly stigmatized. Although the labelling perspective has largely been developed by sociologists, we find proponents of some version of the perspective in a number of different disciplines in the field of mental illness. Of particular note in psychiatry are Szasz (1961, 1970), Laing and Esterson (1964), Laing (1967), and Leifer (1969); psychology is represented by Sarbin (1967a, 1967b, 1972) and Rosenhan (1973); anthropology by Goffman (1961); and sociology by Scheff (1966, 1970, 1974) and Perrucci (1974).

By far the most explicit theoretical statement of how the labelling perspective explains mental illness has been provided by Scheff (1966, 1970). Following Becker, he makes the distinction between rule-breaking and deviance. He then goes on to note that

> the culture of the group provides a vocabulary of terms for categorizing many norm violations: crime, perversion, drunkenness and bad manners are familiar examples. Each of the terms is derived from the type of

AUTHOR'S NOTE: I would like to thank Antonina Gove and Lisa Heinrich for their comments on an earlier draft of this paper.

> norm broken, and ultimately, from the type of behavior involved. After exhausting these categories, however, there is always a *residue of the most diverse kinds of violations* for which the culture provides no explicit label [Scheff, 1966: 34; italics added].

Scheff terms these types of violations residual rule-breaking and then indicates that the violation of these diverse kinds of rules leads to labelling someone mentally ill. He notes that "we can categorize most psychiatric symptoms as instances of residual rule-breaking or residual deviance" (Scheff, 1966: 33). Throughout the remainder of his work, he equates the diverse behaviors of residual deviance with the symptoms of the mentally ill. According to Scheff (1966: 40), there "should be an unlimited number of sources" of residual rule-breaking. In giving an example of residual rule-breaking, he discusses Goffman's position that there is a rule that the individual be "involved" when in public view. According to Scheff (1966: 34-39), if a person is uninvolved or "away" without giving the appropriate signals, he is a residual rule-breaker. Other examples of residual rule-breaking presented by Scheff are the Dada movement and the reactions to LSD-25, to monotony, and to sleep and sensory deprivation. Scheff holds that: (1) acts of residual rule-breaking are frequent and committed by a very wide segment of the "normal" population; (2) they are caused by very diverse (and frequently benign) factors; and (3) they should not be taken as an indication of personal abnormality or disorder. Scheff's point appears to be that we do not need to be particularly concerned with the act of residual deviance or its cause, but that instead we need to focus on the reactions of others to acts of residual deviance. Scheff (1966: 54) explicitly states that the societal reaction is the single most important factor in the stabilization of mental illness.

To explain the public's reaction to an act of residual rule-breaking, Scheff turns to the public stereotype of mental illness. He notes that "stereotyped imagery of mental disorder is learned in early childhood" (1966: 64) and that these "stereotypes of insanity are continually reaffirmed, inadvertently in ordinary social interaction" (p. 67).[1] According to Scheff (1966: 67), an important component of the public stereotype of insanity is the unreasoned fear of the mentally ill, which makes the public unwilling to take risks that would routinely be accepted in ordinary living. He holds that sometimes this stereotype is applied to a person who commits an act of residual rule-breaking and at other times it is not. He notes a general tendency to deny that an act of residual rule-breaking is an indication of mental illness. When denial occurs, residual rule-breaking is presumed to be transitory. However, if for some reason "the deviance of the individual becomes a public issue, the traditional stereotype of insanity becomes the guiding imagery for action"

(Scheff 1966: 82). When this happens, it is assumed that procedures to initiate hospitalization will be quickly taken.

Once a person enters the domain of officials responsible for the hospitalization of the mentally ill, it is argued that he will almost invariably *be* hospitalized. Scheff (1966: 105-155) presents a number of reasons for this supposition based on his research:

(1) Psychiatrists are more sensitive to signs of mental illness than the general public; they tend to see a broad array of persons as disturbed and in need of care.

(2) Once the question of whether or not a person is ill has been raised, officials, following the medical ideology, feel that it is safer to treat someone who may not be ill than it is to release someone who may be ill.

(3) There are a number of features built into the commitment process, such as established routines, lack of facilities, the payment schedule for examiners, etc., which make it difficult to reverse the commitment process.

Scheff's investigation of commitment procedures thus leads him to conclude that "the official societal reaction . . . exaggerates both the amount and degree of deviance," and once the official process is initiated the person is almost invariably routed to a mental hospital (Scheff, 1966: 154).

In summary, Scheff views mental illness as primarily an ascribed status, entry into which is primarily dependent on conditions external to the individual. His formulation is, first, that virtually everyone at some time commits acts that correspond to the public stereotype of mental illness; second, that if these acts become public knowledge, the individual may, depending on various contingencies, be referred to the appropriate officials. Scheff (1966: 182, 100) argues that whether or not this will happen depends upon the marginality of the patient, the patient's lack of power, the nature of the acts of residual rule-breaking, the social distance between the rule breaker and the control agents, the community tolerance level, and the availability of nondeviant roles. Third, once this happens, the person will be routinely processed as mentally ill and placed in a mental institution. This is an original formulation which very neatly gets around a potentially troublesome aspect of the labelling perspective–namely, why does the person commit an act of primary deviance? In most cases, it would be very difficult to argue that the person publicly presents psychiatric symptoms for personal gain or because he or she belongs to a subculture whose values are in conflict with those of the dominant group. Instead, Scheff argues that the psychiatric symptoms are a common phenomenon, that their presentation is unintended, and that only rarely and fortuitously do they cause someone to be labelled mentally ill.

Although Scheff (1970) has presented his theoretical formulation as a sufficient explanation of mental illness, using no qualifiers, we should note that in the introduction to his book he does indicate that his theoretical formulation probably exaggerates the processes of societal reaction and indicates that "ultimately, a framework which encompassed both individual and social systems . . . would be desirable" (Scheff, 1966: 25). It is very clear, however, that Scheff sees the processes of societal reaction as the key processes in the development of mental illness. For example, his final formal hypothesis is, "*Among residual rule breakers, labelling is the single most important cause of careers of residual deviance*" (Scheff, 1966: 92-93; italics in original). Similarly, he states that "the status of the mental patient is more often an ascribed status, with conditions for status entry and exit external to the patient, than an achieved status with the conditions for status entry dependent upon the patient's own behavior" (Scheff, 1966: 129). And finally, he states he has "sought to demonstrate that the behavior or 'condition' of the person alleged to be mentally ill is not usually an important factor in the decision of officials to retain or release new patients from the mental hospital" (Scheff, 1966: 154).

The evidence of the fifties would indicate that one of the tenets of the labelling perspective was correct—namely, that the public was ignorant about mental illness and had a very negative image of persons identified as mentally ill. For example, the studies by Star (1961), Nunnally (1961), and Cumming and Cumming (1957) indicated that during the fifties the public's information about mental illness distorted and exaggerated the amount and type of disturbance. In addition, Nunnally (1961: 46) found that "the mentally ill are regarded with fear, distrust and dislike." In the public conception, mental illness appeared to involve unpredictable and potentially dangerous behavior. Furthermore, there was a halo effect: Once a person was perceived as mentally ill, he or she was not only thought to be unpredictable and dangerous but also "dirty, unintelligent, insincere and worthless" (Nunnally, 1961: 233). These investigations indicated that the public had a negative, highly stereotyped image of mental illness and suggested that the public generally viewed mental illness as a master status that overrode other characteristics of the individual.

Research during the sixties, however, demonstrates that this pattern is no longer as clear as it once was. For example, recent research shows that persons are now more knowledgeable about mental illness and are better able to identify the mentally ill (see Spiro et al., 1973; Crocetti et al., 1974, for a review of the evidence). Furthermore, as Aviram and Segal (1973: 127) and

Crocetti et al. (1974) have shown, there has been a consistent decline over time in the extent to which the mentally ill are rejected. Most striking is the finding by Simmonds (1969: 33) that, among thirteen types of deviance, ex-mental patients were less likely to be rejected than eleven of the other types, including atheists, gamblers, beatniks, alcoholics, and adulterers. In fact, the only category of deviance that was even less likely to be rejected was intellectualism. Thus, although the data from the fifties support the societal reaction view that those perceived as mentally ill are excluded from social interaction, the recent evidence suggests that this view now rests on a questionable empirical base.

THE ISSUE OF WHO IS LABELLED MENTALLY ILL

I will now turn to the characteristics of those who are labelled mentally ill. I will first discuss the labelling process itself. This will give some idea of the rapidity, ease, and reason for labelling and indicate the degree to which there would appear to be an effective selection process which screens out those who are not mentally ill. I will then turn to the individual characteristics of the persons who are labelled mentally ill and then consider their societal attributes. Throughout this discussion, we should remember, according to Scheff, that one can fairly readily be labelled mentally ill for what is intrinsically relatively insignificant behavior, that once the issue of mental illness has been raised it becomes the guiding principle for action, and that officials are predisposed to err on the side of labelling versus nonlabelling. Furthermore, the societal reaction theorists as a group argue that, initially, those labelled as mentally ill do not differ markedly from those who are not labelled, and that it is those on the margin of society who are the most readily labelled (e.g., Scheff, 1966).

The Labelling Process

In a pioneering study, Yarrow et al. (1955) investigated how wives came to define their husbands as mentally ill. The research demonstrated that wives utilized strong defenses to avoid seeing their husbands' behavior as deviant, while making every effort to interpret their husbands' behavior as normal. If that failed, they would minimize the importance of the behavior and balance it off against more normal behavior. Only when a husband's behavior became impossible to deal with would the wife take action to have her husband hospitalized. Even at this time the husband was not always viewed as mentally ill. This pattern is similar to that described by Schwartz (1957:

290), Sampson et al. (1961), Hollingshead and Redlich (1958), Myers and Roberts (1959: 213-220), Jaco (1960: 18). For example, Sampson et al. (1964: 121) state:

> the study groups' wives were grossly disturbed for some time without being defined as mentally ill and without any kind of psychiatric or other professional care. Prior to hospitalization, the wife might have been severely depressed, immobilized, weeping and withdrawn for weeks or even months; she might be unable to perform even routine duties as a housewife and mother most of the time over several years; she might express bizarre, delusional ideas or even noticeably carry on conversations with unseen people without provoking her husband or other relatives to seek professional care or hospitalize her.

Smith et al. (1963) did an analysis of the events precipitating the hospitalization of one hundred schizophrenic patients. Their data suggest that the prospective patients had been disturbed for some time prior to hospitalization. The typical patient had performed more than three critical acts which, in themselves, might appear to warrant hospitalization. The acts that eventually led to hospitalization typically involved "dangerous behavior." Substantially similar results have been reported by Whitmer and Conover (1959).[2]

Even Goffman, who can hardly be considered an advocate of the psychiatric perspective, recognizes that the situation prior to hospitalization tends to be intolerable. As he writes regarding the havoc created by the actions of the mentally ill (1971: 357):

> This havoc indicates that medical symptoms and mental symptoms are radically different in their social consequences and in their character. It is this havoc that the philosophy of containment must deal with. It is this havoc that psychiatrists have dismally failed to examine and that sociologists ignore when they treat mental illness as a labeling process. It is this havoc that we must explore.

Sampson et al. (1964), Yarrow et al. (1955), Myers and Roberts (1959), Hollingshead and Redlich (1958), and Schwartz (1957) all indicate that, although the prospective patient is seriously disturbed, hospitalization is delayed for a considerable period of time. This is also suggested by other studies. For example, Wood et al. (1968: 253) found that sixty-five percent of their patients "reported that they had been ill for longer than one year prior to admission. Most of these patients reported they had been ill for years." Although most families tend to avoid hospitalizing the prospective patient and deny that he or she is mentally ill, this does not mean that they do not treat him or her as a deviant. As Goffman (1971) makes clear in his discussion of the havoc created by the prospective patient, the family has to react to the prospective patient and virtually has to collude against and exclude him or her. As Sampson et al. (1964: 122) describe the process:

> the future patient and her husband moved from each other emotionally, effected patterns of uninvolvement, and reciprocated withdrawal with further withdrawal. The patient moved and was moved toward exclusion, away from interpersonal ties and from any meaningful linkings in social reality. This situation was compatible with very high family tolerance for deviant behavior, primarily because the deviance was ignored by the husband and not visible in the community.

They go on to indicate that

> one important consequence of these accommodative patterns was that the wife did not become accessible to outside help or treatment in many instances until her psychosis was well advanced. By then, her capacity to use help was minimal. Her need was so urgent, her control of impulses and assessment of reality so impaired, her distrust so intense, that any intervention short of hospitalization was too little and too late. A second consequence of these patterns was that other family members had to endure in their homes the presence of a grossly disturbed and sometimes psychotic person for very extended times [Sampson et al., 1964: 123-124].

A very basic position of the societal reaction theorists is that the more powerful a person is the more likely (s)he will be able to avoid (or at least delay) being channeled into a deviant role. However, the literature consistently indicates that persons who occupy a critical and thus a powerful position in the family are more likely to be and are hospitalized more quickly than persons not in such a role. For example, Hammer (1963-1964: 247), in a study of hospitalized patients, found that, of nineteen persons having critical positions in the family, seventeen were hospitalized within a year of the first manifestation of symptoms; whereas thirty-six persons who occupied noncritical positions, only four were hospitalized within the year following the first manifestation of symptoms. Horn (1968: 19-20) found "that the median length of time from the point that the patient was first perceived as 'acting differently' until hospitalization was 36 months for those whose roles were critical and 66 months for those whose roles were noncritical." Similar, if less dramatic, differences were found by Linn (1961: 98). Studies of rehospitalization also consistently suggest that occupying a critical position in the family is positively related to rehospitalization and to the speed with which it occurs (Brown et al., 1962; Freeman and Simmons, 1958, 1963: 94, 97; Angrist et al., 1968: 97; Myers and Bean, 1968: 45).

Before turning to the official screening process associated with persons being involuntarily hospitalized, let us look at persons who voluntarily seek psychiatric care. As will be noted below, most persons who receive psychiatric treatment do so in outpatient clinics, community mental health centers, general hospitals, and private (as compared to public) mental hospitals. Almost all persons receiving such treatment do so voluntarily. Furthermore, a very substantial proportion of persons treated in public mental hospitals are also voluntary patients. From the societal reaction perspective, it is very hard to see why persons would voluntarily stigmatize themselves by seeking psychiatric treatment, particularly when it involved inpatient care. As far as I can determine, the societal reaction theorists have made no attempt to explain voluntary admission to psychiatric treatment aside from an occasional comment that such persons must have been pressured into treatment. However, Kadushin (1969), in his study of why persons go to psychiatrists, found that "only about 5% of the clinic applicants were subjected to heavy pressure to go to a clinic, and only 5% of the applicants to analytic and religio-psychiatric clinics had not themselves actually asked to be sent to a psychiatric clinic" (p. 317).

Similarly, Saenger and Cumming (1965), in a study of outpatient service in all of New York State found that only nine percent of the clinic applicants came because they were told to do so "or else." As Kadushin (1969: 252-253) notes, "These figures are in fact not radically different from those reported in *Personal Influence* for brand shifting (15%), motion picture selection (14%), or fashion change (8%)." Another conceptually possible explanation is that the vast majority of persons seeking voluntary psychiatric care think they are mentally ill even though they are not. That is, these persons have committed an act of residual rule-breaking which had little intrinsic significance but which caused them to apply the stereotype of mental illness to themselves and caused them to seek psychiatric care. However, to me a much more plausible explanation of why persons voluntarily seek psychiatric care is that they are seriously distressed and confused, a finding consistent with my own research (Gove and Fain, 1975) and, as we shall see, with the information on the manifestation of symptoms by psychiatric patients.

In short, the fact that the vast majority of persons who enter the role of the mentally ill do so voluntarily suggests that the labelling perspective cannot, at least in anything like its present form, explain why most people are in the role of the mentally ill.

Still looking at voluntary patients, we might ask whether, as Scheff suggests, psychiatrists act on the assumption of illness and routinely hospitalize a patient who applies for treatment. Mechanic (1962) and Brown (1961: 60) feel that public mental hospitals accept virtually all such patients, but they present no data. To my knowledge there are only two studies that have systematically evaluated hospital acceptance of voluntary patients. Mishler and Wexler (1963) found that the public mental hospital they studied accepted for admission only thirty-nine percent (n = 246) of the applicants, and the private mental hospital accepted fifty-eight percent (n = 137) of the applicants. Similarly, Mendel and Rapport (1969) found that the public mental hospital they studied accepted for admission forty-one percent (n = 269) of the applicants. Although there probably are hospitals that routinely admit all applicants, it is clearly inappropriate to assume this is always or even usually the case.

Let us turn to involuntary patients. Such persons may be thought of as going through three states in their contact with public officials: (1) a screening stage when the police or some other screening agency makes the decision to hold or not to hold the person for examination and possible commitment, (2) an examination by a court psychiatrist or other duly qualified board, and (3) the court hearing when the official decision is made to release the person or to commit him or her to a mental hospital.

First, let us look at the limited data available on the screening stage. A study of police discretion in the apprehension of the mentally ill by Bittner (1967: 280) found that the police, "like everyone else avail themselves of various forms of denial when it comes to doing something about it [mental illness]." Furthermore, it is Bittner's impression that "except for cases of suicide attempts, the decision to take someone to the hospital is based upon overwhelmingly conclusive evidence of illness" (Bittner, 1967: 285). He goes on to note that the police regularly assist persons in the community whom they and others recognize as having a serious mental disturbance while making no effort to have them hospitalized. The largest study of the hospitalization process has been done by Rock et al. (1968) for the American Bar Foundation. Their findings seem to support Bittner. In their words, "given the reluctance of the police and judiciary to act without benefit of medical judgment, and given the fact that medical services are not so organized that they can be deployed for "front line" attention to the potential patient, a condition of circular inertia results" (pp. 94-95).

Tucker (1972a, 1972b), in a recent study of police and hospital records of persons brought to a general hospital for psychiatric treatment, found that seventy-seven percent of the time the police were responding to a complaint and twenty-three percent of the time the police were the ones who initiated action. When the police were responding to a complaint, in the majority of the cases, the other person in the apprehension situations stated that they were related to the subject. When the police brought the prospective patient to the only general hospital in the city that would accept persons brought in by policc, seventy-one percent of the persons were admitted to psychiatric care, with other dispositions being made for the other twenty-nine percent. A follow-up study in another general hospital conducted by Baxter et al. (1968) indicated that those hospitalized in a psychiatric emergency needed to be in a hospital. In looking at the action of the psychiatrists, Tucker (1972b: 15-16) notes,

> First, their decisions about diagnosis and disposition were not affected by the socio-demographic attributes of age, sex and race. Second, the types of other persons present in the apprehension situation, the labels of those others and the labels of the police officers did not seem to affect the *diagnosis* given by the psychiatric residents. Third, the labels of other persons present in the apprehension situations and previous treatment did not seem to affect the *disposition* given by the psychiatric residents. Finally, it appears that these decisions of psychiatric residents were made on information other than that mentioned above in the police reports.

He goes on to note that there was a tendency to hospitalize the patient if others were not available to help the patient, and that there was a correlation between the police officer labelling the person "demented" and disposition (but not the diagnosis). In looking at the screening process, we might note that in the vast majority of the cases someone other than the police had decided that there was something seriously the matter with the patient; the police then evaluated the person and if they decided he was "demented," the person was brought to the hospital, where at least fairly substantial screening again occurred. Before the person would be committed to a mental hospital he or she would still need to undergo an official psychiatric examination and a commitment proceeding.

To my knowledge, there is only one study (Wilde, 1968) of a psychiatric screening agency that presents the agency's response to requests to initiate commitment proceedings. In this study, when someone other than a psychiatrist made a request to initiate commitment proceedings, the screening agency approved the request in only thirty-three percent of the cases (n = 6,000).[3] In contrast, when a psychiatrist made a request, the request was apparently routinely approved–the approval rate for hospital psychiatrists being ninety-eight percent (n = 2,000), and for court psychiatrists one hundred percent (n = 250)–presumably on the assumption that the psychiatrist had carefully and expertly evaluated the need for hospitalization.[4]

Support for the validity of this assumption is provided by the fact that the court psychiatrists examined approximately 1,000 suspected mental cases sent by the jails but requested commitment proceedings on only 250 (Wilde, 1968: 216). These studies clearly suggest that, during the initial screening stage, officials do not assume illness but, in fact, proceed rather cautiously, screening out a substantial number of persons.

Let us shift to the outcome of psychiatric examination of persons held for commitment. Scheff, in his study of these examinations, found them to be unsystematic, arbitrary, and prejudicial. He found that "except in very unusual cases, the psychiatric examiner's recommendation to retain the patient is virtually automatic" (Scheff, 1968: 287). Nonetheless, in each of the studies reviewed, release was recommended for at least some persons (see Table 3.1). Generally such recommendations were relatively rare; however, in

TABLE 3.1
OUTCOME OF THE PSYCHIATRIC EXAMINATION

Wilde (1968: 216-7)		Recommendation of Examiners		
		Release[a]	**Commit**	**N**
		4.8% (200)	95.2% (4000)	4200

Haney and Michielutte (1968)[b]	Examiners' Evaluation of Prospective Patients			
Age	**Competent**	**Temporarily Incompetent**[c]	**Incompetent**	**N**
up to 64	35.7% (158)	13.6% (61)	50.0% (221)	442
65-over	8.5% (11)	3.1% (4)	88.4% (129)	144
Total	29.6% (169)	11.4% (65)	59.0% (337)	571

Kutner (1962)	Recommendation of Examiners		
	Release	**Commit**	**N**
	33%	77%	Not given

Scheff (1968: 284)[d]	Recommendation of Examiners			
	Release	**30 Day Observation**	**Commit**	**N**
	7.7% (2)	23.1% (6)	69.2% (18)	26

a. Over half the requests for commitment came from psychiatrists. If we assume that the court psychiatrists in such cases agreed with their colleagues, then in those cases where the proceedings were initiated by a layman, the proportion of persons for whom commitment is recommended drops to about ninety percent.

b. Although the authors do not explicitly say so, the examining board apparently had the power not only to examine but also to commit.

c. The authors do not indicate whether or not persons judged temporarily incompetent were to be committed to a mental hospital.

d. Elsewhere Scheff (1968: 281) notes that in the examination of 196 court records there was not a single recommendation for release (he does not indicate the outcomes of these hearings). This may be taken as an indication of an almost uniform presumption of illness, but it may be the case that when the psychiatrists recommend the person be released, the officials try to settle out of court by getting the participants to agree to the release of the subject.

the largest study (Haney and Michielutte, 1968) only fifty percent of the persons under sixty-five were found to be incompetent.

When we look at the outcome of the court hearing, we find a similar pattern with most, but usually not all, persons being committed (see Table 3.2). The description of the commitment proceedings by Miller and Schwartz (1966), Wenger and Fletcher (1969), and Scheff (1967) indicate that they are very rapid, that there is rarely any real exploration of the facts surrounding the case and that proper legal procedures are not closely observed. However, the hearings described by Kumasaka et al. (1972) were longer, more thorough, and legally correct. From their experience, Miller and Schwartz (1966: 34) guess that "the judgment of mental illness had already been made earlier in the commitment process and that the hearing was a rubber stamp to an earlier decision." From the rates presented by Wilde (1968), it would appear that those persons who are released are exclusively those for whom the psychiatrists had recommended such action. Wenger and Fletcher (1969: 68) explicitly state this to be the case in their study. Miller and Schwartz (1966: 34), however, found that "the judge reversed the medical recommendation for commitment . . . in nearly one-fourth of the cases." One of the more interesting things about the study by Miller and Schwartz (1966) is that most of the prospective patients did not resist commitment, and those who did resist got special attention. In their words, "Many who resisted commitment elicited the judge's empathy and, as a result, one-half of those who resisted were either released or held over for further study" (Miller and Schwartz, 1966: 29). It is possible that those who did not resist commitment did not do so because they were seriously disturbed, whereas the disorder of those who resisted tended to be less severe.

As we have seen, early in the hospitalization process there appears to be fairly substantial screening, and it is very possible that by the time of the hearing most of the prospective patients have a serious disorder. The study by Kumasaka et al. (1972), which appears to have ample procedural and legal controls, bears on this point. Let us look at the process:

> A patient admitted to Bellevue may be discharged, kept for short-term treatment, or transferred to a state hospital either on a voluntary basis or involuntarily, that is on a two-Physician Certificate. When a two-Physician Certificate (two-PC) is signed by two staff psychiatrists, the certificate is forwarded to the Certification Office of the hospital, which enters the patient's name on the two-PC register. In the last four years, approximately one-third of the patients admitted to Bellevue each year were initially placed on this two-PC status.
>
> After certification, the patient is kept in Bellevue for about another week so that he or any interested party may contest the decision of the

TABLE 3.2
OUTCOME OF COURT HEARINGS (in percentages)

	Proportion of Cases	
Wilde (1968: 216-17)		
Released		**Committed**
4.8 (200)		95.2 (4000)
Miller and Schwartz (1966)		
	Proportion of Cases[a]	
Released	**Held Over**	**Committed**
22 (13)	10 (6)	68 (39)
Wenger and Fletcher (1969)		
	Proportion of Cases	
Released		**Committed**
19.7 (16)		80.3 (65)
Scheff (1967: 113)		
	Proportion of Cases	
Released		**Committed**
0 (0)		100 (43)
Kumasaka (1972)		
	Proportion of Cases	
Released		**Committed**
13.7 (104)		86.3 (653)

a. Of the fifty-eight prospective patients, thirteen were voluntarily seeking admission.

> Bellevue psychiatrists through judicial review. If a court hearing is requested by the patient or someone else, the patient's name is placed on the court hearing schedule compiled weekly at the Certification Office. . . . The patient is then assigned to one of the staff attorneys of the Mental Health Information Service (MHIS) at Bellevue. These lawyers gather information partly from hospital records and partly from independent sources [Kumasaka, 1972: 399].

In 1966 and 1967, approximately twelve percent of the patients on two-PC status requested court hearings. The rate then started to decline and by 1969 only seven percent of the two-PC patients requested court hearings (Kumasaka et al., 1972: 400). This suggests that the overwhelming majority of the two-PC patients acquiesced to commitment, presumably because they were seriously disturbed. I would note that among those who requested hearings a very substantial proportion (almost fifty percent by 1969) were released. Release was generally due to the action of the psychiatrist prior to the hearing, for, as is indicated by Table 3.2, if the hearing actually occurred, an average of only 13.7% of the patients were released.

We might end the discussion of the commitment process by looking at the conclusions of Rock et al. (1968), who have conducted by far the largest and most comprehensive (if somewhat unsystematic) investigation of the commitment process.

> It seems probable that the danger posed by malicious or negligent commitment petitions is exaggerated and that the sanctions are too severe. The more important problem today is not the filing of petitions that are without cause, but rather finding a person willing to petition. We found, generally speaking, that when hospitalization procedures were initiated by close family members, the potential liabilities implicit in the petitioning procedure seldom deterred them from acting, for the family member was not aware in most instances of his own legal position in filing the petition. . . . Our study indicates that the potential penalties concomitant with petitioning may constitute a barrier to the initiation of proceedings by other individuals even when there is a clear need for hospitalization and when no other agent is willing to act [Rock et al., 1968: 86].

They go on to indicate:

> Our broad conclusion [is] that the law as it now stands has effects at preliminary stages that are overly inhibitive. . . . By and large, and most clearly in jurisdictions where commitment is by judicial proceedings, official decisions regarding hospitalization are concerned only with clear-cut cases. This phenomenon goes a long way to explain why the commitment proceedings that do occur are perfunctory [Rock et al., 1968: 122].

INDIVIDUAL CHARACTERISTICS OF PERSONS LABELLED MENTALLY ILL

According to the psychiatric perspective, persons who are reacted to as mentally ill are in fact mentally ill, and they manifest the attributes that mark them as such. In contrast, the labelling perspective, which looks at the societal attributes to explain why an individual is labelled, does not see individuals who are labelled mentally ill as differing intrinsically from those who are not so labelled. In this section, I will look at individuals who are labelled and individuals who are not labelled to see whether or not they differ in (a) their genetic predisposition to mental illness, (b) their manifestation of psychiatric symptoms, and (c) their experience of critical life events which may predispose them to mental illness.

The evidence that schizophrenia has a strong genetic component is compelling. First, as Slater (1968) notes, there is a very consistent rate of schizophrenia across all countries where thorough exams have been conducted. Furthermore, in these countries there has been no change in rate over time. Second, the incidence is higher among family members, and the closer the relationship, the more frequent the incidence (Heston, 1966; Alanen, 1958; Slater, 1968). Third, and more important, children of schizophrenic mothers who have been raised outside their biological family—that is, have been adopted, have much higher rates of schizophrenia than comparably raised controls (Heston and Denny, 1968; Kety et al., 1968; Rosenthal et al., 1968; Wender et al., 1968; Heston, 1970). Fourth, and equally important, monozygotic twins are much more likely to be concordant for schizophrenia than dyzygotic twins (Slater, 1968; Gottesman and Shields, 1972; Kringlen, 1968; Shields, 1968; Gottesman, 1968; Shields and Gottesman, 1972). And finally, as Kringlen (1968) has shown, monozygotic twins are almost always concordant for schizophrenia even when they are reared apart. In short, as Meehl (1972: 368) states when reviewing the evidence presented in Gottesman and Shields (1972), "Nothing but American social science prejudice plus 'establishment psychiatry' brainwashing (given the usual dash of muddleheadedness) can, I think, lead anyone who has read this book to persist in strong doubt of the prime importance of genetic factors in schizophrenia."

There has been much less research done on manic-depressive psychosis. Like schizophrenia, the incidence of manic-depressive psychosis is higher among family members, and the closer the relationship, the higher the rate (Stendstedt, 1952, 1959; Schulz, 1951, Alanen, 1958). This, of course, could very plausibly be due to environmental factors. More relevant is the consistent finding that monozygotic twins are much more likely to be concordant for manic-depressive psychosis than are dyzygotic twins (for a review of the evidence, see Gershon, et al., 1971). Another indicator of a genetic link is that one is able to genetically distinguish between unipolar and bipolar (depressive only and manic-depressive) psychosis (Perris, 1968; Angst and Perris, 1968; Winokur and Clayton, 1967; Reich and Winokur, 1969; Cadoret et al., 1970).

Whether or not there is a genetic link with neurosis is not so great a concern to us, since most persons treated for a neurosis enter treatment voluntarily, and the societal reaction is thus somewhat attenuated. And regardless of its theoretical importance, there has been relatively little investigation of whether or not there is a genetic link in neurosis. What evidence there is does suggest that the link exists, but that it is much weaker than the link associated with schizophrenia or manic-depressive psychosis. As Minor (1973) has shown, there appears to be a higher rate of anxiety neurosis among primary relatives than among the general public. More important is the fact that monozygotic twins are more likely to be concordant for neurosis than dyzygotic twins (see Minor, 1973; for a review, also see Shields, 1954), although the difference between the groups is not huge.

In summary, for the two most serious forms of mental illness, schizophrenia and manic-depressive psychosis, there appears to be a very strong genetic component to the disorders. This finding would appear to run counter to the labelling perspective.

According to the psychiatric perspective, persons who receive psychiatric treatment are mentally ill and should manifest more psychiatric symptoms than those not receiving such treatment. In contrast, the societal reaction perspective suggests that persons receiving psychiatric treatment do not have an underlying psychiatric disorder and thus they should not manifest markedly higher rates of psychiatric symptoms. There have, by now, been a fairly large number of comparisons of the manifestation of psychiatric symptoms by persons in psychiatric treatment and normal controls. The following scales have all indicated that persons in psychiatric treatment are more likely to manifest psychiatric symptoms than those not in treatment:

(1) the HOS Scale developed in the Sterling County Study (Leighton et al., 1963; Matthews, n.d.; Macmillan, 1957; Semmence, 1969; Spiro et al., 1972);
(2) the Langner Scale developed in the Midtown Study (Langner, 1962; Haese and Miele, 1967; Manis et al., 1963; Shader et al., 1971; Gove et al., 1975);
(3) the Gurin Scale (Schwartz et al., 1974; Greenley, 1972);
(4) the General Well-Being Scale developed by Dupuy (Gove et al., 1975);
(5) the Cornell Medical Index (Gunderson and Ronson, 1969);
(6) the KDS-1 developed by Kupfer and Detre (Kupfer et al., 1972);
(7) the Zung Depression Scale (Zung, 1965a, 1965b, 1967, 1969; Gove et al., 1975);
(8) the Hunt Depression Scale (Hunt et al., 1967); and
(9) the Lubin Depression Checklist (Lubin, 1965).

Of all the studies I have been able to locate, in only one group did psychiatric patients not have a higher rate of symptoms than did nonpatients, and that was a group of predischarge patients (Manis et al., 1963). Furthermore, there is an extensive literature dealing with the systematic rating of symptoms by psychiatrists which consistently show that psychiatric patients manifest more symptoms than do nonpatients (e.g., Spitzer et al., 1970).

In summary, there is a large body of data that indicates psychiatric patients manifest significantly more symptoms of mental illness than do nonpatients. We should note, however, that most of the studies show some overlap between the two groups. Thus, although the evidence generally supports the psychiatric perspective, it is possible to interpret the evidence as indicating that some of the difference between the patients and nonpatients are due to societal factors. However, as is suggested by the data in Dohrenwend and Crandell (1970), Seiler (1973), and Schwartz et al. (1973), much of the overlap between the patient and nonpatient groups may be due to the fact that the scales in question generally measure relatively common and nonserious symptoms (i.e., those of neurosis) and ignore the less common and more severe symptoms (i.e., those of psychosis). Thus, it is also possible that different scales, which focused on more severe symptoms, would show much less overlap between the groups.

A basic tenet of psychiatric theory is that stress is related to the onset of mental illness, and, in fact, when we look at the extent to which persons in the community experience stress, there is considerable evidence that such experiences are associated with the manifestation of psychiatric symptoms (e.g., Langner and Michael, 1963; Berkman, 1971; Myers et al., 1971, 1972). If this aspect of psychiatric theory is correct, then we would anticipate that those hospitalized for mental illness would be more likely to have experienced severe stress just prior to hospitalization than would comparable controls. Although this has been a common belief, is a concept that difficult to operationalize. However, the recent studies of critical life events have provided fairly conclusive evidence that persons hospitalized for mental illness are much more likely than comparable controls to have experienced a critical life event just prior to their hospitalization (Paykel et al., 1969; Paykel, 1973; Birley and Brown, 1970; Brown and Birley, 1968; Brown et al., 1973a, 1973b). Of particular importance is the fact that this finding holds up even when we look at events that are completely outside the control of the prospective patient, such as someone losing a job because of a plant closing down. The labelling theorists would probably respond to this evidence by suggesting that the critical event may have focused attention on the prospective patient, with the consequence that people started noticing acts of residual rule-breaking which previously had gone unnoticed. This, of course, is a conceptual possibility, but the fact that such events are also associated with a wide range of stress-related physical disorders (Rahe and Arthur, 1968; Rahe et al., 1964; Rahe et al., 1967; Rahe, 1969) would suggest that it is unlikely.

In summary, the evidence on genetic propensity toward mental illness, the manifestation of psychiatric symptoms, and the recent experience of critical life events indicates a sharp distinction between those labelled mentally ill and those not so labelled. These differences are consistent with the psychiatric perspective, but appear to be inconsistent with the labelling perspective.

Societal Characteristics of Those Labelled Mentally Ill

According to the labelling perspective, after the level of primary deviance is controlled for, the more marginal the person's societal attributes the greater the likelihood that he or she will be channelled into a deviant role. In fact, when societal reaction is treated as a dependent variable, this is perhaps the key prediction. In this section we will look at four indices of the persons's power—namely, the person's socioeconomic status, marital status, sex, and race. If the labelling perspective is correct, controlling for level of primary deviance, we would expect higher rates of psychiatric treatment among those in the lower class, among the never-married, among women, and among blacks.

Socioeconomic status. When one looks at the relationship between social class and mental illness, probably the first thing one notices is that those in the lower classes are more likely to be treated for mental illness, particularly in mental hospitals (e.g., Hollingshead and Redlich, 1958; Kohn 1968; Rushing, 1969). In general, this evidence is consistent with the societal reaction explanation; however, I would note that Rushing (1969) has shown that occupational groups of comparable status often have widely divergent rates of hospitalization, a finding that is not readily explicable by that perspective. More important is the fact that the traditional psychiatric explanations see stress as more common in the lower class, and thus they would also predict higher rates of mental illness in the lower class. Furthermore, their supposition is supported by the fact that most community surveys find higher rates of mental illness among the lower classes (e.g., Dohrenwend and Dohrenwend, 1969).

As both the psychiatric and labelling perspectives see persons in the lower class as having higher rates of psychiatric treatment, we must turn to what these perspectives would predict when levels of primary deviance are controlled for. As we have seen, the labelling theorists would see the lower class as having higher rates after such controls are introduced. In contract, the psychiatric perspective would see the upper class as having higher rates, for, according to their view, socioeconomic resources will help one get treatment. In particular, they presume that such resources will facilitate the correct identification of the disorder and promote prompt and effective action aimed at obtaining the appropriate psychiatric care. As has been shown in Gove and Howell (1974), the evidence on entrance into psychiatric treatment supports the psychiatric perspective and not the societal reaction perspective. As we show in that article, members of the lower class tend to see only a narrow range of aggressive, antisocial behavior as creating a need for psychiatric treatment, whereas persons in the middle and upper class perceive a much wider range of psychopathological behavior as indicating a need for psychiatric care (Gove and Howell, 1974: 89). Thus the evidence on attitudes and knowledge would suggest that persons from the upper classes would seek treatment more quickly and for a wider range of behavior than persons from the lower classes.

Let us examine the relationship between socioeconomic resources and delay in seeking treatment. A basic theme in the classic work by Hollingshead and Redlich (1958) is that members of the lower class are less likely than members of the upper class to identify disturbed behavior as mental illness, that they are more apt to delay seeking treatment and that, when treatment is finally initiated, it is frequently due to the acts of members of the general community, because the patient and his or her family either did not act or acted inappropriately. Myers and Roberts (1959) made a detailed analysis of differences in the onset of illness and paths to treatment of a sample of middle-class and lower-class patients. Among the schizophrenics, they found that in the lower class, "patients were obviously psychotic for over three years before psychiatric referral," whereas among the middle class, "families recognized the patient's classic psychiatric symptoms when they appeared and called a physician," and a psychiatric referral was made in less than a month (Myers and Roberts, 1959: 285). Similar class differences were found among neurotic patients, although the differences were not as marked (e.g., Myers and Roberts, 1959: 283). Furthermore, in my research (Gove and Howell, 1974), I found that low family income was associated with a tendency to delay entrance into psychiatric treatment. These results are supported by Angrist et al. (1968: 97), who found that well-educated patients were likely to be early returnees to the hospital, whereas less-educated patients were more likely to be late returnees. Similarly, Freeman and Simmons (1959) indicate, based on an analysis of the performance of ex-patients and their families' expectations, that middle-class families are less willing to tolerate deviant behavior than lower-class families and are therefore more likely to rehospitalize a former patient.

Turning to the literature on the relationship between class and symptomatology, one finds that it consistently indicates that patients from the lower class typically have a more serious disorder, tending to be more disorganized and violent, whereas the symptoms of the middle-class patients tend to reflect intrapsychic concerns. For example, Myers and Bean, in their study of hospitalized patients, found that "anxiety, depression, obsessions, compulsion and phobias" were much more frequent in the upper classes than the lower classes; while "memory or orientation disturbances, disorganized thought processes, delusions and hallucinations, aggressive verbal behavior and aggressive physical behavior" were more common in the lower class. Myers and Roberts (1959: 285-287) found a similar pattern, even after diagnosis was controlled for, and the pattern is clearly suggested in the cases presented by Hollingshead and Redlich (1958: 172-176). Turner et al., (1969: 294), in a study of schizophrenics drawn from a psychiatric case register, found that for the total sample schizophrenics from the lower class tended to have a more serious pathology than schizophrenics from the upper classes. Shader et al., (1971: 598) found that lower-class patients at a mental health center manifested many more symptoms, as indicated by the Langner scale, than upper-class patients. Similarly, in my own research (Gove and Howell, 1974), I found that at hospitalization patients with a small family income tended to manifest much more serious symptoms than patients with a larger family income.

Marital status. As with class-related variables, the labelling theorists argue that the greater the individual's social or family resources, the greater the likelihood that he or she will be able to avoid hospitalization, particularly in a state mental hospital (e.g., Rushing, 1971; Linsky, 1970). Such theorists assume that interested family members will be able to pressure and manipulate the medical and legal professions to prevent hospitalization. In contrast, the psychiatric perspective suggests that family resources would play an important role in getting a disturbed person into treatment, and that the family's action, by producing a prompt entry, would prevent the development of a severe disorder. For example, they would argue that the disturbance of a person living with his family would be noticed more quickly simply because of his close proximity to others. Furthermore, they would suggest that a person is more likely to assume the responsibility for seeing that someone gets the necessary psychiatric care if close family ties are involved. As we have already seen, this is a premise that has been strongly supported by the study done by Rock et al., (1968). In addition, it has been suggested (e.g., Hammer, 1963-1964) that if one is very dependent on the behavior of another person, as are most married persons, one will be more likely to take action if the person stops performing his or her tasks than if one is not dependent. Again, as has been noted above, this premise is supported, for persons who occupy critical positions in the family are hospitalized much more quickly than persons who do not occupy critical positions.

In our research, Patrick Howell and I divided the patients into three marital categories: those who are married, those whose marriages have been disrupted (the divorced, separated, or widowed), and those who have never been married. We argued, as does Rushing (1971), that the married have most social resources and the single the fewest, with the disrupted category falling between. In general, our data showed that a lack of social resources, as indicated by marital status, was associated with a delay in seeking psychiatric treatment. Furthermore, our data showed that the never married had the most severe disorders and the married the least severe disorders (Gove and Howell, 1974).

In summary, the data on social resources, particularly as indicated by marital status, indicate that such resources are directly related to a rapid entrance into psychiatric treatment.

Sex. In our society, as in most societies, women have a lower status than men. Thus, if we focus on the societal reaction argument that persons on the margin of society are more likely to be channelled into a deviant role, we would predict that women would have a higher rate of treatment for mental illness than men. Indeed, as I have shown elsewhere (Gove and Tudor, 1973), if we limit mental illness to its traditional forms, women in our society do have higher rates of treatment for mental illness. However, it seems highly unlikely that the higher rates for women are due to the processes pointed to by the labelling theorists.

First, when we look at recent community studies conducted in our society, we find that the extent to which women appear to have higher rates of mental illness than men is greater in the community studies than in most of the data on psychiatric treatment, indicating the difference is real (Gove and Tudor, 1973). Second, the data indicate that in western industrial societies prior to World War II men had higher rates of mental illness than women. Similarly, the data suggest that in nonindustrial societies women tend to have lower rates of mental illness than men (Gove and Tudor, 1973). Thus, it does not appear to be their lower status per se which produces the higher rate of mental illness among women in our society. Third, and most important, as the Tudors and I (Tudor et al. 1975) have shown elsewhere, when we look at the actual processes of societal reaction, they tend to work against men more than against women. As has been shown–most clearly by Phillips (1964), but also by Larson (1970) and Fletcher (1969)–men are rejected more strongly for the manifestation of the same disturbed behavior. Even more important is the fact that men are hospitalized for mental illness at an earlier age, and this does not appear to be due to a difference in the time of onset of symptoms but instead to a prompter reaction to the manifestation of symptoms in men (Tudor et al. 1975). Furthermore, the data indicate that men are more likely than women to have a prolonged hospitalization, suggesting a more severe societal reaction to men than women. Thus, when we look at the actual processes of societal reaction, they appear to work against the more powerful and not the weaker sex status.

Race. Nonwhites in our society have lower status than whites and thus, even after controlling for socioeconomic variables and degree of psychiatric disturbance, the labelling perspective predicts that blacks (as a nonwhite group) would have higher rates of psychiatric treatment than whites. Unfortunately, I know of no study that allows us to look at the societal reaction to blacks and whites and allows us to control for either socioeconomic variables or psychiatric condition. However, the available data do allow us to draw some very tentative conclusions.

Fisher's (1969) review of the evidence on racial differences leads him to conclude that, even without controlling for economic factors, the evidence taken in toto does not indicate that blacks have higher rates of hospitalization than whites. His conclusion is supported by the early national data which indicated that blacks had lower rates of admission to mental hospitals than whites (Malzberg, 1940: 225). However, the recent government statistics indicate that, at present, nonwhites have somewhat higher rates of psychiatric treatment than whites in general hospital psychiatric inpatient units (Taube, 1973b), in community mental health centers (Bachrach, 1973), in outpatient psychiatric clinics (Taube, 1970), and in public mental hospitals (Taube, 1971). These differences, while substantial, are not huge and do not control for socioeconomic variables. I would note that the differences in these statistics between whites and nonwhites are relatively comparable to those found in the community survey by Warheit et al., (1973) which, by and large, washed out when socioeconomic controls were introduced. Thus, at present nonwhites do appear to have higher rates of psychiatric treatment than whites, but it is not clear if these differences would persist if socioeconomic controls were introduced.

The literature on hospitalization and commitment does provide at least some indication of whether or not blacks are discriminated against in the hospitalization process. In looking at persons brought by the police to a general hospital for psychiatric treatment, Tucker (1972b) found that the hospital admitted seventy-eight percent of the whites and sixty-six percent of the blacks, a direction that runs counter to that postulated by the labelling perspective. In a similar vein, Baxter et al., (1968) found that the prospective patient's race was unrelated to the decision to hospitalize. In a study of commitment proceedings, Haney et al., (1969) found that being nonwhite was very weakly related to being found competent. In contrast, a study by Fein and Miller (1972) found that being nonwhite was very weakly related to being found incompetent ($r = .07$), but at the same time they found that nonwhites were slightly less likely to be confined prior to the hearing ($r = .15$) and that nonwhites were slightly more likely to have a legal committee at the hearing ($r = .12$).

In summary, the very limited evidence on race indicates that the processes pointed to by the labelling perspective do not result in a marked discrimination against blacks as compared to whites. In fact, what evidence there is does not demonstrate any discrimination. When this limited information is combined with the substantial amount of data which suggests that, when the degree of the disorder is controlled for, hospitalization is more frequent among (a) the upper classes, (b) those with social resources, and (c) men, we find that the labelling perspective is not supported. In fact, the effect of the societal reaction process is in the opposite direction to that postulated.

THE CONSEQUENCES OF BEING LABELLED MENTALLY ILL

Let us now turn to what happens to a person who enters psychiatric treatment, paying particular attention to mental hospitalization. The labelling theorists believe that once a person has gone through a public hearing and has been certified as a deviant and placed in an institution, it is extremely difficult for the person to break out of the deviant status. For a number of reasons the impact of this process is held to be especially pronounced for the mental patient (see Goffman, 1961). First, the mental patient may have been misled, lied to, jailed, and testified against by those (s)he trusted; and by the time he or she arrives at the hospital, (s)he is presumed to feel deserted, betrayed and estranged from family and friends. This condition should promote the acceptance of the mentally ill role. Second, in the hospital the patient is surrounded by severe restrictions and deprivations which are presented as "intended parts of his treatment, part of his need at the time, and therefore an expression of the state his self has fallen to" (Goffman, 1961: 149). Third, the events recorded in the patient's case history are selected in such a manner that they are almost uniformly defamatory and discrediting. These events tend to be public knowledge, and they may be used to keep the patient in his or her place and to validate the mental illness.

Unfortunately, the research in the societal reaction tradition dealing with the effects of hospitalization has focused almost exclusively on what goes on in the hospital. Such studies have apparently focused primarily on long-term patients who make up the bulk of the resident population and tend to ignore the majority of psychiatric patients whose hospitalization is relatively brief. For this reason, much of this literature presents an unrepresentative picture. Furthermore, the societal reaction theorists tend to focus on the mental hospital of the forties and early fifties and almost totally ignore the radical changes that have occurred in the past two decades in psychiatric treatment and hospitalization procedures. For example, according to Scheff (1974: 445), "The need for new research directions in the study of mental illness has long been apparent. Although thousands of studies have been based on the medical model, real progress toward scientific understanding or even a fruitful formulation of the problem is lacking." This was perhaps a viable position in the early fifties, but the revolutionary change Scheff appears to be calling for has been with us for two decades. This revolution originated in psychiatric treatment and is producing drastic modifications and innovations in psychiatric theory (e.g., Snyder et al., 1974). Furthermore, this revolution has been built around medication (e.g., tranquilizers and anti-depressants), which is the classic form of medical innovation, although it has also included other changes such as the open door policy and new psychotherapeutic techniques.

Statistics on Treatment

Let us turn to the statistics on psychiatric treatment, for they have a very decided bearing on the extent to which the institutionalizing processes described by the labelling theorists have a chance to affect most persons entering psychiatric treatment, and they point to problems of the perspective. From 1955 to 1971, there was an increase each year in the number of patients admitted to public mental hospitals. In spite of an influx of patients, each year from 1955 to the present has shown a decrease in the number of patients residing in public mental hospitals (Bethel, 1973). As Bethel (1973: 1) indicates,

> The number of inpatients in the 327 state and county mental hospitals in the U.S. as of June 30, 1972 was 275,995. This represents a drop of 32,029 patients or a ten percent decline over the past year. Thus, for the seventeenth consecutive year this population has declined. Since 1964, the decrease has been accelerating each year and continued to do so in 1972.

This reduction of the patient population, in spite of an increase in admission rate, has been brought about by reducing the average length of stay. Thus, while two decades ago a hospital stay of many months and often many years was common, in 1971 the median length of stay in the United States was forty-one days, and three-quarters of the patients had left within two months (Meyer and Taube, 1973). As is indicated by the data presented in Cannon and Redlich (1973) and elsewhere, in 1955 most persons who received psychiatric care did so in public mental hospitals. By 1970, many more persons were admitted to general hospitals for inpatient psychiatric care than were admitted to public mental hospitals. At that time, their median length of stay in the general hospitals was 11.4 days (Taube, 1973a). Furthermore, almost twice as many persons entered outpatient psychiatric clinics in 1970 as were admitted to public mental hospitals. In addition, in 1970 a very substantial number of persons were admitted to community mental health centers, another recent innovation. Of those admitted to the community mental health centers, eight-three percent received outpatient care and seventeen percent received inpatient care, with the inpatient care lasting seventeen days on the average (Witkin and Bass, 1973; Bass and Witkin, 1973). Thus, since 1955, there has been a tremendous increase in the number of persons receiving psychiatric care, but treatment is now for a brief period of time and tends to be given in the community.

With regard to labelling theory, one might note three things about these statistics. First, labelling theory would predict that the tremendous increase in the number of persons being labelled mentally ill by entering psychiatric treatment should result in a sizable increase in the number of persons in the role of the chronically mentally ill. But, as is indicated by the population in mental hospitals, there has been a marked decline in the number of persons in that role. Second, the hospitalization of the vast majority of mental patients is sufficiently brief that the impact of the institutionalizing process outlined by the labelling theorists should be minimal. Third, the influx in the number of persons entering psychiatric care, including the increase in public mental hospital admissions, can be attributed almost entirely to persons voluntarily seeking treatment. Labelling theory (at least as presently formulated) has no explanation for this influx of voluntary patients.[5]

Institutionalism

However, let us agree that mental hospitals *may* be debilitating places where patients *may* come to accept the preferred role of the insane and *may,* over time, develop skills and a world view adapted to the institutional setting and gradually lose their roles and even interest in the community. The available evidence, however, suggests that this is not a common reaction to the modern mental hospital. For example, Brown et al., (1966: 201) state, regarding their follow-up study of 339 schizophrenic patients, that "institutionalism . . . was almost completely prevented during the five years after admission."

One of the reasons that modern mental hospitals do not routinely produce the debilitating reaction suggested by Goffman (1961) and others is that these investigators have viewed the hospital procedures from the perspective of the mentally healthy middle-class individual. Many of the deprivations Goffman describes are not experienced as such by many mental patients (Linn, 1968). As Mechanic (1969: 89), citing Linn (1968), says:

> Many patients find their hospitalization experience a relief. The community situation from which they come is often characterized by extreme difficulty and extraordinary personal distress. Their living

> conditions are poor, the conflicts in their life are uncontrollable, and their physical and mental states have deteriorated. Such patients are frequently capable of harming themselves or others, or at least damaging their lives in irreparable ways. Thus many patients in mental hospitals report that hospital restrictions do not bother them, that they appreciate the physical care they are receiving, and that the hospital—despite its restrictions—enhances their freedom rather than restricts it.

This finding has been substantiated by Karmel (1969: 141), among others, who found that the patients she studied had a positive reaction to the hospital's procedures, as did the patients studied by Mayer and Rosenblatt (1974).

As we have noted, most mental patients have a brief hospitalization, and we would not anticipate serious institutionalization effects. Karmel (1969) has conducted an important study that bears on this point. She interviewed a panel of mental patients within a day and a half of their hospitalization and then reinterviewed them after they had been in the hospital one month to see if they had undergone a discernible degree of self-mortification. However, instead of her respondents undergoing self-mortification, she found that the self-esteem of the majority of the patients had improved and that there was a slight increase in the extent to which the patients looked to their roles in the community for their social identity.

When we shift to patients who have been hospitalized for a number of years, the effects of institutionalism become more discernible. As Wing (1962), Wing and Brown (1970) and Karmel (1970) have shown, prolonged institutionalization is associated with a growing apathy toward events outside the hospital. Wing and Brown (1970: 80) explain this by noting, "The longer a person persists in one form of activity, or undergoes one form of experience, the more difficult it will be for him to choose any other and the less he will want to do so." Furthermore, in a relatively small minority of patients, there was the development of general apathy and withdrawal. However, contrary to what one might expect if one felt that psychiatric symptoms were primarily a response to cues in the immediate environment, prolonged hospitalization was not associated with changes in symptomatic behavior (Wing, 1962), and the individual does not acquire a social identity based on his or her deviant social role (Karmel, 1970).

Restitutive Processes

The fact that debilitating processes may be present does not mean restitutive processes are not also in operation. The most obvious restitutive process is treatment. Although there are a wide variety of types of treatment, I will only consider two: drug therapy and psychotherapy.

Let us first consider drug therapy, because we can be very brief. The evidence is in on the efficacy of the tranquilizers and antidepressants. They work; they are therapeutic. The evidence to me is incontrovertible, and if anyone has any doubts on this matter, I suggest they look at Klein and Davis (1969).

The evidence on the efficacy of psychotherapy is not nearly so well established. In fact, it has been the position of Eysenck (1952, 1965) and others (e.g., Bandura, 1969; Ullman and Krasner, 1965) that it has been shown that psychotherapy does not have an effect. However, as Kellner (1965) has demonstrated, Eysenck has been both very selective in the studies he has chosen to evaluate and has manipulated their data in a highly questionable fashion. In fact, as Bergin (1966, 1971), Kellner (1967), Meltzoff and Kornreich (1970), and Kernberg et al. (1972) have shown, the cumulative evidence in support of the therapeutic effectiveness of psychotherapy is fairly impressive. For an excellent overview of the evidence and the debate, see Malan (1973).

Although treatment is the most obvious and perhaps the most important restitutive process associated with hospitalization, it is not the only one. An important study by Sampson et al. (1961, 1964), which looked at the patient before, during, and after hospitalization, found that hospitalization initiated major restitutive processes that were not consciously guided by the hospital personnel. It was found that hospitalization interrupted a situation which was experienced as intolerable and, by doing so, it blocked actions which threatened irremediable damage to family life. This interruption was "legitimated by the act of hospitalization which ratifies the wife as ill and in need of special isolation and treatment" (Sampson et al., 1961: 144). This ratification of illness was decisive in blunting and redefining the negative implications of the interruption. The acts leading to the hospital were not viewed as alienative, "but as actions of an involuntary nature required by and serving the present and future interests of the patient and her family" (Sampson et al., 1961: 144). Furthermore, through moral and legal obstacles, the husband was sometimes forced to defer a planned divorce, allowing other solutions to marital difficulties to be considered and attempted.

As hospitalization occurred "at a relatively late state in family and personal disorganization" (Sampson et al., 1961: 143), a number of alienative acts had frequently occurred which seriously jeopardized the resumption of the marriage. In such situations, a certain "undoing" must be accomplished if the marital family is to be restored. Hospitalization was found to facilitate this "undoing" in a number of ways:

(1) It enabled the patient and family to separate the deviant behavior and ideation from the real self of the patient.

(2) Treatment was interpreted as an important and successful "undoing" process. According to Sampson et al. (1961: 148), "patients and their spouses often assigned remarkable diagnostic acumen and therapeutic efficiency to the hospital and they strained to view their eventual release as a carefully determined medical judgment of recovery."
(3) During and following hospitalization, there was a transition period of construction where the family evolved a new "working consensus." During this period, as is consonant with the concept of illness, relatives were advised not to upset the patient, and they in fact tended to avoid touchy subjects.

Hospitalization was also found to have initiated processes which served in a positive way to move the family toward reintegration. In some cases, the removal of the patient from the conflict situation promoted a revival of positive ties and feelings. In many other cases, the dislocation of family life produced by the wife's absence caused considerable problems and "at the first sign of improvement the husband often began to pleasurably anticipate his wife's return and resumption of responsibilities" (Sampson et al., 1961: 152). Furthermore, the hospital, by treating the husband as responsible for his wife and eager for her recovery, put him into a role which frequently reinstituted a relationship of concern and improved marital communication.

THE REACTION PRODUCED BY BEING LABELLED MENTALLY ILL

A very basic tenet of the societal reaction perspective is that the act of labelling someone mentally ill will severely stigmatize the person and cause him or her to be excluded. The early study by Phillips (1963), "Rejection: A Possible Consequence of Seeking Help for Mental Disorders," supported this position. He presented housewives with vignettes describing various forms of disturbed behavior (i.e., that of a normal individual, a phobic compulsive, a simple schizophrenic, a depressed neurotic, and a paranoid schizophrenic) combined with various forms of help-seeking behavior (i.e., no help, clergyman, physician, psychiatrist, and mental hospital). He found that, controlling for the type of disorder, help-seeking behavior was positively related to rejection. This would seem to provide fairly strong support for the societal reaction perspective. However, more recent work does not support the perspective.

A subsequent paper based on the same data by Phillips (1964) shows that, with these respondents, rejection was much more strongly associated with the degree of disturbed behavior than it was with the help source, suggesting that the behavior was more important. Recently there have been five papers (Bentz and Edgerton, 1971; Kirk, 1974; Spiro, Siassi and Crocetti, 1973; Bord, 1971; Schroder and Ehrlich, 1968) which have focused on this issue of disturbed behavior, the label of mental illness, and rejection, using the same general procedures as those Phillips employed. All these studies found that disturbed behavior was associated with rejection. However, *none* of these studies found that the label of mental illness was associated with rejection. In fact, in Bord (1971: 503), the rejection of three of the five subjects (the paranoid schizophrenic, the depressed neurotic, and the phobic compulsive) was greatest when the person was described as having no help source. In summarizing their results, Bentz and Edgerton (1971: 32) state, "Our data strongly support the proposition that persons who attach the label of mental illness to the previously described behavior do not differ significantly from persons not using this label in terms of their willingness to interact at various levels with the mentally ill." And Kirk (1974: 115) states, "Labeling rule-breaking behavior was found to have no influence on rejection independently of the behavior engaged in."

These studies deal with hypothetical cases. There are two studies that I know of which look at the rejection of the mentally ill among relatives of mental patients. The study by Swanson and Spitzer (1970) looked at relatives before hospitalization, during hospitalization, and after hospitalization. The rates of rejection that they found were very low. Schwartz et al. (1974) looked at the rejection of the mentally ill among relatives of former mental patients. They found that "psychiatric treatment *per se* is less important in determining rejection of the mentally ill than is the ex-patient's level of impairment." They conclude that "the policy of masking the psychiatric identity of treatment services is probably warranted only in exceptional circumstances."

In summary, as Kirk (1974: 115) notes, "the cumulative evidence indicates that the societal reaction view—the label of mental illness, in itself, leads to rejection—needs to be modified, if not abandoned altogether."

These studies have dealt with abstract attitudes toward the mentally ill as a group. Now let us turn to the experiences and feelings of actual patients. According to the labelling perspective, the patient is apt to be so stigmatized by having been labelled mentally ill that when he or she returns to the community (s)he will have great difficulties resuming previous interpersonal and instrumental roles. Let us look first at the attitudes of patients and ex-patients toward their hospital experiences. A study of psychiatric patients by Jones et al. (1963) found that patients typically felt that the lay public would not view a person as undesirable because that person had been in a mental hospital. A study by Wood et al. (1968: 250) of hospitalized patients found that "twenty-seven (57%) of the patients said with little hesitation that it was a good thing for their families that they had decided to come to the hospital [and] only four (8%) of the patients felt hospitalization would be bad for the family." In a study of former mental patients, Kotin and Schur (1969: 408) found, "About two-thirds of the former patients felt that their experience had been helpful to them." In my own study of ex-mental patients, I found that out of 298 ex-patients living in the community one year after hospitalization, 84.2% believed they had been helped by their hospitalization while only 13.5% indicated that they had been harmed in some way by hospitalization.

Interestingly, 72% of those who saw hospitalization as having negative effects also saw it as having positive effects. A content analysis of those who indicated they had been harmed in some way by their hospitalization indicated that slightly over one-third were concerned with the stigma of hospitalization (Gove and Fain, 1973). Cumming and Cumming (1965) found, in a study of twenty-two former patients, that 41% felt stigmatized, four expressing shame and five having a generalized expectation of discrimination. They suggest that with the passage of time, or with the occupancy of normal roles, feelings of stigma will disappear. This corresponds to my own impressions. As I stated in Gove and Fain (1973: 500), it was my impression, based on having conducted the interviews with the ex-patients, that "a substantial minority of the ex-patients were initially somewhat embarrassed and uncomfortable about having been in a mental hospital, but they did not perceive the stigma of hospitalization as having any serious or long-run consequences." And, finally, let me take note of the study by Freeman and Simmons (1961) of the feelings of stigma among relatives of ex-mental patients. They found that only 24% (n = 394) of the relatives felt stigmatized. Furthermore, their findings indicate that the feelings of stigma were associated with the perception that the ex-patient is acting in an abnormal fashion and with a fear that persons in the community will discriminate against the family because of the patient's current behavior. In short, the majority of hospitalized mental patients appear to have a positive attitude toward their hospitalization and feelings of stigma do not appear to be a serious issue for most patients.

Now let us turn to four very different studies dealing with the situation of the ex-patient. First, Robins (1966) obtained data on 524 patients seen in a child guidance clinic between 1924 and 1929. Information on 100 controls who had no psychiatric history was also obtained. She then conducted a follow-up study 30 years later. Although she was interested in deviant behavior in general, her results are relevant to us. She found

> that labelling by schools, parents, and referral to a psychiatric clinic seemed to have remarkably little effect on later outcomes. Children

> with severe school discipline problems who were labeled as unacceptable by the school through expulsion or suspension were not significantly more anti-social adults than comparably behaved children allowed to initiate their own school termination (p. 213). Children whose parents did the labelling, by referring them to court, clinic, or initiating their removal from the home, were no more deviant adults than children with similar behavior and similar parents who did not overtly repudiate them (p. 176). Finally, children with few behavioral or subjective symptoms who were nonetheless referred to the clinic and thus labelled "psychiatric cases" had as little adult psychiatric disorder as did the control group of unlabeled school children (50% versus 52% were symptom-free through adulthood, p. 143) [Robins, 1970: 247].

Second, let me discuss a study of my own which involved a follow-up of 429 ex-patients a year after their hospitalization in a state mental hospital (Gove and Fain, 1973). When we look at employment, we find that slightly more men and considerably more women were employed one year after hospitalization than were employed in the period prior to their hospitalization. The reports of housewives showed a tendency for them to improve in their household tasks following hospitalization. Furthermore, when we turn to financial problems, more patients report that they had financial problems prior to hospitalization than following hospitalization. Thus, in terms of instrumental performance, patients were performing somewhat better after their hospitalization than they had been prior to their hospitalization.

It can plausibly be argued that the negative effect of labelling will most strongly manifest itself in the area of social relations. However, our data showed that the patient's relationship with a spouse had undergone a very marked improvement following hospitalization. The same marked improvement in social relations was found when we looked at patients who were not living in the conjugal family. When we looked at the patient's relationships with his or her children, we found that these relationships also tended to improve, although the shift was not so great. Thus, taken in toto, the patients' social relationships showed a very marked improvement following hospitalization. I would also note that a substantial majority of the patients saw their ability to handle problems as improved and saw their general situation as better than it was prior to hospitalization.

Third, let me turn to a very different type of study, that of Angrist et al. (1968), who looked at the experiences of 287 women following their hospitalization and compared them to their neighbors, who were used as controls. One of the first things to be noted is that the ex-patients were not like their neighbors, or a random sample of females in the community. The ex-patients were atypical in their lack of education, their singleness, and their household living arrangements. These factors predated their hospitalization and could not be considered a consequence of being publicly labelled mentally ill. Once the former mental patients and their neighbors were matched on these characteristics, the groups were extremely similar "in the areas of instrumental role performance, role expectations and tolerance for deviant behavior" (Angrist et al., 1968: 161). The ex-patients, however, manifested significantly more psychiatric handicaps. The authors also found that, "as performance (or the ability to perform) degenerates, the expectations of family members are corroded, so they become accustomed to expect less of their relative" (Angrist et al., 1968: 171). This suggests that expectations for poor performance may be determined more by ineffectual behavior than the reverse, a conclusion that appears to be consistent with the work of Freeman and Simmons (1963).

For former patients, probably the most important indicator of continued occupancy of the mentally ill role is rehospitalization. Of the patients in this study, 15% had been rehospitalized after six months; 24% after two years; and 32% after seven years (Angrist et al., 1968). Thus, over two-thirds of these patients had not been rehospitalized after seven years, and probably a significant proportion of these never will be.

What caused rehospitalization? The evidence indicated that, following the initial hospitalization, the readmitted patients had exhibited more deviant behavior and more psychiatric symptoms (particularly extreme and acutely disordered symptoms) than ex-patients who avoided rehospitalization. Furthermore, the data showed that in spite of the fact that the ex-patients had previously been labelled mentally ill, the relatives viewed "readmission as a last resort for behavior which cannot be handled without medical help" (Angrist et al., 1968: 100). In conclusion, the authors (Angrist et al., 1968: 176) state, "The fact that the returnees were decidely sicker than the community patients indicates that intrinsic features of the illness are of greater consequence in precipitating readmission than are the variations in the way significant others perceive, evaluate or tolerate such illness."

Fourth, in a recent article, Eaton (1974) has used mathematical models to examine the hospitalization and rehospitalization experiences of schizophrenics. He looked at three types of explanations of the hospitalization experiences:

(1) the societal reaction or institutionalism model where the hospital experience is seen as tending to produce a readmission,
(2) the therapeutic model where the treatment associated with hospitalization is seen as reducing the likelihood of a readmission, and
(3) a heterogeneity model which assumes that hospitalization has little effect, positive or negative, on prognosis and that hospitalization experiences were due to individual differences among schizophrenics.

This last model, which Eaton (1974: 258) notes is consistent with a g explanation of schizophrenia, assumes that hospital experiences are ind dent random events in time, with heterogeneous propensities for occurre

The data for the study came from the Maryland Psychiatric Case Regi and covered a seven-year period. All schizophrenic episodes severe enough to result in hospitalization were considered. To test the three models, Eaton used a simple Poisson and a compound Poisson process, and compared the actual outcomes with those predicted by the three models. He found that the data supported the heterogeneity (or genetic) model and that "there is very little evidence for positive reinforcement (i.e., the societal reaction model); and institutionalization, if operative at all, is a trivial factor in the recurrence of episodes of schizophrenia."

In summary, these four studies of the consequences of psychiatric treatment, each of which takes a very different approach, find very little evidence in support of the labelling perspective.

DISCUSSION

The labelling perspective does not view the deviant as someone who is suffering from an intrapersonal disorder, but instead as someone who, through a set of circumstances, becomes publicly labelled a deviant and who is forced by societal reaction into a deviant role. In essence, they view the deviant as someone who is victimized. The available evidence, however, indicates that the societal reaction formulation of how a person becomes mentally ill is substantially incorrect. There is very little evidence of victimization. The evidence shows that a substantial majority have a serious disorder quite apart from any secondary deviance that may be associated with the mentally ill role. Furthermore, persons in the community do not view as mentally ill someone who happens to act in a bizarre fashion. On the contrary, they persist in denying mental illness until the situation becomes intolerable. Even after prospective patients come into contact with public officials, a substantial screening occurs, presumably sorting out persons who are being railroaded or who are less disturbed. It is only in the last stages of the commitment process that some ritualization appears to occur, and even here a discernible proportion of persons is sorted out. Perhaps the most telling evidence is that, to the extent to which the individual societal attributes do seem to have an effect on the hospitalization process, their effect is in the opposite direction from that posited by the labelling perspective—that is, controlling for level of disorder, it is the individuals with the most resources who are the most likely to enter the role of the mentally ill.

The evidence also indicates that the societal reaction theorists have overstated the degree to which secondary deviance is associated with mental hospitalization: (1) there appear to be many restitutive processes associated with hospitalization, (2) patients treated in the modern mental hospital typically do not spend enough time in the hospital to become truly institutionalized, and (3) in most cases the stigma of having been a former mental patient does not appear to greatly affect one's performance in the community. In summary, the studies reviewed, while in no way denying the existence of the processes outlined by the labelling theorists, suggest that mental hospitalization, in our present society, does not typically lead to a prolonged occupancy of the mentally ill role. Furthermore, the available evidence indicates that, when former patients continue to have difficulties, these difficulties are generally due to the person's confronting a troubled situation or to some psychiatric disorder, and not to the social expectations of others.

Having made the point that, at least in our society at the present time, the societal reaction perspective not only does not have a general explanation of mental illness, but it does not even point to processes that, at least in the long run, have a marked effect on the *typical* mental patient, let me end on a somewhat cautious note. The very fact that two decades ago mental hospitals had a much larger resident population than at present strongly suggests, at least to me, that the debilitating process described by the labelling theorists had a marked effect on a noticeable number of people in the past. In short, two decades ago the labelling theorist had a much better case than at present. We should be warned, however, that the fact that mental hospitals have greatly improved their procedures does not mean that the problems of the chronically mentally ill have been solved. There is a growing body of evidence that indicates that the institutionalism of the old mental hospital is being transferred, albeit in a modified form, to an institutionalism in the community (e.g., see Wing and Brown, 1970; Chase, 1973; Lamb and Goertzel, 1971; Davis et al., 1972, 1974; Glick et al., 1974). In short, the evidence indicates that, when the chronically mentally ill leave inpatient care, they need support in the community and all too often they do not get it. Simply leaving them alone is not enough.

NOTES

1. At this point, Scheff's argument appears to me to be somewhat inconsistent. I find it difficult to associate a stereotype that is well established and continually reinforced with a set of diverse behavior (acts of residual deviance), whose primary similarity is that no explicit label can be attached to them. For a more detailed discussion of this problem, see Fletcher and Reynolds (1968).

2. The finding of Haney and Miller (1970: 528) regarding critical incidents and the likelihood that a prospective patient will be found incompetent has some bearing on our evaluation of labelling perspective. They defined a critical incident as "the last straw, a behavioral incident involving the deviant which contributes to the decision that the situation is no longer tolerable." Following Scheff (1966: 82), they reason that, as "these incidents tend to be more highly visible, have an element of crisis in them and tend to center attention on the deviant . . . they do much to crystallize the definition of the deviant as mentally ill." They found, however, that this was not the case, for "the direction of the relationship was the opposite of that predicted, with a higher frequency of such incidents among those who escaped the judgement of incompetency."

3. Wilde (1968), from a study of a sample of persons processed by the screening agency, came to the conclusion that there was no relationship between the degree of disturbance and the initiation of procedures. His study, however, suffers from methodological problems, and it can be shown that his conclusion is probably erroneous (see Gove, 1970).

4. I would note that this agency was not deciding on commitment, and, as Wilde (1968: 219) notes, the agency was "expected to approve a petition whenever they felt there is a reasonable probability that the alleged deviant may be commitable."

5. According to the psychiatric perspective, this increase can be attributed to the fact that, as psychiatry started demonstrating that it could effectively treat the painful and disabling symptoms of the mentally ill, persons who were disturbed were more willing to seek treatment.

REFERENCES

Alanen, Yojo

1958 "The mothers of schizophrenic patients." Acta Psychiatrica et Neurologica Scandinavica, Supplementum 124, 33: 31-47.

Angrist, Shirley, Mark Lefton, Simon Dinitz, and Benjamin Pasamanick

1968 Women After Treatment: A Study of Former Mental Patients and Their Normal Neighbors. New York: Appleton-Century-Crofts.

Angst, J. and C. Perris

1968 "Zur Nosologie endogener depressionen: vergleich der ergebnisse zweier Untersuchungen." Archiv fuer Psychiatric und Zeitschrift f.d. ges. Neurologic 210: 373-386.

Aviram, Uri and Steven Segal

1973 "Exclusion of the mentally ill: reflection on an old problem in a new context." Archives of General Psychiatry 29 (July): 126-131.

Bachrach, Leona

1973 "Center and catchment area variations in the age, color and sex distributions of additions to 69 selected community mental health centers, United States, 1971." National Institute of Mental Health, Washington, D.C.

Bandura, Albert

1969 Principles of Behavior Modification. New York: Holt, Rinehart & Winston.

Bass, Roselyn and Michael Witkin

1973 "Outpatient treatment service in federally funded community mental health centers, 1971." Statistical Note 94, National Institute of Mental Health, Washington, D.C.

Baxter, Seymour, Bernard Chodorkoff, and Robert Underhill
1968 "Psychiatric emergencies: dispositional determinants and the validity of the decision to admit." American Journal of Psychiatry 124 (May): 100-104.
Bentz, W. Kenneth and J. Wilbert Edgerton
1971 "The consequences of labeling a person as mentally ill." Social Psychiatry 6, 1: 29-33.
Bergin, A. E.
1966 "Some implications of psychotherapy research for therapeutic practice." Journal of Abnormal Psychology 71 (August): 235-246.
1971 "The evolution of therapeutic outcomes." In A. E. Bergin and S. L. Garfield (eds.) Handbook of Psychotherapy and Behavior Change. New York: John Wiley.
Berkman, Paul
1971 "Life stress and psychological well-being: a replication of Canger's analysis in the Midtown Manhattan Study." Journal of Health and Social Behavior 12 (March): 35-45.
Bethel, Helen
1973 "Provisional patient movement and administrative data state and country mental hospitals inpatient services July 1, 1971 - June 30, 1972." Statistical Note 77, National Institute of Mental Health, Washington, D.C.
Birley, J. L. T. and G. W. Brown
1970 "Crises and life changes preceeding the onset or relapse of acute schizophrenia: clinical aspects" British Journal of Psychiatry 116 (March): 327-333.
Bittner, Egon
1967 "Police discretion in apprehending the mentally ill." Social Problems 14 (Winter): 278-292.
Bord, Richard
1971 "Rejection of the mentally ill: continuities and further developments." Social Problems 18 (Spring): 496-509.
Brown, E. L.
1961 Newer Dimensions of Patient Care. New York: Russell Sage.
Brown, G. W. and J. L. T. Birley
1968 "Crises and life changes and the onset of schizophrenia." Journal of Health and Social Behavior 9 (September): 203-214.
Brown, G. W., T. O. Harris, and J. Peto
1973 "Life events and psychiatric disorders. Part 2: Nature of causal link." Psychological Medicine 3 (June).
Brown, G. W., Margaret Bone, Bridget Dalison, and J. K. Wing
1966 Schizophrenia and Social Care: A Comparative Follow-up Study of 339 Schizophrenic patients. London: Oxford University Press.
Brown, G. W., E. M. Monck, G. M. Carstairs, and J. K. King
1962 "Influence of family life on the course of schizophrenic illness." British Journal of Preventive and Social Medicine 16 (January): 55-66.
Brown, G. W., F. Skleiz, T. O. Harris, and J. L. T. Birley
1973 "Life events and psychiatric disorders. Part 1: Some methodological issues." Psychological Medicine 3 (February): 74-87.
Cadoret, Remi, George Winokur, and Paula Clayton
1970 "Family history studies. VII: Manic-depressive disease versus depressive disease." British Journal of Psychiatry 116 (June): 625-635.
Cannon, Mildred and Richard Redlich
1973 "Differential utilization of psychiatric facilities by men and women, United

States, 1970." Statistical Note 81, National Institute of Mental Health, Washington, D.C.

Chase, Janet
1973 "Where have all the patients gone?" Human Behavior 2 (October): 14-21.

Crocetti, G. M., H. R. Spiro, and I. Siassi
1974 Contemporary Attitudes Toward Mental Illness. Pittsburg: University of Pittsburg Press.

Cumming, Elaine and John Cumming
1957 Closed Ranks. Cambridge: Harvard University Press.

Cumming, John and Elaine Cumming
1965 "On the stigma of mental illness." Community Mental Health Journal 1 (Summer): 135-143.

Davis, Ann, Simon Dinitz, and Benjamin Pasamanick
Davis, Ann, Simon Dinitz, and Benjamin Pasamanick
1972 "The prevention of hospitalization in schizophrenia: five years after an experimental program." American Journal of Orthopsychiatry 42 (April): 375-388.
1974 Schizophrenics in the New Custodial Community. Columbus: Ohio State University Press.

Dohrenwend, Bruce and Dewitt Crandell
1970 "Psychiatric symptoms in community clinics and mental hospital groups." American Journal of Psychiatry 126 (May): 1116-1121.

Dohrenwend, Bruce and Barbara Dohrenwend
1969 Social Status and Psychological Disorder. New York: John Wiley.

Eaton, William
1974 "Mental hospitalization or a reinforcement process." American Sociological Review 39 (April): 252-260.

Eysenck, Hans
1952 "The effects of psychotherapy, an evaluation." Journal of Consulting Psychology 16 (October): 319-324.
1965 "The effects of psychotherapy." International Journal of Psychiatry 1 (January): 99-144.

Fein, Sara and Kent Miller
1972 "Legal process and adjudication in mental incompetency proceedings." Social Problems 20 (Summer): 57-64.

Fisher, Joel
1969 "Negroes and whites and rates of mental illness: reconsideration of a myth." Psychiatry 32 (November): 428-446.

Fletcher, Richard
1969 "Measuring community mental health attitudes by means of hypothetical case descriptions." Social Psychiatry 4, 4: 152-158.

Fletcher, C. Richard and Larry Reynolds
1968 "Residual deviance, labeling, and the mentally sick role: a critical review of concepts." Sociological Focus 1 (Spring): 9-27.

Freeman, Howard and Ozzie Simmons
1958 "Mental patients in the community: family settings and performance levels." American Sociological Review 23 (April): 147-154.
1959 "Social class and past hospital performance levels." American Sociological Review 24 (June): 345-351.
1961 "Feelings of stigma among relatives of former mental patients." Social Problems 8 (Spring): 312-331.
1963 The Mental Patient Comes Home. New York: John Wiley.

Gershon, Elliot, David Dunner, and Frederick Goodwin
1971 "Toward a biology of the affective disorders." Archives of General Psychiatry 25 (July): 1-15.

Glick, Ira, William Hargreaves, and Michael Goldfield
1974 "Short versus long hospitalization: a prospective controlled study: I. The preliminary results of a one-year follow-up of schizophrenics." Archives of General Psychiatry 30 (March): 363-369.

Goffman, Erving
1961 Asylums: Essays on the Social Situation of Mental Patients and Other Inmates. Garden City, N.Y.: Doubleday.
1971 Relations in Public: Microstudies of the Public Order. New York: Harper.

Gottesman, Irving
1968 "Severity/concordance and diagnostic refinement in the Maudsley-Bettlem schizophrenic twin study." Pp. 37-48 in David Rosenthal and Seymour Kety (eds.) The Transmission of Schizophrenia. New York: Pergamon.

——— and James Shields
1972 Schizophrenia and Genetics: A Twin Study Vantage Point. New York: Academic.

Gove, Walter
1970 "Who is hospitalized: a critical review of some sociological studies of mental illness." Journal of Health and Social Behavior (December): 294-303.

——— and Terry Fain
1973 "The stigma of mental hospitalization: an attempt to evaluate its consequences." Archives of General Psychiatry 28 (April): 494-500.
1975 "Voluntary and involuntary hospitalization." Mimeographed.

Gove, Walter and Patrick Howell
1974 "Individual Resources and mental hospitalization: a comparison and evaluation of the societal reaction and psychiatric perspectives." American Sociological Review 39 (February): 86-100.

Gove, Walter and Jeanette Tudor
1973 "Adult sex roles and mental illness." American Journal of Sociology 78 (January): 812-835.

Gove, Walter, James McCorkel, and Terry Fain
1975 "Response bias in community surveys of mental health." Mimeographed.

Greenley, James R.
1972 "The psychiatric patient's family and length of hospitalization." Journal of Health and Social Behavior 13 (March): 25-37.

Gunderson, Eric and Arthur Ronson
1969 "A brief mental health index." Journal of Abnormal Psychology 74, 1: 100-104.

Haese, Phillip and Richard Miele
1967 "The relative effectiveness of two models for the scoring of the mid-town psychological disorder index." Community Mental Health Journal 3 (Winter): 335-347.

Hammer, Muriel
1963-1964 "Influence of small social networks or factors on mental hospital admission." Human Organization 22 (Winter): 243-251.

Haney, C. Allen and Robert Michielutte
1968 "Selective factors operating in the adjudication of incompetency." Journal of Health and Social Behavior 9 (September): 233-242.

Haney, C. Allen and Kent Miller
1970 "Definitional factors in mental incompetency." Sociology and Social Research 54 (July): 520-532.
--- and Robert Michielutte
1969 "The interaction of petitioner and deviant social characteristics in the adjudication of incompetency." Sociometry 32 (June): 182-193.
Heston, Leonard
1966 "Psychiatric disorders in foster-home-reared children of schizophrenic mothers." British Journal of Psychiatry 112 (August): 819-825.
1970 "The genetics of schizophrenic and schizoid disease." Science 167 (January 16): 249-256.
--- and Duane Denny
1968 "Interaction between early life experience and biological factors in schizophrenia." Pp. 363-376 in David Rosenthal and Seymour Kety (eds.) The Transmission of Schizophrenia. New York: Pergamon.
Hollingshead, August and Frederick Redlich
1958 Social Class and Mental Illness. New York: John Wiley.
Horn, Charles
1968 "Critical incidents on contingencies in the career of the psychiatric patients." Research Reports in Social Science 11, 2: 15-24.
Hunt, Stanley, Karl Singer, and Sidney Cobb
1967 "Components of depression." Archives of General Psychiatry 16 (April): 441-447.
Jaco, E. Gartly
1960 The Social Epidemiology of Mental Disorders. New York: Russell Sage.
Jones, Nelson, Marvin Kahn, and John MacDonald
1963 "Psychiatric patients' view of mental illness, hospitalization and treatment." Journal of Nervous and Mental Disease 136 (January): 82-87.
Kadushin, Charles
1969 Why People Go to Psychiatrists. New York: Atherton.
Karmel, Madeline
1969 "Total institution and self-mortification." Journal of Health and Social Behavior 10 (June): 134-141.
1970 "The internalization of social roles in institutionalized chronic mental patients." Journal of Health and Social Behavior 11 (September): 231-235.
Kellner, R.
1965 "Discussion in Eysenck, H. J., the effects of psychotherapy." International Journal of Psychiatry 1 (April): 322-338.
1967 "The evidence in favor of psychotherapy." British Journal of Medical Psychology 40 (December): 341-358.
Kernberg, O. F. et al.
1972 "Psychotherapy and psychoanalysis: final report of the Menninger Foundations Psychotherapy Research Project." Bulletin of the Menninger Clinic 36, Nos. 1 and 2.
Kety, Seymour, David Rosenthal, Paul Wender, and Fini Schulsinger
1968 "The types and prevalence of mental illness in the biological and adaptive families of adopted schizophrenics." Pp. 345-362 in David Rosenthal and Seymour Kety (eds.) The Transmission of Schizophrenia. New York: Pergamon.

Kirk, Stuart
1974 "The impact of labeling on rejection of the mentally ill: an experimental study." Journal of Health and Social Behavior 15 (June): 108-117.

Klein, Donald and John Davis
1969 "Diagnosis and Drug treatment of Psychiatric Disorders. Baltimore: Williams & Wilkins.

Kohn, Melvin
1968 "Social class and schizophrenia: a critical review." Pp. 155-173 in David Rosenthal and Seymour Kety (eds.) The Transmission of Schizophrenia, New York: Pergamon.

Kotin, Joel and J. Michael Schur
1969 "Attitudes of discharged mental patients toward their hospital experiences." Journal of Nervous and Mental Disease 149, 5: 408-414.

Kringlen, Einar
1968 "An epidemiological-clinical twin study on schizophrenia." Pp. 49-63 in David Rosenthal and Seymour Kety (eds.) The Transmission of Schizophrenia. New York: Pergamon.

Kumasaka, Yorihiko, Janet Stokes, and Raj Gupta
1972 "Criteria for involuntary hospitalization." Archives of General Psychiatry 26 (May): 399-404.

Kupfer, David, Thomas Detre, and Millard Amdur
1972 "KDA-1 Scale for symptom discrimination." Psychological Reports 30 (June): 915-919.

Kutner, L.
1962 "The illusion of due process in commitment proceedings." Northwestern University Law Review 57 (September): 383-399.

Laing, R. D.
1967 The Politics of Experience. New York: Ballantine.

Laing, Ronald and Aaron Esterson
1964 Sanity, Madness, and the Family. London: Tavistock.

Lamb, H. Richard and Victor Goertzel
1971 "Discharged mental patients–are they really in the community?" Archives of General Psychiatry 24 (January): 29-34.

Langner, Thomas
1962 "A twenty-two item screening score of psychiatric symptoms indicating impairment." Journal of Health and Human Behavior 3 (Winter): 269-276.

––– and Stanley Michael
1963 Life stress and Mental Health: The Midtown Manhattan Study, Volume 2. New York: Free Press.

Larson, Richard
1970 "The influence of sex roles and symptoms on clergymen's perceptions of mental illness." Pacific Sociological Review 13 (Winter): 53-61.

Leifer, Ronald
1969 In the Name of Mental Health. New York: Science.

Leighton, D. C., J. S. Harding, D. B. Macklin, A. M. Macmillan, and A. H. Leighton
1963 The Chracter of Danger. New York: Basic Books.

Linn, Erwin
1961 "Agents, timing, and events leading to mental hospitalization." Human Organization 20 (Summer): 92-98.

Linn, L.
1968 "The mental hospital in the patient's phenomenal world." Ph. D. dissertation. University of Wisconsin.

Linsky, Arnold
1970 "Who shall be excluded: the influence of personal attributes in community reaction to the mentally ill." Social Psychiatry 5 (July): 166-171.

Lubin, Bernard
1965 "Adjective check lists for measurement of depression." Archives of General Psychiatry 12 (January): 57-62.

Macmillan, A. M.
1957 "The health opinion survey: technique for estimating prevalence of psychoneurotic and related types of disorder in communities." Monograph supplement 7, Psychological Reports 3 (September): 325-339.

Malan, David
1973 "The outcome of psychotherapy research: a historical review." Archives of General Psychiatry 29 (December): 719-729.

Malzberg, Benjamin
1940 "Social and biological aspects of mental disease." New York State, Department of Mental Hygiene.

Manis, Jerome, Milton Brower, Chester Hunt, and Leonard Kercher
1963 "Validating a mental health scale." American Sociological Review 29 (February): 108-116.

Matthews, Margie
n.d. "A preliminary descriptive study of HOS responses in college students and an attempt at validation." M.P.H. thesis.

Mayer, John and Aaron Rosenblatt
1974 "Clash in perspective between mental patients and staff." American Journal of Orthopsychiatry 44 (April): 432-441.

Mechanic, David
1962 "Some factors in identifying and defining mental illness." Mental Hygiene 46 (January): 66-74.
1969 Mental Health and Social Policy. Englewood Cliffs, N.J.: Prentice-Hall.

Meehl, Paul
1972 "A critical afterword." Pp. 367-415 in Irving Gottesman and James Shields, Schizophrenia and Genetics: A Twin Study Vantage Point. New York: Academic.

Meltzoff, J. and M. Kornreich
1970 Research in Psychotherapy. New York: Atherton.

Mendel, Werner and Samuel Rapport
1969 "Determinants of the decision for psychiatric hospitalization." Archives of General Psychiatry 20 (March): 321-328.

Meyer, Nessa and Carl Taube
1973 "Length of stay of admission to state and county mental hospitals, United States, 1971." Statistical Note 74, National Institute of Mental Health, Washington, D.C.

Miller, Dorothy and Michael Schwartz
1966 "County lunacy commission hearings: some observations of commitments to a state mental hospital." Social Problems 14 (Summer): 26-35.

Minor, Gary
1973 "The evidence for genetic components in the neuroses." Archives of General Psychiatry 29 (July): 111-118.
Mishler, Elliott and Nancy Wexler
1963 "Decision processes in psychiatric hospitalization." American Sociological Review 28 (August): 576-587.
Myers, Jerome and Bertram Roberts
1959 Family and Class Dynamics in Mental Illness. New York: John Wiley.
Myers, Jerome and Lee Bean
1968 A Decade Later: A Follow-up of Social Class and Mental Illness. New York: John Wiley.
Myers, Jerome, Jacob Lindenthal, and Max Pepper
1971 "Life events and psychiatric impairment." Journal of Nervous and Mental Disease 152, 3: 149-157.
--- and David Ostrander
1972 "Life events and mental status: a longitudinal study." Journal of Health and Social Behavior 13 (December): 398-406.
Nunnally, Jum
1961 Popular Conceptions of Mental Health. New York: Holt, Rinehart & Winston.
Paykel, E. S.
1973 "Life stress and psychiatric disorder: applications of the clinical approach." Presented at the Conference on Stressful Life Events: Their Nature and Effects, New York, June.
--- J. K. Myers, M. N. Dienelt, G. L. Klerman, J. J. Lindenthal, and M. P. Pepper
1969 "Life events and depression: a controlled study." Archives of General Psychiatry 21 (December): 753-760.
Perris, Carlo
1968 "Genetic transmission of depressive psychoses." Acta Psychiatrica Scandinavica Supplement 203 (November): 45-52.
Perrucci, Robert
1974 The Circle of Madness: On Being Insane and Institutionalized in America. Englewood Cliffs: N.J.: Prentice-Hall.
Phillips, Derek
1963 "Rejection: a possible consequence of seeking help for mental disorders." American Sociological Review 28 (December): 963-972.
1964 "Rejection of the mentally ill: the influence of behavior and sex." American Sociological Review 29 (October): 679-687.
Rahe, Richard
1969 "Life crisis and health change." In P.R.A. May and J. R. Witterborn (eds.) Psychotropic Drug Response: Advances in Prediction. Springfield, Ill.: Charles C. Thomas.
--- and Ransom Arthur
1968 "Life-change patterns surrounding illness experience." Journal of Psychosomatic Research 11: 341-345.
Rahe, Richard, Joseph McKeen, and Ransom Arthur
1967 "A longitudinal study of life-change and illness patterns." Journal of Psychosomatic Research 10: 355-366.
Rahe, Richard, Merle Meyer, Michael Smith, George Kjaer, and Thomas Holmes
1964 "Social stress and illness onset." Journal of Psychosomatic Research 8: 35-44.

Reich, J., P. Clayton, and G. Winokur
1969 "Family history studies. V. The genetics of mania." American Journal of Psychiatry 125 (April): 1358-1369.

Robins, Lee
1966 Deviant Children Grown Up. Baltimore: Williams & Wilkins.
1970 "Letter to the editor." Journal of Health and Social Behavior 11 (September): 247.

Rock, Ronald, Marcus Jacobson, and Richard Janopaul
1968 Hospitalization and Discharge of the Mentally Ill. Chicago: University of Chicago Press.

Rosenhan, David L.
1973 "On being sane in insane places." Science 179 (January): 250-258.

Rosenthal, David, Paul Wender, Seymour Kety, Fini Schulsinger, Joseph Welner, and Lise Ostergaard
1968 "Schizophrenics' offspring reared in adoptive homes." Pp. 337-391 in David Rosenthal and Seymour Kety (eds.) The Transmission of Schizophrenia. New York: Pergamon.

Rushing, William
1969 "Two patterns in the relationship between social class and mental hospitalization." American Sociological Review 34 (August): 533-541.
1971 "Individual resources: societal reactions and hospital commitment." American Journal of Sociology 77 (November): 511-526.

Saenger, Gerhart and John Cumming
1965 Study of Community Mental Health Clinics, Report I, Characteristics of Patients Applying for Service and Factor Determining Acceptance for treatment. Mental Health Research Unit, New York, State Department of Mental Hygiene.

Sampson, Harold, Sheldon Messinger, and Robert Towne
1961 "The mental hospital and marital family ties." Social Problems 9 (Fall): 141-155.
1964 Schizophrenic Women: Studies in Marital Crisis. New York: Atherton.

Sarbin, Theodore
1967a "On the futility of the proposition that some people be labeled 'Mentally Ill.' " Journal of Consulting Psychology 31, 5: 447-453.
1967b "The scientific status of the mental illness concept." In S. Plog (ed.) Determinants of Mental Illness: A Handbook. New York: Holt, Rinehart & Winston.
1972 "Stimulus/response: schizophrenia is a myth, born of metaphor, meaningless." Psychology Today 6 (June): 18-27.

Scheff, Thomas J.
1966 Being Mentally Ill: A Sociological Theory. Chicago: Aldine.
1967 "Social conditions for rationality: how urban and rural courts deal with the mentally ill." Pp. 109-118 in Thomas Scheff (ed.) Mental Illness and Social Progress. New York: Harper & Row.
1968 "The societal reaction to deviance: ascriptive elements in the psychiatric screening of mental patients in a Midwestern state." Pp. 276-290 in Stephen Spitzer and Norman Denzin (eds.) The Mental Patient. New York: McGraw-Hill.
1970 "Schizophrenia or ideology." Schizophrenia Bulletin No. 2 (Fall): 15-19.

1974 "The labelling theory of mental illness." American Sociological Review 39 (June): 444-452.

Schroder, David and Danuta Ehrlich

1968 "Rejection by mental health professionals: a possible consequence of not seeking appropriate help for emotional disorders." Journal of Health and Social Behavior 9 (September): 222-237.

Schulz, B.

1951 "Auszahlungen in der Verwandtschaft von nach Erkrankunssalter und Geschlecht gruppienrten Manisch-Depressiven." Archiv fuer Psychiatrie und Nervenkrankheiten 186: 560-576.

Schwartz, Carol, Jerome Myers, and Boris Astrachan

1973 "Comparing three measures of mental health status: a note on the validity of estimates of the psychological disorder in the community." Journal of Health and Social Behavior 14 (September): 265-273.

1974 "Psychiatric labeling and the rehabilitation of the mental patient, implicative of research findings for mental health policy." Archives of General Psychiatry 31 (September): 329-334.

Schwartz, Charlotte

1957 "Perspectives on deviance–wives' definitions of their husbands' mental illness." Psychiatry 20 (August): 275-291.

Seiler, Lauren

1973 "The 22-item scale used in field studies of mental illness: a question of method, a question of substance, and a question of theory." Journal of Health and Social Behavior 14 (September): 252-264.

Semmence, A. M.

1969 "The health opinion survey." Journal of Royal College of General Practitioners 18 (October): 344-348.

Shader, Richard, Michael Ebert, and Jerold Harnatz

1971 "Langner's psychiatric impairment scale: a short screening device." American Journal of Psychiatry 128 (November): 596-601.

Shields, James

1954 "Personality differences and neurotic traits in normal twin school children." Eugene Review 45 (January): 213-246.

1968 "Summary of the genetic evidence." Pp. 95-126 in David Rosenthal and Seymour Kety (eds.) The Transmission of Schizophrenia. New York: Pergamon.

——— and Irving Gottesman

1972 "Cross-national diagnosis of schizophrenia in twins: the heritability and specificity of schizophrenia." Archives of General Psychiatry 27 (December): 725-730.

Simmonds, J. L.

1969 Deviants. Berkeley: Glendessary.

Slater, Eliot

1968 "A review of earlier evidence on genetic factors in schizophrenia." Pp. 15-26 in David Rosenthal and Seymour Kety (eds.) The Transmission of Schizophrenia. New York: Pergamon.

Smith, Kathleen, Muriel Pumphrey, and Julian Hall

1963 "The 'last straw': the decisive incident resulting in the request for hospitalization in 100 schizophrenic patients." American Journal of Psychiatry 119 (September): 228-232.

Snyder, Solomon, Shailesh Banerjee, Henry Yamamura, and David Greenberg
1974 "Drugs, neurotransmitters and schizophrenia." Science 184 (June): 1243-1253.

Spiro, H. R., I. Siassi, and G. Crocetti
1972 "What gets surveyed in a psychiatric survey? a case study of the Macmillan Index." Journal of Nervous and Mental Disease 152 (February): 105-114.
1973 "Ability of the public to recognize mental illness: an issue of substance and an issue of meaning." Social Psychiatry 8 (February): 32-36.

Spitzer, Robert, Jean Endicott, Joseph Fleiss, and Jacob Cohen
1970 "The psychiatric status schedule." Archives of General Psychiatry 23 (July): 41-55.

Star, Shirley
1961 "The Dilemmas of Mental Illness Cited in the Joint Commission on Mental Illness and Health Action for Mental Health." New York: Science Editions.

Stendstedt, Ake
1952 "A study in manic-depressive psychosis, clinical, social and genetic investigations." Acta Psychiatrica et Neurologica Scandinavica, Supplementum 79: 1-75.
1959 "Involutional melancholia: an etiologic, clinical and social study of endogenous depressions in later life, with special reference to genetic factors." Acta Psychiatrica Scandinavica, Supplementum 127.

Swanson, Robert and Stephen Spitzer
1970 "Stigma and the psychiatric patient career." Journal of Health and Social Behavior 11 (March): 44-51.

Szasz, Thomas
1961 The Myth of Mental Illness: Foundations of a Theory of Personal Conduct. New York: Hoeber-Harper.
1970 The Manufacture of Madness: A Comparative Study of the Inquisition and the Mental Health Movement. New York: Harper & Row.

Taube, Carl
1970 "Differential utilization of outpatient psychiatric services by whites and nonwhites." Statistical Note 36, National Institute of Mental Health, Washington, D.C.
1971 "Admission rates to state and county mental hospitals by age, sex and color, United States, 1969." Statistical Note 41, National Institute of Mental Health, Washington, D.C.
1973a "Length of stay of discharges from General Hospital inpatient units, United States, 1970-1971." Statistical Note 70, Natioanl Institute of Mental Health, Washington, D.C.
1973b "Differential utilization of general hospital psychiatric inpatient units by whites and nonwhites, United States, 1970-1971." Statistical Note 69, National Institute of Mental Health, Washington, D.C.

Tucker, Charles
1972a "Demented persons and psychiatric decisions." Mimeographed.
1972b "Societal reactions and mental illness: an examination of police behavior." Mimeographed.

Tudor, Jeanette, William Tudor, and Walter Gove
1975 "Sex roles and societal reactions to two types of mental disorder." Mimeographed.

Turner, R. Jay, Joann Raymond, Lawrence Zabo, and James Diamond
1969 "Field survey methods in psychiatry: the effects of sampling strategy upon findings in the research on schizophrenia." Journal of Health and Social Behavior 10 (December): 289-297.

Ullman, Leonard and Leonard Krasner
1965 Case Studies in Behavior Modification. New York: Holt, Rinehart & Winston.

Warheit, George, Charles Holzer, and John Schwab
1973 "An analysis of social class and racial differences in depressive symptomatology, a community study." Journal of Health and Social Behavior 14 (December): 291-299.

Wender, Paul, David Rosenthal and Seymour Kety
1968 "A psychiatric assessment of the adoptive parents of schizophrenics." Pp. 235-250 in David Rosenthal and Seymour Kety (eds.) The Transmission of Schizophrenia. Oxford: Pergamon.

Wenger, Denis and C. Richard Fletcher
1969 "The effect of legal counsel on admissions to a state mental hospital: A confrontation of professions." Journal of Health and Social Behavior 10 (March): 66-72.

Whitmer, Carroll and Glen Conover
1959 "A study of critical incidents in the hospitalization of the mentally ill." Journal of the National Association for Social Work 4 (January): 89-94.

Wilde, William
1968 "Decision-making in a psychiatric screening agency." Journal of Health and Social Behavior 9 (September): 215-221.

Wing, J. K.
1962 "Institutionalism in mental hospitals." British Journal of Social and Clinical Psychology 1: 38-51.

Wing, J. K. and G. W. Brown
1970 Institutionalism and Schizophrenia: A Comparative Study of Three Mental Hospitals 1960-1968. Cambridge: Cambridge University Press.

Winokur, G. and P. Clayton
1967 "Family history studies. I: Two types of affective disorders separated according to genetic and clinical factors." Recent Advances in Biological Psychiatry 9: 35-50.

Witkin, Michael and Roselyn Bass
1973 "Inpatient treatment in federally funded community mental health centers." Statistical Note 95, National Institute of Mental Health, Washington, D.C.

Wogan, Michael, Millard Amdur, David Kupfer, and Thomas Detre
1973 "The KDS-1: validity, reliability and independence among symptom clusters for clinic and normal samples." Psychological Reports 32 (April): 503-506.

Wood, Edwin, John Rakusin, and Emanuel Morse
1968 "Interpersonal aspects of psychiatric hospitalization. 1: The admission." Pp. 250-261 in Stephan Spitzer and Norman Denzin (eds.) The Mental Patient: Studies in the Sociology of Deviance. New York: McGraw-Hill.

Yarrow, Marion, Charlotte Schwartz, Harriet Murphy, and Leila Deasy
1955 "The psychological meaning of mental illness in the family." Journal of Social Issues 11, 4: 12-24.

Zung, William
1965a "A self rating depression scale." Archives of General Psychiatry 12 (January): 63-70.

1965b "Self rating depression scale in an outpatient clinic." Archives of General Psychiatry 13 (December): 508-513.

1967 "Factors influencing the self rating depression scale." Archives of General Psychiatry 10 (May): 543-554.

1969 "A cross-cultural survey of symptoms of depression." American Journal of Psychiatry 126 (July): 116-121.

Chapter 4

EXAMINING LABELLING THEORY: THE CASE OF MENTAL RETARDATION

ROBERT A. GORDON

The opportunity to examine labelling theory in the same arena with the IQ test, which has been termed "psychology's most telling accomplishment to date" (Herrnstein, 1973: 62), promises to be revealing. Jane Mercer's application of the labelling perspective to the area of mental retardation affords such a confrontation. Since hers is the most recent, most empirical, and most sophisticated example of the labelling perspective within this particular substantive area, I will deal mainly with her publications (specifically, 1965, 1972, 1973; Mercer and Brown, 1973) but also to some extent with a quite recent one by Beeghley and Butler (1974). Becker (1975), for one, has recently praised her work as "a magnificent and comprehensive study" which analyzes "voluminous data with . . . rigor and on their basis argues some shocking conclusions cogently," and has recommended her analysis as "a model for work of this kind."

In Mercer's work, the societal reaction is considered in the role both of dependent and of independent variable–a distinction made by Gove in his introductory overview. Mainly, her own research is concerned with why certain persons come to be labelled mentally retarded and others do not. Secondarily, she strongly suggests that, in many cases, this labelling consolidates the person's career as a retarded individual, and that without it the problem of mental retardation would be reduced (e.g., Mercer, 1973: 33, 204-205). However, her empirical results pertain only to the first of these two issues, that is, to the societal reaction in the role of dependent variable. The central focus of this review, therefore, will be on those parts of her work that are more germane to that kind of thesis.

CLINICAL VERSUS SOCIAL SYSTEM: TWO PERSPECTIVES, WITH CRITICISMS OF A GENERAL NATURE

In this major section, I am going to introduce, describe, and criticize the basic assumptions and concepts that Mercer (1973) employs. Some of these basic ideas demand lengthy analysis and a review of the relevant literature. Mercer's own empirical work is taken up in the next major section.

Conceptual Framework

Mercer (1973) constantly juxtaposes an individual-differences approach with a labelling approach. This contrast ought to make her study one of special interest to anyone concerned with the broader issues of scientific strategy and the style of investigation deemed appropriate to particular social science disciplines. Implicitly, Mercer's two-dimensional framework poses the question raised by Gove in his introduction: what is the relative proportion of variance associated with the societal reaction model in contrast to other explanations?

In her work, what amounts to an individual-differences dimension is represented by the prevailing approach to mental retardation in our society, termed by Mercer the "clinical" approach. "The clinical perspective classifies mental retardation as a handicapping condition, which exists in the individual and can be diagnosed by clinically trained professionals using properly standardized assessment techniques" (Mercer, 1973: 2). These techniques typically include the IQ test, an instrument which probably represents the accomplishments of the individual-differences tradition in social science better than any other.

In contrast (or competition) with the clinical approach is a new perspective, introduced by Mercer herself, and clearly inspired by the labelling orientation, which she calls the "social system perspective." This new perspective "classifies mental retardation as an acquired social status. Like any social status, that of mental retardate is defined by its location in the social system vis-a-vis other statuses, and by the role prescriptions that define the type of performance expected of persons holding the status" (Mercer, 1973: 2). This is clearly in keeping with Becker's (1969: 8-9) recent statement of the labelling position: "The central fact about deviance: it is created by society. . . . From this point of view, deviance is *not* a quality of the act the person commits, but rather a consequence of the application by others of rules and sanctions to an 'offender.' "

According to the clinical perspective, mental retardation is "an attribute of the individual" and "a case of mental retardation can exist undiagnosed in much the same sense that a case of rheumatic fever can exist undiagnosed. . . . The symptomatology exists as an entity quite apart from whether it has been identified and labelled" (Mercer, 1973: 7). Thus, it might also be said that this perspective places the phenomenon of mental retardation toward the physical reality end of an abstract physical reality versus social reality continuum (Festinger, 1950), whereas the social system perspective places it toward the pure social reality extreme.

The clinical perspective is itself based on two models, according to Mercer. One is the medical *pathological* model, which emphasizes organic conditions "which interfere with the physiological functions of the organism" (Mercer, 1973: 2), and the other is the *statistical* model, which emphasizes simply the fact that one is an outlier in the less desirable direction with respect to a particular normal distribution–in this case, the IQ distribution. Both these models are applied in the field of mental retardation, often by the same professionals, but the first derives mainly from the medical tradition and the second from the psychological. Let us proceed to examine her use of these two models.

Mercer does make strong concessions to physical reality with respect to cases of mental retardation that meet the pathological model. The grossly organic complications which accompany such cases are difficult to argue away. However, she contends that the existence of organic cases, and the dual set of models, lends a spurious authenticity to nonorganic cases identified solely in terms of the IQ test, because "there is a tendency to think in terms of one model while operating with the other" (1973: 5). "Thus," she states, "IQ, which is not a biological manifestation but is a behavioral score based on responses to a series of questions, becomes conceptually transposed into a pathological sign carrying all the implications of the pathological model" (1973: 6).

This may or may not be so as regards pathology. Certainly, the wish of many clinicians to hold open the possibility of a cure for mental retardation in cases where low IQ and its correlates are the only symptoms has often led them to postulate physiological defects where none can be found (see, for example, the discussion of this tendency in Zigler, 1967: 294; Albee, 1972: 201-202). The language of such hopeful workers lends credence to Mercer's notion that one model is contaminated by the other. However, it is now widely accepted since Zigler's clear statement in 1967, which Mercer cites in other connections, that such cases are probably not defective in any special sense, but simply represent the lowermost tail "of the distribution of intelligence that we would expect from the normal manifestations of the genetic pool in our population" (Zigler, 1967: 293; Jensen, 1969: 25-26, 1970a; Albee, 1972: 198-199). This "polygenic" kind of mental retardation, in which the genetic component is understood to reflect the combined action of many genes, is now often called "familial," to distinguish it from cases caused by single-gene effects, chromosomal abnormalities, or brain damage; these latter cases are the ones typically subsumed under Mercer's *pathological* model. Thus, Zigler's influential paper explicitly rejects the applicability of one model to the other, and hence the possibility of the contamination Mercer supposes to exist, while the strong correlation of .90 between genotype and phenotype for IQ among whites (Jensen, 1969: 43, 48, 1970b) renders Mercer's distinction between the two models–based on only one model's being a "biological manifestation"–somewhat tenuous, to say the least. Even the "best guess" of Jencks (1972: 315) in his analysis of heritability implies a genotype-phenotype correlation of .80.[1]

If one wanted to belabor the medical or disease analogy for the familial case, one could point to its biological transmissibility through family lines. For example, one major study shows that when both parents are retarded (defined as an IQ below 70), then nearly forty percent of their children are retarded; when only one parent is retarded, fifteen percent of the children are retarded; and when neither parent is retarded, only one percent of the children are retarded (Reed and Anderson, 1973: 114). These data alone should be sufficient reason for society to take an active interest in this portion of the IQ range.

From the very first, Mercer's (1973: 3-7) characterization of the statistical model is an oversimplification, although I am willing to grant that others, in thoughtless moments, have also occasionally discussed IQ norms in these terms, perhaps to avoid the unpleasant topic of the meaning of low scores (e.g., Kushlick, 1966: 121). Mercer's emphasis on simply deviating from the mean by a certain amount as the major criterion gives this model an arbitrary aspect that would be dispelled by considering why the dimension in question was singled out for attention in the first place. After all, we do not pay much attention to the vast majority of dimensions along which human populations are normally distributed. Once the importance to human affairs of a particular dimension is recognized, however, use of the normal distribution in guiding policy and interpreting cutting points with due regard for the meaning of scores (in the present case, IQ scores) at each point makes a great deal more sense. Either Mercer completely misunderstands the meaning of IQ norms in any particular application, or she is content to let what she calls the statistical model look as ridiculous as possible. Purely statistical norms of the sort Mercer envisages make sense only when the *meaning* of scores (e.g., of IQ 75) has no generalizability to new populations. For IQ scores, this is a question to be settled empirically, quite separate from whether means and variances are the same in all populations. Perhaps Mercer has been confused by the fact that the standardization and validation of tests are often carried out as separate operations, although in practice the results of these operations are brought together in the interpretation of the so-called "norms."

Mercer next distinguishes between the pathological and statistical models according to their trans-societal generalizability. Since the pathological model is founded on the physical reality of gross organic impairment, its criteria would apply as readily in one country as another, she holds. However, as she has conceived them, the norms emerging from the statistical model cannot be safely generalized in this manner to a new population, presumably because it might have a different mean and variance. But this relativistic limitation holds only if Mercer's caricature of the statistical model is accepted, in which norms were based entirely on arbitrary deviations from the mean. If we allow for the possibility that common sense entered into the definition of the norms, so that the correlates of scores were taken into account and not simply the number of cases beyond the cutting point, as scores the norms would have the same meaning in both populations (assuming equal validity of the measurements, which is an entirely separate empirical question, not to be confused with the point at issue here). A person who is six feet tall would remain so regardless of the mean and variance of his population, and regardless of whether his height was expressed as a deviation within some other normative distribution. The same holds true of a score on a test equivalent to, say, IQ 75 when the test remains valid.

Whether or not members of the new population would choose to respond to the scores in the same manner as the normative population is another issue. This issue would fall under the heading of true "cultural relativism," and it is in no way peculiar to the statistical model since it applies to the pathological model equally as well: the new culture, for example, could regard children with Down's syndrome as objects of religious significance.

To give a clear example, imagine the use of height as a predictive test of broad-jumping ability being applied to a Pygmy population after having been normed in the United States. It is quite conceivable, but by no means necessary, that it would predict as accurately for the Pygmies as for U.S. citizens. The former, of course, would have lower predictions, on the average. It is easy to recognize in this neutral example that the attitudes of the Pygmies toward the results is a separate matter. Presumably, they would respond to deviant jumpers with due respect to their own mean. This does not negate the meaning of the predictions, however, if the Pygmies were to compete in a world Olympics, or if we were physical anthropologists studying the universal relation between stature and performance in the human species. The fact that a test has been normed on one population in no way necessitates that its scores have different absolute meanings in another population.

As Cleary et al. (1975: 17) state, "If the data indicate that the test is useful, and something about the limits of its usefulness, the mere fact that the test was originally developed for another population becomes meaningless." Thus, we see that Mercer first permits IQ norms in any practical application to appear more arbitrary than they are in practice, and then she makes them seem more restricted to the normative population than is necessarily the case. One effect of these debilitating descriptions is to provide more room for her to maneuver in with the societal reaction model when she eventually takes up the matter of differential rates of mental retardation among various U.S. sub-populations.

Mercer (1973: 5-19) devotes considerable attention to elaborating the distinction she has drawn between the pathological and statistical models, and hence implicitly between the organic and familial forms of mental retardation, based on her argument that the former reflects a "biological manifestation" and the latter does not. As I have indicated, this dichotomization is specious in view of the high heritability of IQ. Strictly speaking, it is not even essential to her subsequent argument. There was nothing to prevent Mercer from recognizing a strong biological component in both forms of mental retardation, and yet arguing that perhaps the familial form ought to be classified still more separately from the other or even placed outside the rubric of "mental retardation" altogether. Jensen (1970a: 65), for example, who explicitly recognizes the biological role of polygenic causes in familial mental retardation, does exactly this, stating: "It is unfortunate that the label 'retarded' is ever used in connection with [such] individuals."

Why then did she insist on this distinction? First, so classifying the two models places them poles apart on the physical reality versus social reality continuum. This false dichotomy yields a concession to physical reality on the one side–Mercer is clearly not a radical labelling theorist since she does allow that something called "mental retardation" really exists–even while it simplifies her task of applying labelling theory within the mental retardation context, on the other side. Second, by implicating the IQ test itself as the major cause of improper labelling, she implicates whole segments of the institutional structure of our society through the network of middle class professionals who are responsible for administering and interpreting the test. This provides her with an argument that is much more interesting to sociologists and fellow members of the labelling school than the simple one of whether or not familial retardates in the IQ range of, say, 70 to 85, ought to be placed under a particular rubric. Becker (1975), for example, has recently found her "material useful in developing further a theory of the role of professional self-interest . . . in the creation of 'deviants'." Third, although she could simply have skirted the biological issue altogether, her advance labelling of the IQ test as an instrument of apparently pure social reality strengthens her role as champion of minority "underdog" groups, who have differentially high retardation rates according to the test. She therefore prejudices her audience against the test more than would be the case if the audience fully appreciated the issues raised by the high heritability of mental retardation among whites. As Jensen has spelled out, although "there is no *formal* relationship between within-group heritability and between-group heritability," evidence of high within-group heritability creates a probabilistic presumption of genetic differences between groups (1973a: 133-139). We shall see later that the admission of heritability as a factor in familial mental retardation creates special tensions concerning the implications of differences between groups in rates of retardation.

All the gains that I have just identified, however, require that Mercer ignore the literature concerning IQ and genetics throughout her argument. Jensen, for example, is never mentioned. This silence builds so much tension between her position and what is going on elsewhere in science that it is not surprising that she attempts to resolve that tension by finally confronting the genetic issue in her later work (Mercer and Brown, 1973).

Within this context of her main work, we also encounter the first of numerous points at which Mercer raises the issue of cultural loading of IQ tests, based on the fact that their original standardization samples were totally or predominantly white. This adds the question of specific content to her list of criticisms of the statistical model as it is implemented by IQ tests. She argues: "Items and procedures used in intelligence tests have inevitably come to reflect the abilities and skills valued by the American 'core culture' [which] consists mainly of the cultural patterns of that segment consisting of white, Anglo-Saxon Protestants whose social status is predominantly middle and upper class" (1973: 13), and she goes on in the next paragraph to add, "The ability to live amicably with other human beings counts not at all in the psychometric test situation" (1973: 14).

I am not sure whether she is denying the amicability of the group she calls "Anglos" or simply insisting that intelligence tests should measure other traits too, such as "musical ability," which she also mentions. The appeal here, of course, is to the fact that these other attributes are also nice to have, but there is no real reason to construe IQ tests as omnibus measures of everything it is nice for a person to have—or to suggest that Anglos do not treasure these other abilities, too, just because they do value the ability that IQ tests have been especially designed to measure. Finally, she asserts, "The Anglocentrism inherent in the mental tests . . . for diagnosing intelligence has been thoroughly documented" (1973: 14). This statement is accompanied by three citations, none later than 1963 (mistakenly given as 1953).

This issue of cultural bias in the IQ test is more fundamental than any other for understanding Mercer's work. As an issue, it has several variants that are often left implicitly confounded by those who raise it. The simplest but most radical variant is the contention that the importance of IQ *and* its correlates is culturally relative. In order to be consistent, the advocate of this position must permit all of the intellectual, educational, and occupational correlates of IQ to be as subject to cultural whim as the IQ test itself. Much of the superficial plausibility of statements concerning the relativity of IQ tests derives from this irrefutable position. When Mercer points out the IQ tests have "come to reflect the abilities . . . valued by" Anglos, she is implicitly drawing upon this source of plausibility. In practice, where minority groups with low average IQ are involved, no social scientist is willing to entertain a consistent cultural relativism of this sweeping sort. For example, no one is willing to allow groups to experience the high infant mortality rates, starvation, and unmitigated squalor that would accompany their low IQs under this relativistic interpretation. Furthermore, it is inconsistent, unfair, and unrealistic to insist that the larger society inhibit its concern with a subpopulation's hypothetical relativistic attitude toward its own low IQ and yet assume heavy obligations for protecting that subpopulation against the disadvantageous correlates of low IQ. This, clearly, would amount to double-standard cultural relativism. Unless one is willing to assume the full liabilities of this form of argument, it is irresponsible to garner its superficial plausibility in support of versions of the relativistic position that involve issues of a purely empirical nature, such as that to be considered next.

A more practical interpretation of the cultural bias argument holds that specific content in IQ tests gives advantages to one group over another in test scores that are unaccompanied by actual differences in pragmatic intelligence. This is a testable, empirically decidable issue that has nothing to do with value-judgments. Operationally, it implies, among other things, that the tests do not have the same validity for both groups. There is now a considerable body of evidence on this question as it applies to blacks and whites in the United States. In the present context, it seems safe to infer that, in the case of verbal tests, this same evidence holds, a fortiori, for lower-class whites and non-Anglo whites such as American Jews whenever the group in question can be assumed to have a familiarity with English equal at least to that of American blacks. Findings based on nonverbal tests would have even broader applicability, of course. In view of the crucial role of this key issue for dealing with Mercer's work, including the empirical part to come, we will now review the relevant evidence.

Findings Concerning the Validity of Intelligence Tests for Members of Disadvantaged Minority Groups

All standard academic ability tests, which measure abilities with high loadings on the same general factor as IQ tests (Jensen, 1970c: 412-413), predict school and college grades for blacks that are as high as or higher than the grades blacks actually earn. That is, when institutions use tests to select blacks by employing regression equations developed from either entirely white or from mixed samples, they tend to exhibit bias in favor of blacks, if they exhibit bias at all (Boney, 1966; Stanley and Porter, 1967; Hills and Stanley, 1968, 1970; Cleary, 1968; APA Task Force on Employment Testing of Minority Groups, 1969; Thomas, 1971; Stanley, 1971a, 1971b; Temp, 1971; Kallingal, 1971; Pfeifer and Sedlacek, 1971; Cleary et al., 1975). Occasional differences found between blacks and whites in purely correlational studies of validity (e.g., Dalton, 1974) as distinct from regression studies probably reflect artifacts such as curtailment of distributions and restriction of range due to the fact the test was too difficult for the blacks–that is, lacking in sufficient "floor." This possibility was demonstrated empirically by Hills and Stanley (1968, 1970), who showed that the level of the School and College Abilities Test (SCAT) appropriate for school grades 6 to 8 predicted freshman grades better than did the Scholastic Aptitude Test (SAT) at three predominantly black Southern colleges. For especially comprehensive reviews, see Stanley and Porter (1967), Stanley (1971b), Thomas (1971), and Cleary et al., (1975). A general discussion of the relevant issues can be found in Jensen (1970c, 1970d).

The demonstrated validity of intelligence tests for blacks in the area of academic performance would naturally be expected to generalize most strongly to those occupational performances in which similar abilities play a major role. The professions would be obvious examples of such occupations. However, points in the occupational spectrum as far removed from the professions as machine-shop employee in the aircraft industry (Tenopyr, 1967, after Thomas, 1971: 73), medical technician in Veterans Administration hospitals (Campbell et al., 1969), telephone company installation and repairman (Grant and Bray, 1970), and telephone company service representative (Gael and Grant, 1972) have now been explored. Again, the usual tests prove equally valid for blacks and whites, with any bias from using common regression lines to predict objective criteria favoring the selection of blacks (Grant and Bray, 1970: Figure 1). Identical findings prevail within the broad subsociety of military occupations, where aptitude tests have been found "equally effective in predicting performance in job training for blacks and whites. While blacks make lower average scores, their training performance is correspondingly lower, comparable to that of whites with the same level of test scores." The tests relate not only to rate of promotion within the Army, but also to "civilian earnings after separation from service for both blacks and whites" (Maier and Fuchs, 1975: 209). It is generally recognized, moreover, that IQ scores in the lower range are more valid predictors than those in the upper range—for example, persons with extremely high IQs can be found up and down the range of occupations, but extremely low IQ persons are almost never found in upper-status occupations (e.g., Harrell and Harrell, 1945; Stewart, 1947a, 1947b). Another consistent finding of interest is that the reliability of intelligence tests is greatest in the lower range of IQ, below 90 (McNemar, 1942: Tables 17-19; Terman and Merrill, 1960: 10).

The foregoing studies deal with the *external* criteria of test bias. The question of cultural bias can also be explored by examining the internal structure of the tests themselves. As Jensen (1974a: 189) explains, "if test items are culture-loaded, i.e., they call for specific information acquired in a given culture, and if the cultures of the standardization and target groups differ with respect to the cultural information sampled by the items, this should be reflected in various internal indices of bias, such as Culture-group X Item interactions." These interactions can be studied as a single component in appropriate analysis of variance models, and they can also be decomposed for finer analysis into two more basic kinds of evidence. One kind consists of significant differences between the groups in the rank order of difficulty of the items (as indicated by the percent, p, passing each item), and the other "is seen even when the rank order of p values is the same in both groups but the *differences* between the p values of adjacent items are significantly different in the two populations" (Jensen, 1974a: 189). One can also examine the loadings of the items on the first principal component, the choice of distractors for incorrect responses, and the reliabilities within each group. If cultural bias fails to manifest itself in any of these ways, there is very little left for it to consist of, aside from the bare fact of a mean difference between the groups in total score and percentage passing each item. But this fact alone cannot be used to prove bias because it begs the question. Mean differences would have to be backed by evidence of differential predictive accuracy, and we have just seen that such evidence does not exist for blacks and whites in any of the studies that meet acceptable scientific standards.

In two studies, Jensen has closely examined intelligence tests for *internal* evidence of this sort concerning cultural bias. The first of these studies deliberately concerns itself with school children from the very same ethnic populations studied by Mercer (white, black, and Mexican-American) in the same city studied by Mercer (1973: ch. 3)—Riverside, California. This study also deliberately employs two standard tests of intelligence that are generally recognized to differ maximally in their apparent degree of cultural loading, and that happen also to have been employed at some point by Mercer and Brown (1973). These two tests are the nonverbal Raven's Colored Progressive Matrices and the Peabody Picture Vocabulary Test, which is simply a test of recognition vocabulary. Jensen points out that the difficulty of items on the nonverbal Raven cannot be due to their rarity in everyday life, because none of them occurs in everyday life. Their difficulty can only be related to the complexity of mental processes that they involve. The difficulty of vocabulary items on the Peabody, on the other hand, can be shown to be more closely related to their rarity in daily life as measured by the Lorge-Thorndike word count than to their conceptual difficulty (Jensen, 1974a: 192-193). As Jensen notes, there appears to be nothing more difficult conceptually about the hardest item, "culver," than about the easiest, "table." The high cultural loading of the Peabody, of course, does not necessarily mean that it is *biased* in any particular application, even if it does yield mean differences between groups. Bias must be determined by other operations, such as examination of the sensitive internal indicators that I have already mentioned. In any case, these two strategically chosen tests span the known range of cultural loading for standard measures of intelligence.

Jensen's second study (n.d.) of internal criteria focuses on the Wonderlic Personnel Test. This is a test of general intelligence used by more than 6,500 business and industrial organizations for personnel selection and placement. Its content would place it somewhere between the Peabody and the Raven in amount of cultural loading. This study compared blacks and whites only. Since its procedures and findings are identical to those for blacks and whites in the other study, I will not describe them further. However, let me simply point out that findings from the study of the Wonderlic have special and direct practical implications for the occupational sphere, in view of the test's established role within that sphere, while findings from the Peabody and Raven are of greater theoretical interest, because of the extreme contrast between them in cultural loading.

In his study involving the Peabody and Raven, Jensen found all three ethnic groups quite similar to each other on both tests with respect to the various internal indicators described, particularly the most important two, based on item difficulty, which represent two aspects of the ethnic group X items interaction. For both the Peabody and the Raven, the total interaction of ethnic group X items accounted for "an exceedingly small proportion of the total variance" (1974a: 241). Jensen then went on to show that this extremely modest group x items interaction could be eliminated almost entirely if the analysis of variance was based on a minority group and a white group about one or two years younger than the minority group. This shows that the extremely modest groups x items interaction found in the analyses of variance based on ethnic comparisons of the same age can be interpreted as reflecting a mental age x items interaction rather than a cultural differences x items interaction. Jensen maintains that "it would seem far fetched to argue that the groups x items interaction reflects culture bias when such interaction can be greatly reduced simply by comparing ethnic groups that differ one or two years in age" (1974a: 242). Jensen bolsters this argument concerning mental age as the main source of the interaction by demonstrating that it was possible to simulate the results for the comparison between whites and blacks almost exactly by making up a "pseudo-ethnic" group of whites. This involved the comparison of two white groups with each other, one being selected so as to average two years older than the other. "This finding suggests the conclusion that little or none of the group x items interaction in the case of the Negro samples is attributable to cultural differences" (Jensen, 1974a: 242).

Some of Jensen's findings for the Mexican-American group were more complex. There was evidence that performance on the Peabody, which has a high cultural loading, was depressed for this ethnic group relative to their performance on the Raven. This tendency of Mexican-Americans to perform relatively better on nonverbal than on verbal tests of general intelligence has been observed in other studies dating back to 1936, and it can be seen in Mercer and Brown's data comparing the Raven with the Peabody, and the verbal with the performance subscales of the WISC (Wechsler Intelligence Scale for Children), as well as in another separate study by Jensen himself (1973b; Garth, Elson, and Morton, 1936; Mercer and Brown, 1973: Table 1). I would like to observe at this point that Anglo groups can also display such a difference between verbal and nonverbal tests, and that the white population in Riverside does so in fact (Mercer and Brown, 1973: Table 1; Jensen, 1973b: Table 1). This means that, despite efforts at uniform standardization, the nonverbal tests may sometimes be easier, and hence the corresponding gains by foreign-speaking ethnic groups must be viewed in relative rather than absolute terms. Jensen interpreted such relative differences in the present case as an indication of possible bias in the Peabody for Mexican-Americans. The cause of such a potential bias in the Peabody would have to be some factor that depresses all Peabody items about equally, and that does not operate as strongly in the Raven. Jensen suggests that "this factor is verbal and may be associated with bilingualism in the Mexican group" (1974a: 240).

This pattern of verbal-nonverbal differences has been observed elsewhere in studies of intelligence of bilinguals (Darcy, 1963). It represents a group x test-type interaction that corresponds, but on a larger scale, to the group x item interactions within tests that Jensen sought. The interpretation of such interactions among bilinguals presents severe difficulties because of the great potential for confounding between the presence of bilingualism and more fundamental factors. To take a hypothetical example, imagine that two ethnic groups arrive in this country under identical conditions, but that one has less native verbal ability than the other. After one generation the less able group would have progressed less rapidly in learning English, so that it would manifest bilingualism to a greater degree than the more able group (which presumably exchanges its native tongue for English), and this in turn would be confounded with poorer performance on verbal tests of intelligence. Under these conditions, it would be difficult to distinguish between bilingualism as an artifact and bilingualism as a manifestation of the very difference represented by the two kinds of test. It is recognized that simply testing a bilingual group in its ethnically native language does not necessarily eliminate problems of this nature for groups that learn one language in early childhood and another at school (Darcy, 1963). This is one reason for preferring nonverbal tests.

In his other study of these same three ethnic groups, Jensen (1973b) interprets the observed verbal-nonverbal differential for Mexican-Americans within the framework of Cattell's (1971: ch. 5) distinction between crystallized and fluid intelligence, which are viewed by Cattell as two aspects of the general intelligence factor present in varying degrees in all tests. This cogent interpretation is compatible with, but not necessarily identical in all heuristic implications to, the "simple" bilingualism hypothesis. "*Fluid* intelligence is the capacity for new conceptual learning and problem solving . . . independent of education and experience [whereas] *crystallized* intelligence . . . is a precipitate out of experience, consisting of acquired knowledge and developed intellectual skills" (Jensen, 1969: 13). The fluid-crystallized interpretation of differential performance on nonverbal versus verbal tests makes most sense in a genetically homogeneous setting, of course, and especially when applied to changes within the same individuals during their own life-spans. It is easy to see that the applicability of this interpretation to the case of bilinguals could be quite straightforward.

When applied across gene pools, however, the same interpretation runs into the risk that superficially similar differentials in verbal versus nonverbal intellectual performance could also be due to somewhat greater differences in the polygenic substrate for the two abilities than existed in the original normative population. Any such absolute genetic difference in the normative population would in part have been concealed by the norming process itself, which would automatically set the means for both types of performance arbitrarily at IQ 100, regardless of which commanded the greater number of supporting genes. It is even possible for the correlation between the two abilities to remain relatively constant across gene pools, perhaps partly because a large proportion of the supporting genes are common to both types of performance (e.g., McNemar, 1955: 140-141), and yet for there still to be a greater average differencc between the two gene pools in, say, frequency of verbal ability genes than frequency of nonverbal ability genes. However, Jensen's three replications show that even the correlation between verbal and nonverbal ability differs consistently from one ethnic group to another when whites, Mexican-Americans, and blacks are separately considered (1973b: Figure 3; see also Table 4.1, below).[2]

I raise the possibility of there being a genetic substrate even for differences between verbal and nonverbal general ability because we are gradually becoming accustomed to the idea that different ethnic groups exhibit characteristically different profiles across familiar cognitive dimensions, which in turn appear to depend heavily on genetic factors within groups when eventually studied under conditions that make estimates of heritability possible. Lesser, Fifer, and Clark (1965) demonstrated such profile differences across the four cognitive dimensions Verbal, Reasoning, Number, and Space for Chinese, Jews, Negroes, and Puerto Ricans. Although the mean levels of these four abilities changed as socioeconomic status was varied across two levels within each of the four ethnic groups, the key finding was that characteristic profile shapes remained strikingly constant within each ethnic group. For example, the profile for Jews begins with its highest point at Verbal, slopes down for Reasoning, up for Number, and down for Space, giving it the same jagged lightning-stroke appearance at both socioeconomic levels. The profile for Chinese, on the other hand, begins with its lowest point at Verbal, and then rises and remains relatively flat across the remaining three dimensions at both socioeconomic levels. These findings were later replicated in another city by Stodolsky and Lesser (1967). One implication of the differing profiles and their invariance over socioeconomic status is that it would be impossible to match these ethnic groups across all four dimensions simultaneously by equating for or adjusting socioeconomic status. Another implication is that whatever causes the profiles to be different is not associated with those powerful environmental influences sociologists usually group together under the heading of socioeconomic status. Additional evidence that particular test patterns of this sort are attributable to particular ethnic groups has been presented by Flaugher (1971) and Marjoribanks (1972). These findings provide a basis for renewed interest along fresh empirical lines in the diffuse problem that sociologists once conjectured about under the heading of "national character."

In statistical terms, such profile differences are known as "interactions." Similar interactions observed between whites and blacks involving the two cognitive dimensions IQ and associative learning ability (Jensen, 1968, 1970a,

1973b, 1974b; Jensen and Frederiksen, 1973), and between males and females involving IQ, spatial, and numerical ability (Garron, 1970; Helson, 1971; Bock and Kolakowski, 1973; Keating, 1974: 27-28), are simply additional cases in point. When we recognize that such robust interactions are the rule rather than the exception, it puts a new light on the potential interpretation of interactions involving verbal and nonverbal ability, which do not go in the same direction for all non-Anglo populations. Blacks, for example, often exhibit such an interaction, but in the opposite direction; that is, they do better on verbal than on nonverbal tests (Higgins and Sivers, 1958: Table 1; Shuey, 1966: 117-118; Jensen, 1973a: 278-279, 1973b: Table 1). Clearly, it is not automatically the case that the particular example of such interactions frequently found among bilinguals–namely, better performance on nonverbal than verbal tests–is caused by the fact of bilingualism, however plausible this may seem when viewed as an isolated phenomenon.[3]

Now let us take stock of where we stand concerning the issue of cultural loading of IQ tests with respect to the minority ethnic groups in Mercer's study. For blacks, the evidence is overwhelming that cultural bias does not account for intelligence test performance differences between the races. This evidence reflects both external and internal criteria, applies to both academic and occupational settings, and encompasses a range of tests that includes even the Peabody, which clearly represents the extreme among standard tests in amount of cultural loading.

For Mexican-Americans from the same setting in which Mercer conducted her study, we have excellent evidence, based on internal criteria, that cultural bias has a negligible effect on the nonverbal Raven, but that bilingualism might have a consistent, depressing effect on the Peabody. Standard tests such as the Stanford-Binet and WISC, employed by Mercer, would presumably fall between the Raven and Peabody in susceptibility to the effects of bilingualism. I know of no published validational studies employing external criteria of IQ tests for Mexican-Americans. However, the gross facts concerning their performance in the verbally demanding educational sphere are certainly consistent with their poor performance on tests of verbal ability, even according to the statistics presented by critics who contend that the IQ scores of Mexican-American children "have no relation to their ability to learn" (Reynoso et al., 1970: 827-830), whereas occasional reports of their sometimes holding an employment status that is higher than would be expected on the basis of their education is consistent with their relatively better performance on what Jensen regards as tests of fluid intelligence (Horowitz and Schwartz, 1974: 244). Even a sympathetic commentator such as Heller, who quite freely ascribes the academic problems of Mexican-Americans to aspects of the "system," reports that Mexican-American "high school students frequently refer to their difficulties with subject matter in school, and even those who manage to enter college speak of such difficulties" (1966: 91). Mercer herself reports correlations between Stanford-Binet IQ (Form L-M) and ratings by representative members within each ethnic community of children on a "slow-bright" scale that do not differ much between Mexican-Americans and Anglos, thus lending credence to the hypothesis that IQ differences have the same meaning within each community. For Mexican-Americans and Anglos, these correlations were .28 and .34, respectively. For blacks, the correlation was .47. When Mercer (1973: 88) divided her sample in thirds according to social status, the correlations were uniform within each third: .36, .36, and .35. The classic tendency, noted by Mercer, for raters to confound the brightness of children with their chronological age and sex (girls are better behaved and more conscientious) undoubtedly served to decrease these correlations somewhat. Terman (1925: 32-33) found, for example, that if you wanted to identify the brightest child in a class, it was better to seek the youngest than to ask the teacher's opinion.

Jensen (1973b: Table 1) has also administered verbal and nonverbal forms of the Lorge-Thorndike Intelligence Test, which employs a reading level for the verbal test well below the reasoning demands made by the test items, to representative samples of elementary school children in Riverside. On the verbal and nonverbal tests, respectively, Mexican-Americans scored 11.3 and 9.2 IQ points below Anglo children; blacks scored 12.7 and 15.0 IQ points below the Anglos, and thus *lower* than the Mexican-Americans, who were almost a standard deviation below the blacks in socioeconomic status. Jensen demonstrated that, within this tri-ethnic sample, the Lorge-Thorndike nonverbal test is quite close to the Raven in its oblique factor structure. Presumably, therefore, the Lorge-Thorndike nonverbal IQ is about as free of internal evidence of cultural bias for Mexican-Americans and blacks as the Raven; the fact that the Mexican-Americans outscore the blacks, as they did for the Raven but not for the Peabody, is consistent with this inference. Even if the verbal-nonverbal differential were entirely due to bilingual or cultural causes, therefore, evidence from the nonverbal tests indicates that the greater part of the IQ difference between Mexican-Americans and Anglos cannot be traced easily to this source. If cultural bias were as potent a factor in nonverbal tests as Mercer appears to claim for IQ tests in general, this ought to be easily demonstrable by the methods covered in this review.

To be on the safe side, however, I have brought together the relevant materials for a concurrent validational study of ability tests for Mexican-Americans, employing the external criteria of academic achievement and general information, from the Coleman study. These national sample data concerning external criteria thus help fill the one important gap remaining in our assessment of the fairness of ability tests for Mexican-Americans. The Mexican-American sample sizes are within one or two of one thousand; Negro samples are over three hundred thousand; and white samples are close to two million. Table 4.1 shows the correlations, for the three ethnic groups Mercer was concerned with, between nonverbal and verbal ability measures, on the one hand, and tests of reading comprehension, mathematical achievement, and general information, on the other hand. According to the Coleman Report, the general information test probes "areas likely to have become known through out-of-school rather than curriculum activities" (Coleman et al., 1966: 583). The achievement tests are of the standard type used in schools.

TABLE 4.1
CORRELATIONS BETWEEN NONVERBAL AND VERBAL ABILITY MEASURES AND ACHIEVEMENT TESTS FROM THE COLEMAN REPORT, FOR MEXICAN-AMERICANS (M), NEGROES (N), AND WHITES (W)—SIMPLE AVERAGES OVER GRADES APPEAR IN PARENTHESES

		Verbal Ability		Reading Comprehension		Mathematical Achievement		General Information	
Grade 12 (And Averages Over Grades)									
Nonverbal Ability	M	.59	(61)	.59	(59)	.43	(52)	.56	(58)
	N	.57	(55)	.56	(53)	.37	(46)	.57	(54)
	W	.52	(51)	.49	(51)	.51	(53)	.50	(52)
Verbal Ability	M	–		.75	(75)	.45	(59)	.77	(78)
	N	–		.78	(74)	.40	(53)	.78	(78)
	W	–		.77	(75)	.56	(63)	.77	(80)
Grade 9									
Nonverbal Ability	M	.61		.59		.59		.60	
	N	.54		.51		.50		.51	
	W	.54		.53		.58		.53	
Verbal Ability	M	–		.71		.62		.79	
	N	–		.70		.55		.79	
	W	–		.73		.65		.82	
Grade 6									
Nonverbal Ability	M	.62		.58		.54		–	
	N	.55		.53		.50		–	
	W	.48		.50		.51		–	
Verbal Ability	M	–		.79		.71		–	
	N	–		.75		.64		–	
	W	–		.75		.67		–	

SOURCE: Office of Education, 1966, *Supplemental Appendix to the Survey on Equality of Educational Opportunity,* Section 9.10/Correlation tables. Washington, D.C.: Government Printing Office.

Since we may be inclined to put greater stock in the fairness of nonverbal tests for Mexican-Americans, in view of Jensen's findings concerning the Peabody, let us focus first on the performance of the nonverbal ability tests used in the Coleman study. Over the three grades, the Mexican-American sample always has the highest correlation between this test and the verbal and reading comprehension tests. Mexican-Americans also have the highest correlation between this test and the mathematical achievement test two out of three times, and with the general information test one out of two times. There is certainly no indication that nonverbal ability is a less valid measure of school and informational learning for Mexican-Americans than it is for blacks or whites. The verbal ability test also appears to be as valid for Mexican-Americans as for the other two groups. In general, it is even more valid than is the nonverbal test as a predictor of these kinds of dependent variables for all three ethnic groups. Thus, if indeed the verbal test is more subject to bias for the Mexican-Americans than is the nonverbal test, it would appear that this bias is more than compensated for by the superior validity of the verbal test in this context, using these particular instruments. This may very well hold generally, of course.

Table 4.2 shows that relative standing on the criterion variables tends to be commensurate with the relative standing of these ethnic groups on the two

TABLE 4.2
MEANS FOR ABILITY AND ACHIEVEMENT MEASURES FROM THE COLEMAN REPORT, FOR MEXICAN-AMERICANS (M), NEGROES (N), AND WHITES (W)

	Nonverbal Ability	Verbal Ability	Reading Comprehension	Mathematical Achievement	General Information[a]
Grade 12:					
M	31.5	54.0	61.5	44.6	43.3
N	28.0	49.2	58.2	37.5	39.8
W	37.2	66.9	75.6	56.8	55.4
Grade 9:					
M	31.7	42.0	47.7	37.1	40.2
N	30.2	38.2	44.5	34.5	36.8
W	38.1	54.4	61.0	48.2	54.1
Grade 6:					
M	29.1	22.3	28.3	21.8	—
N	29.2	22.5	29.4	21.0	—
W	37.9	35.3	43.3	33.3	—

SOURCE: Office of Education, 1966, *Supplemental Appendix to the Survey on Equality of Educational Opportunity,* Section 9.10/Correlation tables. Washington, D.C.: Government Printing Office.

a. Not given in Grade 6.

ability tests. Thus, not only do the ability tests order individuals within each ethnic group in a way that is consistent with their performances on the criterion variables, but they also predict the level of performance of each group in a consistent way. It might be noted that on several tests at grade 6 (and only at grade 6) blacks score higher than Mexican-Americans. This unusual configuration does not hold at grade 3, so there is no need to suppose that Mexican-American performance relative to blacks improves over the sequence of grades simply because of a high Mexican-American dropout rate. The Mexican-American dropout rate exceeds the black dropout rate markedly only after age 16.0, which normally is after grade 9 (Coleman et al., 1966: Table 6.1.3).

Table 4.3 shows that if the two ability tests are employed to predict Mexican-American performance on the criterion variables in a simple regression equation standardized on whites, they tend to overpredict. That is, the tests would be biased in favor of Mexican-Americans for selection purposes. This can be seen by comparing the predicted means with the actual means, where the predicted values have been obtained by substituting a minority ability mean in the corresponding white regression equation. Because of its much greater validity, the bias is always less for the verbal than for the nonverbal test, despite the problematic nature of the former where bilinguals are concerned. This indicates that it might be a mistake to substitute non-

TABLE 4.3
PREDICTION OF MEXICAN-AMERICAN ACHIEVEMENT SCORES BY NONVERBAL AND VERBAL ABILITY TESTS OF COLEMAN REPORT, USING REGRESSION EQUATION FOR WHITES

	Reading Comprehension	Mathematical Achievement	General Information[a]
Grade 12:			
Observed M-A mean	61.5	44.6	43.3
Predicted by Nonverbal	68.9	49.7	50.3
Predicted by Verbal	64.0	48.1	46.8
Grade 9:			
Observed M-A mean	47.7	37.1	40.2
Predicted by Nonverbal	53.6	41.6	47.8
Predicted by Verbal	49.9	40.2	43.5
Grade 6:			
Observed M-A mean	28.3	21.8	–
Predicted by Nonverbal	34.3	26.7	–
Predicted by Verbal	29.9	24.7	–

a. Not given in Grade 6.

verbal for verbal tests in such cases, just because one is less culturally loaded, unless they are comparable in validity, too, or unless the validity of the new test exceeds the validity of the test it replaces.

The data in Tables 4.1, 4.2, and 4.3 clearly put nonverbal and verbal ability tests that are less culturally loaded than the Peabody on the same footing for Mexican-Americans as for blacks insofar as the concurrent prediction of academic achievement and general knowledge is concerned. Since the black-white ability differences in Table 4.2 are approximately equivalent to the usual one standard deviation difference in ability between these two groups, which comes to about 15 points nationwide on the IQ scale, it would appear that the Mexican-Americans average about 12.1 and 12.3 IQ points below whites on the nonverbal and verbal tests, respectively, over the three grades. When differences in tests, testing conditions, and the sampling of populations are given due weight, Jensen's Lorge-Thorndike results for Riverside, California, Mexican-Americans, which locate them 9.2 (nonverbal) and 11.3 (verbal) IQ points below Anglos, are certainly in line with the more general data of the Coleman Report. It appears that there is, in fact, a substantial valid IQ difference between these populations, and that it means pretty much what a similar IQ difference would mean between two groups of Anglos insofar as performance is concerned. For the remainder of this review, therefore, I intend to regard the presence of substantial IQ differences, on the order of at least 10 points, between Anglos and the two minority groups studied by Mercer as a settled matter, her characterization of IQ tests as culturally biased notwithstanding.

I would like to emphasize at this point that once it is established that IQ scores have the same or nearly the same functional meaning in all these populations, we are subject to virtually all of the unfavorable practical consequences that are commonly and mistakenly identified only with the equally controversial issue of genetic differences. Nothing reported so far concerning IQ differences between Mercer's populations depends on genetic differences. The issue of whether these IQ differences are environmentally or genetically determined is quite separate from the issue of whether the scores mean the same for these groups in everyday life. If the differences are valid and prove extremely resistant to remedial measures by environmental means—as they have proven for blacks (Jensen, 1969, 1973a; Page, 1972; for special insight into the limited meaning of IQ changes in remedial programs, see Bereiter, 1970: 284)—then it makes little difference in everyday life whether they are genetic or not.

With these fundamental matters out of the way, we can now complete our consideration of Mercer's conceptual apparatus and then turn to a more informed consideration of her empirical results.

Final Remarks Concerning the Social System Framework

Mercer states (1973: 22):

> The term *normal* from a social system framework does not refer to an individual's statistical position in relation to his peers nor to the absence of pathological signs. Normal behavior is role performance that conforms to the norms and expectations of the social system being studied. Deviant behavior is behavior that varies sufficiently from the expectations of the group to trigger group strategies aimed at coping with the deviance. Thus, the extent of deviation is determined not only by the behavior of the individual, but also by the norms used by the definer in making his judgments.

Most of this, of course, is a truism. It leaves out, however, that usually there is at least some relation between statistical distributions and the perception of what is normal or deviant, even if the classifying decision is not self-consciously derived in a statistical manner. Humans, as perceivers, do respond to central tendencies and deviations from them, and they interpret these perceptions according to the implications they hold for positive or negative reinforcement along the underlying dimension in question. Some dimensions, obviously, are more important than others. Psychometric instruments simply represent an effort to sharpen these judgments and reduce the time and cost involved in making them (Terman, 1925: 1). Ultimately, the human meaning of many judgments can be traced to the common responsiveness of the species to certain basic forms of positive or negative reinforcement that have been programmed by its biological nature. This common biological nature produces a tendency toward convergence in such judgments that Mercer's social system perspective never takes into account, and even seems at times deliberately to ignore. Such an omission undercuts one important source of common ground for resolving conflicts.

According to Mercer's social system perspective, "What is 'normal' depends on the norms of the particular social system in which the person is functioning at any given time" (Mercer, 1973: 22). "Mental retardation cannot be conceptualized as an abstract category transcending social systems, for it is tied to a . . . specific social system" (1973: 30), such as the school, the family, and the neighborhood. But it is one thing to recognize that definitions do vary according to context (e.g., Mercer, 1965), and quite another to elevate this observation into a principle for establishing the most useful meaning of such definitions in a complex society. The application of Mercer's theoretical view to complex societies amounts to the acceptance of an extreme form of local relativism, with no mechanism for resolving conflicting claims and no basis for recognizing legitimate priorities by appealing to general principles. The notion of legitimacy implied by this approach is always so local, and hence so subjective, that there is nothing to be gained even by introducing the concept. As Gove observed in his overview, labelling theorists have taken cognizance only of the priority of "power." Their failure to find a place for a more general conception of legitimacy, which would transcend any strictly local application, stems from their failure to give sufficient weight to both sides of any labelling decision in terms of its meaning to society as a whole, including, perhaps, members as yet unborn, who have no power, but who outnumber the living at any given time. Thus, even when Mercer refers to "a corps of professional diagnosticians" as "legitimate labellers" of the retarded (1973: 33-34), she means "legitimate" only in the eyes of the middle-class power structure and of anyone else who happens to agree with it. These "legitimate labellers" defend "the integrity of the normative structure of formal organizations" (1973: 34). Apparently, they never use their instruments and technical expertise to protect anyone who has been mistakenly labelled by his local system as "retarded" by pointing out that he or she does in fact have an adequate IQ, because Mercer describes them only as "charged . . . with the task of identifying persons who are violating societal norms" (1973: 34). It is quite typical of critics of IQ tests to overlook, for example, their important role in discovering talented individuals without regard to social background and personal appearance more efficiently than any other process ever devised (see, for example, Cleary et al., 1975: 32-35).

The failure to grapple with the problem of legitimacy in labelling analyses sidesteps the heaviest responsibility of social scientists, who could conceivably equip themselves to play the role in society of honest referees, prepared to defend their "calls." This tacit rejection of the very possibility of legitimacy that is implicit in the standard labelling approach goes deeper than Becker's (1967) refusal to accept the "credibility hierarchy," a refusal which under some circumstances, at least, could conceivably be legitimated.

This lack even of the recognition of the possibility of legitimacy in combination with extreme local relativism yields an unappealing and even corrosive view of society as comprising nothing but autistic conflict groups, the least ignoble being those who can best defend their claims to "underdog" status. It is my impression that even the ardent conflict theorist allows for meaningful exchange and compromise between opposing parties in order to arrive at common goals. From this standpoint, the indifference of the labelling school to the problem of legitimacy leads to an impoverished analysis of the larger social system, which suddenly seems to have no functional prerequisites at all.

I do not want to suggest here that I have any simple solution to the problem of identifying which, if any, of several conflicting viewpoints is sound or legitimate. However, by imagining simple cases, and considering how they would be handled by Mercer, I believe it is possible for the reader to sense that it is not the answer I am concerned with, but rather the attitude toward the question. Her attitude seems to be that the social scientist has no special role to play in tracing the implications of alternative policies, so that parties to a seeming conflict of interest are provided with a deeper understanding of their common interest and of the relevant facts on all sides. Instead, she seems content to portray the viewpoint of each local "underdog" context as though that viewpoint could never be inimical to the well-being of the complex society in which the disagreeing enclave is embedded and on which it often depends in greater measure than its own members realize.

The extreme relativism inherent in the labelling approach also makes for a rather unsteady platform from which to analyze society. In practice, members of the school steady their platforms by adopting a local point of view—usually that of the underdog (see Becker, 1967; Schur, 1971: 168). Mercer tends to do the same. One could imagine, for example, a savage analysis of what it is that her local social systems regard as "normal" and that the middle class regards as "retarded," simply as part of a complete presentation of the anarchic perspective she espouses. This, of course, we do not get (for hints of what it might be like, see the sympathetic but unsentimental study of mildly retarded persons by Edgerton, 1967).

If the main purpose of her theoretical apparatus is simply to legitimate her assumption of a particular, iconoclastic viewpoint, she could just as well have moved directly to it. This would have eliminated the need for passages such as the following, where, having defined a retardate as a person who plays the role of retardate in some social system, Mercer casually divorces having a low IQ from the list of possible role prescriptions, thus enabling her to state: "If a person does not occupy the status of mental retardate, is not playing the role of mental retardate in any social system, and is not regarded by any of the significant others in his social world, then he is not mentally retarded, irrespective of the level of his IQ" (1973: 28). All this says is that if having a low IQ does not define retardation, then having a low IQ does not define retardation. In its original form it is a mildly stupefying tautology, whose main accomplishment seems to be the exclusion of IQ test results from the arena of any social system.

Finally, it appears that the labelling perspective can be distracting as well as uneconomical. A classic case in point is Mercer's conclusion that the "corps of professional diagnosticians" constitutes "the single most important social system in the sociological study of mental retardation" (1973: 35). This is like stating that the single most important entity in the study of cancer is the pathologist who performs biopsies. It seems to me that a far more important social system, even for sociologists (who have a long tradition of studying assortative mating) could very well be what geneticists call "the breeding system." After their own large-scale study of mental retardation, Reed and Reed (1965: 48) stated, "One inescapable conclusion is that the transmission of mental retardation from parent to child is by far the most important *single* factor in the persistence of this social misfortune." They came to this conclusion after finding that "the one to two percent of our population composed of fertile retardates produced 36.1 percent of the retardates of the next generation" (1965: 48). Epidemiological data of this sort, not to mention surveys of attitudes toward mental retardation, are certainly of a kind that a sociologist might gather. Mercer's claim, therefore, that the diagnosticians are the most relevant social system in the *sociological* study of this subject harks back to artificial definitions of the proper province of sociology which take as their base some restricted or "sociological" portion of the total variance—thereby yielding results whose relevance to practical concerns is inevitably ambiguous and probably exaggerated.

EMPIRICAL WORK BY MERCER

Epidemiological Survey of Formal Organizations

Mercer carried out what she calls "a social system epidemiology" by asking 241 public or private organizations in Riverside to nominate all mentally retarded persons known to them. Deliberately, the term "mental retardate" was left undefined. This yielded 812 traceable retardates, who had been nominated a total of 1,493 times. After grouping the organizations into eight meaningful types, it was found that the "public schools" had yielded 340 retardates nominated by no other type of organization, and 429 in total (1973: Table 2). These last two numbers constitute 42% and 53% of the Riverside total.

Had the three ethnic groups contributed retardates to the total pool of nominees in proportion to their share of the population in Riverside, the index for each would have been 1.00. Instead, there was disproportionality. Indices for Anglos, Mexican-Americans, and blacks stood at 0.66, 3.37, and 1.57, respectively. Among the "public school" nominees, there was even greater ethnic disproportionality: 0.45, 4.74, and 2.29, respectively. Several of the organization types, however, did not exhibit this disproportionality. The "Department of Mental Hygiene" and various "medical facilities" had only a slight underrepresentation of Anglos, while "private organizations for the mentally retarded" and "religious organizations" had a slight overrepresentation of Anglos. There were also disproportions in varying measures among the eight organizational types with respect to the socioeconomic status of their nominees.

Mercer then assessed "whether an organization emphasizes medical or statistical norms by analyzing the nature of the data available in" its files for the retardates. "If an organization has a medical diagnosis for a large percentage of its nominees, then it is using medical norms. If it has an IQ . . . it is using statistical norms" (1973: 59). Most organizations, of course, used both, in varying degree. After comparing the ranking of the organizational types according to their degree of ethnic and socioeconomic disproportionality with their ranking according to the type of norm employed, Mercer concluded that "the medical-pathological model is less likely to produce socioeconomic and ethnic disproportions in the labeling and that heavy reliance on the statistical model without concomitant use of the medical model is associated with such disproportions" (1973: 61). Organizations that reported "learning problems" rather than health or physical disability problems also tended to rank high in socioeconomic and ethnic disproportionality.

I want here to indicate that the topical headings of Mercer's empirical presentation thus far parallel five "aspects of normative structures" described earlier in her theoretical presentation of the social system perspective (1973: 23). I think it is instructive to know that what comes next was presented under one of these headings–"Level of Expectation." Here, Mercer asserts, "The lower the mean IQ and the larger the mean number of physical disabilities of persons holding the status of mental retardate, the less stringent the demands of a system" (1973: 62). In other words, the classification of higher IQ, able-bodied individuals as "retarded" would be tantamount to more stringent demands. I mention the topical heading because her discussion at this point seems to be motivated to a greater degree than at other points by the prior existence of the theoretical outline based on labelling theory.

In the course of this particular discussion, Mercer reports that retardates nominated by the organizational types "law enforcement" and "public schools" had the highest mean IQs, 70.3 and 67.4, and the lowest average number of physical disabilities, less than 1.0 in each case. According to her argument, therefore, these organizations had the most stringent norms. The organizational types "private organizations for the mentally retarded," "Department of Mental Hygiene," and "medical facilities" had the lowest mean IQs, ranging from 42.5 to 50.4, and the highest average number of disabilities, ranging from 2.5 to 3.9. Consequently, these had the least stringent norms. There is clearly a 20- to 25-point IQ difference between these extremes, and a large difference in average number of physical disabilities.

The argument here is of interest mainly because I regard it as symptomatic. Clearly, the criterion for classification as retarded is in the nature of a cutting point, especially for the unidimensional IQ variable (disabilities are multidimensional). But one cannot infer the location of a cutting point from the mean of those selected without knowing the shape and location of their distribution, which reflects in turn the shape and location of the distribution exposed to the selection process. Yet, this is exactly what Mercer is doing. Despite her claims, all of the agencies involved could be employing exactly the same cutoffs—that is, the same norms—and yet be receiving different kinds of eligibles, with the result that they differ from each other on the average with respect to the IQs of their retardates. Mercer's overeagerness to infer normative differences from mean differences at this point looks to me very much like an instance in which the labelling model exercised negative heuristic influence over the analysis. It is consistent with the general attitude toward group differences throughout her work, in which attention is called repeatedly to differentials as though they were evidence, ipso facto, that something was awry in the social system.

Ostensibly inexplicable differentials of the sort that Mercer reports between ethnic groups and between socioeconomic levels in the number of retardates, and between formal organization types in mean levels of intellectual competence and physical disability, typically play an important role in all labelling approaches. Cast in familiar terms of contingency table analysis—say, of the association between minority versus Anglo ethnic status, and retarded versus nonretarded status—these differentials are formally equivalent to interactions. When they are sufficiently mysterious, such interactions enable the more quantitatively oriented labelling theorist to concede that some aspect of the phenomenon in question exists in physical reality (there really is such a thing as mental retardation), without compromising his or her claim that the phenomenon is also in important measure a product of pure social reality. Mercer's entire discussion of the various differentials she observed, for example, is conducted under the major heading "Comparative Normative Structures." (1973: 58). Attribution of an effect to norms rooted only in social reality has important rhetorical implications. If there is any indication that the effect is a harmful one, audiences are inclined to regard the norm as changeworthy, and to dismiss the resistance of those who hold the norm as symptoms of delusion. (See, for example, the attitude toward the white middle class taken by Beeghley and Butler, 1974: 752.)

The persuasiveness of differentials as evidence of the intervention of social reality rests heavily on the assumption that they do not reflect real differences between the groups being classified. Scheff (1966: 155-168), for example, was sensitive to this issue in his study of differential mental hospital release rates, and so he attempted to control for relevant attributes of the patients that might affect release before concluding that the differences were in fact due to "social contingencies." Even then, these contingencies were recognized to be of a highly practical sort–e.g., availability of nursing homes, etc. The validity of arguing by exclusion, of course, depends on our ability to identify and measure adequately all of the variables it is relevant to control. In the present case, however, the need to deal with these troublesome issues has been minimized by Mercer's dismissal of the IQ test as culturally biased. It can be seen, therefore, that the scientific status of the IQ test plays a crucial role in determining the ease of the form of argument that she has adopted.

Many social scientists are unprepared to anticipate the dramatic effects that even small differences in mean can have on the relative proportions of cases falling beyond a certain cutoff in the tails of normal or approximately normal distributions. Differences in variance produce similar effects, of course. In considering the differentials among the three ethnic groups in retardation rates, we have to take into account that we are dealing with approximately normal distributions which vary in the size of their standard deviations, and which are often as much as one standard deviation apart.

Table 4.4 indicates the percentage of each ethnic group that would be "retarded" at each of two IQ levels often suggested as major cutting points in discussions of the retarded (e.g., Mercer, 1973: 130-131). These percentages were developed by referring the means and standard deviations of three IQ tests given to samples of Riverside school children by Jensen or by Mercer to a table of areas under the normal curve (Jensen, 1973b: Table 1; Mercer and Brown, 1973: Table 1). The bottom half of Table 4.4 presents minority/Anglo ratios that tell us the number of minority retardates implied for each Anglo retardate in equal-sized populations under the foregoing conditions. These ratios are obtained simply by dividing a minority percentage in the top part of the table by its associated Anglo percentage. In the bottom righthand corner of the table there appear for comparison three more sets of minority/Anglo ratios that express the various ethnic differentials observed by Mercer in the course of her social system epidemiology.

It is evident from Table 4.4 that the percentage retarded fluctuates quite a bit from test to test. This is because means and standard deviations differ, which is not surprising since the tests measure somewhat different specific factors despite their high loading on general intelligence. It is also the case that two samplings of the population are involved. Changes in the ordering of the ethnic group percentages from one IQ level to the other can also be observed. Such changes are to be expected, since the mean and variance combine in a complex manner to produce these percentages, and the relative influence of these two parameters varies according to the segment of the range under consideration. Although Mexican-Americans are often close to the blacks in mean IQ, they produce more retardates at several segments of the range than the blacks because of their larger variance. This larger variance of Mexican-Americans is typical of whites in general in contrast to blacks, and in the Lorge-Thorndike data the Mexican-American standard deviations are closer to the Anglo standard deviations than to the black standard deviations.

TABLE 4.4
PERCENTAGES OF RETARDATES IMPLIED AND OBSERVED IN RIVERSIDE, ACCORDING TO VARIOUS TESTS AND CRITERIA, BY ETHNIC GROUP, AND ASSOCIATED MINORITY/ANGLO RATIOS

	Lorge-Thorndike Nonverbal (Jensen, 1973b)	Lorge-Thorndike Verbal[a] (Jensen, 1973b)	WISC Full Scale (Mercer and Brown, 1973)	Observed (Mercer, 1973)
	Implied Percentage Below IQ 85			
Black	25.1 (N=556)	38.2	28.8 (N=180)	–
Mexican-American	14.7 (N=668)	35.2	31.9 (N=180)	–
Anglo	4.6 (N=698)	12.1	2.9 (N=180)	–
	Implied Percentage Below IQ 70			
Black	4.2	5.8	3.8	
Mexican-American	1.9	6.3	5.7	
Anglo	0.4	1.2	0.1	
	Minority/Anglo Ratio (Anglo/Anglo = 1.00)			
Below IQ 85:				
Black/Anglo	5.46	3.16	9.93	–
M-A/Anglo	3.20	2.91	11.00	–
Below IQ 70:				
Black/Anglo	10.50	4.83	38.00	–
M-A/Anglo	4.75	5.25	57.00	–
Mercer's 812 Nominated Retardates:				
Black/Anglo				2.39
M-A/Anglo				5.12
Mercer's Subset of 429 Retardates Nominated by Public Schools:				
Black/Anglo				5.07
M-A/Anglo				10.50
Mercer's Study of 71 School Children Referred in Past Year:				
Black/Anglo				7.22
M-A/Anglo				10.40

a. The sample sizes for the Lorge-Thorndike Verbal test are the same as for the Nonverbal test.

The minority/Anglo ratios in the lower part of Table 4.4 also fluctuate markedly. Each of these ratios depends on double the number of parameters of any single percentage, and furthermore the ratio statistic often magnifies the effects of minute percentage differences occurring within the denominator, especially when the denominator percentages are as low in absolute value as they are for Anglos.

The important understanding to be gained from Table 4.4 is that all of the IQ test results portray ethnic differentials of about the same magnitude as those actually observed by Mercer. We cannot hope to match Mercer's differentials exactly because we do not know precisely what processes besides IQ operated to produce 812 retardates under 50 years of age in a city of 84,000-130,000 (Mercer, 1973: 276; Mercer and Brown, 1973: 56). We are also relying on the normal approximation here, and not all of the actual IQ distributions are necessarily precisely normal. In the South, the black IQ distribution has been observed to be skewed to the left (Kennedy, Van De Riet, and White, 1963: 68-69). The point is, *any one* of these sets of differentials, all of which have been generated by applying uniform cutoff "norms" to our best estimates of the IQ distributions of the three ethnic groups, would have been sufficient to trigger Mercer's concern and subsequent interpretations, because her implicit model for comparison purposes is one of equiproportionality. Since the familial form of mental retardation is accounted for simply as an aspect of the distribution of individual differences in IQ, we can see that this one type alone is responsible for a major part, if not all, of the ethnic differential in retardation rates, and not necessarily any differences in diagnostic norms from situation to situation. Once the validity of IQ scores for these three ethnic groups is established, differentials follow automatically at any common cutoff point one would wish to select within the range of interest pertinent to retardation.

Now I would like to turn attention to the remaining interactions noted by Mercer—those involving socioeconomic status and type of organization. In 1966, Kushlick stated:

> It has long been known that parents of severely subnormal children are *evenly distributed* among all the strata of industrial society, while those of mildly subnormal subjects come predominantly from the lower social classes.
>
> There is now evidence which suggests that mild subnormality in the absence of abnormal neurological signs . . . is virtually confined to the lower social classes. Indeed, there is evidence that almost no children of higher social class parents have IQ scores of less than 80, unless they

> have one of the pathological processes mentioned above [1966: 130-132; emphasis added; see also Jensen, 1970a: 37-38].

We can now recognize that when Kushlick distinguishes between severe retardation with neurological signs and mild retardation without such signs, he is referring to the same two types noted by Zigler (1967), one of which I will simply call "organic" for short, and the other of which is the "familial" variety. Zigler reports that the organic type gives rise to a separate IQ distribution outside the white normal distribution, which descends only to about IQ 50. This separate IQ distribution is somewhat normal, with a mean of about 35 and a range from 0 to 70. Zigler (1967: 292) states, "The retardate having an extremely low IQ (below 40) is almost invariably of the physiologically defective type." Zigler informs us that this type comprises only about twenty-five percent of all retardates in predominantly Anglo populations that are representative with respect to socioeconomic status. Mercer was aware of Zigler's two-group taxonomy, and of this proportion, because she quotes this section of his paper and cites the classic sources for the proportion (Mercer, 1973: 69-70, 223). She does not, however, cite Kushlick.

We see, therefore, that we have one type, representing a small fraction of all retardates, characterized by extremely low IQ and gross, often massive, physical anomalies. This type is distributed evenly by social class, presumably because the various factors producing it are themselves unrelated to social class. It seems reasonable to suppose these factors would also be unrelated to ethnic group, inasmuch as all white parents seem to be equally at risk in this respect. And we also have a second, much more frequent, type characterized by mild retardation, no physical abnormalities, and a strong relation to social class.

Clearly, the relation of the second type to social class reflects the well-established relation between social class and IQ (Herrnstein, 1973: 116). The mean differences between social classes are formally equivalent to the mean differences between ethnic groups in Mercer's research. The lower the mean IQ of any group, regardless of whether it is defined on an ethnic basis or on a socioeconomic basis, the greater the area in its lower tail extending below any particular IQ cutoff, and hence the greater the prevalence of familial retardates in the group. Keep in mind, however, that the prevalence of the other, organic kind of retardate remains relatively constant, regardless of the mean IQ of the population, because this form of retardation is due to factors unrelated to those which determine the rest of the population's IQ. Now let us see what kind of differentials result from a model based on both forms of retardation.

It is clear that the familial-organic "mix" of retardates will vary widely as a function of population IQ. In higher IQ populations, we can expect to find that practically all of the retardates are of the severe, physically abnormal, "organic" variety. However, since these severe retardates are in general a minority of all retardates, we can expect to find that, in low IQ populations, whose modes are close to the retardation cutoff, the retardates are predominantly of the milder, familial type. The IQ and physical disability score distributions actually observed by Mercer fit these expectations. Anglo retardates average 2.18 physical disabilities, as compared to 0.99 and 0.81 for Mexican-Americans and blacks, and the latter two groups have a greater proportion of mildly retarded persons in the 60-79 IQ range (Mercer, 1973: Table 4).

The superimposition of a small constant proportion of severe, organic cases upon the results in Table 4.4 would of course not disturb the ethnic differentials very much. By substantially augmenting those Anglo denominators in Table 4.4 in which the proportions of familial retardates are close to zero, the organic cases would reduce ratios that now appear unrealistically large to more reasonable levels. Beyond that, it does not take much imagination to see that these simple facts concerning the two major retarded types are fully capable of accounting for all of the remaining interactions noted by Mercer—without the necessity for imputing any variation whatever in "norms" across formal organizational settings. The differences between organizational types in mean IQ, average number of physical impairments, and reliance upon medical or psychometric criteria, which Mercer invokes to infer differences in "norms," would simply reflect differences in intake and clientele. Medically oriented agencies, such as the "Department of Mental Hygiene" and "medical facilities," would be more apt to receive as cases the highly visible organic types, and private agencies catering to the middle classes would also take in a disproportionate share of organic cases, because this is the most common type within that social class. To the extent that such private agencies functioned as charitable agencies, they would also probably be inclined to respond more to medical, organic cases, particularly if this was the type of case they were set up to deal with in the first place because of their middle-class origin. Hence, medically oriented and other types of organizations specializing in the treatment and diagnosis of organic retardates would show little or no evidence of ethnic differentials because there is little or no ethnic differential in this form of retardation. It is natural, therefore, that the "Department of Mental Hygiene" and "medical facilities" would have only a slight underrepresentation of Anglos, while "private organizations for the mentally retarded" and "religious organizations" would have only a slight overrepresentation. Whether Anglos were slightly underrepresented or slightly overrepresented in the files of such organizations might hinge simply on whether the organizations were public or private ones. Many of the severely retarded organic cases, of course, would be screened out before entering public school (Kushlick, 1966: 128). This would leave the public schools and the law enforcement agencies as the major specialists in the detection and diagnosis of familial retardation, as many observers have noted (Kushlick, 1966: 129; Jensen, 1970a: 36). Since agencies would be inclined to use criteria appropriate to the form of retardate they encounter, and since the familial type does not entail physical anomalies, it is to be expected that the schools and similar agencies would less often record medical information of this type. This would account for the bare facts which led to Mercer's conclusion "that heavy reliance on the statistical model without concomitant use of the medical model is associated with such disproportions" (1973: 61). But there is no evidence here for Mercer's opening claim, plausible though it may seem, that "mental retardation cannot be conceptualized as an abstract category transcending social systems, for it is tied to a specific status and role in a specific social system" (1973: 30).

From a theoretical standpoint, it is important to note that it was her labelling perspective that led Mercer to infer differences in norms to account for these differentials—that is, to infer differences in social situations from one organizational type to another—and to implicitly assume no differences in the individuals involved. However, the underlying reality definitely points to differences associated with individuals that are quite capable of accounting for all of the differentials without any need to suppose the existence of differences in organizational norms. These would appear to be quite different interpretations of the differentials, with widely divergent implications for public policy and the channeling of an aroused public concern.

Mercer's Analysis of Referral and Testing within the Public Schools

In light of my discussion of the factors underlying disproportionality in the distribution of retardates in the city as a whole, it should not be surprising that a similar ethnic and socioeconomic disproportionality was found within the public schools (see Table 4.4, above). In a separate analysis, Mercer focused on the process of referral and testing within the public schools, and reported the following information. School personnel such as teachers and principals refer children to the Pupil Personnel Department for a variety of reasons. Two of the many reasons are to determine whether the child should be classified as gifted or as retarded, depending on the case. In the course of the one year studied in detail, 31% and 8.3% of the referrals, respectively, concerned potential giftedness or retardation (Mercer, 1973: 110). This fact establishes the large proportion referred for giftedness—more than were referred for any other single reason. If a child was referred for either of these two reasons, the chances were nine out of ten that he or she would be given an IQ test (1973: 113).

Mercer's study of the referral process begins with "all 1,234 children referred for *any reason* to the Pupil Personnel Department during a single school year" (1973: 97; italics added). She reports:

> The 1,234 children referred to the Pupil Personnel Services were similar in ethnic distribution and socioeconomic status to the total population of the school district. This pattern continued until the point in the labeling process at which the intelligence test was administered. *As soon as the intelligence test was used, the higher failure rate of children from lower socioeconomic background and from minority homes produced the disproportions characteristic of classes for the mentally retarded.* Apparently, there is no ethnic or socioeconomic bias in the type of children referred by the principal-teacher team or tested by the school psychologist. The disproportionate number of low-status and minority children in special education classes first appears at the juncture in the referral process when standardized intelligence measures are used for diagnosis [1973: 115; italics in original].

And still later:

> Ethnic disproportions appear only at the point in the labeling process at which the IQ test is administered. Minority children are not referred by teachers at a higher rate than their percentage in the population, nor are they tested at a higher rate [1973: 117].

As incredible as it may seem, Mercer is including those children referred for testing because the teacher suspects they are gifted as part of the population "at risk" for being labelled "retarded" when given the IQ test. This produces the equiproportionality which supposedly holds all through the referral process only to vanish suddenly with administration of the IQ test. "All children referred during that year faced the risk of being tested by a psychologist and found eligible for placement in the status of mental retardate" (1973: 110). "Those referred for the 'gifted' program tended to come from significantly higher socioeconomic levels and Anglo homes" (1973: 114).

It is not hard to understand why the inclusion of referrals for giftedness should manage to achieve equiproportionality for Anglo referrals as compared with minority referrals made mainly for other reasons. In several of her Riverside studies, Mercer reports WISC IQs for samples of Anglo school children of 106.9 (1973: 240) and 107.5 (Mercer and Brown, 1973: Table 1). She also tells us that the median Anglo IQ, based on the school testing program, ranged from 106 to 108 (1973: 240). If we take IQ 107 as a representative value for these convergent estimates, we find that it is 22 points above the IQ of 85 at about which the question of retardation might begin to arise (for possible referral), and only 23 points below IQ 130, which has been the IQ of the average Ph.D. in the natural sciences (Wolfle and Oxtoby, 1952), and which is the criterion in Riverside for placing pupils in classes for the gifted (Mercer, 1973: 104). (Note the relation of the criterion to its meaning in the real world rather than to just the size of the percentile.) Because their IQ distribution has its center so high in the range, Anglos apparently overlap the zone in which teachers suspect giftedness in pupils to an extent sufficient to compensate for their underrepresentation among referrals motivated by the possibility the pupil is retarded.

By failing to distinguish among reasons for referral to the Pupil Personnel Department in defining the population "at risk," Mercer succeeds in concentrating the onus of diagnosis on the IQ test. In view of the facts in her surrounding discussion, it is probable that similar differentials were *already* apparent in the judgments of experienced teachers—as reflected in the composition of the pool of suspected retardate referrals. Hence, her failure to distinguish among reasons almost certainly deprives the test of the consensual validation it would have received from this source. Mercer's policies here represent a continuation of the tactic which effectively places the IQ test outside any interpersonal social system. But Jensen's (1973a: 263) research shows that teachers' ratings of pupil intelligence correlate .66 with Lorge-Thorndike Verbal IQ even if recorded before any testing of the pupils. Mercer's own earlier analysis (1973: 105-107) of grades and of teachers' spontaneous comments concerning "74 of the children referred by teachers and placed in special classes" for the retarded shows that even before referral they were already visibly inferior in mental ability to a group of regular classroom children matching them in ethnic status.

The implications of Mercer's policy materialize in an article by Beeghley and Butler (1974: 746), which parallels Mercer's thinking throughout, and which apparently employs some of the same data she collected. The lack of disproportionality in teacher referrals reported by Mercer indicates to these authors that the ultimate differentials in retardation rates cannot be attributed to "individual racism" and therefore they must be due to "institutional racism." They go on to point out that "the only means of altering a discriminatory situation deeply embedded in institutional structures is by decisively altering that structure" (1974: 752). This portent of drastic action of unspecified nature probably points more clearly than any other single statement to the extent of the divergence in policy implications between Mercer's interpretations and those presented here. In turn, this visible divergence suggests some of the ways in which scientific analysis can bear upon the legitimacy of opposing positions in a conflict situation for, as nearly as I can determine, few if any of these differences in policy implications stem from differences in value-judgments per se.

Mercer next focused on the 134 children referred for testing and found eligible for placement in special classes for the retarded by virtue of the fact that their IQ was under 80. Of the 134 who were eligible, only 81 were recommended for placement; within the subset of 134 eligibles there was a percentage difference of 23.0 points between Anglos and minorities in being recommended for placement; Anglos were less likely to be so recommended. We are also informed that the average IQ of eligible children not recommended for placement was not significantly higher than that of the children recommended–71.4 versus 69.0. Here, of course, the analysis is directly astride that segment of the decision zone in which ambiguity is at its maximum for the small proportion of all cases falling within it. Mercer certainly leaves us with the impression that there is something sinister about the fact that relatively fewer eligible Anglos were recommended for placement. Our interpretation of how sinister this might be would depend on our evaluation of the utility of being in a special curriculum (e.g., Katz, 1973), given that one is eligible. We should not let the fact that no one wants to be retarded prejudice our judgment of this utility. That would be like letting our antipathy toward being hospitalized prejudice our judgment of the utility of being in the hospital given that one is seriously ill. Perhaps the diagnosticians felt they were favoring the minority children by awarding them scarce places. In any case, Mercer made no attempt to ascertain the reasons behind this slight differential, and thus let the decision-makers speak for themselves, which would certainly have been in accord with the relativistic approach she applies elsewhere. It is conceivable that experience has taught the psychologists that low-scoring Anglo children "improve" more over time than minority children if tested at a later time, and thus it is best to let some of them remain where they are. This perception would correspond to our realistic expectation that the putative retardates who happen to be Anglos would regress upward toward the mean between testings more than minority members. Given the eligibility criterion of IQ 80, and the WISC IQs of these ethnic groups (Mercer and Brown, 1973: Table 1), the Anglo, black, and Mexican-American eligibles would be at least 2.31, 0.97, and 0.84 standard deviations from the means of their respective groups, and the amount of regression would be proportional to the distance from the mean. This also happens to be the order in which they fall, from lowest to highest, in the percentage recommended for placement of those eligible (48.4%, 73.1%, 75.0%).[4]

Survey of Neighbor and Family Nominees

In order to compare the labelling process within formal organizations with that of members of the community, Mercer conducted a household survey. In the course of the interviews, respondents were asked if they knew of any retarded persons in Riverside. They also rated children in their own household on several scales. One of these, the "bright-slow" scale, was considered a measure of intelligence. The sixteen percent of children receiving the lowest ratings on the "bright-slow" scale were designated as "family nominees," and the retarded persons actually named as such were designated "neighbor nominees." Mercer found that neither of these two classes of nominees reproduced any of the ethnic or socioeconomic differentials previously noted. She concluded, "This finding indicates that the labelling of large numbers of persons from low socioeconomic levels and minority ethnic groups as subnormal is a characteristic of the clinical perspective that is not shared by lay persons in the community" (1973: 85).

The psychological impact of this apparent discrepancy between persons in the community and clinicians builds on the seeming disarray and lack of consensus among even middle-class agencies that was uncovered by Mercer's earlier social system epidemiology. However, I have already demonstrated that the ethnic and diagnostic differentials exhibited in that connection cannot be used to infer supposed differences in norms among agencies.

In the present context of the household survey, it should be noted that, when the known attributes of actual retardates on her central register from the organizational study were regressed on the number of nominations these retarded persons received from neighbors, IQ was the most significant single variable ($r = -.31$). Number of physical disabilities was second ($r = .24$). I have already called attention to the correlations within each ethnic group between IQ and the "bright-slow" ratings, which emerged when the Stanford-Binet was given to a subsample of the children rated. These sets of data indicate that persons in the community are sensitive to IQ differences, but they do not tell us much about their sensitivity to level of IQ given that there are substantial differences in IQ level among the three ethnic communities and, of course, the social classes. Now let us examine these analyses more closely.

Mercer chose the lowest sixteen percent of the ratings on her "bright-slow" scale as a cutting point for family nominees because this is the percentile that would correspond to an IQ of 85, one standard deviation (15 points) below the mean (100), in the white, normative population on which IQ tests have been standardized. IQ 85 is the highest of the various IQ criteria of mental retardation generally put forward (1973: 130-131).However, her actual Riverside sample was chosen so that "all geographic areas and socioeconomic levels in the community were represented in their proper proportion" (1973: 83), and this community does not correspond to the white normative sample in those parameters which would cause the sixteenth percentile to be equivalent to IQ 85. Our best estimates of the relevant parameters, given the means, standard deviations, and ethnic proportions presented at various points by Mercer (1973: 49; Mercer and Brown, 1973: Table 1), and a formula for combining these in order to arrive at the values for the composite (McNemar, 1955: 26), is that children in Riverside as a whole have a WISC mean IQ of 105.4 with a standard deviation of 13.2. The sixteenth percentile of this distribution would fall approximately one standard deviation below its mean, at IQ 92.2. In order to cut the Riverside population at IQ 85, Mercer should have set her cutting point 1.54 standard deviations below the mean IQ, or at the sixth percentile.

Cutting the Riverside ethnic groups at IQ 92.2 is tantamount to cutting blacks, Mexican-Americans, and Anglos at the 50.8, the 52.8, and the 9.8 percentiles, respectively. These values may be compared with the percentages generated by actually cutting at WISC IQ 85, in Table 4.4 (above). At IQ 85, we obtained minority/Anglo ratios of 9.93 for blacks and of 11.00 for Mexican-Americans. At IQ 92.2, however, we obtain reduced ratios of 5.18 and 5.39, respectively. Thus, even if the "bright-slow" scales correlated perfectly with IQ, the minority/Anglo differentials actually to be expected were reduced to 52.2% and 49.0% of the value they would have had, had Mercer chosen a cutting point more relevant to the issue of mental retardation. It can also be seen from the minority/Anglo ratios in Table 4.4 (above) that lower cutting points produce even larger ratios, e.g., 38.00 and 57.00 at IQ 70. By aiming at IQ 85 to start with (but hitting IQ 92.2), Mercer chose a cutting point that has recently been recommended as realistic in contemporary industrial society (See Mercer, 1973: 130; Jensen, 1970a: 36), but which is not actually implemented in Riverside, where the IQ cutoff for placement in a special class was not higher than 80 in the public schools (1973: 104). Thus, the differentials she observed among labelled retardates in Riverside apply to a segment of the IQ range in which such differentials would be expected to be much larger than is the case in the segment she investigated with her "bright-slow" scale, which produced no differentials. It must be remembered, too, that the "bright-slow" scale was a weak measure of intelligence, as such measures go even *within* the Anglo sample, where it correlated .34 with IQ (Mercer, 1973: 88). Lack of validity reduces the ability of an instrument to differentiate between criterion groups.

Our interpretation of the lack of differentials in neighbor nominees must also take into account that such responses from the community may not automatically represent the authentic appraisal of the subject. What would be the result, for example, if members of the community were asked to nominate persons with tuberculosis? Katz (1973: 136) states, "The predominant cultural stereotype of the mentally retarded is that of a person suffering from a severe mental and physical handicap and requiring constant supervision or institutionalization." If this is indeed the case, then it would account for the lack of social differentials in response to being asked in a survey whether one knew of any retarded persons. The stereotype clearly describes the organic type of retardate, which does not necessarily produce differentials. On the other hand, we could side with Mercer against Katz and maintain that what he dismisses as a "stereotype" is in fact the community "norm."

Rather than dwell on this dilemma, let us consider another problem, which pertains to the "bright-slow" ratings as well. Going back to my neutral example of the Pygmies, let us suppose they were asked whether there were any really poor broad-jumpers in their neighborhood. Naturally, we would expect that they would respond in terms of their adaptation to their own Pygmy mean, rather than in terms of Olympic standards which would probably classify the entire Pygmy community as poor broad-jumpers. It certainly seems likely that a process of this sort must have been operative in the ethnic samples, since two of them were at least 15 IQ points below the third. Is it not reasonable to suppose that each individual views the world from the vantage point of his own IQ, and that where there is a mean difference in the vantage points there is also a mean difference in outlooks upon the world? We have evidence, after all, that analogous processes operate within academic settings which vary in their selectivity (Davis, 1966; Alexander and Eckland, 1975), and we know from a national survey of secondary school students that responses of blacks are distributed about the same as those of whites (or are higher) when asked where they stand in relation to the "average" in intelligence (Brim et al., 1969: Table 7.7). Again, it is possible to take a totally relativistic view of these matters, but fairness demands that one embrace double-standard cultural relativism frankly, with all its inconsistencies, if that is what one intends, for the lesson of the data is that the Pygmies will not produce their proportional share of Olympic broad-jumpers, no matter how they feel about it, and that similar effects will obtain as the result of group differences on the more vital IQ dimension.

More restricted, but equally interesting models capable of accounting for Mercer's lack of differentials in the neighbor nominee data would involve rater-ratee interactions built up out of assumptions such as: retardates do not nominate retardates. Interactive processes such as this would tend to reduce differentials sharply—that is, make groups more alike than they are in fact, since the size of the error is a function of the proportion retarded. This and the previous model would tend to shade into each other as one allowed that a nonretardate does not nominate retardates who are adjacent to him in IQ, and so on.

Mercer summed up her various findings concerning the labelling process within four broad areas (1973: 120-121). These areas refer to the differentials and the absences of differentials that I have discussed so far, and which I have shown could be accounted for entirely on the basis of known facts concerning the individual-differences dimension operating within the context of a uniform norm, rather than as the result of variations in the situational dimension for which there is little or no evidence beyond the differentials themselves. Before I introduce in the next section some additional findings—from the individuals dimension—that round out my explanation of why Mercer found no differentials in her analyses of neighbor and family nominees. I want to present the conclusions she drew, from her summary. In these conclusions, she attributes all of the effects, which I need not repeat here, to situational causes:

> Anglocentrism, institutionalized and legitimated by the diagnostic procedures used in the formal organizations of the community, appears to be the most pervasive pattern in labelling the mentally retarded in the community.
>
> Anglocentrism is a specific form of ethnocentrism. Ethnocentrism refers to the tendency . . . for persons to believe that the culture of their own group is superior to that of other groups. Ethnocentrism leads people to act as if the language, history, life style, and values of their own group are the "right" and "good" standards by which the behavior of all other persons ought to be measured [1973: 121].
>
> We conclude, therefore, on the basis of our social system epidemiology of mental retardation in the community, that institutionalized Anglocentrism is a recurring pattern in the labelling process, a pattern that is closely linked with the statistical definition of "normal" and the IQ test [1973: 123].

This general position has been vigorously seconded by Beeghley and Butler in their own recent article, where they conclude, *"The most important structural factor contributing to the disproportionate labeling of children as mentally retarded is the testing process itself,"* which they regard as "an archetypal example of institutional racism" (1974: 747-748). The only thing remarkable about their article, which deals with the same three ethnic groups, and which finds essentially the same ethnic disproportions in retardation rates after massive school integration as existed before, is their treatment of the psychological literature. They manage to ignore all of the validational literature I have cited, and they devote far more attention than it deserves to the now thoroughly discredited study by Rosenthal and Jacobson (1968) called *Pygmalion in the Classroom* (on which, see Thorndike, 1968; Snow, 1969; Elashoff and Snow, 1971; and the review of this literature in Jensen, 1973a: 260-264). Elashoff and Snow report that not one of nine studies attempting to replicate or demonstrate teacher expectancy effects on IQ has succeeded (1971: 158). Beeghley and Butler (1974: 749) also assert that the ethnicity of the test administrator has been shown to effect test scores, but here they ignore the comprehenisve review of this literature by Sattler (1970), who found that there was no support for such a statement. Jensen (1974c) has recently completed a study of this same effect involving 9,000 children, virtually the entire enrollment of the participating elementary school system. He too found no evidence that the race of the examiner was of any consequence. Beeghley and Butler do not mention Jensen at all.

A Contrasting Approach Recognizing Individual Differences

In the preface to a recent book, Jensen (1972: 4-6) describes how he first became interested in those topics with which his name is now popularly linked. One of his graduate students pointed out that mentally retarded children (with IQs under 75) from minority groups often seemed far brighter than white middle-class retarded children in the same special classes. The student asked Jensen if there was a more culturally fair IQ test that might reveal this brightness. He had tried all the existing ones, but they had not worked. Jensen went down to the playground to observe such children for himself, and received the same impression–minority children "appeared much brighter socially and on the playground, often being quite indistinguishable in every way from children of normal IQ except in their scholastic performance and in their scores on a variety of standard IQ tests" (1972: 6). Middle-class retardates, however, appeared dull in every respect, not just in school.

In subsequent research, Jensen developed tests that revealed the nature of the cognitive difference between these two groups of retarded youngsters. It turns out that the minority retardates are superior to white middle-class retardates in this IQ range with respect to associative or rote learning ability, measured by traditional tests such as digit span and others since developed by Jensen. These "direct learning" tests differ from IQ tests, which emphasize the ability to manipulate abstract or conceptual material rather than "how fast the child could learn something new right in the test situation itself" (Jensen, 1970a: 66). Evidence for this interaction between the two kinds of ability, which Jensen calls "Level I" (associative) and "Level II" (IQ), and race and socioeconomic status now exists for blacks, Mexican-Americans, and whites (Jensen, 1968, 1970a, 1972: 281-293, 1973b, 1974b; Jensen and Frederiksen, 1973).[5]

These research findings provide a plausible account of why it is that many lower-class children, including children of "disadvantaged" minority groups, seem to be retarded in school, but then go on to lead a reasonably normal life in the community once they exit from school. School draws heavily on Level II abilities, and school performance was in fact what the IQ test was devised to predict. What predictive value IQ tests have in other areas, such as occupation, simply reflects the fact that they draw on the same ability that is required to perform well in the classroom, which in turn was designed to prepare pupils to fill jobs in the occupational world (Jensen, 1969: 5-16).

Middle-class white children with low IQs, however, do not typically display this nonacademic form of brightness. This is because the correlation between the two forms of ability is higher among middle-class than among lower-class white children or children of black or Mexican-American extraction (Jensen, 1969: 286-288). Hence, when a middle-class child has a low IQ, it is likely that (s)he is also deficient in associative learning ability. Jensen hypothesizes that this higher correlation in the middle class and among whites reflects a tendency for the two abilities to be selected together genetically (1972: 290-291). This plausible hypothesis would fall under what is called "the theory of correlated responses to selection for polygenic characters," which has been developing among geneticists for some time (e.g., Haskell, 1954).

Out of this body of research, Jensen (1970a) has elaborated what he calls "a theory of primary and secondary familial mental retardation," This theory now introduces an important conceptual distinction within the familial category of retardate, which accounts for the fact that severe familial (non-organic, that is) retardates often require institutionalization, whereas other familial retardates, often viewed as "mildly" retarded, but with the same IQs, function reasonably well in the community once out of school. For example, in 1966, Kushlick commented on the same phenomenon:

> The IQ range 50-70 or 75 has been suggested as diagnostic of the grade of mild subnormality. This has not proved useful, either clinically or administratively. There are many people in this IQ range who are never dealt with as subnormal and who do not appear to have problems arising from their low intelligence, and there are people of IQ well over 70 who are being dealt with by the services for the abnormal [1966: 128].

According to Jensen's theory, the more severe "primary" familial retardate is deficient in Level I ability, whereas the more self-sufficient "secondary" retardate is deficient mainly in Level II (IQ). Impairment in both levels also seems to be present in the few severe, organic cases tested by Jensen (1970a: 68), and since primary familial retardates with IQs over 85 or so seem to be rare (1970a: 61-62), they too are typically deficient in both levels.

Quite clearly, these discoveries also contribute to our understanding of the lack of differentials among Mercer's neighbor nominees. Although the theory predicts that middle-class familial retardates ought to be more often visible in the community, because they are more often of the primary kind, familial retardates are probably too rare altogether in the middle class for this to tip the differentials among neighbor nominees so that the middle class would be overrepresented. And although familial retardates are more numerous among lower-class and some minority groups, they are predominantly of the secondary kind, which merges into the lower-class community when out of school, and hence escapes nomination. These outcomes constitute a situational source of variance, but one that is more in the nature of an individuals x situations interaction than of a simple main effect.

Some of the major features of this interaction were anticipated years ago by the anthropologist Ralph Linton, in the course of drawing his classic distinction between ascribed and achieved statuses:

> Fortunately, human beings are so mutable that almost any normal individual can be *trained* to the adequate performance of almost any role. *Most of the business of living can be conducted on basis of habit, with little need for intelligence and none for special gifts.* Societies have met the dilemma by developing two types of statuses, the *ascribed* and the *achieved.* Ascribed statuses are those which are assigned to individuals without reference to their innate differences or abilities. They can be predicted and trained for from the moment of birth. The achieved statuses are, as a minimum, those requiring special qualities. . . . They are not assigned to individuals from birth, but are left open to be filled through *competition and individual effort.* The majority of the statuses in all social systems are of the ascribed type and *those which take care of the ordinary day-to-day business of living are practically always of this type* [Linton, 1936: 115; italics added].

Of course, "those which take care of the ordinary day-to-day business of living" are the roles which secondary retardates return to, and perform normally in, when they are not in the achieved status system of the school or in the occupational hierarchy of a modern industrial society.

Jensen's introduction of a second cognitive variable implies that improvement of the prediction of occupational performance in the lower IQ, lower occupational range is possible. Implicitly, it also suggests that IQ tests might be a shade less valid for predicting minority performance within an extremely narrow segment of the lower occupational range because minority familial retardates are predominantly of the secondary kind, which often copes well with nonintellectual tasks. So far, validity studies have not plumbed this lowermost range, but that is because IQ tests are not actually employed for selection within it in everyday life, and so there has been no controversy over their value. In civilian life, the major practical application of IQ tests within this low range seems to be in the "prediction" and diagnosis of retardation, and here both Jensen and Mercer, as well as others, seem to agree that they do not predict the incompetence of minority members quite as well as they do the incompetence of white middle-class children.[6] Using an individual-differences approach, Jensen's tactic has been to find a variable that improves the prediction. Using a labelling approach, Mercer's tactic has been to destroy the existing prediction throughout a large portion of the range, by setting what amount to quotas for those diagnosed as retarded in minority groups (1973: ch. 17).

Lest there be any doubt that there is a prediction to be destroyed, let me point out that the IQ is still highly related to performance in school; Jensen also reports that many secondary retardates are to be found in regular school classes in low SES neighborhoods, where "their scholastic performance is usually commensurate with their low IQs" (1970a: 67).[7]

It is important to realize that, although Mercer plays heavily upon our sentiments in her book by referring to the status of retardate as a "dis-esteemed" status, which is occupied disproportionately more often by under-dog groups, whose children are "exposed to a much higher risk of achieving" this status (1973: 120-121), she herself is not altogether against labels. Elsewhere, she states,

> But it would be a mistake to drop all labels, all special classes. One of the great achievements in public education in the last twenty years has been the development of special-education programs, and we do not think they should be abandoned hastily. Many minority-group children are still going to need help if they are to do well in the mainstream of public education; they will need help whether or not we call them retarded. Relabeling is not a panacea [1972: 96].

Now let us see how consistent Mercer's appreciation of special classes is with her own recommendations that we employ "pluralistic norms" in diagnosing able-bodied (i.e., nonorganic) children to be placed in these special classes. In accordance with her recommended policy (1973: 188, ch. 17), a child would have to score within the lowest three percent of his own ethnic group, both on an IQ test and again on a test of adaptive behavior (which the two minority groups also failed to pass at highly disproportionate rates; 1973: 160). Adaptive behavior is in fact usually taken into account in diagnosing retardation; Mercer's suggestion simply requires that a relative rather than an absolute standard be used. (Just how these principles might apply to a child from an interethnic marriage is a complication, incidentally, that is never considered.)

For simplicity, I shall consider only the IQ criterion in examining this issue. In effect, an individual would have to score 1.89 standard deviations below the mean of his ethnic group (on both dimensions) to qualify for special classes. In Riverside, this is equivalent to IQs of 65.8, 68.6, and 85.0 for Mexican-Americans, Blacks, and Anglos, respectively. There is nearly a twenty-point spread among these criteria. Quite clearly, if IQs mean the same in all groups insofar as academic performance is concerned, Mercer's policy can only result in extremely sloppy diagnosis for the purpose of assigning pupils to special or regular classes.

Taken at face value, much of Mercer's evidence is certainly consistent with observations of others, indicating that low IQs do not mean exactly the same thing in all ethnic groups insofar as the performance of routine living tasks is concerned (1973: 190), how physically disabled one is, or how one is perceived in the neighborhood or playground (1973: ch. 6, and p. 177). This is because of variation in the "mix" of retarded types from one social category to another. However, other evidence demonstrates quite conclusively that IQs mean very much the same thing in all categories insofar as scholastic performance is concerned. Yet Mercer uses the evidence of differential validity in the out-of-school settings as the basis for formulating policy to be applied within schools, precisely the setting where IQ tests are equally valid for all groups.

This validity in schools was obscured, it will be recalled, by Mercer's policy of counting potentially gifted Anglos as part of the referral population "at risk," thus enabling her to claim later that the deficiencies of minorities "are limited primarily to performance in formal test situations" (1973: 191). Clearly, by focusing exclusively on the label she has lost sight of the underlying reality to which the different validations pertain.

The final significance of this is not fully appreciated until we realize also that Jensen's primary retardates often have IQs well up in the borderline range—that is, 70-84—which falls entirely above Mercer's minority group cutoffs. In evaluating the import of a change of from 2 to 20 points in IQ, one must not be misled by the instability of individual IQ scores, which are sometimes ambiguous because of fluctuations of about this order of magnitude. In policy decisions concerning populations of individuals, we are in effect dealing with infinite sample sizes, and hence the standard error of (the mean) IQ is zero for all practical purposes. Consequently, the *average* impact of a change in policy is equivalent in many ways to what it would be if each person's IQ were measured with absolute precision.

To obtain a sense of the meaning of Mercer's policies in the case of primary retardates, I turn to a report by Edgerton, an anthropologist, who closely studied forty-eight patients who had been released from an institution for the mentally retarded. These patients were "near the upper limit of the mildly retarded range in intelligence" and also "the most socially competent and most intellectually able of the patients" to have been admitted to the hospital in the ten years prior to Edgerton's research. "If any group of persons once institutionalized as being mentally retarded could be expected to have an opportunity for successful independent living outside an institution it was persons in this cohort" (Edgerton, 1968: 79). Thirty-five percent of them had IQs of 70 or more, and 16.7% had IQs of 80 or more. Two of the seven Mexican-Americans in the group had IQs over 80. Jensen would regard these as primary retardates. Secondary retardates, he points out, are not usually perceived as retarded once they leave school, and are seldom institutionalized (1970a: 65-66).

How did these former patients fare when helped to rejoin the community? One's first impression, according to Edgerton (1968: 79), was that they were "coping with life in a modern city . . . rather well." Would this also have been the perception of uninvolved neighbors if Mercer had asked them? (We gain insight into the sensitivity of the "neighbor nominee" criterion from Mercer's own description of the incompetence of an IQ 47 woman who was *not* named by her employer as a retarded individual; see 1973: 216.)

Edgerton then points out that the former patients have problems. First, they live in dread of being found out as retarded. Mercer has referred to this aspect of Edgerton's study as follows (1973: 33):

> When a person has been assigned the status of retardate by a professional diagnostician and has been systematically socialized to the role, it is difficult for him to escape the status even in thinking about himself. The struggle of ex-patients from an institution for the mentally retarded to escape the status of the mental subnormal is movingly described by Edgerton.

This does not convey the full flavor of Edgerton's observations. These patients were not simply trying to conceal the fact that they had once been institutionalized; that is, they were not simply trying to shed a past label or a past role that was no longer applicable. The label they were trying to avoid was spontaneously regenerated constantly in the course of social interaction: "They do not escape detection when their public exposure becomes face-to-face, when it is prolonged, or when problematic social situations must be confronted. In such instances the former patient is found out; his incompetence becomes quite evident" (Edgerton, 1968: 80). For example, a patient with an IQ of 83 was found a job in a bakery. His new employers described him as follows: "God, he is stupid. At first he almost drove us nuts. He couldn't follow simple instructions and we had to tell him everything a hundred times. He couldn't even learn how to grease a pan. He worked hard, though, and was honest, so we kept him. Besides, we don't pay him too much" (Edgerton, 1967: 176). Evidently, when labelling theorists tell us someone is trying to escape a label, what they often mean is that he is trying to escape the thing in itself.

Second, every one of the former patients had acquired the assistance of a benefactor "without whose aid they could succeed in none of these things. In my judgment, it is the case that only three of these former patients have been able to maintain themselves in the community without the significant intervention of benefactors in their lives" (Edgerton, 1968: 80).

Third, Edgerton emphatically states that "for the ex-patient in this study, any distinction between 'intellectual' and 'social' competence is factitious. In the course of these ex-patients' everyday lives, the two competencies–intellectual and social–cannot be separated" (1968: 81).

Quite clearly, Mercer's "pluralistic norms" are not only inappropriate for predicting the scholastic performance of secondary retardates, but they are also inappropriate, as Edgerton's work shows, for many borderline IQ primary retardates who are even more severely handicapped. In view of Schur's (1971: 26-27) comments concerning the special role of "sensitizing concepts" in labelling theory, it is ironic that an individual-differences approach has led to the discovery of methods for diagnosing these conditions in a manner more sensitive to the needs of the individuals concerned, whereas a labelling approach has led to the development of less sensitive methods. It is of interest to note that Mercer (1973: 123) reports the passage of a bill through the California legislature which mandates procedures similar to those "pluralistic" ones she herself has suggested.

A Solution to the Problem of Mental Retardation or Simply a Stupefying Tautology?

Mercer tells us:

> Social problems are not self-defined. A particular condition is a social problem only as persons in a society regard it as problematic. In a very

> real sense, the issue of the choice of criterion for determining mental retardation is precisely that of defining the limits of a social problem . . . called mental retardation. If the criterion level is high, then the scope of the problem is greatly expanded. If the criterion level is low, relatively few persons will be rated as subnormal and the scope of the problem will shrink [1973: 204-205].

The question to be raised, however, concerns the aspects of "the problem" that still remain unchanged after the definition is manipulated. If it is also an aspect of "the problem" that persons with low IQs are concentrated in the lower range of socioeconomic status (Mercer, 1973: 166-167), and in the lower range of educational achievement (1973: 166), and among those who depend on others for their daily sustenance (1973: 181), then changing the *definition* of the problem will not change the *size* of the problem. Concepts are created to help us manipulate the real world symbolically, but labelling theory seems to foster the illusion, by distracting us from the reality underlying the label, that any manipulation of the symbol creates a corresponding manipulation in the real world.

The recognition that simply unlabelling a category of persons once labelled "retarded" does not automatically make them equivalent in all respects to persons labelled "normal" brings to light a shortcoming in Mercer's proposals that is probably characteristic of many labelling approaches to deviance. For example, if children with IQs of 70-80 are not put in special classes, where do we put them? A new category of class could be created, between the special class and the regular class, but then this becomes tantamount to a tracking system, a solution already under heavy attack because minorities appear disproportionately in the lower tracks. If we place such low IQ children in the regular classes, so that an IQ range of 70 to 130 often exists within the same room, it means that at age ten we are dealing with academic mental ages ranging from seven to thirteen within the same instructional setting. I personally doubt that the "open classroom" philosophy does more than paper over the severe problems produced by this much heterogeneity. At the present time, for example, the Baltimore school system is under attack because it plans to lower the cutoff for keeping pupils in regular classes from IQ 75 to 70 (Miller, 1975). One of the critics is a black school board member with a Ph.D. in the natural sciences—apparently, the opinion of minority group members is not monolithic on these matters (a fascinating prospect totally neglected by Mercer).

In principle, Mercer had two strategies open to her for dealing with the embarrassing correlated disadvantages of low IQ that remain after we have changed "the size" of the problem by changing the label.

(1) She could have adopted a sweeping relativism, by defining the correlates too as no longer problems. However, poverty and low academic achievement are taken far too seriously by social scientists to be dealt with in this frivolous manner. Labelling theorists tend to reserve this tactic for the afflictions of the middle class.

(2) She could have granted that the correlates of low IQ do remain as problems, and insisted just the same that the middle class has no right to concern itself with the IQs of others, although it does have an obligation to protect low IQ persons from experiencing correlated disadvantages. This boils down to the double-standard cultural relativism that I described earlier, which quickly becomes either intellectually untenable or socially unrealistic once it is made explicit.

With both of these courses obviously foreclosed, there was only one intellectual avenue possibly remaining open to Mercer: confront the correlation between low IQ and other disadvantages directly but demonstrate that its directionality is such that differentially low IQ is the effect, not the cause. The intellectual necessity of advancing such an argument in order to protect her labelling analysis accounts in part, I suspect, for the heavily one-sided nature of her persistent attack on the IQ test.

The essence of this attack can be illustrated by statements concerning the test's validity, from her own summary account of her work (see also 1973: 236): minority persons "are being labelled mentally retarded . . . because they have not had the opportunity to learn the cognitive skills necessary to pass Anglo-oriented intelligence tests. . . . Yet their behavior outside of the test situation belies their test scores" (Mercer, 1972: 44). The first part of this statement suggests that by providing opportunities to learn the cognitive skills it would be possible to remove the IQ deficit, and thus, it would also be possible to transform a minority person's IQ into a higher one which has the same predictive validity which that IQ score would have for whites. This has not yet proven to be the case (Jensen, 1969, 1973a; Bereiter, 1970: esp. 284; Page, 1972). The second part of the statement misrepresents the generality of the contexts in which some differential validity was found. As I have already made clear, there was no evidence, either in Mercer's work or elsewhere, of differential validity in the crucial area of educational achievement. All the evidence had to do with routine role performances within the minority community itself.

A genetic explanation of group differences in IQ would be the ultimate in validation, and counterarguments to Mercer's claims such as those I have just mentioned always have some effect on the a priori plausibility of the genetic case. There is reason to suspect, furthermore, that these counterarguments exert more leverage than usual when applied to the matter of mental retardation. It is one thing to entertain environmentalist hypotheses for 15-point IQ differences in the abstract, or, for example, in the range 110 to 125. It is quite another to do so when faced with the heartbreaking intractability of IQs in the extremely low range, under 80, where the greatest remedial effort has been concentrated, especially when the theory of familial mental retardation already contends, with little serious challenge, that the corresponding phenomenon in whites is genetically caused (Zigler, 1967). Individuals in this extremely low IQ range are sensed to be so different by middle-class persons that glib environmentalism loses much of its appeal.

One cannot easily accept a genetic explanation of familial retardation for the same apparent phenomenon within minority groups, however, without implicating the remainder of their population distribution under the normal curve in the same explanation. Both segments are clearly part of the same distribution, and as a result, for explanatory purposes, the highly differential proportion in the retarded tail tends to drag the rest of the distribution with it. These implicit phenomenological reactions generate an especially high degree of tension concerning the broader question of genetic differences between groups, therefore among persons working in the area of ethnicity and retardation, where differential rates between groups are clearly manifest.

Thus, the need to establish IQ as a variable that depends more heavily on the environment in the case of minority groups, and the special tensions concerning the genetic hypothesis within the area of the sociology of mental retardation, make it almost unavoidable that Mercer consider genetics.

Mercer first raises the topic of genetics in discussing the relation between the IQ and genotypes:

> The IQ is ordinarily treated as a measure of an individual's intellectual capacity, his mental ability. Obviously, intellectual ability cannot be measured directly, because that would require assessment of the genetic component of performance, the genotype. . . . The clinical perspective is based on the assumption that it is possible to make valid inferences about the genotype from a properly normed and administered intelligence test [1973: 235-236].

But this is a total misrepresentation, which criticizes the IQ test for not being able to do something it was not even designed to do (i.e., measure genotypes "directly"). Elsewhere, Mercer herself states correctly that "the original purpose for 'intelligence' testing was to predict which children would succeed academically" (Mercer and Brown, 1973: 58). Inferences are made from intelligence tests on the basis of their *predictive validity*, against a background of knowledge concerning the stability of this validity–i.e., how likely the predictive validity is to be suddenly altered by an attempted intervention. The quite separate empirical question of the genetic sources of this stable validity arises only after prediction has been found dependable. Thus, the "intellectual capacity" that the tests measure, and which is employed for prediction, is a property of the phenotype, not of the genotype as Mercer claims. The genetic question simply concerns the extent to which the phenotype is determined by the genotype. There is little reason to suppose this issue would be of any less moment in the case of the performances measured by "intelligence" tests had they been called something else, Mercer's penchant for purely semantic arguments notwithstanding (e.g., Mercer and Brown, 1973: 58). In whites, as I indicated earlier and as is well known by now, the extent of this determination by the genotype has proven quite substantial. This finding haunts the discussion of stubborn intergroup differences. In the final section, I examine Mercer and Brown's attempt to lay the genetics issue to rest.

Mercer and Brown's Empirical Investigation of Possible Genetic Differences Between Groups

The authors confront the latent genetics issue squarely by explicity conceding that pluralistic assessment procedures such as those proposed by Mercer (1973) "are based on the assumption that the distribution of the genetic potential for learning is essentially identical in all racial and ethnic groups" and that IQ test differences are due to differential exposure to the content of the tests prior to examination (Mercer and Brown, 1973: 57). How this question of exposure would apply to nonverbal test differences is never considered, although the authors' own data suggest IQ differences on the nonverbal Raven between Anglos and Mexican-Americans, and Anglos and Blacks, of 9.6 and 11.3 points, respectively, in Riverside (Mercer and Brown, 1973: Table 1). The assumption of no genetic differences relevant to IQ (there are other kinds of learning, as Jensen's research shows) is just that– an assumption–which must be made in the face of the fact that these populations are certainly not genetically the same in all respects. The proportion of genes from Caucasian ancestry in urban California Mexican-Americans has been estimated, for example, at 0.679 ± 0.056 (Reed, 1974), the remainder being of Indian ancestry. Although a one standard deviation difference between groups looms large on the scale of human affairs, differences of this magnitude are not necessarily large on the scale of nature. Against the background of their assumption of genetic uniformity between groups, and a willingness to concede that IQ test scores do reflect a genetic component within ethnic-cultural groups, the authors set out to test whether "differences between the average IQ test scores of different ethnic-cultural groups can be accounted for entirely by environmental factors" (Mercer and Brown, 1973: 58).

The basic data for this analysis consist of WISC IQ and other test scores for equal-sized samples of children from each ethnic group in Riverside, and a wealth of environmental background information obtained from their parents. The authors demonstrate that, when from four to nine environmental background variables are partialled out of the correlation between ethnic status and IQ, this correlation vanishes, thereby "accounting" for the Anglo-minority difference. To succeed in reducing the number of control variables from all nine to only four in the analysis containing Mexican-Americans, they explored "all possible combinations" of the environmental factors. However, in the analysis containing blacks, they had to retain all nine in order to accomplish the reduction of the correlation between ethnicity and IQ (1973: 94). It must be recognized that the use of so many control variables, and the act of searching among so many for optimal combinations, capitalizes on chance.

However, it is more important to know that the background variables included such items as "residence in minority neighborhood," "occupational status of the head of household," and "geographic locale of parents' birthplace." Clearly, the first and third of these could be code-words for ethnicity itself, since the third took into account the distinction between Mexico and the U.S. South, on the one hand, and the rest of the United States, on the other hand, and the first accomplishes on the neighborhood level what the third attempts on the continental level. Moreover, all of the mentioned correlations have been corrected for attenuation, but our understanding of the reliabilities employed for doing so in the case of some of these unusual, ad hoc, variables is minimal. Whereas the two Anglo-minority ethnic-IQ correlations were both .56, correlations between many of the background variables and the Anglo-minority ethnic dichotomies were higher: "residence in minority neighborhood" correlates .69 with Anglo-Mexican-American, and .84 with Anglo-black, for example. In the case of controlling for this variable, one suspects that ethnic status is being partialled out of itself, thereby leading to the commission of what I have elsewhere called "the partialling fallacy" (Gordon, 1967, 1968). "Occupational status of the head of the household" also correlated substantially with the Anglo-Mexican-American (.64) and the Anglo-black (.87) dichotomies. This and "residence in minority neighborhood" were controlled in both the four-variable and nine-variable analyses.

The potency of these two variables is indicated by the fact that they correlated more strongly with ethnic status than with any of the other control variables (Mercer and Brown, 1973: Table 5).

In the case of controlling "occupational status of the head of the household" so as to cause both of the ethnic-IQ correlations to vanish, we must take into account a peculiarity of the Anglo sample. Mercer and Brown (1973: 73) describe this sample as follows: "The Anglo children in Riverside come mainly from middle and upper middle status homes. Their fathers are mainly white collar and professional workers and have more than a high school education." This description, plus other information that I will present, suggests that the parent generation was highly selected and therefore of a higher mean IQ than the children, who would have regressed downward toward the mean of the general white population.

Before establishing the parents' IQ, let us establish the children's. The analysis we are examining uses WISC IQ, where Anglo children averaged 107.5 (Mercer and Brown, 1973: Table 1). Elsewhere, Mercer (1973: 240, 284) has given us other IQ results for Anglo children: 106.9 on a WISC, 105.6 on the Stanford-Binet, and 106 to 108 in the school testing program.

What empirical evidence have we of the parents' IQ? We are told that the adults in one of Mercer's (1973: 284) community surveys averaged 116.8. This statistic may also reflect small proportions of minority group members, which would make the Anglo adult mean somewhat higher still. We also know that the Anglo parents usually have had more than a high school education, and the average Wechsler-Bellevue IQ of typical college freshmen in the past has been between 116.5 and 119.5 (Plant and Richardson, 1958: Table 1). Burt's (1961: Table 1) estimates for England show a mean IQ of 115.9 even for persons in clerical occupations, and a mean IQ for the children of persons in clerical jobs of 107.8 (which is quite close to that of Anglo children here). This is without counting in Burt's "lower" or "higher" professionals, with still higher IQs, who would probably correspond to at least some of the Anglo fathers in the present study. The actual values reported for Riverside are exactly consistent with what would be expected on the basis of these data from elsewhere. Thus, there is good reason to suspect a higher IQ, of about 8 IQ points, for the Anglo adults than for the Anglo children, who would then be exhibiting the classic phenomenon of regression toward the general mean, to be expected in view of the empirically well-established (single parent) parent-child correlation of .5 for IQ (Erlenmeyer-Kimling and Jarvik, 1963: Figure 1). Burt's numerical example showing this effect is presented in Table 4.5. The amount of regression to be expected can also be derived from a genetic model using the best available estimates of heritability (in the

TABLE 4.5
BURT'S ILLUSTRATION OF REGRESSION TOWARD THE MEAN

Occupational Class		Mean IQ of Adults	Mean IQ of Children
I.	Higher Professional	139.7	120.8
II.	Lower Professional	130.6	114.7
III.	Clerical	115.9	107.8
IV.	Skilled	108.2	104.6
V.	Semiskilled	97.8	98.9
VI.	Unskilled	84.9	92.6

SOURCE: Burt, Cyril, 1961, "Intelligence and social mobility." *British Journal of Statistical Psychology.*

narrow sense) and of the assortative mating correlation. This result would be consistent with Burt's example and all other aspects of present concern, however, so there is no point in introducing additional material.

We have no reason to suspect that the children in the minority samples are regressing, but if they were, and the regression happened to be upward, this would only strengthen the argument I am about to make. It can be assumed, therefore, that the average IQs of the minority fathers are the same as those of the minority children.

A regression effect here for Anglos means that the IQ separation between the fathers of the ethnic groups is much greater than what the IQ separation between the children would directly suggest. In turn, this means that the socioeconomic difference between the fathers applies to an Anglo-minority IQ difference between the fathers of about 25 points, but is being used in the authors' analysis to explain the smaller Anglo-minority IQ difference between the children, of about 16 points. Since there would be more between-group variance (a higher point-biserial correlation) associated with the greater IQ difference than with the smaller IQ difference, the effect of partialling father's socioeconomic status out of the IQ-ethnic correlation for children is considerably magnified. To be fair, Mercer and Brown should have used a sample of Anglo children whose mean IQ equalled their population mean; in this way the fathers would have exhibited the same mean IQ as the children, and the effect of ethnic differences in father's occupational status would not have been exaggerated. The effects and considerations I am describing, but operating in reverse, would also have influenced their accompanying demonstration that partialling IQ out of the correlation between ethnic status and sociocultural variables did not cause the correlation to vanish (Mercer and Brown, 1973: Table 5).

Using the IQ of the fathers rather than of the children to calculate the point-biserial correlation between IQ and ethnicity would not only have involved a greater between-group variance, as I have indicated above, but also a smaller within-group variance in IQ. Burt (1961: 12-14) has shown that in regressing from the mean of their fathers, the variance of the children within any selected stratum becomes much greater than that of their fathers. Both of these two effects—the increase in between-group variance and the decrease in within-group variance—contribute to an increase in the point-biserial correlation. Given these considerations, there is a good chance that the ethnic-IQ correlations of .56 for both minority-Anglo comparisons would have increased so as to equal the higher values attained by the correlations between parental occupational status and ethnicity. If they did rise to this level, neither of these correlations would have been superior to the other as a factor causing the other to vanish, as simple inspection of the numerator of the formula for partial correlation will show.

Of course, all of their analyses are really only an exercise to show that environmental variables that are confounded with potential genetic differences in the parental generation "could" account for ethnic differences in IQ, although in places the authors use the results to impugn genetic hypotheses more than their own evidence would warrant. When such a demonstration succeeds, it leaves their initial assumption of no genetic differences between groups looking more tenable. However, the casualness of the underlying assumptions here—the use of variables that are code-words for ethnic status, the many predictors, and the regression artifact, not to mention the fact, of which the authors seem to be aware, that nothing can really be determined from such a potentially confounded analysis concerning the genetic contribution to between-group differences—contrast markedly with the stringent set of five conditions they insist must be met by other researchers in order for their genetic comparisons to be valid (1973: 60-61, 75).

These five conditions are intended to embrace the full range of cultural, environmental, educational, and motivational factors which might possibly influence IQ test performance. According to the authors, individuals or groups must be equated with respect to these five conditions if their genetic potential is to be compared fairly. If genetic potential does influence any of these factors, it would of course be impossible to match groups with respect to them without also matching their IQ genotypes, thus vitiating the research. Contrary to the authors' claims, there are other conceivable, ethically acceptable designs by use of which the existence of genetic IQ differences between groups *must* be equated with respect to these five conditions if their genetic

We see, therefore, that the labelling approach has finally carried Mercer into the genetics controversy, but that nothing has really been resolved by her analyses, which are questionable on many counts. This leaves all of the questions raised along the way concerning her policies for diagnosing the retarded and her appraisal of IQ tests still to be answered.

AN EVALUATION OF THE CONTRIBUTION OF LABELLING THEORY TO OUR UNDERSTANDING OF MENTAL RETARDATION

Labelling theorists sometimes reply to their critics by claiming that the critics misunderstand the theory and therefore fail to appreciate its true elegance. It is hard to find anything elegant that this approach has contributed to the work I have reviewed. Mercer's results do lend support to the idea that many persons seem retarded only within the school context, and that there is an interaction in this respect with ethnic group and socioeconomic status. Her data also point to the existence of at least two and perhaps three types of retardate, which also interact with ethnic group and social status (see Mercer, 1973: ch. 15). Furthermore, she promotes the idea that we should review our policies concerning the labelling of retardates, with an eye toward possibly easing the stigma of those in certain categories. It probably also is true that a useful analytic dimension is added by recognizing that definitions of retardedness may vary according to context, perhaps making the retarded individual more comfortable in some respects, but possibly insulating him from aid in other respects. This useful distinction between being retarded and being in the retarded role was made by Mercer in an earlier publication (1965), but it seems to have become blurred, for polemical purposes, in her later work where we are encouraged to believe that manipulating the role affects the reality.

It is not necessary, however, to be a labelling theorist in order to make these basically sound observations. All of them have been made, sometimes more astutely, by persons who are not identified with labelling theory.[8] When such effects are noted by persons outside the labelling tradition, the observations are presented without the distracting and perhaps even destructive criticisms of social institutions that so often seem to accompany the labelling point of view regardless of whether or not the criticisms can be sustained by scientific analysis. Becker (1975), for example, has himself said of Mercer's work, "I can't imagine a more damning critique of intelligence testing and those who would like to base social policy on its results." His laudatory review of Mercer's work suggests that the labelling field lacks the resources to adequately evaluate its own work.

Since the positive aspects of Mercer's work are not necessarily linked to the labelling approach, it is difficult to see that these aspects of her work should be credited to labelling theory. On the other hand, virtually all of the errors of interpretation, analysis, and of recommended policy that I have noted appear to have been inspired by Mercer's determination to apply the labelling approach. It is possible that in other hands the theory would have come off looking better. However, Mercer is far more sophisticated in her empirical methodology than the average labelling theorist, and Becker's unreserved praise of her work gives no indication that he would have done better. It would appear, therefore, that the fundamental lack of respect for the meaning of real human differences that this approach fosters has led her repeatedly to erroneous conclusions despite her use of "hard" methodology. In this sense, the labelling approach to mental retardation has repeatedly proved to have negative heuristic value, and we can only wonder at its value when used by persons whose methods are less subject to outside appraisal.

NOTES

1. This correlation becomes apparent in Jencks' analysis when the covariance is combined with the genetic variance and it holds whether one includes these two components in the numerator of one's definition of "heritability" or not. "Heritability" is an analytic concept, and, hence, subject to various definitions just as are measures of association. Many persons do consider it more realistic to keep these two components together (e.g., Jensen, 1969: 38-39, 1973a: 368-369), but others would prefer to look at two smaller numbers rather than one larger one in these matters.

2. Jensen found that, in replications over three grades, the size of the correlations between verbal and nonverbal tests differed consistently from ethnic group to ethnic group (1973b: Figure 3); from largest to smallest correlations, the groups were ordered white, Mexican-American, and Negro. Jensen regarded this correlation as reflecting the association between fluid and crystallized intelligence within each group. However, in Table 4.1 in this chapter, these same ethnic populations are ordered Mexican-American, Negro, white at each of three grade levels with respect to the size of correlations between verbal and nonverbal tests. The meaning of this totally different order is unclear, and the change could be an artifact of insufficient range in tests of the Coleman et al. study (1966). It does indicate, however, that the interpretation of differences in such correlations is anything but a settled matter, as Jensen himself would certainly agree.

3. Let me mention in passing an experience that I have had concerning one of those recently discovered interactions. Although the evidence for sex-linkage in spatial ability, which is also predictive of success in quantitative thinking, is quite strong, and the genetic model is capable of accounting not only for the entire difference between the sexes but also for other peculiarities of the data that alternative explanations do not handle well (Bock and Kolakowski, 1973), this evidence has not received wide publicity, and nonmathematically oriented women that I have spoken to about it seem naturally to experience the difference as being entirely determined by environment, and to regard my information with suspicion. The paper which presents the evidence is itself fairly mathematical, and so when I refer these nonmathematical women to this paper, I detect in myself a feeling of futility. I mention this to point up the special role that highly mathematical women could conceivably play in disseminating such information

across the boundaries of the male-female gene pool, and the weird problems we can expect to encounter sometimes in communicating evidence from one genotype to another when the evidence concerns a difference between the two genotypes in the ability to understand the evidence.

4. It is conceivable that the school psychologists had evolved the policy of taking this expected amount of regression into account by converting observed IQs into regressed true scores based on the mean and IQ test reliability of each group in question. Goldstein, Moss, and Jordan (1965; after Farber, 1968: 86, 168), for example, found that children who gained at least 10 IQ points after having been diagnosed as retarded at the age of six were more likely to be Caucasian than Negro, and to be from families without other retarded children (i.e., higher in IQ).

5. It is of interest to note that an experimental class established for black children in Newark by the black militant LeRoi Jones (who adopted the Swahili name Imamu Amiri Baraka), also stresses rote learning techniques (Butterfield, 1971): "Mr. Jones has also devised a special set of teaching methods, stressing discipline and rote, collective response, which are said to be better adapted to black children. During a recent history lesson, the teacher, Mama Asali, asked: 'What part of Africa is Ethiopia in?' The students responded loudly, in unison, 'East Africa.' 'What did Malcom X preach?' Mama Asali then asked. 'Black nationalism,' the students quickly answered. The questions and answers were then repeated in identical fashion for several minutes. Mama Asali frequently interjected 'tatadali,' meaning please and 'asante,' thank you. 'We call this method collective education,' Mama Asali explained. A slight woman with a pleasant smile and a soft . . . voice, Mama Asali believes that 'this method is more suitable for black children. It teaches collectively, not individually,' she continued. 'The students don't have to feel left out or in competition. Individualism is a white man's idea. We want to reduce the conflict that individualism and competition produces and achieve consensus.' "

6. When all spheres of life are considered, the major practical application of testing within the low IQ range occurs as part of military selection programs. From July 1950 through December 1968, blacks were rejected for military service by the Army at a rate 4.7 times the white rate for failing the Armed Forces Qualification Test alone (Office of the Surgeon General, 1969: Table 9). That is, 36.6% of the blacks, as opposed to 7.8% of the whites, failed the test. It will be noted that the ratio here is comparable to those in Table 4.4 above.

7. Reactions within the Armed Forces to Project 100,000, which was initiated in 1966 by former Defense Secretary McNamara, suggest that this validity also remains strong in the occupational sphere. The project directed the services to accept applicants (100,000 per year) in the AFQT percentile range between 10 and 30 who otherwise would have been rejected because of low mental qualifications. Disproportionate numbers of such applicants would have been black. Over the years, racial problems have been visibly intertwined with other complaints against Project 100,000 recruits (Homan, 1969; The Sun, 1971; The Evening Sun, 1972, 1973). The comment by Hauser (1973: 141) is revealing: "It was true that the vast majority made good soldiers, spokesmen said, but the effort required to make them so oftentimes exceeded the benefits of their service."

8. In the field of gender identity, for example, a dramatic effect of gender labelling in early childhood has been discovered, which, to my knowledge, is never even mentioned by labelling theorists (Money, Hampson, and Hampson, 1957; Stoller, 1968).

REFERENCES

Albee, George W.
1972 "A revolution in treatment of the retarded." Pp. 195-209 in J. McVicker Hunt (cd.) Human Intelligence. New Brunswick, N.J.: E. P. Dutton.
Alexander, Karl and Bruce K. Eckland
1975 "Contextual effects in the high school attainment process." American Sociological Review 40 (June): 402-416.
APA Task Force on Employment Testing of Minority Groups
1969 "Job testing and the disadvantaged." American Psychologist 24 (July): 637-650.
Becker, Howard S.
1963 Outsiders: Studies in the Sociology of Deviance. New York: Free Press.
1967 "Whose side are we on?" Social Problems 14 (Winter): 239-247.
1975 "Book review of *Labelling the Mentally Retarded* by Jane Mercer." Social Forces 53 (December 1974): 370.
Beeghley, Leonard and Edgar W. Butler
1974 "The consequences of intelligence testing in the public schools before and after desegregation." Social Problems 21 (June): 740-754.
Bereiter, Carl
1970 "Genetics and educability: educational implications of the Jensen debate." Pp. 279-299 in Jerome Hellmuth (ed.) Disadvantaged Child, Vol. 3: Compensatory Education: A National Debate. New York: Brunner/Mazel.
Bock, R. Darrell and Donald Kolakowski
1973 "Further evidence of sex-linked major-gene influence on human spatial visualizing ability." American Journal of Human Genetics 25: 1-14.
Boney, J. Don
1966 "Predicting the academic achievement of secondary school Negro students." Personnel and Guidance Journal 44 (March): 700-703.
Brim, Orville G., Jr., David C. Glass, John Neulinger, and Ira J. Firestone
1969 American Beliefs and Attitudes about Intelligence. New York: Russell Sage.
Burt, Cyril
1961 "Intelligence and social mobility." British Journal of Statistical Psychology 14 (May): 3-24.
Butterfield, Fox
1971 "Experimental class in Newark school is indoctrinated in black subjects." New York Times (April 10): 34.
Campbell, Joel T., Ronald L. Flaugher, Lewis W. Pike, and Donald A. Rock
1969 "Bias in selection tests and criteria studied by ETS and U.S. Civil Service." ETS Developments 17 (October): 2.
Cattell, Raymond B.
1971 Abilities: Their Structure, Growth, and Action. Boston: Houghton Mifflin.
Cleary, T. Anne
1968 "Test bias: prediction of grades of Negro and white students in integrated colleges." Journal of Educational Measurement 5 (Summer): 115-124.
--- Lloyd G. Humphreys, S. A. Kendrick, and Alexander Wesman
1975 "Educational uses of tests with disadvantaged students." American Psychologist 30 (January): 15-41.

Coleman, James S., Ernest Q. Campbell, Carol J. Hobson, James McPartland, Alexander M. Mood, Frederic D. Weinfeld, and Robert L. York

1966 Equality of Educational Opportunity. Washington, D.C.: Government Printing Office.

Dalton, Starrette

1974 "Predictive validity of high school rank and SAT scores for minority students." Educational and Psychological Measurement 34 (Summer): 367-370.

Darcy, Natalie T.

1963 "Bilingualism and the measurement of intelligence: review of a decade of research." Journal of Genetic Psychology 103 (December): 259-282.

Davis, James A.

1966 "The campus as a frog pond: an application of the theory of relative deprivation to career decisions of college men." American Journal of Sociology 72 (July): 17-31.

Edgerton, Robert B.

1967 The Cloak of Competence. Berkeley: University of California Press.

1968 "Anthropology and mental retardation: a plea for the comparative study of incompetence." Pp. 75-87 in H. J. Prehm, L. A. Hamerlynck, and J. E. Crosson (eds.) Behavioral Research in Mental Retardation. Eugene: Rehabilitation Research and Training Center in Mental Retardation, University of Oregon.

Elashoff, Janet D. and Richard E. Snow

1971 'Pygmalion' Reconsidered. Worthington, Ohio: Charles A. Jones.

Erlenmeyer-Kimling, L. and Lissy F. Jarvik

1963 "Genetics and intelligence: a review." Science 142 (December 13): 1477-1479.

Farber, Bernard

1968 Mental Retardation: Its Social Context and Social Consequences. Boston: Houghton Mifflin.

Festinger, Leon

1950 "Informal social communication." Psychological Review 57: 271-282.

Flaugher, Ronald L.

1971 "Patterns of test performance by high school students of four ethnic identities." Project Access Research Report No. 2. Educational Testing Service, Princeton, N.J.

Gael, Sidney and Donald L. Grant

1972 "Employment test validation for minority and nonminority telephone company service representatives." Journal of Applied Psychology 56 (April): 135-139.

Garron, David C.

1970 "Sex-linked, recessive inheritance of spatial and numerical abilities, and Turner's syndrome." Psychological Review 77, 2: 147-152.

Garth, Thomas R., Thomas H. Elson, and Margaret M. Morton

1936 "The administration of non-language intelligence tests to Mexicans." Journal of Abnormal and Social Psychology 31, 1: 53-58.

Goldstein, Herbert, James W. Moss, and Laura J. Jordan

1965 The Efficacy of Special Class Training on the Development of Mentally Retarded Children. Urbana, Ill.: Institute for Research on Exceptional Children, University of Illinois.

Gordon, Robert A.
1967 "Issues in the ecological study of delinquency." American Sociological Review 32 (December): 927-944.
1968 "Issues in multiple regression." American Journal of Sociology 73 (March): 592-616.

Grant, Donald L. and Douglas W. Bray
1970 "Validation of employment tests for telephone company installation and repair occupations." Journal of Applied Psychology 54 (February): 7-14.

Harrell, Thomas W. and Margaret S. Harrell
1945 "Army general classification test scores for civilian occupations." Educational and Psychological Measurement 5: 229-239.

Haskell, Gordon
1954 "Correlated responses to polygenic selection in animals and plants." American Naturalist 88 (January/February): 5-20.

Hauser, William L.
1973 America's Army in Crisis: A Study in Civil-Military Relations. Baltimore: Johns Hopkins Press.

Heller, Celia S.
1966 Mexican American Youth: Forgotten Youth at the Crossroads. New York: Random House.

Helson, Ravenna
1971 "Women mathematicians and the creative personality." Journal of Consulting and Clinical Psychology 36, 2: 210-220.

Herrnstein, R. J.
1973 I.Q. in the Meritocracy. Boston: Little, Brown.

Higgins, Conwell and Cathryne Sivers
1958 "A comparison of Stanford-Binet and colored Raven progressive matrices IQs for children with low socioeconomic status." Journal of Consulting Psychology 22 (December): 465-468.

Hills, John R. and Julian C. Stanley
1968 "Prediction of freshman grades from SAT and from level 4 of SCAT in three predominantly Negro state colleges." Pp. 241-242 in Proceedings of the Seventy-Sixth Annual Convention, American Psychological Association.
1970 "Easier test improves prediction of black students' college grades." Journal of Negro Education 39 (Fall): 320-324.

Homan, Richard
1969 "Services report on project for low-intelligence recruits." Chicago Sun-Times (July 13): 46.

Horowitz, Ruth and Gary Schwartz
1974 "Honor, normative ambiguity and gang violence." American Sociological Review 39 (April): 238-251.

Jencks, Christopher
1972 Inequality: A Reassessment of the Effect of Family and Schooling in America. New York: Basic Books.

Jensen, Arthur R.
1968 "Patterns of mental ability and socioeconomic status." Proceedings of the National Academy of Sciences 60 (August): 1330-1337.
1969 "How much can we boost IQ and academic achievement?" Harvard Educational Review 39 (Winter): 1-123.

1970a "A theory of primary and secondary familial mental retardation." International Review of Research in Mental Retardation 4: 33-105.
1970b "IQ's of identical twins reared apart." Behavior Genetics 1, 2: 133-148.
1970c "Selection of minority students in higher education." University of Toledo Law Review 1970, 2 and 3: 403-457.
1970d "Another look at culture-fair testing." Pp. 53-101 in Jerome Hellmuth (ed.) Disadvantaged Child, Vol. 3: Compensatory Education: A National Debate. New York: Brunner/Mazel.
1970e "Can we and should we study race differences?" Pp. 124-157 in Jerome Hellmuth (ed.) Disadvantaged Child, Vol. 3: Compensatory Education: A National Debate. New York: Brunner/Mazel.
1972 Genetics and Education, New York: Harper & Row.
1973a Educability and Group Differences. New York: Harper & Row.
1973b "Level I and level II abilities in three ethnic groups." American Educational Research Journal 10, 4: 263-276.
1974a "How biased are culture-loaded tests?" Genetic Psychology Monographs 90: 185-244.
1974b "Interaction of level I and level II abilities with race and socioeconomic status." Journal of Educational Psychology 66, 1: 99-111.
1974c "The effect of race of examiner on the mental test scores of white and black pupils." Journal of Educational Measurement 11 (Spring): 1-14.
n.d. "An examination of culture bias in the Wonderlic Personnel Test." Unpublished manuscript.

--- and Janet Frederiksen
1973 "Free recall of categorized and uncategorized lists: a test of the Jensen hypothesis." Journal of Educational Psychology 65, 3: 304-312.

Kallingal, Anthony
1971 "The prediction of grades for black and white students at Michigan State University." Journal of Educational Measurement 8 (Winter): 263-265.

Katz, Elias
1973 "The mentally retarded." Pp. 132-153 in Don Spiegel and Patricia Keith-Spiegel (eds.) Outsiders USA. San Francisco: Rinehart.

Keating, Daniel P.
1974 "The study of mathematically precocious youth." Pp. 23-46 in Julian C. Stanley, Daniel P. Keating, and Lynn H. Fox (eds.) Mathematical Talent: Discovery, Description and Development. Baltimore: Johns Hopkins Press.

Kennedy, Wallace A., Vernon Van De Reit, and James C. White, Jr.
1963 "A normative sample of intelligence and achievement of Negro elementary school children in the Southeastern United States." Monographs of the Society for Research in Child Development 28, 6.

Kushlick, Albert
1966 "Assessing the size of the problem of subnormality." Pp. 121-147 in J. E. Meade and A. S. Parkes (eds.) Genetics and Environmental Factors in Human Ability, New York: Plenum Press.

Lesser, Gerald S., Gordon Fifer, and Donald H. Clark
1965 "Mental abilities of children from different social-class and cultural groups." Monographs of the Society for Research in Child Development 30, 4.

Linton, Ralph
1936 The Study of Man. New York: Appleton-Century-Crofts.

McNemar, Quinn
1942 The Revision of the Stanford-Binet Scale. Boston: Houghton Mifflin.
1955 Psychological Statistics. New York: John Wiley.

Maier, Milton and Edmund F. Fuchs
1975 "Effectiveness of selection and classification testing." U.S. Army Research Institute for the Behavioral and Social Sciences Research Report, 1973 (September), No. 1179. Catalog of Selected Documents in Psychology 5 (Winter): 209.

Marjoribanks, Kevin
1972 "Ethnicity and learning patterns: a replication and an explanation." Sociology 6 (September): 417-431.

Mercer, Jane R.
1965 "Understanding career patterns of persons labelled as mentally retarded." Social Problems 13 (Summer): 18-34.
1972 "IQ: the lethal label." Psychology Today 6 (September): 44-47, 95-97.
1973 Labeling the Retarded. Berkeley: University of California Press.

--- and Wayne Curtis Brown
1973 "Racial differences in I.Q.: fact or artifact?" Pp. 56-113 in Carl Senna (ed.) The Fallacy of I.Q. New York: Third Press.

Miller, Sue
1975 "Regular class plans for IQ's of 70 hit." The Evening Sun (Baltimore, February 5): D22.

Money, John, Joan G. Hampson, and John L. Hampson
1957 "Imprinting and the establishment of gender role." Archives of Neurology and Psychiatry 77 (March): 333-336.

Office of Education
1966 Supplemental Appendix to the Survey on Equality of Educational Opportunity, Section 9.10/Correlation Tables. Washington, D.C.: Government Printing Office.

Office of the Surgeon General
1969 Supplement to Health of the Army: Results of the Examination of Youths for Military Service, 1968. Washington, D.C.: Medical Statistics Agency, Office of the Surgeon General, Department of the Army.

Page, Ellis B.
1972 "Miracle in Milwaukee: raising the IQ." Educational Researcher 1 (October): 8-16.

Pfeifer, C. Michael, Jr. and William E. Sedlacek
1971 "The validity of academic predictors for black and white students at a predominantly white university." Journal of Educational Measurement 8 (Winter): 253-261.

Plant, Walter T. and Harold Richardson
1958 "The IQ of the average college student." Journal of Counseling Psychology 5 (Fall): 229-231.

Reed, Elizabeth W. and Sheldon C. Reed
1965 Mental Retardation: A Family Study. Philadelphia: W. B. Saunders.

Reed, Sheldon C. and V. Elving Anderson
1973 "Effects of changing sexuality on the gene pool." Pp. 111-137 in Felix F. de la Cruz and Gerald D. LaVeck (eds.) Human Sexuality and the Mentally Retarded. New York: Brunner/Mazel.

Reed, T. Edward
1974 "Ethnic classification of Mexican-Americans." Science 185 (July 19): 283.

Reynoso Cruz, Jose Alvarez, Albert F. Moreno, Mario Olmos, Anthony Quintero, and William Soria
1970 "La raza, the law, and the law schools." University of Toledo Law Review 1970, 2 and 3: 809-846.

Rosenthal, Robert and Lenore Jacobson
1968 Pygmalion in the Classroom: Teacher Expectation and Pupils' Intellectual Development. New York: Holt, Rinehart & Winston.

Sattler, Jerome M.
1970 "Racial 'experimenter effects' in experimentation, testing, interviewing, and psychotherapy." Psychological Bulletin 73 (February): 137-160.

Scheff, Thomas J.
1966 Being Mentally Ill: A Sociological Theory. Chicago: Aldine.

Schur, Edwin M.
1971 Labeling Deviant Behavior: Its Sociological Implications. New York: Harper & Row.

Shuey, Andrew M.
1966 The Testing of Negro Intelligence. New York: Social Science Press.

Snow, Richard E.
1969 "Unfinished Pygmalion." Contemporary Psychology 14 (April): 197-199.

Stanley, Julian C.
1971a "Predicting college success of the educationally disadvantaged." Science 171 (February 19): 640-647.
1971b "Predicting college success of educationally disadvantaged students." Pp. 58-77 in Stephen J. Wright (ed.) Barriers to Higher Education. New York: College Entrance Examination Board.

——— and Andrew C. Porter
1967 "Correlation of scholastic aptitude test score with college grades for Negroes versus whites." Journal of Educational Measurement 4 (Winter): 199-218.

Stewart, Naomi
1947a "A.G.C.T. scores of Army personnel grouped by occupation." Occupations 26 (October): 5-41.
1947b "Relationship between military occupational specialty and Army general classification test standard score." Educational and Psychological Measurement 7 (Winter): 677-693.

Stodolsky, Susan S. and Gerald Lesser
1967 "Learning patterns in the disadvantaged." Harvard Educational Review 37 (Fall): 546-593.

Stoller, Robert J.
1968 Sex and Gender. New York: Science House.

Temp, George C.
1971 "Validity of the SAT for blacks and whites in thirteen integrated institutions." Journal of Educational Measurement 8 (Winter): 245-251.

Tenopyr, M. L.
1967 "Race and socioeconomic status as moderators in predicting machine-shop training success." Presented at the meeting of the American Psychological Association, Washington, D.C., September 1967.

Terman, Lewis M.
1925 Mental and Physical Traits of a Thousand Gifted Children. Genetic Studies of Genius, Vol. 1. Stanford, California: Stanford University Press.
––– and Maud A. Merrill
1960 Stanford-Binet Intelligence Scale: Manual for the Third Revision Form L-M. Boston: Houghton Mifflin.
The Evening Sun
1972 "Hearings resume on race trouble within Navy." (Baltimore, November 24: A2.
1973 "Navy quietly weeding out misfits and malcontents," (Baltimore, February 3: A3.
The Sun
1971 "Army wants fewer with low I.Q.'s." (Baltimore, October 26): A1.
Thomas, Charles L.
1971 "The relative effectiveness of high school grades and standardized test scores for predicting college grades of black students." Unpublished Ph.D. dissertation, Department of Education, Johns Hopkins University.
Thorndike, Robert L.
1968 "Review of Rosenthal and Jacobson's 'Pygmalion in the Classroom'." American Educational Research Journal 5 (November): 708-711.
Wolfle, Dael and Toby Oxtoby
1952 "Distributions of ability of students specializing in different fields." Science 116 (September 26): 311-314.
Zigler, Edward
1967 "Familial mental retardation: a continuing dilemma." Science 155 (January 20): 292-298.

Chapter 5

SOCIETAL REACTION AND PHYSICAL DISABILITY: CONTRASTING PERSPECTIVES

RICHARD T. SMITH

The societal reaction perspective, an approach to the study of deviance, has been suggested as an explanation of chronic illness behavior, including behavior associated with physical disabilities (Freidson, 1965: 71-99; Safilios-Rothschild, 1970: 109-125). That societal reaction or labelling occurs is not at issue; what is in question is the explanatory power of this approach to our understanding of the labelling process and its consequences as it relates to the physically impaired and disabled.

How relevant the societal reaction approach is to interpreting disability behavior will be examined in light of the conventional model of chronic illness behavior (see Kassebaum and Baumann, 1965). The same basic paradigm of labelling will be used for the purpose of contrasting the two approaches. This will allow us to observe the similarities and to take note of the exceptions.

In the basic labelling model, we can distinguish two stages: one is the process that results in labelling; the other, the consequences of labelling. Key issues related to the labelling process include the definition of deviance, the role of disease in illness behavior, primary interactions (that lead to societal response), and society's response to illness behavior, in particular the response of official agents of social control. Issues related to consequences include the effects of labelling on subsequent illness behavior, both positive and negative, such as deviant careers, *de*labelling, and *re*labelling. Furthermore, there is the issue of contingencies—that is, to what extent do contingent factors impede or facilitate labelling and subsequent outcome.

LABELLING AND ITS CONSEQUENCES

The Societal Reaction Perspective

Scheff's (1966) work on mental illness is cited as an example of the application of the societal reaction approach to illness behavior. Other critiques of the societal reaction perspective have been made on the issues involved–notably by Gibbs (1972), Gove (1970, 1973), and Fabrega and Manning (1972). The present interpretation is an attempt to place Scheff's approach in perspective and to provide a means of contrast with the conventional or traditional approach to the study of illness behavior, as exemplified by Parsons (1951), Mechanic (1962), and Suchman (1965) applied to sickness behavior; by Kassebaum and Baumann (1965) and Gallagher (1974) applied to chronic illness behavior; and by Nagi (1969) applied to disability. In turn, this will suggest some of the fundamental differences inherent in the application of societal reaction to physical illness and the disabled.

Scheff's major concerns focus on (a) society's response to deviant behavior, in particular, the likelihood of misclassifying behavior, (b) the structural determinants (contingencies) which may influence the direction of mislabelling, and (c) the negative consequences of labelling as well as the negative consequences of false labelling (induced deviancy), both of which may lead to deviant careers. For Scheff, the focus on mental disorder provides a uniquely appropriate set of conditions to formulate the propositions of the societal reaction model. In this sense, it counters the critics who contend that labelling theory has a tendency "to focus upon bizarre or exotic behavior of groups" (Fabrega and Manning, 1972: 93).

What are these conditions? For one, the basis for assessing mental disorder is primarily behavioral (Clausen, 1972), and the signs and symptoms are vague and ambiguous. Scheff (1966: 33-34) refers to psychiatric symptoms as acts of "residual rule-breaking." Thus, the likelihood of misclassification, of errors in judgment, by society's labellers may be enhanced under conditions of ambiguous signs and uncertain normative guidelines. This is why Scheff places significant emphasis on errors in diagnosis (Scheff, 1966: 105-113, 1963). Furthermore, the act of rule-breaking is taken as given, and de-emphasized by shifting attention to the *reaction* of others, especially the role of formal agents–those who apply the rules of deviance (Scheff, 1966: 32-33). This shift is in keeping with the notion of primary deviation (Lemert, 1967: 17, 40); by definition, acts of rule-breaking occur in diverse ways, tend to be episodic, are usually denied by self and others as deviant, and therefore are of transitory significance (Scheff, 1966: 51). In the societal reaction approach, the concern is with rule-breaking behavior that is visible and so labelled.

Accordingly, Scheff accepts Becker's (1973: 9) definition: "Deviance is *not* a quality of the act the person commits, but rather a consequence of the application by others of rules and sanctions to an 'offender.' " The focus, then, is on the role of "moral entrepreneurs"–the agents of social control–and their position of power in the labelling process (Becker, 1973: 162-163).

This, in turn, leads to consideration of another condition. To what extent do social factors influence society's response to deviant acts and, therefore, what might influence the response of decision makers? Scheff maintains this is of crucial importance and is central to all perspectives on deviant behavior. Are there "contingencies which lead to labeling that lie outside the patient and his behavior?" (Scheff, 1974: 448). Prominent among these contingencies are the type, degree, amount, and visibility of the act, the power and social distance of the individual vis-à-vis the agents of control, and the availability of alternative roles (Scheff, 1966: 96-100).

In seeking to answer this question, the societal reaction perspective suggests that there are contingencies that influence the labelling process. Stated as a general rule, resources favor the avoidance of labelling while the lack of resources influences the likelihood of false labelling. Thus, those in disadvantaged positions in society, individuals lacking resources with the imputation of undesirable differences, are more likely to be adversely effected. This false classification can lead to deleterious consequences–for example, induced deviance–at least in the field of mental illness. On the other hand, those with resources are more likely to be classified on the basis of desirable traits, that is, to avoid being labelled ill, and hence avert the negative consequences. This is shown in Table 5.1.

From the societal reaction perspective, "Labeling is the single most important cause of careers of residual deviance" (Scheff, 1966: 92-93). Once labelled, correctly or incorrectly, the individual is likely to "proceed on a career of chronic deviance" (Scheff, 1966: 88). The effect of labelling is so pervasive that it tends to be irreversible; for the individual, this leads to the

TABLE 5.1
SOCIETAL REACTION MODEL IN MENTAL ILLNESS
(Errors in Classification as a Function of Contingencies)

Societal Response	Rule-Breaking Acts	
	Engage	Not Engage
Label		Without resources (false labeling)
Not label	With resources (labeling avoidance)	

"organization of social roles and self-regarding attitudes" around deviance—what Lemert (1967: 40-41) terms secondary deviation. Presumably, this precludes the likelihood of delabelling (recovery) or relabelling (rehabilitation) as viable alternatives to initial labelling. Why the irreversibility of labelling and subsequent pattern of deviant careers? As Scheff views the process, labelled individuals are "punished when they attempt the return to conventional roles" and "rewarded for playing the stereotyped deviant role" (1966: 87, 84).

In summary, the formulation of the societal reaction model is uniquely served by its application to the particular set of conditions related to mental illness.

The Contrasting Perspective

To what extent is the societal reaction perspective, and the propositions formulated, applicable to physical illness and the chronically impaired? Setting aside for the moment the issue of deviance theory and illness behavior, we are confronted with a different set of conditions in viewing the process of labelling in relation to physical disease and chronic illness behavior, and in viewing the consequences in relation to the physically disabled. The criteria for assessing chronic illness are not primarily manifested in behavior but include disease manifestations which have biologic and physiologic bases (Fabrega and Manning, 1972: 100-104). The condition of illness and subsequent illness behavior tend to be less ambiguous and involve more definitive guidelines. The likelihood of misclassification, of errors in judgment, by those applying the rules may be reduced. Under these circumstances, "residual rule-breaking behavior" needs to be viewed as primary illness behavior associated with physical signs and symptoms.

Primary deviance, rather than being of transitory significance, is central to the concept of chronic illness behavior. Illness behavior, in general, is viewed as a way in which an individual behaves when he or she perceives in him- or herself a condition of health impairment (Mechanic, 1962). Furthermore, significant others may facilitate the process of labelling through reactions designed to reinforce the person's sense of pending illness (Suchman, 1965; Kassebaum and Baumann, 1965; Gallagher, 1974). Indeed, Freidson (1961: 146-147) emphasizes the significance of the "lay referral system" in the labelling process prior to any contact with official agents of social control. In light of these suggestions and the available evidence, chronic illness behavior cannot be viewed simply as a function of behavior that is visible and so labelled by control agents.

Society's reaction to physical illness behavior occurs in a manner more in keeping with the medical model of labelling rather than with the societal reaction-deviance model. In part, this is a function of the likelihood of acceptance of the label rather than the likelihood of avoidance of the label. An individual may seek to be labelled as physically impaired and disabled in order to legitimate his claim for societal support and assistance (Haber and Smith, 1971). Furthermore, the structural determinants (contingencies) tend to operate in the opposite direction from that suggested by Scheff. The emphasis is on positive consequences and labelling tends to favor the advantaged. Also, errors in labelling (false positives) tend to favor the advantaged. Given the same type of impairment, those rejected (not labelled) may likely exhibit social attributes deemed marginal or undesirable by control agents. Moreover, the more ambiguous the chronic illness signs and symptoms, the greater the likelihood of labelling misclassification to favor the advantaged, that is, to be accepted as disabled.

This general pattern of errors in classification for the physically impaired is illustrated in Table 5.2. The pattern it shows is suggested by data derived from Nagi's (1969: 66-90) study of disability applicants seeking legitimation of, and compensation for, chronic impairments. Nagi's work is one of the best examples of empirical evidence documenting the influence of contingencies in society's response to the physically impaired and disabled. The evidence is presented in Table 5.3.

As Nagi (1969: 72) states, "The lower the socioeconomic, educational, or intellectual-functioning levels, the greater the likelihood of change in decisions from denial (non-disabled) to allowance (disabled)." In effect, the fewer the resources, the greater the error of initial rejection or nonlabelling. This type of error (false negative) accounts for nine percent of the applicant population. Those changed to denial status (false positives) are more likely to

TABLE 5.2
MEDICAL MODEL IN PHYSICAL ILLNESS
(Errors in Classification as a Function of Contingencies)

Societal Response	Chronic Illness Behavior	
	Engage	Not Engage
Label		With resources (false labeling)
Not Label	Without resources (labeling denied)	

TABLE 5.3
INITIAL DETERMINATION AND VALIDATION OF CHRONIC IMPAIRMENT STATUS

Initial Determination of Chronic Impairment	Validation of Chronic Impairment	
	Disabled (allowance)	Non-disabled (denial)
Disabled (allowance)	54%	5%
Non-disabled (denial)	9%	33%

Adapted from Nagi (1969: 60, Table 9).

command resources (Nagi, 1969: 73, Table 12). The error rate is only five percent. This pattern is further supported by the finding that clients who do not submit their own evidence and therefore must rely on agency facilities to document evidence of disability (use of agency consultative services) are more likely to be initially rejected, while clients submitting their own evidence (use of outside services) have a greater likelihood of being labelled with disabling impairments (Nagi, 1969: 79). In general, induced "deviancy" (falsely classified as disabled) is greater for those in advantageous circumstances.

Finally, this alternative perspective suggests that labelling has beneficial consequences and a diminished likelihood of irreversible deviant careers. Once labelled, the disabled individual may engage in deviant behavior such as rejection of the label or rejection of services, perhaps preferring passive dependence and secondary gain, or the individual may be constrained in his pursuit of alternative pathways through rejection and avoidance by others. More typically, legitimation of disability by society's agents provides mechanisms of alternative pathways to recovery (delabelling) or adaptation to the chronic sick role through rehabilitation (relabelling). Through constitutive rules and acceptable alternatives (Lemert, 1967: 19-20), normative adaptation to incapacity may take place. In the model of disability, "Normalization of exceptional behavior is provided for within the framework of reciprocal role obligations, as a means of facilitating role maintenance and social control" (Haber and Smith, 1971: 89).

A classic example is in society's response to cardiovascular disease—a major disabling condition. In labelling the cardiac sufferer disabled, society provides supportive services, in the form of restorative therapy and rehabilitation, designed to assist the individual toward full recovery (delabelling) or to some modified alternative level such as adaptation to the chronic sick role (relabelling). This process occurs under conditions of normalization–the chronically impaired and disabled are legitimately exempted from responsibilities but must conform to the constitutive or modified rules applied to reciprocal role obligations.

Numerous examples of positive societal responses to disabling chronic illness, in terms of recovery and adaptation, can be cited from the literature. Again, the cardiac disabled can be used for illustrative purposes. Rates of recovery (delabelling) for heart disease range from as low as twenty-five percent to as high as ninety percent of the population labelled (Croog et al., 1968: 142). These rates vary depending on disease factors, such as severity and other complications, as well as contingent social factors, such as availability of, and access to, the medical care system, quality of care provided and accuracy in diagnosis by medical agents.

Adoption of the chronic sick role constitutes a form of adaptation and is viewed as a meaningful alternative to full recovery or complete dependence. Characteristic traits of adaptation include reduction or alteration in work activity, diet control, changes in personal habits such as smoking, and adjustments in family relations. Much of this evidence is based on follow-up studies (Croog et al. 1968; Monteiro, 1973).

However, this evidence is presented primarily to illustrate the positive consequences of society's initial response to labelling the physically disabled. Those who "manage deviance" apparently do not channel the behavior of the disabled into deviant careers; rather, much of the effort of these agents is directed toward beneficial outcomes.

In addition, the support of significant others, those identified as other than official agents of social control, may constitute the difference between deviant careers and successful adjustment as suggested by studies of the chronically impaired in the recovery process (Croog et al., 1972; New et al., 1968; Hyman, 1972; Garrity, 1973). In these studies, evidence is presented that higher levels of social integration of the patient with family and peers leads to the likelihood of recovery or successful adaptation, and at a more rapid rate. This pattern is similar to that observed by Gove and Howell (1974) in their study of hospitalized mental patients.

Furthermore, this suggests that the individual is not a passive agent in coping with the consequences of physical disability (Lorber, 1972: 423). Labelling, as a legitimating function, may enhance the disabled's claim on others for support and assistance. As a group, Alcoholics Anonymous not only furthered its cause by having the label legitimated–that is, by relabelling alcoholism as a disease–but used the label to further the organization's goals. Once labelled, the group employed the helper therapy principle to assist others (Riessman, 1965). A similar case can be found among the disabled as suggested by those who call their group the "Committee for the Rights of the Disabled" (Smith, 1973: 286). Also, heart clubs and the Disabled American Veterans have organized to protect and promote their respective interests. In general, self-help groups seem to flourish as a reaction to labelling.

THE CONCEPT OF DEVIANCE IN LABELLING

Finally, one key issue that deserves attention is the definition of deviance. This is fundamental in the conceptualization of illness behavior, especially in relation to the physically impaired. In the societal reaction approach, as well as in the medical model approach, individuals who experience long-term incapacitating illnesses are identified as deviating from societal norms because of role performance failure.

For most physical illnesses and ensuing incapacities, individuals are not held responsible, and although viewed as undesirable by society, they are not grossly stigmatized or segregated (Freidson, 1965: 95). Yet, for Freidson, disability results in social deviance because of its persistence, its chronicity. This leads society to react by labelling such behavior, thereby producing deviance, and then proceeding to manage the consequences by channeling the disabled into deviant careers. In effect, deviance in disability is viewed as "conduct which violates sufficiently valued norms" (Freidson, 1965: 73) and therefore requires the imposition of negative sanctions.

Safilios-Rothschild (1970: 114-115) states a similar view:

> [The disabled] can best be analyzed and explained by means of the general theory of deviance. As with all other deviants, it is not so much their actual physical disability that is the key, but rather society's reaction to it. The disabled are not intrinsically deviant because of their disability, but because those around them label them 'deviant' since they impute to them an undesirable difference. The resulting limitations render an individual more or less dependent—and therefore deviant—since he must break the norm of adult independence and self-reliance.

On this basis, the unemployed, welfare recipients, minority groups, and the aged—in effect, a major segment of society—are deviant, since by definition they are "norm breakers." Perhaps it is the idea that illness poses a threat to society, and societal reactions are directed toward the maintenance and control of this form of deviance. However, it need not be imputed as norm violating behavior in the sense of negative sanctioning and negative consequences. The suggested alternative approach has been stated earlier. In essence, disability is a process of normalization of exceptional behavior with institutionalized provisions for recovery and adaptation. At least this approach avoids the implications of negativism so apparent in the general labelling perspective.

REFERENCES

Becker, Howard S.
1973 Outsiders. New York: Free Press.

Clausen, John A.
1972 "The sociology of mental disorder." Chapter 7 in H. E. Freeman et al. (eds.) Handbook of Medical Sociology. Englewood Cliffs, N.J.: Prentice-Hall.

Croog, Sydney, Sol Levine, and Z. Lurie
1968 "The heart patient and the recovery process." Social Science and Medicine 2: 111-164.

Croog, Sydney, Alberta Lipson, and Sol Levine
1972 "Help patterns in severe illness: the roles of kin network, non-family resources and institutions." Journal of Marriage and the Family 34: 32-41.

Fabrega, Horacio, Jr. and Peter K. Manning
1972 "Disease, illness and deviant careers." Pp. 93-116 in R. A. Scott and J. D. Douglas (eds.) Theoretical Perspectives on Deviance. New York: Basic Books.

Freidson, Eliot
1961 Patients' Views of Medical Practice. New York: Russell Sage.
1965 "Disability as social deviance." Chapter 4 in M. B. Sussman (ed.) Sociology and Rehabilitation. Washington, D.C.: American Sociological Association.

Gallagher, Eugene B.
1974 "Lines of reconstruction and extension in the Parsonian sociology of illness." Unpublished manuscript.

Garrity, Thomas F.
1973 "Vocational adjustment after first myocardial infarction: comparative assessment of several variables suggested in the literature." Social Science and Medicine 7: 705-717.

Gibbs, Jack P.
1972 "Issues in defining deviant behavior." Pp. 39-68 in R. A. Scott and J. D. Douglas (eds.) Theoretical Perspectives on Deviance. New York: Basic Books.

Gove, Walter R.
1970 "Societal reaction as an explanation of mental illness: an evaluation." American Sociological Review 35: 873-884.
1973 "Societal reaction theory and disability." Unpublished manuscript.

--- and Patrick Howell
1974 "Individual resources and mental hospitalization: a comparison and evaluation of the societal reaction and psychiatric perspectives." American Sociological Review 39: 86-100.

Haber, Lawrence D. and Richard T. Smith
1971 "Disability and deviance: normative adaptations of role behavior." American Sociological Review 36: 87-97.

Hyman, Martin D.
1972 "Social isolation and performance in rehabilitation." Journal of Chronic Diseases 25: 85-97.
Kassebaum, Gene G. and Barbara O. Baumann
1965 "Dimensions of the sick role in chronic illness." Journal of Health and Human Behavior 6: 16-27.
Lemert, Edwin M.
1967 Human Deviance, Social Problems and Social Control. Englewood Cliffs, N.J.: Prentice-Hall.
Lorber, Judith
1972 "Deviance as performance: the case of illness." Chapter 26 in E. Freidson and J. Lorber (eds.) Medical Men and Their Work. Chicago: Aldine-Atherton.
Mechanic, David
1962 "The concept of illness behavior." Journal of Chronic Diseases 15: 189-194.
Monteiro, Lois A.
1973 "After heart attack: behavioral expectations for the cardiac." Social Science and Medicine 7: 555-565.
Nagi, Saad Z.
1969 Disability and Rehabilitation. Columbus: Ohio State University Press.
New, Peter K. et al.
1968 "The support structure of heart and stroke patients: a study of the role of significant others in patient rehabilitation." Social Science and Medicine 2: 185-200.
Parsons, Talcott
1951 The Social System. New York: Free Press.
Riessman, Frank
1965 "The 'helper' therapy principle." Social Work 10: 27-32.
Safilios-Rothschild, Constantina
1970 The Sociology and Social Psychology of Disability and Rehabilitation. New York: Random House.
Scheff, Thomas J.
1963 "Decision rules and types of error, and their consequences in medical diagnosis." Behavioral Science 9: 97-107.
1966 Being Mentally Ill. Chicago: Aldine.
1974 "The labeling theory of mental illness." American Sociological Review 39: 444-452.
Smith, Richard T.
1973 "Health and rehabilitation manpower strategy: new careers and the role of the indigenous paraprofessional." Social Science and Medicine 7: 281-290.
Suchman, Edward H.
1965 "Stages of illness and medical care." Journal of Health and Human Behavior 6: 114-128.

Chapter 6

LABELLING AND CRIME: AN EMPIRICAL EVALUATION

CHARLES R. TITTLE

Contemporary students of deviance are primarily interested in the social reactions that are generated in response to rule-breaking or which define certain behaviors as deviant. Studies of societal reaction have focused on a variety of issues. Some social scientists have attempted to specify the consequences of their own activity for the people who are directly involved in doing something about deviance (Skolnick, 1966; Blumberg, 1967; Ross, 1973), while others have tried to establish the consequences for the individuals or groups that are the object of such efforts (Lemert, 1967; Schwartz and Skolnick, 1962; Buckner, 1971). A number of social scientists have concerned themselves with how social actions to deal with rule violations affect the amount and kind of deviance that occurs within a given population unit (Andenaes, 1966; Zimring and Hawkins, 1973; Tittle and Logan, 1973). And still others have focused attention on the way in which various reactions to deviance contribute to or undermine the ability of social groups to survive and maintain themselves (Erikson, 1966; Turk, 1969; Connor 1972). Nevertheless, the main intellectual inspiration for societal reaction research has been the scheme variously referred to as the labelling "perspective," "approach," "orientation," or "theory." In this paper, I will attempt to evaluate the empirical adequacy of labelling theory as it bears on adult crime.

DIFFICULTY OF THE TASK

The task at hand is especially difficult for two reasons. First, any empirical assessment of a theory requires that specific, testable propositions be derivable from the abstract ideas that constitute its core. In the case of labelling, it is not only difficult to derive specific empirical assertions (Gibbs, 1966, 1972; Schur, 1971: 154-158), but the advocates themselves unashamedly claim to eschew precise propositional statements (Becker, 1973: 6; Schur, 1971: 35) in favor of "sensitizing observations" (Schur, 1971: 27) which "jostle the imagination, to create a crisis of consciousness which will lead to new visions of reality" (Scheff, 1974: 445). Indeed, we are told that the particular strength of labelling theory lies in its resistance to formalization and in its vagueness and ambiguity, since such features alert us to important aspects of social life which are themselves relativistic and elusive (Schur, 1971: 14). Labelling theory is touted as a heuristic orientation for stimulating thought, for generating new insights, and for producing intellectual "understanding" for those who employ it. Hence, if one takes these claims seriously, one must concede that empirical tests of labelling theory are both impossible and ridiculous.

Second, even if one ignores these claims and attempts to marshall evidence relevant to things that seem to be suggested by labelling theory, one immediately encounters a sparcity of data. Not only have there been few direct tests of labelling ideas, but the inherent vagueness of the labelling concept (Gibbs, 1972) makes it difficult to bring to bear data that were gathered for other purposes. According to Schur (1971: 23-27), labelling involves attempts to "deal with" or "do something about" behavior which departs from normative expectations. There are said to be degrees of being deviant which are presumably created by various degrees of "dealing with" or "doing something about" the behavior. But labelling theorists also speak of "successful application of labels and of nonconforming behavior which is "perceived" as deviant (Becker, 1963: 9, 20). This implies that the concept of labelling involves more than "doing something about" nonconforming behavior; rather, it suggests that the essence of a label is in the acceptance by an audience of a deviant identity on the part of a nonconformist who has been "dealt with." Furthermore, it is conceivable that an audience may come to accept a deviant definition even without distinct efforts having been made to "deal with" or "do something about" the deviance. Thus Schur (1971: 22) tells us that labelling may involve "all diverse societal definitions of and response to behavior."

The problems of using such vagaries in empirical research are clear. In attempting to measure degrees of labelling, are we to focus on the efforts to "deal with" nonconformity, on the degree to which those efforts have resulted in a collective definition of deviant character, or simply on collective definitions of character regardless of whether they have involved any distinguishable efforts to do something about nonconformity? If one tries to measure degrees of labelling, one must assume that some reactions indicate greater degrees of "doing something about" than others. But it is impossible to devise a defensible continuum which includes any possible societal response to behavior. If one moves directly to measurement of collective definitions, one is forced to assess public opinion with respect to each individual case studied. This is a practical impossibility since there are no meaningful guidelines in labelling theory about the limits which define an audience. What constitutes a public for a given deviant act or potential deviant person is presently unknown.

In view of these problems, it is hardly surprising that most researchers have simply assumed that the imposition of any sanction or any official act of negative classification constitutes labelling. Imprisonment (Lemert, 1967), hospitalization for mental illness (Rushing, 1971), being placed on probation (Fisher, 1972), being convicted or fined for drunken driving (Marshall and Purdy, 1972; Lovald and Stub, 1968), being convicted of a felony (Chiricos, Jackson, and Waldo, 1972), being dishonorably discharged from the military (Williams and Weinberg, 1970), and being classified as an alcoholic (Trice and Roman, 1970) have all been accepted as indicators of labelling without any consideration being given to whether such negative classifications actually resulted in general attribution of deviant character to those so classified or to the degree of "doing something about" which such official acts represented.

Although operational assumptions like this are apparently essential for empirical tests, they are at the same time likely to render those tests tautological. For example, in considering the postulate that labelling leads to secondary deviance (a postulate which almost all labelists would endorse, at least if stated in nondeterministic terms), if it is found that negatively classified individuals repeat the behavior for which they were labelled, proponents will applaud the power of the labelling perspective. On the other hand, should it be discovered that those who are negatively classified actually engage in the behavior less frequently, proponents will maintain that the label obviously did not stick. In short, it is easy to assume that subsequent deviance constitutes an effect of labelling as well as being evidence that labelling has occurred. But if labelling cannot be ascertained independent of its presumed effect, then the proposition in question is incontrovertible and thereby unscientific.

Moreover, even if it could be agreed that sanctioning or negative classification were equivalent to labelling, systematic data to enable tests of propositions concerning it are lacking. Consider again the postulate of secondary deviance. The most obvious data bearing on this question are those concerning criminal recidivism. It is generally conceded that arrest or incarceration is more likely to indicate labelling than almost any other social reaction. Most people consider any contact with the law as evidence of criminal character, especially if that contact eventuates in actual incarceration: and stigmativation of offenders is well known (Schwartz and Skolnick, 1962). Therefore, if labelling produces further rule-breaking, it should be discernible from the rate of criminal recidivism. Unfortunately, this approach has a number of practical weaknesses.

For one thing, meaningful recidivism data are impossible to obtain. Rearrest is a poor indicator because ex-convicts are more likely to be arrested independent of actual criminal conduct. In fact, arrest may indicate little about guilt. In an FBI follow-up study in *Uniform Crime Reports* of all individuals released from custody in 1963, only forty percent of those rearrested within a four-year period of time had been reconvicted at the end of that period, and extrapolation suggests that, despite a high rearrest rate, overall reconviction for the entire population of releasees for the indefinite future would not exceed thirty-five percent (see Tittle and Logan, 1973: 389). This rate obtains despite the fact that the widespread practice of plea bargaining makes it more likely that previously convicted people will be reconvicted, albeit on a lesser charge than the police would like. Hence, arrest does not necessarily signify criminal conduct just as criminal behavior may not result in an arrest. Arrest and criminality are only tenuously connected. Furthermore, people may be arrested for many things which are different from that for which they were incarcerated. Being arrested for gambling cannot be accepted as evidence of recidivism for a burglar, although some might argue that any form of subsequent deviance will establish the power of labelling.

Although recommitment to prison is probably a better reflector of recidivism than is rearrest, it too is defective. Recommitment rates may indicate further criminality, but they also reflect parole revocation for noncriminal activity such as unmarried cohabitation, failure to report to a parole supervisor, or leaving a jurisdiction without permission. In addition, figures concerning return to prison are probably inflated because the probability of reconviction is greater for those with criminal backgrounds. Under the plea bargaining system, a former inmate threatened with prosecution is very likely to plead guilty even if he has engaged in no illegal conduct (Newman, 1966; Blumberg, 1967). On the other hand, it is undoubtedly true that much recidivism never results in reimprisonment.

But even ignoring these considerations, using rates of recommitment as an indication of recidivism is frustrating because of the sparcity of systematic data. Return to prison rates must be estimated from prison records or from a relatively small number of career studies. Basing estimates on the proportion of recidivists in prisoner populations seriously exaggerates the overall degree of recidivism. Repeat offenders accumulate in prison and are disproportionately represented in any inmate population because they have longer sentences and are less likely to be paroled (Wilkins, 1969: 48-49). Follow-up studies give a better indication of the extent of recommitment, but they are too few in number and too weak methodologically to give a firm basis for conclusions.

For these reasons, judgments about labelling drawn from recidivism figures must be tempered. But even if recidivism data were reliable, information about the rate of deviance prior to adjudication would still be needed to determine if labelling leads to greater or lesser amounts of deviance. There are no systematic data of this type, although FBI follow-up figures do compare rearrest for those who were incarcerated (and therefore probably more likely to be labelled) with rearrest rates for those who were acquitted, dismissed, or only fined (drawn from *Uniform Crime Reports* of 1968, p. 38). Hence, what might at first blush appear to be quite adequate data for assessing one postulate from labelling theory actually are extremely weak, and so it is with data relevant to any proposition that might be suggested by labelling theory.

IMPORTANCE OF PROCEEDING

Despite these problems, it behooves the sociological community to conceptualize labelling ideas within a testable format and to assess them with whatever data happen to be available at any given time. Every "orienting stance" must ultimately lead to real theory if it is to have long-range scientific value. Scientific explanation demands continuous specification of vague ideas into more precise postulates, and comparison of theoretically generated predictions with real world outcomes. It is only through a continuing formulation-test-feedback process that theoretical inadequacies can be identified and corrected. Scientific theories do not emerge full blown. They are built as provocative ideas are refined and made more precise through the vehicle of empirical testing. In this way, sensitizing concepts become parts of genuine theories that serve the ends of science.

There are other good reasons to defy the theoretical disclaimers issued by labelists. For one thing, they are not themselves consistently committed to the stance that labelling is not a theory in the scientific sense. Protestations notwithstanding, labelling advocates do attempt to state propositions which can be tested with empirical data, and they frequently cite studies that are said to be supportive of or consistent with the principles of labelling (Wilkins, 1965). For example, after denying that the labelling perspective qualifies as a theory and after depreciating the value of empirical tests, Scheff (1974: 450) goes on to evaluate empirical evidence concerning "propositions" about mental illness derived from this nontheory, concluding that "the balance of evidence seems to support labelling theory." Similarly, Becker lauds labelling theory as merely "a way of looking at a general area of human activity" but clearly hypothesizes that the act of criminal labelling provokes abnormal actions (the degree of which must be established by empirical research) (Becker, 1973: 5-6). Labelists seem to want it both ways. It is not a theory when criticized, but when the evidence looks favorable, ideas that were previously only "sensitizing" suddenly become testable. This cat-and-mouse game must soon give way to straightforward theoretical statements and confrontation of empirical issues.

Furthermore, even if the original intent of labelling theorists was merely "orienting," it is clear that many followers and working researchers assume that labelling constitutes at least a rudimentary theory or have taken steps to move it in that direction. Thus, several studies purport to have tested propositions drawn from labelling theory (Chiricos, Jackson, and Waldo, 1972; Gove, 1970; Marshall and Purdy, 1972; Fisher, 1972) and some disciples matter-of-factly state features of labelling theory as if they were empirically established axioms (Trice and Roman, 1970; Payne, 1973). Since this divergence exists between what theorists say and what theorists and others do, it is important to assess our knowledge lest the sociological community draw unfounded conclusions.

Finally, although available data are meager, they are better than unfettered speculation. Even poor data can discipline mental inclinations, inspire creative approaches to the acquisition of more adequate information, and serve a theory-building purpose by forcing us toward precision. Scanty data may insult fine ideas, but failure to be empirically accountable undermines intellectual integrity.

THE THEORY

Despite variations in the work of different labelling theorists, there appear to be two common ideas that emerge from this literature (Hagen, 1973). Although some labelists have focused on the process of rule-making at the societal level, most have been concerned with the causes and consequences of negative classification of individuals by social control agencies. Theorists maintain that official labelling (classification of a person as one who is a fit subject for official management) results from the interplay of a number of variables, only one of which is actual rule-breaking. They tend to emphasize the importance of other variables such as personal resources, power, and physical or social attributes (Gove, 1970; Becker, 1963: 18; Quinney, 1970: 217; Steffensmeier and Terry, 1973) of the individual (which will hereafter be referred to as social disadvantages). Thus one of the major tenets of labelling theory is that the probability of being officially classified as a deviant is more heavily influenced by other variables, particularly social disadvantages, than by actual rule-breaking.

Second, labelists argue that official classification as a deviant has pejorative consequences which result in rule-breaking by those who are labelled. Being labelled is said to generate negative reactions by others, including attribution of bad character and stereotypical behavioral expectations. These reactions, in turn, limit opportunities for conforming participation and produce changes in the self-image. Limited opportunities for participation and altered self-image lead ultimately to rule-breaking (Erikson, 1962: 312; Lemert, 1967: 41; Trice and Roman, 1970). The second major idea of labelling theory, therefore, is that official negative classification is a self-fulfilling prophecy—it actually causes rule-breaking behavior. But more than that, labelling theory seems to specify the process by which this result is produced.

These two major ideas can be translated into specific testable propositions, but until the theoretical ideas are sharpened, the derivable propositions cannot be precise. For example, it would be desirable to state something like: "In situation X (with features ABC) labelling will be explained 30% by rule breaking behavior, 40% by power of the individual, 20% by life style of the individual, and 10% by idiosyncratic variables." Or: "Official classification as a deviant of type R will increase the probability of rule breaking of type R (in situation X with features ABC) 60% above what would have occurred in the absence of labelling." Development at this point, however, only justifies propositions like the following: "Other variables will account for more of the variance in labelling than will actual rule breaking." Or: "Official classification as a deviant will increase the probability of rule breaking more often than it will decrease it."

THE EVIDENCE

Proposition One

It is not entirely clear whether labelling theorists intend to say that disadvantage variables will have *some* effect on labelling or whether they mean to imply that their effect will be greater than the effect of actual rule-breaking. The more stringent interpretation seems desirable for two reasons. First, if labelling theory says only that disadvantage variables will have *some* effect on official classification, then all the excitement generated by the approach has been misplaced. Everybody can agree that justice is not totally blind and sociologists have been aware of prejudice and discrimination for generations. The novelty of the labelling approach seems to lie in its postulation and theoretical justification of various forms of discrimination as the fundamental basis for police and judicial decisions. Second, to say only that disadvantage variables will have some effect is too imprecise to be of scientific value. Surely the theorists are not interested in only a one percent effect, but it is impossible to state exactly what level of effect they are suggesting. Without precision, researchers are left with only two choices. They can investigate the effect of disadvantage variables in different situations and conclude that any effect whatsoever supports labelling theory. But, again, this renders the theory uninteresting and almost certainly incontrovertible. Or they can interpret the proposition more rigorously by conceptualizing it in a comparative framework. Thus, whatever effect disadvantage variables have, it must be greater than the effect of rule-breaking alone.

It is clear, however, that the more rigorous interpretation of proposition one means that little systematic evidence in the criminological literature can be brought to bear. A valid test would (1) hold constant actual rule-breaking and observe the relationship between labelling and disadvantages, and (2) compare the magnitude of that association with the one observed when disadvantages are held constant and the level of actual rule-breaking and labelling are associated. To my knowledge, only three studies even approaching these criteria have been reported.

Hindelang (1974) investigated decisions by commercial establishments to refer to the police people who were caught shoplifting. Although such referral is not exactly the same as labelling by official agencies, it is a good indicator, since referral will almost certainly result in a police record and perhaps even conviction. Hindelang found that the relationship between the level of rule-breaking (value of objects stolen) and labelling, holding constant age, race, and sex, was greater than the relationship between these characteristics and labelling when the value of the goods stolen was held constant. Alternatively, he showed that the value of the goods stolen, what was stolen, and how it was stolen all predicted the probability of referral better than did the personal characteristics of the offender. This study is not a perfect test of the proposition in question because it does not include socioeconomic status, a key disadvantage variable, and because did not consider a combination of the disadvantage variables relative to a combination of the actual rule-breaking bariables (instead it treated each of both kinds of variables as an autonomous factor). Nevertheless, the evidence reported is the most rigorous available, and it is contrary to labelling predictions.

A second study focused on decisions by store detectives in a California department store to refer shoplifting cases to the police. Cohen and Stark (1974) found that controlling for the value of the goods stolen eliminated all relationship between referral and age, sex, race, or class. Such controls did not, however, eliminate the relationship between employment status and referral. The store detectives were more likely to refer the unemployed in all circumstances, apparently on the theory that being unemployed was a good sign of being a professional thief. Moreover, these authors found that the amount stolen accounted for more of the variance in referral than did any other variable, although the difference between the amount of variance accounted for by it and employment status was not large.

The Cohen and Stark study, while ostensibly quite powerful, is in fact somewhat defective for our purposes. While the study reports the relationship between the disadvantage variables and labelling (controlling for rule-breaking), it does not show the other half of the coin–the relationship between the value of the theft and referral, controlling for the disadvantages. Moreover, although the authors did compare amounts of variance explained by rule-breaking and each disadvantage variable, they neglected to compare the predictive power of the amount stolen with a combination of the disadvantage variables. Although the findings are not compelling in view of the methodological criteria set forth, they are nevertheless at variance with labelling expectations.

A third study examines variations in the imposition of a label of "adjudicated guilty" among probationers. In Florida the law allows those convicted by a court and placed on probation to be classified at the discretion of the judge as having been adjudicated not guilty. Chiricos, Jackson, and Waldo (1972) measured the relationship between such guilty labels and a large number of social characteristics. Only in the case of race, however, did they control for actual rule-breaking and observe variations by disadvantage. Even then, though, the actual magnitudes of the associations are not reported. The reader is simply told. "White defendants are spared the sting of felony adjudication more often than blacks at *every* level of age or education, for *every* type of offense, attorney, plea, or court, and regardless of the extent of the defendants' prior criminal record" (p. 537). Moreover, the opposite association is not calculated at all. The authors do control for social characteristics and find a relationship between prior convictions and labelling, but it is difficult to know what this means in the present context. Thus, even though " 'prior contact' variables appear in this sample analysis to be more strongly related to adjudication status than any other cluster of variables in the study" (p. 562), prior contact could be taken as evidence of the extent of actual rule-breaking or as evidence of prior labelling. It could be interpreted as showing that having been labelled in the past is the most powerful determinant of present labelling, but even this may be spurious, since actual rule-breaking is not considered as one of the other variables in the analysis that led to that particular conclusion. Hence, the data appear to be simply uninterpretable as far as a rigorous test of the proposition in question goes.

Of the three studies most nearly approaching ideal methodological conditions, one is uninterpretable and the other two can offer only weak data. Thus, if we insist on rigorous evaluation, we will have to conclude that the empirical status of the first labelling proposition, at least as far as crime goes, is currently unknown. Within the methodological limitations noted, however, the evidence tends to be contrary to labelling predictions.

Even though studies which meet ideal methodological criteria are desirable, they are not the only ones of relevance for assessing the proposition in question. Any study that shows *no* relationship between disadvantage variables and labelling can be important in evaluating the validity of the proposition, although studies which do find an association between disadvantage variables and labelling are of little use in establishing the proposition as it is stated in its stringent form (Popper, 1959, 1963). This is so because supporting evidence requires not only the demonstration of a positive association between disadvantage variables and labelling, but also that this association is stronger than that between labelling and actual rule-breaking. A demonstration that there is no association between disadvantage and labelling, on the other hand, would be contrary to the theory regardless of the magnitude of any alternative association. Thus, in the absence of comparative evidence on the two alternative associations, one can never prove the validity of the labelling proposition even though it is possible to reject it convincingly.

My survey of the literature turned up at least four studies that report no evidence of variations in labelling by disadvantage factors. Green (1960) investigated variations in sentencing by age, sex, and race in Philadelphia. He found that control for type of offense, number of prior felony convictions, and number of bills of indictment reduced to nonsignificance any relationship between these social characteristics and the nature of the sentence. This study is not as strong as it could be for two reasons. First, Green does not examine variations in sentencing by socioeconomic status of the offender, a key variable in the labelling perspective. Second, he deals only with the sentencing stage of the criminal justice process. It is possible that the effect of social variables might manifest themselves only at earlier points in the justice process. Nevertheless, within these limitations, the evidence is contrary to labelling expectations.

In a later study, Green (1964) reanalysed the Philadelphia data in order to take into account the make-up of offender-victim combinations. He examined variations between crimes involving black offenders and white victims, black offenders and black victims, and white offenders and white victims for the crimes of robbery and burglary. Controlling for type and seriousness of offense and other jural considerations, he found no differences among the offender-victim combinations except that offenders in the b-b combinations were sentenced a little more severely for robbery than were others. Green argues, however, that this slight variation is the result of a lower percentage of "single" as opposed to multiple charge robberies within this grouping (although he did not control this variable systematically). Again, the analysis is limited by the absence of control for socioeconomic status and by concentration only on sentencing. But the findings are clearly contrary to labelling principles which would predict considerable variation among the combinations, particularly between the b-w and w-b types.

Third, Bensing and Schroeder (1960) analyzed homicide data in Cleveland by suspect-victim racial combinations as well as by the race of the suspect only. Considering only the race of the offender, the data indicated almost identical percentages of each race convicted as charged, convicted of a lesser offense, and not guilty. Analysis by suspect-victim types did show that black offenders in cross-race combinations were more often convicted as charged, were convicted less often on a lesser charge, and were less often acquitted than were white suspects. But the authors maintain (without systematic control) that this is probably due to the fact that a larger proportion of the blacks were charged with more serious felony counts such as killing a police officer or killing while perpetrating a crime. As in the previous cases, the study is limited because it considers only race and because it does not include all steps in the criminal justice process. In addition, it is limited in applicability because it is concerned only with homicide cases. But again within the limitations of the data, it challenges the validity of the labelling proposition.

Finally, Wolf (1965) examined variations in sentencing of capital cases by age and race in New Jersey, controlling for type of murder. He found no statistically significant differences between racial or age categories in sentences. As before, there is no consideration of socioeconomic status, other stages in the legal process, and other types of offenses, but the data are contrary to the labelling position.

Data relevant to the proposition that disadvantage variables have greater effect on official classification as a criminal than does actual rule-breaking therefore consist of three comparative studies and four negative test studies. All of these suffer interpretative and methodological weaknesses, but they nevertheless place the labelling proposition on shaky ground. As far as I have been able to determine, there is no positive test of the proposition, although there is this negative evidence.

However, since labelling theory is so imprecise and unformalized, it might be well to consider the amount of positive evidence that exists for the weak form of proposition one. Any study which demonstrates a nonspurious relationship between disadvantage variables and labelling would be supportive of the idea that variables other than actual rule-breaking have *some* effect on labelling, provided we can safely assume that the disadvantages preceded the official classification. In considering correlational data of this type, it is important to remember that they are of evidentiary value only if relationships can be shown not to be due to some intervening variable such as the amount or seriousness of actual rule-breaking. For example, data show that arrest varies by race, but unless the actual amount or seriousness of criminal behavior is controlled, one cannot know if this variation is attributable to differential handling by control agents or to real crime. This point would seem obvious, but over the years numerous studies in sociology have purported to demonstrate racism, sexism, ageism, or classism simply on the basis of categorical variations in some phenomenon, just as many studies have attributed causation to race, sex, age, or class without attempting to eliminate the effects of extraneous variables.

I have been able to locate a total of seventeen systematic studies relevant to the hypothesis that variables of social disadvantage have *some* effect on criminal labelling and that meet the minimum methodological criteria set forth. They include the seven investigations reported above in connection with the stringent form of the labelling proposition and ten additional studies.

Although Hindelang's (1974) study shows that behavioral variables are more important than disadvantage in labelling of shoplifters, his data do reveal some variation by age, sex, and race even when the value of the goods stolen is held constant. The Chiricos, Jackson, and Waldo (1972) research is uninterpretable in terms of the stringent form of the labelling proposition, but it would have to be counted as positive evidence for the weaker form, since they did find that blacks were more often adjudicated guilty than whites even when age, education, type of offense, prior criminal record, and type of attorney, plea, or court were held constant. Similarly Cohen and Stark (1973) reported evidence contrary to the rigorous labelling proposition but they did find that the probability that an apprehended shoplifter would be reported to the police varied by employment status of the individual even when the value of the goods stolen was controlled (although they offered a plausible nonlabelling explanation of this).

Of the additional ten studies, the one by Marshall and Purdy (1972) appears to be the strongest. These authors gathered self-report data concerning the frequency and seriousness of drinking and driving. They then examined the relationship between conviction and social characteristics, holding constant drinking/driving behavior. Consistent with labelling predictions, they found variations by age, sex, race, and socioeconomic status even when the degree and seriousness of rule-breaking were controlled. In the case of age and sex, however, the direction of the relationship indicated that the most disadvantaged received the most favorable treatment.

A second study (Steffensmeier and Terry, 1973) reports results of an experiment in which shoplifting episodes were contrived to enable measurement of the extent to which observers would report the theft, either on their own or when quizzed by a "store detective." They found that customers more often reported acts of theft when the thief's appearance indicated nonconventional or disadvantaged life styles. The relevance of this investigation is contingent upon two assumptions. First, we must assume that customer reports of theft to store personnel is an adequate indication of official labelling. This is a fairly stringent assumption, since other studies of shoplifting indicate that the majority of cases are not reported to the police by store detectives even when they personally observe the offense. Second, we have to assume that the value of the goods stolen as well as the way in which the thefts occurred were constant across all conditions in the experiment. The authors do not say this was the case, but it seems logical that they would have staged a similar theft in each case.

In addition to these studies, investigations of the judicial process provide some supportive, although weak, evidence for the hypothesis that disadvantage variables have some effect on criminal labelling. Hagen (1974) summarizes the character and results of twenty studies of judicial functioning. Eight of them are applicable to our discussion here because they involve at least one control for spuriousness and they deal with sentencing, which is an aspect of the labelling process (studies of executions and later court intervention, such as appellate review, are not relevant). These eight studies involve a total of sixteen tests concerning sentencing, including ten of racial variations, two of interracial combinations, two of socioeconomic variations, and one of age and sex. Seven of them control for type of offense, and four control for prior record of the suspect.

Although these investigations found some evidence of variations by social disadvantage in the direction predicted by the labelling perspective, the highest association in any of the sixteen tests was only .06, and only three of the sixteen showed a statistically significant relationship between disadvantage and labelling within all categories of the control variables. Moreover, none of these studies employed adequate controls to rule out the possibility of spuriousness. The controls that were used were exceptionally crude, and none of the studies took into account legally relevant aspects of the crimes such as number of indictments, way in which the crime was committed (cruelty, extenuating circumstances), or characteristics of the victims (children, policemen, relatives). Thus, these eight provide some positive evidence, but it is difficult to place much confidence in them.

Taken as a whole, then, thirteen studies support the argument that social disadvantage has *some* effect on labelling, while four contradict it. The weight of the evidence, therefore, is in favor of the weak form of the labelling proposition. These systematic data are supplemented in this conclusion by suggestive but nonsystematic and uncontrolled studies. Ethnographic research on the police suggests the intervention of social disadvantage variables into the decision to arrest (Skolnick, 1966: 86; Rubinstein, 1973: 264). And observational studies of judicial functioning point up the role of disadvantage in determining legal handling (Blumberg, 1967; Sudnow, 1965). For example, Foote's description of the administration of vagrancy laws in Philadelphia suggests that one's social status heavily influenced whether he would be classified as a vagrant, regardless of his actual behavior (Foote, 1956).

In sum, the available evidence, although suffering from many methodological defects, is contrary to the thesis that disadvantage variables have more influence on criminal labelling than does actual rule-breaking, but it is generally consistent with the view that disadvantage variables have some effect on labelling. Thus, the stringent and more interesting form of the labelling proposition is negated by the data, while the weak and essentially nonnovel form of the proposition is found to have some empirical grounding.

Proposition Two

One can conceptualize the active, or causal, aspect of labelling in several forms, varying in complexity as well as rigor. The most demanding version of the proposition would postulate a fairly complex chain specifying that (1) labelling leads to crime through several causally linked, sequential steps including negative reactions from others (in the form of limitation of opportunities for participation), transformation of self-image, and association with other criminals. A less complex but still rigorous version would state that (2) labelling causes crime (without saying how) or (3) labelling has a stronger independent effect on criminal behavior than any other variable. A still less demanding version would be that (4) labelling has *some* effect on crime.

As with the first proposition, it is impossible to say which of these versions best captures the essence of labelling theory as presently formulated. But, as before, there are good reasons to conceptualize the theory in something besides the weakest form. To say only that labelling has *some* effect in producing crime is so imprecise that it tells us very little, even if true.

Moreover, hardly anyone (even before the advent of labelling theory) has ever doubted that official classification as a criminal has a negative effect on the future behavior of some. If this is all that labelling theory predicts, it is neither novel nor enlightening enough to merit the attention it has gained.

Although the first form of the proposition is the most interesting, it is not really necessary to test it until less stringent versions have been shown to be empirically tenable. Even though some have tried to evaluate various parts of the proposed causal chain (cf. Hagen, 1973), it is superfluous to bother with linkages if there is no connection between the first and last variables in the chain. For these reasons, I will devote my attention to the other hypotheses. But testing any of these hypotheses, even the least demanding, requires something approximating an experimental design. In order to establish that labelling has some effect on criminal behavior, it is necessary to compare those who are labelled with those who are not (or compare degrees of labelling) in terms of subsequent criminal behavior, making sure that both groups are alike in all other relevant ways, including prior crime, social characteristics, cultural influences, and normative commitments. This necessitates measures of criminal behavior for those who come in contact with the law as well as those who do not. I know of no such data in the criminological literature (cf. Gold, 1970: 106-108, for an approximation in delinquency research), but studies of probation have some of the necessary features.

If being convicted, imprisoned, and then paroled is indicative of more severe labelling than is simple conviction and probation, and if the labelling proposition is correct, then probationers should have lower recidivism rates than similar parolees. The two best studies of this type are by Beattie and Bridges (1970) and Babst and Mannering (1965). The first compared for a one-year follow-up period the success of probationers with those who were released from California jails, controlling for county, sex, age, prior record, and offense. In addition, they controlled simultaneously for several pairs of the variables. The results showed that sixty-five percent of the probationers had no subsequent arrests or technical violations during the follow-up period, while only forty-one percent of those who had been incarcerated were free of further difficulties. If one assumes that the supervision required for probationers was not a significant variable in their conforming behavior, the data are consistent with the labelling proposition.

Babst and Mannering compared violation rates of probationers with those of parolees who were similar in original disposition, county of commitment, type of offense, number of prior felonies, and marital status. They found that first offense probationers had lower violation rates than did parolees (twenty-five percent versus thirty-three percent), but for second offenders the rates were approximately equal (forty-two percent versus forty-four percent). For those who were multiple offenders, parolees had lower violation rates (fifty-two percent versus forty-nine percent). Thus, overall, there appears to be almost no difference in this study between the violation rates of those more and those less severely labelled, a finding that is contrary to the labelling argument.

But these are not ideal tests of the hypothesis. First, arrest or parole violations are defective indicators of criminal behavior. As pointed out earlier, there is only a tenuous connection between arrest and guilt, and parole violation reflects a large number of noncriminal acts or omissions. Moreover, supervision rules, and therefore the grounds for violation, may not be comparable for those who were placed on probation and those who were incarcerated. Second, all the subjects in these two studies had been convicted of a crime. In effect, the authors were comparing subsamples of a population who had all been criminally labelled. The real effect of labelling may be observable only when those who have not been labelled are compared with those who have. Finally, while some precautions were taken to ensure that the comparison groups were alike prior to labelling, the controls were minimal. It is possible that any number of uncontrolled variables could have differentiated the comparison groups and influenced the outcomes. Indeed, offenders are often selected for probation because the court believes they are less likely to be recidivists. Presumably there are differentiating criminogenic factors which are apparent to the courts, but which are not taken into account in these studies. It is precisely for this reason that the bulk of probation studies are useless for the purposes at hand. While many investigations show that probationers have lower recidivism rates than do incarcerees (Levin, 1971; Wilkins, 1969: 14-15), they do not employ sufficient control to ensure that pre-selection did not determine the outcome.

Although not free of methodological defects (Ward, 1972), the follow-up study reported in the Careers in Crime section of *Uniform Crime Reports* during the late 1960s is a much closer approximation to the experimental ideal than other studies. The FBI report in 1968 showed rearrest rates for all people released from custody in 1963, with the data broken down by type of release. Rearrest rates were substantially *higher* (ninety-one percent versus thirty-six percent to seventy-four percent for various categories) among those who escaped being labelled (were acquitted or had their cases dismissed) than among those who were labelled (incarcerated, fined, or placed on probation). These data are superior to the others because they are based on the same criterion of recidivism for all comparisons (although not the best criterion), they apply to a national population, and they permit comparisons of the labelled with the nonlabelled rather than forcing attention on categories that differ in degree of labelling. There is no way of knowing if people released under the various conditions differed in criminogenic characteristics prior to contact with the law, but it seems likely that they would have differed, if at all, only with respect to evidentiary characteristics of the crime. Moreover, it is hardly reasonable to assume that those who were acquitted or had their cases dismissed were *more* criminogenic than those who were convicted. Any preselection that might have occurred would, therefore, have favored the labelling hypothesis. Thus, although not ideal, these data are the strongest of their kind, and they are strikingly contrary to labelling expectations.

An alternative strategy for evaluating the labelling proposition is to compare the recidivism rate of labelees with an estimate of the recidivism rate of all those who commit crimes. If the general recidivism rate were determined purely by chance, the odds of being a repeater would be .5. Of course, recidivism is probably not a simple chance occurrence. Since many systematic variables may influence the likelihood of a subsequent offense, the actual probability of general recidivism may be less than fifty percent, or it may be considerably greater than fifty percent. With appropriate data, we could establish the actual probability that an individual who commits a crime will repeat, but in the absence of such data our best estimate is pure chance. Thus, if labelling has any effect on crime, it should be reflected in a recidivism rate among the labelled that is greater than chance (fifty percent), and if we are to draw a strong inference concerning the effect of labelling, the recidivism rate of labelees should be substantially greater than that predicted by chance (much greater than fifty percent). Furthermore, even if the actual general recidivism rate were known to be somewhat less than fifty percent, support for those versions of the labelling proposition which imply an almost inevitable pejorative outcome would require that the recidivism rate of labelees far exceed fifty percent.

Inadequacy of data concerning the recidivism question has already been discussed; nevertheless, the most defensible evidence is inconsistent with the labelling hypothesis. Although rearrest figures are approximately sixty-five percent, FBI data suggest that reconviction for those released from custody in 1963 will be only thirty to thirty-five percent for the indefinite future (see Tittle and Logan, 1973: 389), even though plea bargaining increases the probability of conviction for those with previous records. Moreover, recommitment studies show that rates of return to prison for any reason vary from place to place, but that the average is less than fifty percent. Glaser's review of eleven recommitment studies prior to 1964 showed that the average return rate is approximately thirty-five percent (Glaser, 1964: 25-26). Since his review, five additional follow-up studies have been reported. Metzner and Weil (1963) traced inmates released from the Massachusetts Correctional Institute at Concord and found that fifty-six percent were recommitted within two and one-half years, half for technical parole violations. Carney (1967) found an overall return rate for the Massachusetts Correctional Institute at Norfolk of fifty-five percent, but again half of these were returned for technical parole violations. Kolodney et al. (1970) report a recommitment rate of sixty-seven percent for California prisoners, and a follow-up of a sample of releasees from Connecticut prisons (Simon and Cockerham, 1974) shows that sixty-eight percent were reimprisoned for new crimes. In addition, Kassebaum, Ward, and Wilner (1971) traced California releasees for a three-year period, using parole disposition, based largely on rearrest information, and found that fifty-six percent of the releasees were completely clean or associated only with technical parole violations or misdemeanors (pp. 222-223). Thus, sixteen follow-up studies show failure rates varying from twenty-four percent to sixty-eight percent with the average being forty-four percent, a figure that is inflated because a large percentage were returned for technical parole violations in several of the studies. Recidivism rates, then, do not appear to support the labelling argument.

Case materials also call into question the causal power of labelling by showing that many criminal careers occur without labelling, that labelling often comes after rather than before adoption of a criminal career, or that criminal careers may not follow even when labelling takes place. As Mankoff (1971) points out, most check forgers, marijuana users, and embezzlers adopt careers without labelling ever taking place. Most pickpockets and bunco artists develop their career patterns before rather than after labelling (Sutherland, 1937). Studies suggest that shoplifters seldom repeat the crime (Cameron, 1964; Cohen and Stark, 1974), and most offenders do not reappear in court for public drunkenness (Lovald and Stub, 1968).

In sum, of the three studies most nearly fulfilling necessary methodological criteria, one favors the labelling argument while two are contrary to it. General studies of recidivism do not confirm labelling expectations that more than half will be recidivists, and case materials provide many exceptions to labelling predictions. The weight of the evidence, then, is contrary to the idea that labelling leads to crime in the general case or that it is the most important variable in the production of criminal careers. Nevertheless, the data do not justify dismissal of the ideal that labelling may have *some* effect on criminal behavior. Although the absence of experimental evidence and of data do not justify dismissal of the idea that labelling may have *some* effect tive conclusions about cause, the incidence of rearrest, recommitment, and technical violations among all categories of labelled people forces us to at least take seriously the argument that being officially labelled has a crime-generating effect. The evidence, therefore, contradicts rigorous forms of the second labelling proposition, and it is insufficient to establish even the weak statement that labelling has some effect on crime. But it is also impossible to rule out the likelihood of some effect.

CONCLUSION

Neither of the major propositions of labelling theory finds much support in the available data concerning crime. It does not appear that disadvantage has more influence on criminal labelling than actual rule-breaking, nor does it appear that labelling leads generally to crime or even that it increases the probability of rule-breaking more often than it decreases it. The most that can be concluded is that social disadvantages may have some effect on labelling and that labelling may have some influence in producing criminal behavior. On the basis of the present evidence, then, only the weakest implications of the perspective can be sustained, and even they lack firm support.

This does not mean, however, that we can reject the labelling approach. For one thing, the data concerning this question are extremely poor. Not only has there been comparatively little research, but that which has been done suffers from crippling methodological defects. Not a single good test of either of the major propositions of labelling theory currently exists in the criminological literature. Moreover, most of the research does not even attend to the most fundamental requirements of scientific methodology. The truth is, we simply cannot judge the empirical adequacy of the labelling theory with any confidence at the present time. Hence, it would be foolish to conclude that it is unfounded. But by the same token, it is even more foolish to accept it as if it were tried and proven.

Second, although present evidence does not favor any rigorous hypotheses drawn from labelling theory, it does suggest that something may be there. The basic problem is that labelling theory is so grossly formulated that it almost invites empirical negation. Before we can really judge the merits of the perspective, it must be refined so that specific limited hypotheses can be derived and tested. The major objective of labelling theorists ought to be to specify the conditions under which social disadvantages or other variables will affect official criminal classification and to specify the circumstances under which labelling will produce rather than deter crime (cf. Tittle, 1975). Until this refinement takes place, empirical tests will remain gross, and we will run the risk of throwing out the plant without ever having given it a chance to blossom. A wise theorist, like a wise gardener, must not fear to prune and shape, or even to graft.

Finally, as Schur has pointed out, the perspective may be far more cogent in its ability to explain macro-sociological phenomena. This paper has not addressed labelling propositions concerning lawmaking and -breaking at the societal level, but has instead confined itself to questions concerning labelling individuals as criminals. It would be a mistake to judge the general merits of an approach on the basis of an evaluation confined to only one level of analysis. Nevertheless, it should be noted that thc problems of deriving precise macro-sociological propositions from the labelling perspective and then putting them to empirical tests appear even more formidable than those encountered in considerations at the micro level.

The lessons are clear. Labelists must get down to serious theoretical business. Evasiveness, lauding of ambiguity, and hiding behind a façade of sensitizing concepts will no longer suffice. Researchers, on the other hand, must apply themselves with more facility and care. The meagerness and sloppiness of research on a question of this importance is embarrassing.

REFERENCES

Andenaes, J.
1966 "The general preventive effects of punishment." University of Pennsylvania Law Review 114: 949-983.
Babst, D. V. and J. W. Mannering
1965 "Probation versus imprisonment for similar types of offenders." Journal of Research in Crime and Delinquency 2 (July): 60-71.
Beattie, Ronald H. and Charles K. Bridges
1970 Superior Court Probation and/or Jail Sample. Sacramento: Bureau of Criminal Statistics, Department of Justice.
Becker, Howard S.
1963 Outsiders. New York: Free Press.
1973 "Labelling theory reconsidered." Pp. 3-32 in S. Messinger et al. (eds.) The Aldine Crime and Justice Annual, 1973. Chicago: Aldine.
Bensing, Robert C. and Oliver Schroeder, Jr.
1960 Homicide in an Urban Community. Springfield, Ill.: Charles C. Thomas.
Blumberg, Abraham S.
1967 Criminal Justice. Chicago: Quadrangle.
Buckner, H. Taylor
1971 Deviance, Reality, and Change. New York: Random House.
Cameron, Mary Owen
1964 The Booster and the Snitch. New York: Free Press.
Carney, F. J.
1967 "Predicting recidivism in a medium security correctional institution." Journal of Criminal Law, Crimonology, and Police Science 58 (September): 338-349.
Chiricos, T. G., P. D. Jackson, and G. P. Waldo
1972 "Inequality in the imposition of a criminal label." Social Problems 19 (Spring): 553-571.
Cohen, L. E. and R. Stark
1974 "Discriminatory labeling and the five-finger discount." Journal of Research in Crime and Delinquency 11 (January): 25-39.

Connor, W. D.
1972 "The manufacture of deviance: the case of the Soviet purge, 1936-1938." American Sociological Review 37 (August): 403-413.
Erikson, K. T.
1962 "Notes on the sociology of deviance." Social Problems 9 (Spring): 307-314.
1966 Wayward Puritans. New York: John Wiley.
Fisher, S.
1972 "Stigma and deviant careers in school." Social Problems 20 (Summer): 78-83.
Foote, C.
1956 "Vagrancy-type law and its administration." University of Pennsylvania Law Review 104 (1956): 603-650.
Gibbs, J. P.
1966 "Conceptions of deviant behavior: the old and the new." Pacific Sociological Review 9 (Spring): 9-14.
1972 "Issues in defining deviant behavior." Pp. 39-68 in R. A. Scott and J. O. Douglas (eds.) Theoretical Perspectives on Deviance. New York: Basic Books.
Glaser, Daniel
1964 The Effectiveness of a Prison and Parole System. Indianapolis: Bobbs-Merrill.
Gold, Martin
1970 Delinquent Behavior in an American City. Belmont, Calif.: Brooks/Cole.
Gove, W.
1970 "Societal reaction as an explanation of mental illness: an evaluation." American Sociological Review 35 (October): 873-884.
Green, E.
1960 "Sentencing practices of criminal court judges." American Journal of Correction 22 (July/August): 32-35.
1964 "Inter- and intra-racial crime relative to sentencing." Journal of Criminal Law, Criminology and Police Science 55 (September): 348-358.
Hagen, J.
1973 "Labelling and deviance: a case study in the sociology of the interesting." Social Problems 20 (Spring): 447-458.
1974 "Extra-legal attributes and criminal sentencing: an assessment of a sociological viewpoint." Law and Society Review 8 (Spring): 357-383.
Hindelang, M. J.
1974 "Decisions of shoplifting victims to invoke the criminal justice process." Social Problems 21 (April): 580-593.
Kassebaum, Gene, David Ward, and Daniel Wilner
1971 Prison Treatment and Parole Survival: An Empirical Assessment. New York: John Wiley.
Kolodney, Steven et al.
1970 A Study of the Characteristics and Recidivism Experience of California Prisoners. San Jose: Public Systems Incorporated (as described in Levin, 1971).
Lemert, E. M.
1967 "The concept of secondary deviation." Pp. 40-64 in Human Deviance, Social Problems, and Social Control. Englewood Cliffs, N.J.: Prentice-Hall.
Levin, M. A.
1971 "Policy evaluation and recidivism." Law and Society Review 6 (August): 17-46.

Lovald, K. and H. R. Stub
1968 "The revolving door: reactions of chronic drunkenness offenders to court sanction." Journal of Criminal Law, Criminology and Police Science 59 (December): 525-530.

Mankoff, M.
1971 "Societal reactions and career deviance: a critical analysis." Sociological Quarterly 12 (Spring): 204-218.

Marshall, H. and R. Purdy
1972 "Hidden deviance and the labelling approach: the case for drinking and driving." Social Problems 19 (Spring): 541-553.

Metzner, R. and G. Weil
1963 "Predicting recidivism: base-rates for Massachusetts Correctional Institution Concord." Journal of Criminal Law, Criminology and Police Science 54 (September): 307-316.

Newman, Donald J.
1966 Conviction: The Determination of Guilt or Innocence Without Trial. Boston: Little, Brown.

Payne, W. D.
1973 "Negative labels: passageways and prisons." Crime and Delinquency 19 (January): 33-40.

Popper, Karl
1959 The Logic of Scientific Discovery. New York: Basic Books.
1963 Conjectures and Refutations: The Growth of Scientific Knowledge. New York: Basic Books.

Quinney, Richard
1970 The Social Reality of Crime. Boston: Little, Brown.

Ross, H. L.
1973 "Law, science and accidents: the British road safety act of 1967." Journal of Legal Studies 2 (January): 1-78.

Rubenstein, Jonathan
1973 City Police. New York: Farrar, Straus & Giroux.

Rushing, W. A.
1971 "Individual resources, societal reaction, and hospital commitment." American Journal of Sociology 77 (November): 511-526.

Scheff, T. J.
1974 "The labelling theory of mental illness." American Sociological Review 39 (June): 444-452.

Schur, Edwin
1971 Labeling Deviant Behavior: Its Sociological Implications. New York: Harper & Row.

Schwartz, R. D. and J. H. Skolnick
1962 "Two studies of legal stigma." Social Problems 10 (Fall): 133-142.

Simon, S. and W. Cockerham
1974 "State's prisons fail to deter or help most criminals." Hartford Courant 137 (February 24): 1 ff.

Skolnick, Jerome J.
1966 Justice Without Trial: Law Enforcement in Democratic Society. New York: John Wiley.

Steffensmeier, D. J. and R. M. Terry
1973 "Deviance and respectability: an observational study of reactions to shoplifting." Social Forces 51 (June): 417-426.

Sudnow, David
1965 "Normal crimes: sociological features of the penal code in a public defender office." Social Problems 12 (Winter): 255-276.

Sutherland, Edwin H.
1937 The Professional Thief. Chicago: University of Chicago Press.

Tittle, C. R.
1975 "Deterrents or labeling?" Social Forces 53 (March): 399-410.

--- and C. H. Logan
1973 "Sanctions and deviance: evidence and remaining questions." Law and Society Review 7 (Spring): 372-392.

Trice, H. M. and P. M. Roman
1970 "Delabeling, relabeling, and alcoholics anonymous." Social Problems 17 (Spring): 538-546.

Turk, Austin T.
1969 Criminality and Legal Order. Chicago: Rand McNally.

Ward, P.
1972 " 'Careers in crime': the FBI story." Journal of Research in Crime and Delinquency 7 (July): 207-218.

Wilkins, Leslie T.
1965 Social Deviance. Englewood Cliffs, N.J.: Prentice-Hall.
1969 Evaluation of Penal Measures. New York: Random House.

Williams, C. J. and M. S. Weinberg
1970 "Being discovered: a study of homosexuals in the military." Social Problems 18 (Fall): 217-227.

Wolf, E.
1965 "Abstract of analysis of jury sentencing in capital cases: New Jersey, 1937-1961." Rutgers Law Review 19: 56 (as described in Hagen, 1974).

Zimring, Franklin E. and Gordon J. Hawkins
1973 Deterrence: The Legal Threat in Crime Control. Chicago: University of Chicago Press.

Chapter 7

LABELLING THEORY AND JUVENILE DELINQUENCY: AN ASSESSMENT OF THE EVIDENCE

TRAVIS HIRSCHI

It is not easy for a traditional student of delinquency to approach labelling theory with an open mind.[1] Labelling theorists are not kind to the traditional approach: they typically begin with a flat denial of the validity of most of the research the traditional approach has produced; in most cases, they do not hesitate to infer and condemn the values and politics of their opponents; they typically insist on confusing a description of a set of conditions with approval of these conditions. Further, and perhaps worst of all, labelling theorists often appear with little effort to have won the battle. Students are enthralled; the journals begin to bulge with "critiques," "tests," "appreciative reviews," and all the other perquisities of theoretical victory.

One is reminded of Sheldon Glueck's (Glueck and Glueck, 1964: 243) complaint about differential association: "The theory of differential association . . . fails to organize . . . the findings of respectable research and is . . . so general and puerile as to add little or nothing to the explanation . . . of delinquency."

If we care for those who suffer, we should put ourselves for a moment in Sheldon Glueck's shoes. What do we see from his vantage point? For several decades, he has been sifting and sorting data on delinquency. Not once in all this time has he seen a trace of "differential association." Yet this theory dominates the field and, even worse, is frequently used to call into question the results of his own research. Little wonder he is upset! Given such provocation, we can only admire his restraint.

For much the same reasons, it would be easy for me to begin a review of the evidence on labelling theory with a conclusion even stronger than Sheldon Glueck's indictment of differential association: The labelling theory of delinquency fails to *recognize* the results of competent research and is so general and *sophisticated* that one wonders how anyone could ever possibly have taken it seriously.

But that would be too easy. As a theory, the labelling approach to delinquency is not entitled to reverential awe, to undue concern for its "proper" interpretation, or to the benefit of every doubt. As a theory, it is, however, entitled to that respect we reserve for attempts to help us see the world clearly through the confusion about us.

For that matter, insofar as it is a theory, the labelling approach can be diagrammed on blackboards, listed as a set of propositions on sheets of yellow paper, and fed into computers; the names, insights, and politics of its authors can be separated from it and altogether forgotten. The same is true of the theories to which it is opposed. In other words, it is possible to state the predictions of these various theories as though they were the creation of a single mind, as though all other considerations but the results of research were irrelevant.

This, of course, is the faith of the naive empiricist, of those who respond to requests to evaluate the labelling theory by carefully sifting the empirical evidence bearing on its adequacy. Whether such faith is justified, only time can tell.

Let us take this faith to the first labelling theory, and, as of now, the only attempt by a labelling theorist as opposed to a researcher to apply the theory directly to the causation of juvenile delinquency. This theory is found in Frank Tannenbaum's *Crime and the Community* published in 1938. Tannenbaum, a historian himself,[2] begins his discussion with a brief history of criminological thought. His interpretation of this history, and the conclusions he draws from it, are very close to those of later labelling theorists.

"The outstanding characteristic of all criminological discussion," he tells us, "has been the assumption that there was a qualitative difference between the nature of the criminal and that of the non-criminal." In Tannenbaum's view, this assumption has its origins in the contrast between "God on the one side and the Devil on the other." The good-evil distinction was carried over into the classical school with its moral agent choosing freely to do wrong. It was continued by Lombroso with his savages "born by accident in the wrong century." In fact, Tannenbaum tells us, "Regardless of the changes that criminological theory has undergone, this underlying contrast has persisted under one or another . . . disguise." "Abnormal" may have replaced "evil," and "normal" may have replaced "good," but the fundamental attitude toward the criminal remains unchanged.

Hypotheses based on the good-evil distinction have, in Tannenbaum's view, shared a common fate. They have all proved false. For example, with the demise of Lombroso's theory there developed a substitute statistical technique which purported to measure something called "intelligence." Eventually, of course, it was shown that "whatever 'intelligence' is, it has no demonstrated relationship to crime."[3] At the time Tannenbaum was writing, "a new body of theories was being developed to describe not the mental but the emotional deficiency of the criminal." No delay was necessary for Tannenbaum to pass final judgment on these new theories. They have, he says, "no greater validity than the theories they attempt to supersede" (1938: 3-6).

In the end, then, Tannenbaum is able to say that he "rejects all assumptions that would impute crime to the individual in the sense that a personal shortcoming of the offender is the cause of the unsocial behavior. The assumption that crime is caused by any sort of inferiority, physiological or psychological, is here completely and unequivocally repudiated" (1938: 22).

Let us consider the problem Tannenbaum sets for the would-be naive empiricist. The empiricist naturally assumes that "inferiority" is a question of evidence, that to answer it he must go to the research literature on delinquency. Such literature can be, and perhaps should be, measured in cubic yards. Yet there is little point in attempting to reduce the volume of this research by clarifying the meaning of such terms as "shortcoming" or "cause," since neutral language and scientific sophistication are not the issues: If Tannenbaum is able to reject *future* research, he is certainly going to have no difficulty with the always relatively innocent research of the past.

Subsequent events confirm that careful examination of the research literature would be a waste of time. Thirty years after Tannenbaum, another labelling theorist, Dennis Chapman (1968: 4), feels able to advance in all seriousness the thesis that "apart from the factor of conviction there are no differences between criminals and non-criminals." And, of course, research reporting discovery of differences between criminals and non-criminals continues unabated.

If nothing is to be gained by examining research on individual differences, nothing is to be gained by remaining agnostic on this question, by dismissing it as mere ideological dispute. The question of differences is empirical, and the labelling theorist's answer is simply wrong. Reliable differences between delinquents and nondelinquents are not hard to find (see Nettler, 1974).

It is one thing to *deny* differences between delinquents and nondelinquents. It is something else again to ignore such differences. All theories ignore a great deal, and, for that matter, what a theory denies is not necessarily relevant to the truth of what it asserts.

We can, then, take the position that the labelling theorist's denial of individual differences is only a tactical mistake, that he or she is free to ignore such differences if (s)he wishes, and that therefore we do not have to attend further to this question. Having said this, we can return to Tannenbaum.

Unfortunately for our good intentions, Tannenbaum does not cooperate. *Before* completely and unequivocally rejecting "personal shortcomings" as causes of delinquency, he himself lists and appears to accept a long series of such personal shortcomings as being implicated in its production: physical defects, overcrowding, family inadequacy, poor eyesight, truancy, undernourishment, and even, by inference, "intelligence."

How can Tannenbaum get away with an analysis of the causes of crime he would almost surely reject if they were presented by someone who did not share his "point of view"? The answer is in the question: those who impute "an evil nature to the evil-doer" are, it appears, wrong, whatever the causes of crime they adduce; those able to see that we all enter the world free of sin and that our criminal behavior is, as it were, constructed in a process of interaction with persons already present when we arrived, only those able to grasp these facts are able properly to interpret the results of research.

Tannenbaum's insight is fundamental and is, I think, the heart of the persuasiveness of the labelling theory: If the world did not exist as it does, the so-called causes of delinquency would not operate as they do. There may be, for example, nothing inherently "criminogenic" about being intellectually incompetent. If parents, teachers, playmates, and employers did not react differentially to such people, their lack of competence might have no (or, at least, fewer) implications for crime. And so on through the whole list of positivistic "causes." Put in Tannenbaum's (1938: 25) words, "The criminal . . . is a product, he is the very bone and fiber of the community itself."

Unless positivists are savages born by accident in the wrong century, there should be no difficulty in reconciling their point of view with this insight. In fact, no reconciliation is necessary. The positivists tell us that all their assertions are of the nature "if x, then y," where the "if x" summarizes a set of conditions. In other words, when the positivist says "intellectual incompetence is a cause of delinquency," he or she means "*given* the familial, educational, and occupational structure of American society, intellectual incompetence is a cause of delinquency." The range of conditions under which intellectual incompetence will cause delinquency is itself an empirical question; the labelling theorist's conclusion that since the relation holds only under certain conditions it holds under no conditions at all is, well, not prerequisite to pursuit of his or her concerns.

Once again, then, it appears that a good deal of the disagreement between the traditional and labelling approaches is only apparent, that resolution of their differences is either very easy or unnecessary. In the end, the labelling theorist too must make assertions about what is going on "out there," and these assertions will be the heart of the theory. What are Tannenbaum's assertions?

Tannenbaum (1938: 19-20) tells us that efforts at social control, such things as arrest, punishment, and treatment, create the criminal.

> The process of making the criminal, therefore, is a process of tagging, defining, identifying, segregating, describing, emphasizing, making conscious and self-conscious; it becomes a way of stimulating, suggesting, emphasizing, and evoking the very traits that are complained of. . . . The entire process of dealing with the young delinquent is mischievious in so far as it identifies him to himself or to the environment as a delinquent person.

This is clear enough. And it is greatly to Tannenbaum's credit that he is willing to make such assertions. Most labelling theorists are much less willing to do so.

What evidence does Tannenbaum cite in support of these assertions, and the almost automatic treatment implication of them that "the less said about it [the bad behavior] the better" (1938: 20)? Curiously enough, there is almost nothing in the way of anecdote, let alone evidence in the famous chapter in which the theory is set forth. The nearest Tannenbaum comes to evidence in this chapter is a quotation from John Dewey's *Human Nature and Conduct* to the effect that if one is a hard drinker trying to quit it will pay to think about and keep busy doing something other than drinking. To find the evidence upon which Tannenbaum bases his theory of delinquency, we must go elsewhere in his lengthy book, especially to the chapter entitled "Education for Crime." What this chapter tells us about "the process of making the criminal" can perhaps be understood from a quotation from the introductory section (Tannenbaum, 1938: 51-52; italics added):

> Education for crime must be looked upon as habituation to a way of life. As such it partakes of the nature of all education. It is a *gradual adaptation* to, and a *gradual absorption* of, certain elements in the environment. As an educational process it depends upon instruction, stimulus, approval, companionship, conversation, idealization. It has its elements of curiosity, wonder, knowledge, adventure. Like all true education it has its beginnings in play, it starts in more or less random movements, and builds up toward techniques, insights, judgments, attitudes. It gradually takes on constructive skills. *It depends upon companionship and approving judgment.* Like all education it utilizes the material and ideal elements in the environment; it could not come to pass otherwise. It uses what there is to be found in the neighborhood. These may be such humble things as junk heaps, alley ways,

> abandoned houses, pushcarts, railroad tracks, coal cars. It begins with the easy things that can be picked up, pilfered, carried off, eaten, disposed of. *It requires companionship and encouragement.* It is a social process, like all education for life. Friends, companions, brothers, gangs, participate, *encourage,* amuse, tease, praise, *blame,* compensate. . . . For the career of the criminal to develop there must not only be the friends in the gang, the habits of the older companions already prepared to make certain adjustments through previous instruction, but *there must also be the support of the older generation.* There have to be intermediaries or the career would have no outlet. . . .
>
> For the career to mature and the habits to be crystalized, there must and there do exist certain other items in the environment. There is *approval, from parents, older members of the family, or other experienced people.* There must also be a certain attitude toward the police, toward private property of foreign agencies, like railroads. . . . There must also be older criminals who utilize the youngsters as messengers, lookouts, go-betweens. There is also necessary a preexisting sense of values: the younger boys must learn to approve, respect, imitate, and crave the companionship of, the older and more experienced members of the criminal fraternity.

Tannenbaum's theory of crime has all the characteristics of those theories now said to suffer from an "embarrassment of riches" (Matza, 1964: 21-27). It is not that he has failed to construct a criminal, but that he has constructed a full-time, around-the-clock criminal. We would certainly expect much more criminality from Tannenbaum's criminal than we are now able to observe or infer. Perhaps more important, it is clear that Tannenbaum is able to construct a criminal without the use of the labelling factor.[4] In fact, it might be said that he has thus far created the criminal several times without even mentioning the dire effects of labelling. When he does introduce labelling, it is almost as an afterthought. Here is the key passage: "All this is essential, and with it there must also be present the conflict between the marauding youngsters who in their random and mischievous movements intrude, destroy, annoy, and pilfer and the older and more settled element in the neighborhood who chase, shout, throw things, and call for police protection" (1938: 52).

The reactions of the settled members of the community are only one of perhaps a score of conditions apparently necessary for the person to become a career criminal. (And since "approval" is as important as "conflict" in *creating* the criminal, Tannenbaum is no help to those who would choose between a condemnatory and an approving stance.)

Tannenbaum provides little to illustrate the effects of negative community attitudes. And he produces nothing to substantiate the dire effects of arrest. His delinquents, and he quotes many of them on a variety of topics, do not seem to have been overly impressed by these experiences.[5] In fact, I am impelled to quote the only reference I could find to these allegedly traumatic events: "There were about twelve guys in the gang, and we split up in small groups to go stealing. There wasn't a day that somebody didn't get pinched. *You don't think anything about an arrest in that neighborhood*" (1938: 66).

Imprisonment is, of course, another matter. Tannenbaum devotes much attention to the effects of this experience. The source of data is, by and large, reports from boys themselves. For example: "I was green at first, and the boys petted and pitied me, but I was well on the way to Crookdom at the end of my second month in that place" (1938: 72).

Further repetition of the stories of how people are transformed into hardened criminals by the depraving atmosphere of the institution is not necessary. We all know many of these stories. They are often gruesome, and the conclusions drawn from them by the boys, and by Tannenbaum, are certainly plausible. However, after reading all of them, we cannot conclude that they are evidence relevant to the question. On the contrary, we must conclude that they are not relevant, that Tannenbaum has produced no evidence that tends toward verification of his theory. Horror stories of experiences in prison may be true, and they may be used to account for its detrimental effects once such effects have been established, but until such time they are just empirical noise. The inclusion of these stories reflects the labelling theorist's desire to understand the meaning of events to their participants, but true concern for such understanding would lead to inclusion of at least some of the "how I learned my lesson" stories that are also abundantly available from the correctional experience (Lofland, 1969). To establish the effects of arrest, or prison, or any other labelling experience, we must compare persons differentially exposed to these experiences, something Tannenbaum does not do.[6]

In brief, then, Tannenbaum's version of labelling theory was not based on the results of research. He presents no evidence directly relevant to his thesis that attempts to control delinquency merely intensify or amplify it. The material he does present seriously questions, or, at the very least, seriously reduces the importance of his labelling hypothesis. If we were to adopt the decision rule Tannenbaum employs when dealing with the theories of others—when in doubt, dismiss—there would be no question about our reaction to his theory: "It is a good story. But there is no evidence it is a true story. We should therefore employ our research resources elsewhere."

And that is what actually happened. Delinquency research essentially ignored Tannenbaum's theory until recently, when the pressure of the prestigious works of Lemert (1951) and Becker (1963) eventually became too heavy to ignore.[7]

When labelling theory did reappear as a guide to research, or at least as a guide to the research literature, the question it posed was not Tannenbaum's, but was rather a prior question concerning the processes of selecting persons to the delinquent role.

If the control reaction (or the delinquent stereotype) "creates" the delinquent, the bases of this reaction (or the stereotype) in the characteristics and behavior of the "offender" is clearly a central research question. To what extent is the official reaction to delinquency based on the delinquent behavior of the child and to what extent is it based on extraneous considerations?

These questions are in several respects prior to the question of delinquency amplification. They are also crucial to the dispute between the traditional and labelling views. To the extent that the social reaction is an accurate assessment of the delinquency of the child, opportunities to *create* and to *amplify* delinquency are limited. To the extent that the social reaction is an accurate assessment of the delinquency of the child, the "radical positivist's" (see Taylor et al., 1973: 14-19) fondness for studying delinquents identified for him by agencies of the state is justified, after all.

Two bodies of research have dealt with these questions. The first, research on self-reported delinquency, has apparently been a great boon to the labelling perspective. The second, research on police or official bias in the processing of delinquents, has not proved so helpful. Let us begin with self-report research.

SELF-REPORT RESEARCH

The first account of systematic research on self-reported delinquency was published by F. Ivan Nye, James F. Short, and Virgil J. Olson (1958). This research reported no consistent differences in delinquent behavior by socioeconomic status of the family. At the same time Nye, Short, and Olson demonstrated that juveniles in state institutions were disproportionately lower class. Their research procedure has since been repeated many times, with basically the same results: Children from the lower socioeconomic classes appear no more likely to commit delinquent acts; children from the lower socioeconomic classes are, however, more likely to end up in court and in the reformatory. Black children, too, appear to be overrepresented in official statistics (e.g., Akers, 1964; Williams and Gold, 1972).[8]

A corollary form of research has focused on the volume of undetected delinquency in general populations of adolescents as compared to the volume in samples of adolescents having passed through various stages of adjudication (Erickson and Empey, 1963).

The more balanced accounts of the results of this research from a labelling perspective conclude that "the behaviors we now call delinquency are *extremely common throughout the entire society*" (Schur, 1973: 82). Less-balanced accounts picture the results as a clear-cut, definitive victory for the labelling theory:

> Studies of 'hidden' or undetected crime of the past decade have challenged the traditional distinction between criminals and non-criminals, showing that those who become officially known as criminals are merely a small biased sample of the universe of persons who commit crimes selected to fulfill a scapegoat function. . . . "What makes a person 'criminal' is not the fact that he has committed a crime (because non-criminals have done that also) but the fact that he was caught, tried, convicted and punished" [Doleschal and Klapmuts, 1973: 610, quoting Kutchinsky].

The step from this conclusion to the delinquency amplification portion of labelling theory is very short indeed: "It is becoming increasingly clear that most criminals are created through a process of discriminatory selection, ostracizing stigmatization, and dehumanizing punishments" (Doleschal and Klapmuts, 1973: 612).

The findings of self-report research do pose problems for the traditional perspective. This perspective has relied heavily on the assumption of a strong negative relation between social class and delinquency, and various theoretical adjustments have been required. However, this much is certain: The traditional perspective has survived the self-report technique and has, in fact, thrived on it. Further, the results of self-report research are, in the main, consistent with the results of research based on official measures of delinquency, when the focus is on correlates or causes (Nettler, 1974: 82).

These facts pose problems for the unqualified interpretation of self-report research as vindicating the labelling view. These problems, in turn, lead us to question the labelling theorist's interpretation of the results of self-report research. They interpret this research as showing that delinquency is "extremely common," that "noncriminals" have also committed criminal acts, that "most youngsters . . . engage in acts that could be labeled delinquent" (Schur, 1973: 157). The grain of truth in this interpretation is then allowed to obscure larger, more important, and more accurate truths: What self-report research does show is *variation* in the frequency and seriousness of delinquent behavior. At one end of the continua of frequency and seriousness are a good many boys and especially girls who have done little or nothing in the way of delinquency. They are almost saints. And anyone attempting to apply a delinquency "label" to them would stand a good chance of being accurately labelled a nut.[9] As we move along our continua of frequency and seriousness of delinquent acts, the number of boys and especially girls who are still with us diminishes rapidly. The proportion having been picked up by the police also begins to increase with some rapidity, but on the whole we are not yet dealing with persons sufficiently "delinquent" that they would be considered candidates for reformation in an institution. Finally, we get to boys and very few girls who have committed a good many delinquent offenses. The chances that they have been picked up by the police on more than one occasion are very good, and there is a strong likelihood that a juvenile court judge might consider placement of some kind were they to come before him or her repeatedly in a short span of time. Finally, there is a very small group (almost all boys) not around for interviewing or filling out questionnaires. Some are already in institutions. Others are currently being sought. If located, we can safely guess that some of them would remember (and may actually have committed) fewer delinquent acts than some of their cohort who have not had so much trouble with officials—but, on the whole, their self-reported delinquent behavior will be consistent with their troubles with officials. The members of this group are, to complete the story, almost crooks. And anyone so labelling them would stand a good chance of merely stating the obvious.

Studies of hidden or undetected crime have *not*, then, challenged the traditional distinction between criminals and noncriminals. They have challenged the "all or none" view of this distinction repeatedly (but almost always unjustly) imputed to the positivists.[10] The interpretation of these studies by anti-positivists suggests that the "all or none" view of criminality has survived, however. It is now in the sole possession of the anti-positivists—who have moved everyone to the "criminal" side of the ancient dichotomy. (This makes things easier for a theory that requires a large pool of potential delinquents.) Unfortunately, if we adopt this view we are no longer able to see the difference between a broken pencil and a broken skull, and we are forced to ignore much good research which shows important and systematic differences between those who commit many and those who commit few delinquent acts.

Since everyone does not do it with equal frequency and seriousness, the conclusion that "most criminals are created through a process of discriminatory selection, ostracizing stigmatization, and dehumanizing punishments" is, at least, premature.

If the data will not support the view of the labelling theorist that variation in delinquency is simply created by differential response to persons whose behavior is identical, still the discrepancies between behavioral and official measures of delinquency would seem to provide the theory room to operate.

There are other good reasons for thinking the theory should find in juvenile delinquency an ideal situation. As everyone knows, the juvenile justice system was explicitly constructed to give the kindly agents of the state a relatively free hand in dealing with the problems of children. This system was authorized to take into account the needs of the child, his or her probable future behavior, and so on through a long list of considerations that would seem to allow or even require bias or discrimination on the part of officials. As Edwin Schur (1973: 121) puts it, "The philosophy of the juvenile court . . . virtually ensures that stereotypes will influence judicial dispositions."

Given the philosophy of the juvenile justice system, and given that "attention . . . to what *others* are doing or have done and not simply to what the deviating individual has done–is clearly a hallmark of the labeling approach," (Schur, 1971: 28), we would expect to find considerable support for at least one aspect of labelling theory in research on official processing of juveniles. What does this research show?

SELECTION OF DELINQUENTS BY THE JUVENILE JUSTICE SYSTEM

Research on the processing of juveniles by official agencies shows that, on the whole, the major determinant of the severity of the social reaction is the seriousness and frequency of the child's delinquent behavior.[11] It shows, further, that the system is inclined to err in the direction of labelling the guilty innocent.[12] In other words, the system appears to follow a legal rather than a medical model of decision-making: It appears to assume that incorrectly labelling a child delinquent is a potentially costly mistake. Some of those who have done research into what others do to the child have characterized an important part of the juvenile justice system, the police, as overwhelmingly *reactive* rather than *proactive*, as responding to complaints about juvenile misbehavior rather than seeking out such misbehavior on the part of the child (for a useful summary, see Hagan, 1972). The labelers are not nearly as aggressive as the labelling theory leads us to expect, and the child labelled delinquent is much more likely to deserve the label than this theory suggests.

The most widely cited study of police discretion in the labelling literature is probably Piliavin and Briar's "Police Encounters with Juveniles" (1964), which investigates the effects of the child's demeanor on the severity of disposition in the field. References to this study in the literature typically exaggerate the findings in the direction of the labelling theory. For example: "*Demeanor* has . . . been shown to be a factor in differential arrest rates among first and minor offenders by Piliavin and Briar, in that truculence and uncooperativeness were shown to be more crucial than offense in the use of police discretion over outcome" (Downe and Rock, 1971).

The statement that demeanor was more important than offense takes on a different meaning when it is recalled that offense did not vary in this study. Therefore, anything and everything will be more important than offense in determining the severity of disposition. Piliavin and Briar (1964: 209) themselves contribute to such misreading of their results. They say: "Analysis of the distribution of police disposition decisions about juveniles revealed that in virtually every category of offense the full range of official disposition alternatives available to officers was employed."

If we are concerned with the relative contribution of offense and demeanor to severity of disposition, we must be wary of such facts. Piliavin and Briar's statement is consistent with a relation between offense and severity of disposition that we might be able to characterize as *incredibly* strong.[13]

In the Piliavin and Briar study, four percent of cooperative and sixty-seven percent of uncooperative boys were arrested by the police, with arrest being the most serious disposition available. Relations of this magnitude are rare in social science research, but it is not good policy to question a relation on the grounds that it is too strong. It is fair to say, however, that studies which focus on the "error" component in official decision-making without simultaneous consideration of the "accuracy" component tell us little about either. If, as Piliavin and Briar suggest, the seriousness of the offense and prior record were important police considerations, we would have to remove the effects of these variables before we could adequately judge the independent contribution of demeanor.

Subsequent research by Black and Reiss (1970) has considerably reduced the importance of the demeanor component in arrest. For one thing, antagonistic behavior toward the police was relatively rare. For another, the difference in the probability of arrest between "civil" and "antagonistic" boys was less then ten percent rather than the more than sixty percent difference reported by Piliavin and Briar. Finally, Black and Reiss found that juvenile suspects who were *very* deferential to the police were also slightly more likely to be arrested. Although Black and Reiss too were unable to control for the seriousness of the offense, they make it clear that seriousness was an important element in the decision.

Even so, fairness requires that we grant demeanor some impact on the extent of official processing independent of the "delinquency" of the child. It makes sense that it should have at least some potential impact, and such a finding would offer an opportunity to examine further the "deviance amplification" portion of labelling theory.

What does it mean in our culture to be a "delinquent"? What, in other words, does the process of "creating the delinquent" create? The labelling theorist's answer to the latter question is presumably that what is created is the *stereotype* of the delinquent. The person becomes the thing he or she is alleged to be. The gap between the stereotype and what the person really is is filled in by the labelling process. The assumption, then, is that the stereotype is in error (for a critical examination of this assumption, see Mackie, 1973).

What is the stereotype of the delinquent? One element of the stereotype is that the delinquent is tough, mean, disrespectful of authority. Piliavin and Briar's research is clear on this point. But if, as their research also shows, the police select such persons for the delinquent role, it can hardly be said that the effort at control created them. On the contrary, it appears they were "out there" all the time, and the police, according to this research, have merely located and certified their existence. As yet, then, we have no evidence that the police are any more "responsible" for the existence of persons who fit the stereotype of the delinquent than the scientist is responsible for the weight of a rock he or she holds.

(It could be argued, of course, that such "toughness" is not "delinquency." I am inclined to agree, but since such an argument presupposes the existence of delinquency, I am not sure it could be made by a labelling theorist. There is a further evidential problem: "Toughness" toward the police has been shown to be strongly correlated with "delinquency" [Hirschi, 1969: 200-202]. Therefore, even if we found that those overselected by the police were more likely subsequently to be "delinquent"–i.e., to commit delinquent acts–we would still have difficulty ascribing this difference to the actions of the police. Methodological problems of this sort are not evidence against a theory. They do, however, raise a worthwhile question: How is the labelling theorist able to "observe" processes whose workings tax the most sophisticated research designs we are able to construct?)

Subsequent steps in the official processing of juveniles include the possibility of referral to probation, to the juvenile court, and, eventually, commitment to an institution. Several studies have addressed the question of extralegal bias at these points, focusing especially on the effects of race and socioeconomic status (Terry, 1967; Thornberry, 1973; McEachern and Bauzer, 1967; Goldman, 1963; Hohenstein, 1969; Cohen, 1974; Wolfgang et al., 1972). All find the legal variables to be strongly related to severity of disposition. Most conclude that the extralegal variables have no independent effect on severity of disposition when the legal variables (e.g., seriousness of offense, number of prior offenses, attitude of complainant) are taken into account (e.g., Terry, 1967; McEachern and Bauzer, 1967). The exception is a study of Thornberry (1973) based on the excellent data collected in Philadelphia by Wolfgang, et al. (1972).[14] Thornberry (1973: 98) concludes that the effects of race and socioeconomic status "did not disappear when the legal variables were held constant."

It is possible to question Thornberry's finding on methodological grounds. For example, it is only elliptically true that the legal variables were "held constant." The categories of "number of previous offenses" used in the tables are "none," "1-2," and "3 or more." Since nonwhites in the total sample had committed considerably more delinquent offenses than whites, it follows that, with the exception of "none," the nonwhites have a higher *average* number of previous offenses within each category. (Perhaps not incidentally, the difference in severity of disposition between whites and nonwhites is smallest in the "none" category, a finding contrary to the usual finding that discretion is reduced as the frequency and seriousness of offense increases.) This residual variation would, then, account for some of the variation in severity of disposition attributable to race, which variation is not strikingly large to begin with.

Still, it is unlikely that refining the analysis would remove all of the white-nonwhite differences in severity of disposition. Wolfgang et al. (1972: 230) report "splitting and splicing" the same data in a variety of ways without eliminating the difference." The basic finding is certainly plausible. It stands to reason that, at least at some time in some jurisdictions, nonwhites, lower-class kids, and kids from broken homes are going to be more likely to receive extensive processing. If we admit an occasional reliance on extralegal considerations, we can raise the question of the implications of such a fact for the labelling theory.

We could say Thornberry's data show that, at least in some jurisdictions, *lower-class kids, blacks, and perhaps kids from broken homes are more likely to receive, free, the treatment and rehabilitative services of the state.*

I summarize such facts in these terms to emphasize that their interpretation is a matter of evidence rather than bald theoretical assertion. To assume that discrimination is prima facie evidence of or for labelling is to beg the important and interesting questions.[15] If the treatment of delinquents works, if attempts to rehabilitate them are successful, if, in other words, they are able to lead richer and fuller lives as a consequence of an affirmative action policy, we may of course call such effects "labelling," but the theory will have survived only because it is consistent with all possible configurations of events.

DOES TREATMENT WORK?

The Quakers played an important part in the institutionalization of the treatment perspective in the United States. In 1971, the Quaker authors of the *The Struggle for Justice* (American Friends Service Committee, 1971) report being pleased that treatment of offenders has proved unsuccessful. The Attorney General of the United States is quoted as saying that although he was "a firm believer in rehabilitation and probation when he was working in Ohio 20 years ago," he is now convinced that the concept of rehabilitation is a "myth" (Times Record, 1974). The positivists are generally credited with supplying the scientific rationale for the treatment perspective. Sheldon and Eleanor Glueck (1968: 166), positivists indeed, reported on a fifteen-year follow-up of almost 500 delinquents:

> Another basic matter to be inferred from the evidence is that the efforts of the sociolegal apparatus to 'reform' and 'rehabilitate,' or at least 'deter,' the offenders involved, do not seem on the whole to have done as much good as the operations of Mother Nature and Father Time.

In 1973, Eugene Doleschal and Nora Klapmuts (self-designated Consciousness III Criminologists, who would here be called labelling theorists) seem pleased to report the following:

> True successes in rehabilitation have been virtually non-existent. A survey of all studies of correctional treatment published between 1945 and 1967 found that the present array of correctional treatment efforts has no appreciable effect—*either positive or negative*—on the recidivism rates of convicted offenders. In another review of numerous correctional programs, Robison and Smith concluded that there is no evidence to support claims of superior rehabilitative efficacy of any correctional alternative over another. This conclusion is supported by

> the most sophisticated research studies: generally, the more rigorously scientific the methodology the less likely is success to be reported [1973: 610].

My inclination in the face of such apparent unanimity is to think otherwise. My background also inclines me in the same direction—that is, toward a defense of treatment on the grounds that it has never really been given a fair chance. (For a summary of the responses of positivists to the alleged failure of the treatment perspective, see Doleschal and Klapmuts, 1973: 609.) Further, I know competent social scientists of divergent theoretical persuasions whose enthusiastic and optimistic support of a particular treatment strategy I would be reluctant to dismiss out of hand. Finally, my limited acquaintance with the literature on treatment suggests the possibility that not every success reported there can be easily explained away.

Still, it seems to me that, for present purposes, the conclusion that treatment does not work is sufficient. In fact, I would like very briefly to summarize three excellent studies that seem to support this conclusion. The first is the justly famous Cambridge-Somerville Youth Study (McCord and McCord, 1959). The plan of this treatment program was to prevent delinquency from ever developing. To this end, pairs of young boys were carefully matched and then randomly assigned to experimental and control groups. The experimental group was exposed over a six-year period to the best treatment then (1939-1945) available. After many years of careful collection of follow-up data, and careful analysis, the conclusion remains the same: Boys exposed to treatment were as likely subsequently to commit criminal acts as boys denied such tender loving care.

In the Silverlake Experiment, Empey and Lubeck (1971) were able to employ random assignment and compare boys in a community treatment program with institutionalized controls. The "spontaneous remission" rate for both groups was very high (about seventy-three percent did not commit delinquent acts during the follow-up period), but Empey and Lubeck (1972: 200) conclude that the "outcomes [for the two programs] were essentially the same."

The Provo Experiment involved random assignment to various levels of treatment or diversion. Again, although large reductions in delinquent activity were achieved in all programs, Empey and Erickson (1972: 200) remain cautious about attributing differential effects to various levels of treatment. For example, they say:

> The evidence . . . indicates almost always that community intervention is at least as effective as incarceration.

> The more intensive experimental program at Provo did not seem to be greatly superior to regular probation.

These studies are rightly seen as bearing on the treatment perspective. They are, and they will remain, serious blows to this perspective. Treatment does not seem to matter, whether it comes before or after a pattern of delinquency has been established. Further, it appears that no matter what is done to "delinquents," in the days that follow they almost invariably, as a group, get better.[16]

In the traditional or positivistic approach to delinquency, there is no necessary connection between theories of causation and programs of treatment. If the broken home causes delinquency, this does not mean that after the child has become delinquent it would be useful to repair the break. The traditional perspective can thus survive the failure of treatment programs, and it has clearly done so.

Can the same be said of the labelling perspective? The error in most discussions of labelling and delinquency, it seems to me, enters with the assumption that relevant data are not currently available. In fact, the treatment perspective has been intensively researched. The literature is full of assessments of the effectiveness of various correctional programs for delinquents. We have seen that the widely shared conclusion is that all of them have no effect on subsequent delinquency.

If treatment programs have no effect, then they have no effect. Now recall the fundamental assertions of the labelling theory: The process of creating the criminal is a process of tagging, segregating, emphasizing, evoking. The entire process is mischievious. And so on. Apparently, these assertions are not true. Evidence that the juvenile justice system has no effect on the subsequent delinquency of the child is not evidence that it has effects elsewhere.

Unfortunately for the labelling perspective, its theory of causation is directly linked to and can be tested by evaluation of the treatment program it recommends. This program is explicit in the theory: "The less said about [the bad behavior] the better" (Tannenbaum, 1938: 20). Or, "Leave the kids alone wherever possible" (Schur, 1973: 155). This treatment program has been more or less incidentally tested many, many times. Treatment and correctional alternatives can be ranked in terms of how much they say to the child; in terms of the extent to which they leave kids alone. When we rank them in these ways, we discover, since "treatment" does not work, that differential "labelling" also and by definition also has no effect. We may of course decide on a number of grounds that it is best to leave kids alone. But we cannot justify this choice on the grounds that paying attention to them is deleterious, that "stigmatization" is going to increase the probability of delinquency.

SUMMARY AND CONCLUSIONS

A good deal of this paper is devoted to Tannenbaum's original labelling theory of delinquency because the "grounding" of a theory is rightly taken to be an important clue to its ability to survive subsequent testing. Unless a theory can organize the empirical generalizations of the past, there is little reason to hope that it will be able to predict the empirical generalizations of the future. The lack of evidence for Tannenbaum's labelling theory, and the minor role this theory plays in his own explanation of juvenile delinquency, are thus cause for serious concern.

Tannenbaum's theory focuses on delinquency amplification resulting from the action of officials. Research subsequent to Tannenbaum has focused on the extent to which the social reaction is based on the behavior of the child (primary deviance) as opposed to the conceptions of officials (the delinquent stereotype). This research shows that the major determinant of the social reaction is the delinquent behavior of the child. Although many "potential delinquents" do not receive the official processing, they may, in some sense, have earned, the "victims" of official processing tend to have it coming. Subsequent research has thus shown that the potential for delinquency amplification in the system as it now operates is limited by the basic accuracy of the labels it applies. (An accurate label presumably has little effect.)

Research on the treatment of delinquents generally reveals little or no effect, one way or the other. The main finding appears to be that "spontaneous remission" occurs in the bulk of cases. While the treatment perspective can take little comfort from these facts, they seem to be even more damaging to the labelling theory, which predicts both positive harm from excessive treatment and progressive amplification of "delinquency" with the passage of time.

Delinquency appears in many ways to provide an ideal setting for application of labelling notions. Delinquents are, after all, young and therefore presumably impressionable; in dealing with them, the agents of the state have, in comparison with adult criminals, a relatively free hand. And so on. Yet the labelling theory appears to be off the mark on almost every aspect of delinquency it is asked to predict or explain. Perhaps it is because "by and large, types of deviation that tend not to be repeated or to undergo elaboration are difficult to 'explain' in labeling terms," (Schur, 1971: 27) and delinquency is just such a deviation. But I am more inclined to think it is because labelling theory has prospered in an atmosphere of contempt for the results of careful research. Little wonder that such research is now returning the compliment!

NOTES

1. The terms I use to refer to approaches "opposed" to labelling theory include "traditional," "conventional," and "positivist." By and large, these are the terms used by labelling theorists themselves in characterizing their opponents. Stripped of its association with Lombroso, the most accurate is probably "positivist"–in the sense that until, say, ten years ago, all criminology was positivistic in orientation.

2. Tannenbaum's debt to the Chicago school, particularly to the work of W. I. Thomas and Frederick Thrasher, is apparent. In this respect, Tannenbaum and later labelling theorists have common ancestry. His theory is not an example of independent invention.

3. Illustrative of the gap between labelling theorist and traditional research is the statement of Clara F. Chassell (1935: 470) published three years before Tannenbaum's assertion that intelligence has no demonstrated relation to crime: "The relation between morality and intellect in the general population . . . may be expected to fall below .70."

4. Consistency is not Tannenbaum's long suit. Even in the chapter in which he presents his labelling theory, he tells us, "By the time the individual has become a criminal his habits have been so shaped that we have a fairly integrated character whose whole career is in tune with the peculiar bit of environment for which he has developed the *behavior and habits that cause him to be apprehended*" (1938: 21; italics added).

5. Recent research is consistent with Tannenbaum's failure to find material illustrative of his main thesis. After interviewing boys with recent police and court contacts, Foster et al. (1972) conclude, "Little empirical evidence can be found to support the notion delinquent boys who have encountered public intervention actually perceive at the time of intervention the negative effects attributed to stigma, either in terms of interpersonal relationships with family, friends, or teachers, or social structural limitations in terms of education or employment."

6. Tannenbaum employs the strictest of methodological standards when criticizing the work of others. Unfortunately, he does not hold himself to such standards.

7. Note that (if I am correct) the "return" of labelling theory to the delinquency area did not result so much from the pressure of research findings or from the existence of otherwise inexplicable facts as from the pressure of "important theory." The "every man his own theorist" syndrome does not characterize delinquency research.

8. The results of research on socioeconomic status and self-reported delinquency are often characterized as "contradictory," and there is much discussion in the literature of ways and means of resolving these contradications. Actually, from a broader perspective, the results are remarkably consistent. Only occasionally is socioeconomic status found to be related to delinquent behavior; in these cases the relations are uniformly weak and, more importantly, are both positive and negative.

9. Williams and Gold (1972: 215) report on a national sample of adolescents: "Since 60 percent of the total group had a zero score on seriousness of delinquent behavior, they were assigned to the 'less seriously delinquent' category."

10. Recall the "God and Devil" underpinnings of positivism described by Tannenbaum. More recently, Matza (1964: 11-12) has argued that one of the defining characteristics of the positivist view is that it assumes that the delinquent is "fundamentally

different" from the law-abiding. Even some of its critics now grant that this conception of positivism is simply in error. To the positivist, "criminality is a . . . continous trait of the same kind as intelligence, or height, or weight" (Eysenck, 1970: 62, quoted by Taylor et al., 1973: 25).

11. "The disposition pattern for juvenile suspects clearly follows the hierarchy of offenses found in the criminal law, the law for adults" (Black and Reiss, 1970: 68).

12. "Even when the police have very persuasive situational evidence they generally release juveniles in the field; but, when they do arrest juveniles, they almost always have evidence of some kind" (Black and Reiss, 1970: 74).

13. For a brief discussion of police disposition practices in the city studied by Piliavin and Briar, based on an independent set of data, see Hirschi (1969: 68).

14. The Thornberry (1973) and Wolfgang et al. (1972) studies report basically the same results from a common body of data. Thornberry's published analysis is slightly more detailed than Wolfgang's and is therefore considered here.

15. I do not propose that "generous interpretations of racial differences in disposition" are more valid than those which assume prejudice and bias (cf. Wolfgang et al., 1972: 220-221). Here, as elsewhere (a fact labelling theorists should appreciate), discrimination is a complex business whose workings are not well described or even necessarily properly evaluated by attaching a label to them. For example, Cohen (1974: 289) concludes that his findings "largely contradict the assumption of the . . . labeling theorists with respect to who is apt to be accorded severe sanctions ('labeled') and on what bases these sanctions are accorded by social control agents." Yet the juvenile justice system Cohen studied produces the input-output differences that made labelling theory plausible in the first place, and the processes producing these differences could, *after the fact,* be interpreted using a labelling perspective.

16. Studies by Gold (1970) and Williams and Gold (1972) suggest that apprehension by the police produces an increase in the number of offenses subsequently committed. In both studies, an apprehended offender was matched with an unapprehended offender on such things as sex, race, age, date of offense resulting in apprehension, number of prior offenses, and subsequent delinquent activity examined. In both studies, the apprehended offender was likely to have committed subsequently a greater number of offenses than his unapprehended control. (In the "national [1969] study, this was true for 20 of the 35 pairs, with 5 committing an equal number, and 10 committing fewer offenses during the period following apprehension"; in the 1970 study, "the data demonstrate that in 11 of the 20 pairs, the apprehended youngsters went on to commit more offenses than the unapprehended youngsters, in four they committed less, and in five the same number.") Since both studies suffer from the same design problem, the striking similarity in results may well be grounds for suspicion rather than confidence. In both studies it was found that "the more delinquent the youngster is, the more likely he is to be apprehended." In other words, the apprehended offender pool is "more delinquent" than the pool of unapprehended offenders. Thus, when a "match" is achieved between apprehended and unapprehended offenders on number of prior offenses, it is likely that the apprehended offender is "less delinquent" than the entire pool of apprehended offenders, and it is also likely that the unapprehended offender is "more delinquent" than the entire pool of unapprehended offenders from which he or she is drawn. Therefore, it is also likely that, when compared on some further measure of delinquency (such as the number of subsequent offenses), both groups will *regress* "toward the mean of the particular population to which they belong" (see Edwards, 1954: 259-288). Such regression effects made the results of these two studies at least in

part a statistical necessity. In the first of them (Gold, 1970), Gold refers to Edwards (1954) and acknowledges the possibility of regression effects. He reports that "two additional procedures were followed to guard against being misled. First, apprehended youngsters were matched with another set of unapprehended youngsters, with the same result. Second, the analysis was run backward: apprehended youngsters were matched with a set of unapprehended youngsters who committed an equal number of offenses subsequent to the formers' apprehension; then the number of offenses prior to the apprehension date were compared. Apprehended youngsters were reliably less delinquent prior to their apprehension than their controls" (Gold, 1970: 113). Since the first of these procedures merely replicates the questionable design, it does nothing to increase confidence in the results. On the contrary, it may merely establish the robustness of the regression phenomenon. The second procedure seems reasonable in principle as a device to assess the extent of the regression problem. However, the description of this analysis and of the results does not provide sufficient detail to allow anything more than speculation. And the failure to repeat the procedure in the Williams-Gold study is inexplicable given previous acknowledgement of the problem. I conclude that these studies have not demonstrated an "apprehension effect."

REFERENCES

Akers, Ronald L.
1964 "Socio-economic status and delinquent behavior: a retest." Journal of Research in Crime and Delinquency 1: 38-46.

American Friends Service Committee
1971 The Struggle for Justice. New York: Hill & Wang.

Becker, Howard S.
1963 Outsiders. New York: Free Press.

Black, Donald J. and Albert J. Reiss, Jr.
1970 "Police control of juveniles." American Sociological Review 35 (February): 63-77.

Chapman, Dennis
1968 Sociology and the Stereotype of the Criminal. London: Tavistock.

Chassell, Clara F.
1935 The Relation Between Morality and Intellect. New York: Columbia University Press.

Cohen, Lawrence E.
1974 "Conferring the delinquent label: the relative importance of social characteristics and legal factors in the processing of juveniles." Ph.D. dissertation. University of Washington.

Doleschal, Eugene and Nora Klapmuts
1973 "Toward a new criminology." Crime and Delinquency Literature (December): 607-626.

Downes, David and Paul Rock
1971 "Social reaction to deviance and its effects on crime and criminal careers." British Journal of Sociology 22 (December): 351-64.

Edwards, E. L.
1954 "Experiments: their planning and execution." Pp. 259-288 in G. Lindzey (ed.) Handbook of Social Psychology. Reading, Mass.: Addison-Wesley.

Empey, LaMar T. and Maynard L. Erickson
1972 The Provo Experiment. Lexington, Mass.: D. C. Heath.
Empey, LaMar T. and Steven G. Lubeck
1971 The Silverlake Experiment. Chicago: Aldine-Atherton.
Erickson, Maynard L. and LaMar T. Empey
1963 "Court records, undetected delinquency and decision-making." Journal of Criminal Law, Criminology and Police Science 54 (December): 456-469.
Eysenck, Hans
1970 Crime and Personality. London: Paladin.
Foster, Jack Donald et al.
1972 "Perceptions of stigma following public intervention for delinquent behavior." Social Problems 20 (Fall): 202-209.
Glueck, Sheldon and Eleanor Glueck
1964 Ventures in Criminology. Cambridge, Mass.: Harvard University Press.
1968 Delinquents and Nondelinquents in Perspective. Cambridge, Mass.: Harvard University Press.
Gold, Martin
1970 Delinquent Behavior in an American City. Belmont, Calif.: Brooks/Cole.
Goldman, Nathan
1963 The Differential Selection of Juvenile Offenders for Court Appearance. New York: National Council on Crime and Delinquency.
Hagan, John L.
1972 "The labeling perspective, the delinquent and the police." Canadian Journal of Criminology and Corrections 14 (April): 150-165.
Hirschi, Travis
1969 Causes of Delinquency. Berkeley: University of California Press.
Hohenstein, William F.
1969 "Factors influencing the police disposition of juvenile offenders." Pp. 138-149 in Thorsten Sellin and Marvin E. Wolfgang (eds.) Delinquency: Selected Studies. New York: John Wiley.
Lemert, Edwin M.
1951 Social Pathology. New York: McGraw-Hill.
Lofland, John
1969 Deviance and Identity. Englewood Cliffs, N.J.: Prentice-Hall.
McCord, William and Joan McCord
1959 Origins of Crime. New York: Columbia University Press.
McEachern, A. W. and Riva Bauzer
1967 "Factors related to disposition in juvenile police contacts." Pp. 148-160 in Malcolm W. Klein and Barbara G. Myerhoff (eds.) Juvenile Gangs in Context. Englewood Cliffs, N.J.: Prentice-Hall.
Mackie, Marlene
1973 "Arriving at 'truth' by definition: the case of the stereotype inaccuracy." Social Problems 20 (Spring): 431-447.
Matza, David
1964 Delinquency and Drift. New York: John Wiley.
Nettler, Gwynn
1974 Explaining Crime. New York: McGraw-Hill.
Nye, F. Ivan, James F. Short, and Virgil J. Olson
1958 "Socioeconomic status and delinquent behavior." American Journal of Sociology 63 (January): 381-389.

Piliavin, Irving and Scott Briar
1964 "Police encounters with juveniles." American Journal of Sociology 70 (September): 206-214.
Schur, Edwin M.
1973 Radical Non-Intervention: Rethinking the Delinquency Problem. Englewood Cliffs, N.J.: Prentice-Hall.
1971 Labeling Deviant Behavior. New York: Harper & Row.
Tannenbaum, Frank
1938 Crime and the Community. Boston: Ginn.
Taylor, Ian et al.
1973 The New Criminology. New York: Harper & Row.
Terry, Robert M.
1967 "Discrimination in the handling of juvenile offenders by social-control agencies." Journal of Research in Crime and Delinquency 4 (July): 218-230.
Thornberry, Terence P.
1973 "Race, socioeconomic status and sentencing in the juvenile justice system." Journal of Criminal Law and Criminology 64: 90-98.
Times Record
1974 Troy, New York. October 1.
Williams, Jay R. and Martin Gold
1972 "From delinquent behavior to official delinquency." Social Problems 20 (Fall): 209-229.
Wolfgang, Marvin, M. Figlio, and T. Sellin
1972 Delinquency in a Birth Cohort. Chicago: University of Chicago Press.

Chapter 8

BEYOND SECONDARY DEVIANCE: NEGATIVE LABELLING AND ITS EFFECTS ON THE HEROIN ADDICT

WILLIAM E. McAULIFFE

Conflict between the needs of individual actors and the social order is always a fundamental problem for sociological analysis, and today nowhere is the struggle more desperate or the issues so in need of clarification than in the case of narcotics addiction. Systems of socialization and social control as means of tempering and channeling egoistic desires must be more elaborate where pleasures are greater and therefore the incentive to resist more powerful. Drug-induced pleasure may be the strongest of all, even beyond sexual pleasure, and attempts to avoid its controls are to be expected. This resistance, often including a wide range and extensive amounts of criminal activity, makes addiction a particularly interesting topic for the study of secondary deviance.

Addiction and the Two Kinds of Secondary Deviance

In what he refers to as the "broad interpretation" of the secondary deviance perspective, Schur (1971) has distinguished two levels of analysis: the first, which I shall refer to as the "societal-reaction" level, is said to include "all diverse societal definitions of and responses to the behavior"

AUTHOR'S NOTE: I wish to acknowledge the help of Robert A. Gordon, who designed and directed the addict study, Joseph Adams, who recruited and interviewed the addicts, Susan G. Doering, who helped in ways too numerous to mention, and Neil S. Coleman, who took part in the data analysis.

(p. 22); and the second, "direct negative labelling," occurs at the social-psychological level. Most discussions of addiction have been conducted at the societal-reaction level, focusing upon what is usually known as the "criminalization" of addiction (e.g., Schur, 1964). In fact, although direct negative labelling of addicts is frequently mentioned (e.g., Rubington, 1968) and handy anecdotes describing it are used as illustrations of the labelling process, its consequences in terms of secondary deviance and social control have only rarely been discussed in detail (e.g., Ray, 1961; Glatt et al., 1967: 23). Consequently, there is no fully articulated labelling theory of addiction, and many basic empirical questions concerning the labelling of addicts also remain unanswered: Who in a community knows about the addict's deviant identity? How do the various members of the addict's world react to this discovery initially, and over the long run? What is the addict's response to this negative labelling, especially when he or she may actually define the label in positive terms? Fortunately, I am able to present original data from a recent study of addicts to help fill these gaps. After doing so, we shall be in a better position to evaluate the secondary deviance approach to drug addiction, including issues at the societal-reaction level of analysis.

METHODS

The respondents in this study were fifty-nine male addicts (thirty white and twenty-nine black) recruited in Baltimore over a period of four years from 1966 to 1970. Inspection of an ecological study of drug arrest rates (Nurco and Balter, 1969: 93-96) had revealed that addicts were concentrated by race and class into distinct islands of contiguous census tracts or "epidemic areas" (Chein et al., 1964: 39), and that these areas could serve as clusters for sampling purposes. Within each of four clusters, our participant observer found the main "copping site"—the bar, parking lot, or street corner where the addicts congregated to buy drugs or simply to hang out (Hughes and Jaffe, 1971). By personal contacts made primarily through a methadone program, he gained entry into the addict communities in each place, and when sufficient rapport was achieved (see Berk and Adams, 1970, for the techniques employed), he interviewed respondents over twenty-one years of age who were currently dependent on illicitly obtained opiates and who had long histories of addiction. A structured interview schedule was used, and the interviews were tape recorded.

Most urban addicts can be reached by using copping sites as fieldwork stations (Hughes et al., 1971), and samples thus recruited have been representative of the modal patterns of known heroin addict populations in all major respects. The respondents in our sample were all lower class, and most were currently unemployed and involved in crime. Only a small number (eight) were married heads of household. The respondents' extensive experience with opiates is described in Table 8.1. The gross length of time since physical dependence was 8.7 years on average, with a range of 1-24 years, and thus, all have been addicts long enough for labelling and societal-reaction processes to occur. When asked to complete the sentence "I am ______," the only response given by more than one respondent was "I am *a drug addict,*" which twenty-four of the subjects gave. Clearly, they have adopted the addict self-concept as a result of their own or someone else's labelling.

TABLE 8.1
DRUG ABUSE CHARACTERISTICS OF ADDICT RESPONDENTS

Characteristic	Mean	Range	SD
Age first tried an opiate, excluding codeine (years)	18.3	14-27.5	3.00
Age first recognized physical dependence (years)	20.2	15-28	3.09
Length of onset: first use to physical dependence (years)	1.9	0.0-8.5	2.04
Length of dependence: time since first recognition of dependence (years)	8.7	1-24	5.97
Daily cost of habit (dollars)	34.4	5-150	28.5

RESULTS

Being labelled "junkie" should, according to the theory, block legitimate opportunities and cause adoption of the addict role, with its normative expectations and behavioral guidelines. These structural changes have parallels at the interpersonal level, where the information-control techniques of the "discreditable" must be dropped for strategies appropriate for the "discredited" (Goffman, 1963). The extensiveness of these processes depends in part on what Goffman calls "knownaboutness"–that is, how widely a deviant's social identity is known. Being known about is not only a function of the deviant's own efforts to flaunt or conceal his discrediting trait and of the audience's interest in it, but is also a function of the efficiency of the record-keeping and transmitting systems. Recognizing individual variation in all these factors, one may still attempt to sketch broad trends for particular forms of deviance. In the case of addiction, for example, if we are to know how much to attribute to the effects of labelling, we can begin by testing our sense of how much labelling there actually is.

Our interview schedule contained a number of items on this issue. Information was obtained concerning public agencies, neighbors, friends, parents, and extended family. Respondents were asked whether their addict identity had been discovered, and if so, what had been the reaction. I will present results from these questions first. Addiction, it turns out, is generally a rather obtrusive form of deviance in the case of the street addict, and an enormous amount of stigmatization results. In the next section, I shall discuss the addict's response to the labelling process. Over the long run, it seems that the amount of secondary deviance produced may be minor compared to the amount of pressure placed on the addict to get out of the deviant life.

PUBLIC AGENCIES

In secondary-deviance analyses of other forms of deviance, such as mental illness, labelling by public agencies and institutions has been a topic of special interest, so I shall begin by examining it in the case of the addict. We asked our respondents whether they had ever been known as an addict to any public agencies and if so, which agencies.[1] The results are presented in Table 8.2.

Local police (particularly the narcotics squad) identified and recorded the names of ninety percent of these addicts, far more than any other public agency in Baltimore, and nearly all the respondents (ninety-three percent) said they became known to one or more criminal-justice agencies (which also include the Federal Bureau of Narcotics and Dangerous Drugs, courts, probation, parole, and prisons). Similar findings were reported by Robins and Murphy (1967: 1583). They found that every respondent who admitted regular heroin use in an interview study had a public record concerning drugs, and ninety percent had records relating to drugs with the police. Epidemiologists involved in developing narcotics registers in New York (Fishman et al., 1971: 566) and in Baltimore (Nurco and Balter, 1969) also found that the police were the source of the largest number of addict names. (Therefore, it is safe to assume that our asking about police specifically could not account for our results.)

It will be interesting to consider for a moment the details of an addict's becoming known to the police. From Table 8.2 it can be seen that only twenty-four percent of the sample were also known to the courts and correctional system, and in their answers only eight other respondents who

TABLE 8.2
AGENCIES TO WHICH ADDICTS ARE KNOWN

Agencies	% Known to Agency (N=59)
Criminal justice:	
Police	90
Federal Bureau of Narcotics and Dangerous Drugs	20
Courts and correctional system (parole, probation, prisons)	24
One or more criminal justice agency	93
Treatment:	
Methadone and other independent local programs	41
State mental hospitals	41
General hospitals	31
Public Health Service Hospital (Lexington)	20
Out-of-state general hospitals	8
One or more treatment agency	81
Miscellaneous	19

Number of Separate Agencies to Which an Addict Was Known	Frequency
0	1
1	6
2	15
3	13
4	9
5	8
6	4
7	0
8	2
9	1
	59

said they were known to the police also specificially mentioned being arrested and charged for a drug violation. Consequently, many may have been identified in so-called "investigations," private degradation ceremonies conducted for and by the members of the narcotics squad. Seven respondents actually reported that they were "pulled up" for an investigation only. Addict associates, who fear being informed upon, are probably the only other persons who even care or are aware of the occurrence of these events. Apparently, during these interrogations, it is the addict who usually applies the label to himself,[2] and one is tempted to infer that he had already adopted the addict role.[3] However, as we shall see below, addicts often value their deviant label, and my own observations suggest that being "pulled up" by the narcotics squad is an important part of feeling one is a "sure-enough junkie" and of claiming to be one among addict peers.

Public agencies other than those connected with the criminal justice systems also are involved in identifying and recording the names of drug abusers. The respondents in our study mentioned thirty-nine different agencies by name, and only nine were criminal justice institutions. Nearly four hundred different agencies report names to the New York Narcotics Register (Fishman et al., 1971), and Nurco and Balter (1969: 358) found that by canvassing many social agencies in Baltimore they were able to identify a sizable number of drug abusers not known to the police. It is notable, however, that they also commented that some agencies (e.g., schools) did not know and did not want to know who was using drugs, and other agencies (e.g., social work) were not interested in sharing information they had.

Most of our respondents (eighty-one percent) were known to one or more treatment agency, of which methadone programs and detoxification treatment at state mental hospitals were the most popular (forty-one percent naming each). Relatively few, twenty percent, made the trip to Lexington. Before methadone maintenance, detoxification in state mental hospitals was virtually the only treatment available locally.[4] When I talked with addicts about this form of treatment, they indicated that stays in these hospitals were often very brief, in part because the addicts did not like "being put in with all those crazy people."

One aspect of being on a methadone program or going to Lexington is the opportunity to mingle with so many other addicts, which has obvious consequences for full development of an addict's identity and feeling of social support (Schur, 1971: 1). Another relevant feature of methadone maintenance which has not been discussed before is an interesting form of labelling negotiation in which the usual roles are reversed. In an instance of it I once witnessed, a middle-class occasional heroin user whom I had known since high school approached me for help getting on a methadone program. He explained that although he had never been physically dependent, he felt he could not longer control his desire for the drug. He was afraid he would soon get arrested if he continued using heroin, and he wanted to get on a program instead. After unsuccessfully trying to convince him to try a drug-free therapy, I went along with him to a methadone program, one which happened to serve primarily black lower-class drug addicts. The intake clerk, herself a patient, first asked my friend how bad his habit was. He began explaining his situation when she interrupted, "You're not strung out? You can't get on this program, because you're not an addict."

"What do you mean? I am an addict! I know whether I'm an addict or not," he replied angrily. The clerk smiled at him but remained unconvinced, and when further discussion proved futile, we left. A resourceful, white, middle-class male had thus failed in his effort to secure the highly deviant label he hoped for and, ironically, his rejection came at the hands of a black, lower-class female. As far as my friend was concerned he was acting like an addict and sincerely felt he was entitled to the label. I learned a few days later that he had been accepted by another methadone program set up in a middle-class, white area. He had learned what to say in the labelling negotiation.

Though this form of status negotiation may not be commonplace, the discussions between doctor and methadone patient for setting the dosage level of medication are similar, since in making a claim for large amounts of medication the addict is admitting to more deviance than the doctor may be willing to give him or her credit for. A related form of status negotiation, in which the individual makes assertions about his or her own deviant behavior which the audience may consider exaggerated, is an important part of gaining acceptance in an addict group by a drug novice. Yet this same user is likely to have resisted the "junkie" label when (s)he first experienced withdrawal sickness. Although knowing about withdrawal symptoms, the beginner may be unable or unwilling to recognize them in him- or herself at first. In many of our cases, another addict was credited with first applying the label. As Lindesmith (1968) was first to point out, from a labelling perspective this realization should have ramifications for the individual's self-concept and adoption of the addict role. Gillespie (1969) has found, however, that withdrawal symptoms had not been experienced by British heroin users who, like my friend, nevertheless considered themselves addicts. A whole range of criteria–including the amount of the largest dose ever taken, being unable to resist using the drug, and being "registered" at an addict clinic–were employed by the respondents as indicators of being addicted (also see Glatt et al., 1967). In some of these cases too, individuals sometimes sought the label and other times wanted to avoid it, depending on their purposes.

In classic public labelling episodes, such as in the case of commitment of the mentally ill, the deviant label on an unwilling recipient can result in his or her internalization of the public image and a consequent intensification of the behavior in question along with adoption of other aspects associated with the social role. Our data suggest that this was not the pattern in the case of the addict, although public labelling occurred frequently. The addict has usually adopted the addict label and role long before the first contact with the police or a treatment agency, and when he or she did appear before them, it was usually the addict who claimed the label rather than having it thrust upon him/her. The addict did so either to obtain preferred treatment (see McAuliffe and Gordon, 1974, on the addict's use of the sick role) or to claim a rightful status. Since many have been practicing addicts for two years or more, this official confirmation should have little impact psychologically. It is therefore unlikely that these episodes by themselves had any major effect on the addicts in terms of their self-concept, drug use, or subcultural participation, although below we shall see that being publicly labelled may have reverberations within the addict's informal social network.

Theoretically, another consequence of public labelling episodes would be that the individual's name was placed "on the record" of some agency, which then could use the information to block opportunities in the legitimate world and otherwise control him. The potential for such control would depend upon the thoroughness of the record-keeping systems, which, as we can see in the lower portion of Table 8.2, is considerable. Only one respondent of fifty-nine claimed not to be known to any agencies as an addict. At the other extreme, one respondent had his name recorded by nine different agencies. The mean number of agencies per respondent was 3.4. Thus, almost all street addicts admit their deviant identity to a public agency at least once, and usually the process is repeated many times. Of course, some sharing of information between agencies occurs, for example, when police inform the welfare department that a child has been born to an addicted mother, and when methadone programs check whether any of their patients are getting medication from more than one program.

Data from narcotics registers give perhaps the best indication of how efficient a public detection system can be. The names of fifty-three percent of the persons who died from narcotics overdoses were found listed in the New York Narcotics Register (Leveson, 1972), and the Maryland Narcotics Register has a substantially better percentage, approximately eighty percent (personal communication from Howard Silverman). Since overdose victims have abbreviated careers, we can view these percentages as the lower bound of the probability of becoming publicly labelled in the case of street addicts.

Although we collected no systematic data on the effect that being known to a public agency had on the addict, some general conclusions are possible. The fact that so many different treatment agencies are available and that they rarely share information or at least would not refuse treatment on the basis of an addict's experience with another agency shows that an addict has a large store of treatment opportunities to use up. In addition, the records of treatment agencies are rarely available to the public, so little control results on that count. Firsthand experience handling addicts as a probation officer has also convinced me that the information system between criminal justice agencies is relatively inefficient and exercises less control over an individual than is sometimes supposed. Nevertheless, arrest and incarceration for drug offenses and related crime cannot help but reduce the individual's opportunities in the legitimate world (see Ward, 1973: 29-32).

Unofficial Labelling of Addicts

Although most addicts apparently come into the public eye a number of times during their careers, these contacts are still relatively rare events, occurring an average of only once every 2.5 years in our sample. By contrast, our respondents crossed paths with labelling nonaddict members of their community every day. Passing as "normal" by other kinds of deviants is apparently rather easy in some cases, but we do not know how often addicts try and are able to pass on a full-time or regular basis. There is a widely held belief that certain types of addicts (e.g., white, middle-class) do manage to remain hidden at least from public view, and in fact there was recently a group of older addicts who had maintained a low community profile in New Orleans but who were drawn out by the availability of free methadone (Pascarelli, 1972). On the other hand, street addicts, such as the respondents in our study, should be among the most visible, not only to the official agencies but also to the immediate community. We shall see, however, that their deviant status is not known universally, and perhaps what is more important, the reactions to this knowledge seem to vary considerably.

Forming Impressions of Deviants

How attaching a label to a person affects the impression his or her audience has is a fundamental part of societal-reaction theory. Goffman (1963), for example, assumes that the audience judges each individual against a set of ideals. Discovery of a marked discrepancy between the actual person and the ideal is discrediting, and this bad news may be brought to the attention of the rest of the collectivity in a variety of ways, including a formal degradation ceremony. According to Garfinkel's (1972: 55) analysis, if the accusation sticks, the individual "becomes in the eyes of his condemners literally a different and *new* person. It is not that the new attributes are added to the old 'nucleus.' He is not changed, he is reconstituted." We should realize that this same cognitive process should also be the way by which the deviant forms a self-conception.

Garfinkel's views closely parallel ideas found in the social-psychology literature under the rubric of "personality impression formation." The earliest work in this area was done by Solomon Asch (1946), who also believed that each new bit of information resulted in a completely new gestalt or reinterpreted cognitive structure. He claimed to have demonstrated that changing only one of six adjectives describing a hypothetical person caused subjects to infer a wide range of different traits. However, few psychologists have been satisfied with Asch's conclusions, primarily because of the unpredictability they implied, and in subsequent studies of impression formation most researchers have employed additive or averaging models to predict their results (Fishbein, 1967: 489; Anderson, 1971). These same models have also been of interest to sociologists trying to explain prestige (Himmelfarb and Senn, 1969) and to those studying the formation of impressions of groups (Rosnow and Arms, 1968). In most cases, the additive models have predicted the experimental results reasonably well, although introducing elements with extremely low ratings (which is what a stigma is) into the trait sets has resulted in noticeable departures from simple linear models (Willis, 1960; Bossart and Di Vesta, 1964).

One exception to the additive models is Hamblin's multiplicative power function (Hamblin and Smith, 1966), which is the miltivariate extension of Stevens's Psychophysical Law (Stevens, 1960). According to this model (which seems to embody the interactive feature of Garfinkel's and Asch's hypotheses), a handsome, intelligent, considerate, and wealthy heroin addict would probably receive a low evaluation despite his four very positive traits. The rather benign treatment accorded physician addicts (Winick, 1964) suggests, however, that valued traits do have compensating force.

Whichever proves to be the correct model of the cognitive integration process, values placed on individual traits will continue to determine the inputs into the system. Evidence from a study by Gordon et al. (1963) indicates that the acceptability of deviant images increases as one moves across social levels from middle-class to lower-class gang boys. We should expect, therefore, that in lower-class neighborhoods, especially those in which substantial proportions of deviants reside, the opinions held of addicts would be considerably less severe than we might suppose based on our own reactions. These results also suggest that individuals are judged by their audiences in comparison to a particular reference group rather than a set of abstract social ideals, as Goffman (1963) had proposed. Results from early community-studies research on perceptions of social class (Davis et al., 1941) and from studies of anchoring effects in clinical judgments (Orcutt, 1964) also point to past experiences rather than ideals as references. Serious questions exist therefore concerning the assumptions employed by Goffman (1963) and by Garfinkel (1972) in their contributions to the theory of labelling.

Neighbors. In the neighborhoods of Baltimore from which we took our sample, heroin addiction has been a problem for decades. Adaptation to this chronic problem has produced a "culture of addiction," which includes not only a well-developed addict subculture but also an overall community climate which allows addiction to flourish and grow. Since sustained collective efforts against addicts are absent, community members learn to recognize and avoid these sinister elements in their area (Hughes et al., 1974). The weight of their disapproval is felt by the addict as an aggregate of their individual reactions and opinions, rather than as an organized effort.

To find out how the climate of opinion among the neighbors affects addicts, we asked our respondents, "What would most of the non-addicts in your neighborhood think if they knew you were an addict?" Unfavorable opinions by neighbors were reported by ninety percent. Of the remaining respondents, one thought that the older residents would react unfavorably, but *younger* people would look up to him as an expert on drugs. Three others thought that as long as they did not actually harm or "meddle" with people, opinions of them would remain neutral. Another said that his neighbors would not believe he was taking drugs, and so we can infer that he was passing as a nonaddict. In contrast to him, thirteen respondents began their answers by announcing that most or all of the neighbors already knew and their reactions were unfavorable. The following was one example:

R54: Well, everybody knows I'm an addict.
I: What do they think of you?
R54: Some shy away. Yeah, a guy gets tired of getting beat. You take advantage of people if you can, you know, if you're sick you have a tendency to.
I: What about the rest of the people?
R54: Most people are scared. The average person, the one that like doesn't know anything about drugs, is scared of drug addicts. They think of sex fiends and stuff like that, which is not true. And they label them "dope fiends," things like that.
I: When we were coming out of the car you mentioned that like you don't mind being called "junkie" or "drug addict," but that you don't like "dope fiend"?
R54: No, I don't like the word "fiend." It sounds like you'd do *anything,* and it's just not true.

The various negative reactions by neighbors are summarized in Table 8.3. The modal response (thirty-five percent) was to ascribe to the respondent all the faults typically associated with the addict stereotype. For example, one respondent said that people would start "locking their doors at night thinking the big bad junkie was going to steal the house or something." Or, "that I'd kill somebody for ten dollars for a shot. That's what is said, isn't it?" Most of these respondents, as in the excerpt above, resented having these traits imputed to them, and argued that the stereotype was not true, at least not for them. This finding, of course, confirms for addicts the emphasis placed on

TABLE 8.3
NEGATIVE REACTIONS OF NEIGHBORS IF ADDICT'S DEVIANT IDENTITY WERE EXPOSED

Reactions	% (N=52)
Unfavorable:	
Would ascribe to him stereotypic traits	35
Would not want to associate with him	23
Distrustful or fearful	11
Disappointed, but sympathetic	8
Lose respect	6
Miscellaneous	6
Not unfavorable	11
	100

stereotyping in labelling analysis, but as respondents such as R54 pointed out their reputations are not entirely undeserved. Being fearful of the respondent and avoiding him were the next most frequent responses (given by eleven percent and twenty-three percent, respectively) and are obviously closely related to the addict stereotype. Individually, the residents are powerless to remove these threatening and actually punishing persons from their neighborhoods, but they can make their own homes and children off bounds for the addict. They have little incentive to find out whether or not the stereotype is true, and as the addicts themselves stress, the extra precautions taken by the residents make it that much harder for an exploitative addict.

The most systematic study of the relationship between addicts and their neighborhood was reported by Hughes et al. (1974). In one Chicago neighborhood in which a copping site was located, they interviewed six persons from each of four categories: residents, businessmen, representatives of social agencies, and policemen. Residents held attitudes similar to the ones our addicts reported for Baltimore. Only one suggested that the neighborhood should organize to do something. The others simply avoided the "dangerous crowd at the street corner," and it was not clear to the authors that the residents knew that the streetcorner people were addicts. All the business people, on the other hand, were conscious of the addict population and its negative economic effects on them, but were more interested in accommodation than concerted action. Hughes et al. did report, however, that in other neighborhoods in Chicago they had observed individual businessmen obtain sufficient police pressure to drive the addicts away temporarily.

Family. Earlier, I called attention to the fundamental psychological processes which are operative whenever one encounters another person: a number of characteristics, either social or personal, are integrated into an overall identity, and behavior appropriate for it follows. In the present context, as we have just seen, when the resident of an area learns that someone living nearby is a heroin addict, the resident invokes a conception of what an "addict" is like. The weight accorded this notion should depend on what else one knows about the individual, for the more one knows, the less one must infer from the social identity. Agencies and neighborhood residents may know little about an individual, and in the case of persons who become addicts, what they do know is also likely to be unfavorable, if not as serious. We should expect, therefore, that the general concept of addict would play an especially important part in determining their reactions to an individual. On the other hand, if this analysis is correct, the reactions of close friends and family should be less influenced by the popular image. In the discussion which follows, I shall examine whether this inference is supported by the data.

The extent to which a respondent's deviant status was known to friends and family was gauged from the respondent's answers to a series of questions asked about each. For friends, we first determined whether the respondent had any nonaddict friends, and if so, we found out whether the friends knew about the addiction and what their reaction was or what the addict thought it would be if the friends found out. For family, we asked a parallel set of questions. The results are summarized in Table 8.4.

Members of the immediate family usually had learned that the respondent was an addict. If a respondent were either married or living with someone—and twenty-one were—the other person always knew. Addiction was also not easily concealed from parents, especially mothers (eighty-one percent knew). On average, in the case of male addicts, mothers found out 2.1 years after sons began and shortly (0.2 years) after the sons first recognized they had withdrawal sickness. Fathers knew in a smaller percentage of cases (sixty-six percent), but this lesser percentage was entirely due to the absence of many fathers due to death, divorce, or separation. Eighty percent of the *available* fathers were aware that sons were taking heroin, but they discovered it somewhat later than the mothers, 3.0 years after experimentation started and 0.8 years after dependence.

One would suppose that discovery of a son's heroin abuse prior to his becoming deeply involved in it would be important in preventing eventual addiction, but we found that early detection had occurred frequently among addicts-to-be. Heroin use was discovered *before* physical dependence in twenty cases (2.5 years before for the mothers and 2.3 years for the fathers); yet the families could not prevent eventual addiction. In three additional cases, one parent learned almost immediately after the son first tried heroin,

TABLE 8.4
KNOWLEDGE OF RESPONDENT'S ADDICTION BY FAMILY AND NON-ADDICT FRIENDS, AND THEIR REACTIONS

	Family Members			Non-addict friends	
Extent of Knowledge	Mothers %	Fathers %	Relatives %	Female Friends, Wives, or Girlfriends %	Male Friends %
"They know" or "Most know"	81	66	46	71	68
"Some know" or "a few know"	–	–	14	12	8
"They don't know"	12	15	25	3	5
"Not sure if they know"	2	0	7	2	0
No answer[a]	5	19	8	12	19
	100	100	100	100	100
N = 59					

Reactions By Those Who Know	Mothers	Fathers	Relatives	Female Friends, Wives, or Girlfriends	Male Friends
Rejection	6	23	6	2	0
Disapproval	19	3	14	22	16
Said get off drugs	33	18	29	41	53
Did or said nothing to him	6	21	29	12	13
Acceptance	5	5	–	8	11
Miscellaneous	31	30	22	14	7
	100	100	100	100	100
N	48	39	35	49	45

a. Due to either no nonaddict friends, parents unavailable or deceased, or question not asked in error.

but did not inform his or her spouse until after physical dependence occurred. All twenty-three addicts reported that their parents' discovery resulted in no more than an emotional outburst followed by pleadings, warnings, or idle threats. One father surrogate (the respondent's grandfather), who was informed only after dependence was already established, said he would take the respondent to a hospital but did not carry through with his declaration. In another case, the father convinced his wife to "leave him be" when she wanted to take her son to a hospital.

For the labeling approach to addiction, discovery of drug use by parents represents a critical episode, especially when it occurs before the individual's psychological attachment to the drug is so great as to overshadow other considerations. Tolerance, support, and discretion above all are one course for the parents. With luck, the youth will lose interest in drug use if just left alone. A different course is to seek professional assistance (social worker, police, psychiatrist, or treatment program) to help the individual. But, in so doing, the parents will expose their son to stigmatizing labels and risk a deepening of his commitment to drug use. Obviously, the practical import of labelling theory would hinge on the relative success of the first course over the second. In criticism leveled at Gove (1970), Scheff (1974: 446) argues that since cases in which nonintervention was tried have not been examined, one cannot fairly judge the success of intervention. But in the case of drugs, nonintervention is the rule rather than the exception, it seems. For not one of these twenty-three addicts, who had been using for only 0.6 years when drug use was discovered, was anything done, and as we shall see in a moment, intervention was tried by the parents in only two cases in the entire sample. Of course, we do not know whether intervention would have been any more successful in these other cases, but the results for nonintervention do not bespeak its superiority either.

Let me now consider the results for the sample as a whole. The most negative reaction, rejection of the son, was reported for nine of the fathers and three of the mothers. Rejection usually meant that the respondent was asked to move out or not to visit any more unless he stopped using drugs. In some cases, it was punctuated by a fight between father and son or with advice for the son to take an overdose. Rejection also took more subtle forms, not unlike the reactions to the addict by neighbors. One respondent, R57, had chosen to stay with his sister in Baltimore after his parents had left to live in West Virginia. In the following excerpt, he is responding to questions concerning his family life with his sister:

I: How did you get along with her?
R57: I got along real good with her up, up until about the last two years.
I: What happened then?

R57: Well, they just didn't trust me or anything anymore. And they were afraid I was going to rob them or something, which I never have. But I'm pretty sure that's what the problem was. They knew I was on drugs, and they were afraid I would steal something of their stuff.

Even though his sister knows a great deal about R57, she apparently doesn't know to what extent previous behavior is still a valid guide now that he is "no longer himself."

Reactions of mothers were generally less severe but more relentless than were fathers'. Three of the nine respondents who reported that their mothers disapproved complained of constant lecturing or nagging about stopping, and ten percent of the addicts' wives were also said to nag constantly. This continuous pressure without cutting family ties may have had beneficial effects over the long run.

Many of the parents (sixteen mothers and seven fathers) urged, advised, or begged the respondents to stop using drugs and offered to help them with whatever problems arose as a result of their being addicted. Two respondents were actually taken to a hospital or doctor by their parents, and hospitalization was suggested in five other cases. But since the sons had already been dependent in many cases (two and a half years on the average for those already dependent when their parents found out), the prognosis would have been poor. In fact, in five of these cases, the parents learned their son was addicted only because he was in jail or in a hospital.

The weak emotional ties often found between lower-class men and their sons is reflected in the fact that outright rejection was the fathers' modal response (twenty-three percent), and the next most frequent reaction by fathers (twenty-one percent) was to say nothing at all. This silence, respondents sometimes explained, could be expected, since their father had almost never talked to them. Their fathers' disapproval had always been conveyed to them by their mothers.

Four parents were said to have accepted their son's addiction after a short period, and many more seemed to be willing to accept or assume some of the responsibility for the transgressions of their sons (as indicated most frequently by a willingness "to help"). However, in two other cases, one of the parents was upset because of the dishonor the son's addiction brought to an otherwise unblemished family name.

Parents' shame also probably accounts for the ten cases in which the immediate family has known about the respondent's addiction for years and yet their relatives still do not know. In another six cases, only some of the relatives have been told. In forty-six percent of the interviews, the respondent said his drug use was known throughout his extended family, and the relatives most commonly reacted either by advising the respondent to try to get off drugs (twenty-nine percent) or in one respondent's words, by "minding their own business" (twenty-nine percent). It seemed that the relatives simply had to avoid rejecting or confronting the respondent because of a desire to keep their ties with his parents intact. Although relatives did not discuss his addiction with the respondent directly, they frequently advised the parents as to what should be done. In only two instances did a respondent report that he had been disowned by his relatives.

In general, when family members first learned that the respondent was a drug addict, they reacted with shock and dismay, anticipating that severe problems would follow. Both parents usually learned to tolerate his deviant status, although the father often did so in silent disapproval while the mother continued to urge the respondent to stop. Relatives also disapproved, but tolerated the deviance. While some stereotyping was evident, most of the families' reactions seemed to reflect most of all their general relationship with the respondents. There is evidence that, once "discredited," the addicts tried to minimize the impact of drug use on the relationship with their families by using a technique which Goffman (1963) has called "covering." The obtrusiveness of the drug-use stigma was reduced by the addicts' taking only a maintenance dose whenever they planned to visit with their families. Instead of upsetting their parents by nodding out in front of them, the addicts tried to appear as normal as possible. It was also considered disrespectful by the addicts to be heavily intoxicated (nodding) in the presence of their parents, especially their mothers (see McAuliffe, 1973). Covering was also said to be used during interaction with nonaddict friends and other nonaddicts such as a probation officer (although my own experiences as a probation officer showed that covering was often not employed, and addicts sometimes nodded out while sitting in my office).

Male and Female Friends. When asked whether drug use had any bad effects on their "social life," which was interpreted as peer-group socializing with *nonaddict* friends and acquaintances, all but two respondents said that it had. Five males specifically mentioned that they had lost close friends or girlfriends because of drugs, but the most common response by far (forty-eight percent) was simply: "People don't want to socialize with drug addicts." The respondents seem to be suggesting that they have been victims of avoidance reactions to the addict label, although we shall see below that the respondents were not always faultless in these instances either. The few nonaddict friends the respondents have retained or have made since becoming dependent almost always know about the drug use. They disapprove of it and advise or encourage their addicted friends to stop, but to remain close they have learned to tolerate the deviance.

Only four respondents indicated by their remarks that they were passing as "normals" among their nonaddict friends. One was described earlier, and another simply did not see his nonaddict friends very often. The remaining two respondents were able to pass because they were conventional in almost all respects except that they used drugs. They were both employed full time—one had been for the entire four years he was an addict, and the other for eighty percent of the time. They both fired small amounts ($11 and $6, respectively) only once a day, were involved in no criminal activities, and had never been arrested. One lived with his wife and child, and besides other addicts only she and his mother knew he used heroin. He was also the respondent who was not known by any agency. The other addict claimed that parents, relatives, neighbors, and friends did not know. The only agency that knew he was an addict was a methadone program. These two respondents also showed the lowest interest of all in obtaining euphoria from the heroin they used.

The impression one gets from these cases is that failing to adopt the usual addict life style can protect an addicted user from the costs stemming from exposure rather than exposure causing adoption of the life style.

Among female friends, as we have already learned, are numbered twenty-one wives or common-law girlfriends. A large percentage (forty-seven percent) of the addicts are divorced or separated primarily because of drugs, and others have lost long-time girlfriends for the same reason. In a couple of these cases, the addict points out that his girlfriend or wife is willing to accept him back if he would stop. Sixty-five percent of the current group of female friends disapprove of drug use and continue to pressure the addict to abstain. As one subject puts it, "Not a day goes by my wife doesn't have something to say about it." The rest (twenty percent) either explicitly or implicitly (by their silence) accepted it. In one case, the addict points out that his girlfriend was aware of his addiction when they began seeing one another and therefore had no reason to complain.

All told, the data show that the respondents are under a tremendous amount of pressure, either explicit or implicit, from their families and friends to stop using heroin as soon as possible. Some addicts point out that there is an unstated agreement not to broach the topic, but the addicts do not doubt that the disapproval remains. Exceedingly strong disapproval inevitably results in an end of the interpersonal relationship, since there is little that nonaddicts, even parents, can do directly to force the respondents to abandon the habit. In our society, only public agencies and parents of minors command the moral force needed to coerce the deviant drug user into conforming. Others must "mind their own business and let them go to hell if that is what they want," as one policeman told me.

DISCUSSION

Systematic data on the labelling of heroin addicts has been hitherto unavailable, and a number of important facts have come to light as a result of our analysis. Unlike many deviants, few street addicts pass as normal in their communities, and almost all are known to public agencies.[5] In a special check of the names of our respondents through the files of the Maryland Narcotics Register, eighty percent were positively identified, and failure to identify the rest appeared due to the paucity of the identifying information we had on them. When we asked the addicts themselves, only one said he was unknown to any agency. Labels were not attached to these addicts by the agencies until long after the respondent had defined themselves as addicts. Other studies (e.g., Robins and Murphy, 1967: 1594) found, for example, that first arrest for narcotics use did not occur until an average of two or more years after the onset of physical dependence.

When informal social relations were considered, we found that wives always knew about their husbands' addiction, and the addicts' mothers usually knew. Addiction was often a cause of divorce or separation, and those wives who did not break off kept pressure on their husbands to stop. The addicts said that their desire to live a normal married life was a major reason for wanting to get off drugs. Many friends were lost as a result of the respondents' involvement with drugs and even those nonaddicts who were willing to remain friendly merely tolerated the addicts' deviance. Enthusiastic support was never described. While relatives of the addicts did not approve of addiction, they directed their pressure at the addicts' parents. The only family members who were known to reject the addicts outright were their fathers, and this seemed to be a function of the generally poor relationships between sons and fathers in these families. Neighbors, who often knew that the respondents were addicted, avoided them whenever possible.

The general pattern which emerges from these findings is that almost everyone who matters in the addict's informal social life finds out, and they either reject him or they keep pressure upon him to stop, some by nagging and others merely by giving him advice to abstain. Absent were direct attempts to force him to stop or instances of full acceptance. What we found, in effect, was a grinding war of attrition against the addict.

Societal Reaction to Addiction

A major difficulty in evaluating secondary-deviance theory in the context of drug addiction is that there are almost no serious attempts to analyze addiction fully in terms of the perspective or to develop explanations based on the theory's central concepts. In a recent review of theories of drug dependence by Mahon (1974), fourteen different theories were identified, but labelling was not one of them. One analysis which did employ the general concepts of the theory was Ray's (1961) work on relapse, which will be discussed below. Of course, there has been a lot of attention given to the relationship between addiction and crime, but with few exceptions (such as an unpublished dissertation by Gillespie, 1969; Schur, 1964) the issues have not been discussed in the context of secondary-deviance theory (see, for example, Musto, 1973; Inciardi and Chambers, 1974). Even Schur, who has probably devoted more attention than anyone else to the connection between secondary deviance and drug addiction, does not provide one with the detail needed for a full evaluation of the theory. In truth, the observation that addicts commit crimes to get money for drugs is undeniable[6] but trivial and uninteresting from the point of social theory, and it is understandable that so little attention has been given to that theoretical point. In the absence of a definitive treatment, it seems best to try to piece together the elements of the secondary-deviance approach to addiction from the writings of Lemert (1967), Lindesmith (1965), and Schur (1964).

In an article concerned primarily with refining the concept of "secondary deviation," Lemert (1967: 50) discussed the drug problem. He began by expressing doubt that "the laws themselves cause addiction," and then stated, "More plausible are the assertions that laws and policy determine access to drugs, their forms of use, the attributes of the addict population, their degree of contact with criminals and other deviants, their involvement in other deviance, and the particular kind of self-concept held by addicts." These ideas apparently stemmed mostly from Schur's (1964) comparison of British and American policies toward narcotics addiction. In more general terms, Schur (1964: 81) had attributed addict crime, involvement in trafficking, and development of an addict subculture to the nature of the societal reaction to the addict. Lindesmith (1965: 131) reached similar conclusions primarily from his historical analysis of the effects of the Harrison Act of 1914, which he claimed "drastically [reduced] the flow of new addicts from medical practice or through the use of legal drugs. On the other hand, by shutting off the supply of legal drugs for the countless users without criminal records it forced them to the illicit traffic and into the underworld." Addicts, according to Lindesmith, are fundamentally law-abiding, "but become what they are because of the way they are treated," and finally, "The size of the problem is connected with an inappropriate plan for dealing with it" (1965: 137). In the remainder of this section, I shall consider the evidence relevant to this composite of views.

Understanding of the evidence is facilitated by recognizing that there is an essential difference between "medical" addicts and "subcultural" addicts (also see Lindesmith, 1965: 128) and the types of problems they produce. While the defining characteristic of the medical addict is that he became dependent upon opiates as the result of medical treatment (including self-treatment) of an illness or even a psychological problem, the differences between the *average* medical and subcultural addict run much deeper. The medical addict is likely to be an older, upper-income professional male or female who uses only one drug (not heroin or drugs noted for their euphoriant potential) obtained from legal sources only and who *avoids involvement in any kind of illegal activities.* The medical addict is also known to respond well to treatment. These differences are usually so large and closely related that a typology is probably the appropriate conceptual tool at this point, although in the course of our research on contemporary heroin addicts we have found that some of them are similar to medical addicts in many respects (McAuliffe and Gordon, 1974; McAuliffe et al., 1974).

Criminalization of the American Addict

Prior to March 1915, when the Harrison Act took effect, both types of addict existed in the United States. Although medical addiction was widely regarded as the larger problem of the two (Terry and Pellens, 1970: 107-117, 121), especially from a national perspective, there can be no doubt that there was also a substantial subculture of drug users, which did not include Chinese opium smokers. Terry and Pellens (1970: 84-85), for example, reported that heroin use during that period was found primarily among young males who were "frequenters of underworld districts," and that heroin was "used principally as the result of dissipation and is commonly combined with cocain [sic]." Widespread heroin use was still confined primarily to the Northeast then (Terry and Pellens, 1970: 509), even though subcultural addicts had discovered its greater euphoriant value (1970: 84, 384), and so the proportion of heroin users among addicts in Jacksonville, Florida, where Terry and Pellens were located, was still small (five to six percent). However, 30.4% of Jacksonville's addicts in 1913 had become dependent "through dissipation and evil associates" (Terry and Pellens, 1970: 110). Only small percentages of heroin addicts were also found in Tennessee in 1914 (Musto, 1973: 101), but in New York City and in Philadelphia the proportion of subcultural addicts was apparently considerable (Terry and Pellens, 1970: 112-113, 471). A description of the New York subculture emerged from a study of 1,000 addict prisoners published in November 1914 (Terry and Pellens, 1970: 112):

> The number of victims who directly trace their addiction to physicians' prescriptions is very small; I found but twenty [two percent] . . . . Most of these victims were women. . . . Other prisoners have stated that they

> had been induced by friends to take a 'sniff' of the drug, which was variously termed 'happy dust,' 'snow,' etc. . . . Several individuals have come to the conclusion that selling 'dope' is a very profitable business. These individuals have sent their agents among the gangs frequenting our city corners. . . . There is scarcely a poolroom in New York that may not be called a meeting place of drug fiends. . . . The number of young people addicted is enormous. I have come in contact with individuals sixteen and eighteen years of age, whose history was that they had taken a habit-forming drug for at least two years.

Even though punitive laws were only just coming into effect, all the features of a criminal-addict subculture were already developed: addiction was spread by association for the purpose of obtaining pleasure; there was an *addict* argot; addicts were involved in drug dealing (also see Musto, 1973: 95); there was an association between drug use and criminality and underworld recreation; addiction was a problem of poor, urban youth. These conclusions were borne out by studies of New York addicts a few years later (Waldorf et al., 1974: 28-29; Musto, 1973: 158; Lindesmith, 1965: 142; Helmer and Vietorisz, 1974: 19-20).

Thus, in the early 1900s, America had two serious addiction problems: one was medical, stemming from the incautious administering of opiates by physicians and from the ready availability of proprietary medicines containing opiates, and the other was a growing subcultural epidemic. Lindesmith (1965: 128) himself admits that the Harrison Act greatly reduced the incidence of medical addicts, but he claims that the law transformed existing medical addicts into subcultural addicts and furthermore that punitive laws such as it *"recruit"* new subcultural addicts. The nature of the law determines the type of addict and the magnitude of the problem, according to Lindesmith. In support of this inference, he points to the correlation between the relative proportions of subcultural and medical addicts in a country and the severity of its drug policies. But, surely, Lindesmith has the causal force going in the wrong direction. American and British experience indicates that drug laws have been made more severe in attempts to deal with *existing* problems which seemed to be getting out of hand. In the United States when there were virtually no controls, a serious addiction problem (estimated at 200,000 addicts) developed, and individual states began to respond to it even before the federal government did (Musto, 1973: 91). States such as New York and Massachusetts, which had particularly large problems, passed their own restrictive laws (Musto, 1973: 91-120, 308). On the other hand, the British developed their mild policies in 1926 and then again in 1961 when there was almost no drug problem to speak of in terms of both the addict type and the number of addicts (Glatt et al., 1967: 23, 102), but only four years later, after the situation had worsened, was a more restrictive policy adopted. Lindesmith also seems to miss the point that a large *proportion* of subcultural addicts can be obtained merely by reducing the *number* of medical addicts, without recruiting a single new subcultural addict.

Pre-1914 Addicts. What happened to the existing medical addicts after 1914? Lindesmith (1965: 131) and other writers (e.g., King, 1974: 22; Kramer, 1972: 43) claim that the pre-1914 law-abiding addict became a criminal with passage of the Harrison Act, and therefore represents a pure case of criminalization. But what proof is there? None of these authors, nor any others I have been able to find, presented any evidence on this point. Perhaps they considered it to be obviously true, a matter of simple logic if one merely assumed that any addict will do whatever is required to obtain drugs, and that only high-cost illicit drugs are available. Following 1914, there was a large decline in overall addict prevalence in some locales (O'Donnell, 1967: 77), and the character of the addict population became almost entirely subcultural. While it is freely granted that one reason for these changes was that the production of new *medical* addicts was halted by the law, is it not also possible that many or even most of the pre-1914 medical addicts stopped using drugs because it was against the law?

Let us examine the assumptions behind the criminalization argument. Would medical addicts break the law rather than abstain? Were illegal drugs the only ones available? Consider for a moment the many elderly, respectable women who had become addicted through the use of over-the-counter proprietary medicines or through a physician's treatment. Would they wander into the back alley in some slum to cop heroin? Probably not. In actuality, however, supplies of legal drugs remained available to many persons long after 1915, when the Harrison Act went into effect. According to Musto (1973: 151), drugs could be obtained from physicians without much difficulty until about 1919, and after that forty narcotic clinics dispensed drugs for brief periods. Even then, well-to-do addicts received drugs from physicians (Musto, 1973: 151). In fact, it was the supply of the subcultural addict which was hit first, as indicated by the following quote from the head of the New York City narcotics squad in April 1915:

> The poor victims who have been getting dope from peddlers on the street are having a pretty tough time. . . . There is a panic among them. . . . Those who have been getting their drugs from dope doctors and fake-cure places are not so hard hit, because these traffickers have not been touched by the laws, but the poor people, the men and women we call the "bums," who have always bought from street peddlers, are really up against it [Musto, 1973: 107].

Although most physicians did become increasingly careful about prescribing narcotics, O'Donnell (1967: 78) contends that doctors' fears of prosecution were unwarranted, in Kentucky at least, since a small minority of physicians continued to dispense narcotics for decades with little legal trouble.

O'Donnell (1969) found that medical addicts in Kentucky tended to rely mostly on legal sources. Only thirteen percent of the addicts in his sample who became addicted through treatment of illness eventually came to depend primarily on illicit sources for drugs. By comparison, fifty-six percent who became addicted through alcoholism and ninety-two percent through pleasure-seeking used mainly illegal drugs. The assumption that all addicts will do almost anything to obtain the drugs they crave was refuted by the Kentucky study, since the addicts differed greatly in what they would be willing to do. O'Donnell (1969: 215) observed:

> When narcotics became more difficult to obtain in Kentucky, then, very few moved to other places, . . . most did not resort to other methods which were feasible, like drug store burglaries, forging prescriptions, or "making" doctors. . . . Many, but probably not all would buy from peddlers. . . . The reasons why most subjects have never tried forgery or burglary to obtain narcotics [were:] . . . Some said it was because they considered it illegal, or wrong. Others, including some who had used these methods in the past, said they stopped because they were likely to be caught, and feared punishment.

Thus, it seems that few who were not already deviants or recruits into deviant subcultures in Kentucky actually turned to illegal sources, and, when they did, they did not necessarily become underworld figures or criminals. Even now, some subcultural addicts refuse to become involved in any crime besides drug use (Chambers, 1974: 130-131; Winick, 1964; also see our data below), and the Vietnam experience has shown us how relatively easy it is for addicts to abstain when conditions change. It seems quite likely, then, that many of the pre-1914 medical addicts remitted before the legal faucet was finally turned off completely.

Today's Addict Population. Although we do not know precisely how many law-abiding addicts were criminalized back in 1914 and shortly thereafter, it is clear from the nature of the addict population today that almost all heroin addicts are deviant prior to drug dependence and are not mere victims of an innocently acquired habit and unreasonable laws. The number of medical addicts is a miniscule proportion of the addict population and has been so for quite some time (McAuliffe and Gordon, 1975). The rest of the addict population consists of subcultural types who tried heroin even though they knew that using it violated a rather severe law and that heroin was for society at large the most taboo drug of all (in contrast to the general approval or tolerance of marijuana). In most cases, they already had extensive experience using other illegal drugs (Whitehead et al., 1972) and usually had been previously involved in other kinds of crime as well (Chambers, 1974: 126). Robins (1973: 39), for example, found that narcotics use in Vietnam was predicted by pre-service drug use and arrest history. So, deviance and crime are already a regular feature in the lives and self-concepts of persons who become addicted long before actual dependence. As might be expected, we have found that our respondents were already participating in a heroin-using subculture before they first tried the drug, and when the first dose was sometimes unpleasant, the experienced users informed the neophytes that their reaction was not uncommon and that they should try again.

The demographic characteristics of the current addict population (young, male, minority, urban, lower-class) parallel the demographic characteristics of criminal populations in general. Particularly interesting is the sex ratio. Although Manheimer et al. (1969: 13) found that women tend to take legally prescribed psychoactive drugs more than men (suggesting a greater or at least an equal need), when the drugs are illegal (e.g. marijuana) males outnumbered females among the users. One explanation is that women are less willing to break the law and therefore avoid using illegal drugs (O'Donnell, 1969). Even though there are just as many females as males who are poor, urban, young, alienated, minority-group members, etc., male addicts have outnumbered female addicts by a ratio of between three to one and five to one with amazing regularity since 1914 (Terry and Pellens, 1970: 471-474; Waldorf, 1973: 159; Newman et al., 1974: 190; Winick, 1965). A similar sex ratio is found for juvenile delinquents in general (Gordon, 1973; Gordon and Gleser, 1974). Furthermore, prior to the Harrison Act female addicts often outnumbered male addicts, or the numbers were approximately equal, but not among the pleasure-seeking heroin and cocaine users, where males predominated (Terry and Pellens, 1970: 470-472), and in England prior to the recent rise of subcultural addiction females were in the majority (Schur, 1964: 72), whereas after 1960 male addicts were more common there (Glatt et al., 1967: 18). Since in neither case did changes in the law bring about the sex differences, it seems more plausible to infer that at least in the beginning the subcultural addict is addicted because he is a criminal rather than that he is a criminal because he is addicted. Furthermore, when women do become addicted, *they are much less likely to become involved in crime* to support their habits (Chambers, 1974: 131), although for both sexes there does appear to be a considerable increase in motivation which leads the criminal addict to commit illegal acts at high rates (Gould, 1974: 63-67).

The British Situation. Claims by Schur (1965: 154; 1964: 81) that adoption of a medical approach to addiction by the British had prevented addict crime, formation of an addict subculture, the spread of addiction and the development of a black-market distribution system for drugs have been shown to have been largely incorrect or overstated even when first made (see Glatt et al., 1967, for a point by point refutation), and in any case are clearly at variance with the British experience over the last decade (Drug Abuse Council, Inc., 1973: 14; Stimson, 1973: 73) and with the high rates of crime found for American methadone patients (Chambers, 1974: 139-140).

Even if complete medicalization were achieved and addict crime did go down to a minimum, the best the addict could hope for, it seems, would be a deviant status akin to mental patient or alcoholic. It is unlikely that addiction will ever be destigmatized, since it is not a condition which is considered desirable by many persons, if anyone. Addicts have a very high mortality rate, and on that ground alone controls may be warranted. Heroin has become the leading cause of death among teenagers in New York City, according to Bentel et al. (1972: 60). Even in England, where addicts know precisely what they are taking most of the time and the drugs are pure, the estimated death rate is ten times the average English mortality rate (Drug Abuse Council, Inc., 1973: 15). Other undesirable features include interference with employment routines (see below), serious health complications, and a variety of other minor complaints such as constipation and sexual dysfunction. Long before strict controls were imposed, addiction was considered an evil, and persons who were addicted sought treatment to relieve them from the condition (Musto, 1973: O'Donnell, 1967: 77). This by itself should also alert us to the limitations of maintenance as an ultimate solution, and to the fact that labelling of addicts will continue to be of interest no matter what the outcome of the decriminalization movement.

Labelling and Addiction

Secondary deviance among heroin addicts is special in that it involves an entirely different kind of behavior undertaken largely to sustain a commitment to a primary deviance, drug use. Unlike the physically disabled, mentally retarded, and so on, addicts and behavioral deviants like them have the option of reverting to conformity when confronted by social sanctions. As the result of our current policies and the attitude these foster concerning recreational opiate use, most people *do,* after all, refrain from getting involved with heroin. This was also true for roughly fifty percent of the soldiers in Vietnam, even though heroin was *readily available* to all and the usual social controls were not operative (Robins et al., 1974a). The main purpose of our current laws is, of course, to reduce availability. Of those who do experiment with opiates, it is estimated that from twenty to seventy-five percent do not continue, and there is some evidence that fear of the ultimate consequences is a deciding factor. In one of our interviews, for example, a respondent described a friend who tried heroin a few times, liked its effect, but decided not to go on using it because he was afraid others might find out and ostracize him. Schasre (1966: 27) also found that a substantial proportion of forty neophyte heroin users who had stopped did so because of the direct or indirect effects of addiction controls. Police detected tell-tale needle marks on the arms of two of the adolescent respondents. The boys were admonished, and then released to the custody of their parents. That was enough to get them to forswear drugs for good. Others stopped out of fear of arrest when a friend was convicted on drug charges (four) or because their supplier had gotten arrested (nine). Pressure from girlfriends was the deciding factor in two more cases. The most interesting of all were nine respondents who stopped when they first realized they were physically dependent. This realization had been identified by Lindesmith (1968) as crucial for adoption of the addict role, but, for these adolescents at least, it was the event which led them to reject deviant drug use altogether. These last findings were also confirmed in a study by Shearn and Fitzgibbons (1973).

Even after addiction is well established, social controls can be remarkably effective under certain conditions. In a study of ninety-eight addicted physicians, Winick (1964: 266) found, "Once confronted by state or federal authorities, the physicians usually said they were relieved to be caught . . . they had been hoping someone would help them to stop drug use." Although there was little publicity in these cases, some stigmatization occurred since all but one either had their licenses to practice revoked (eight) or were placed on probation (eight-nine). Seventy-four percent were treated in a private hospital, and eleven percent went to Lexington. Although over half of the sample relapsed at least once, most who went to Lexington did not. This contrasts sharply with the usual experience of subcultural addicts at Lexington, almost all of whom relapse. The prognosis for physician addicts is good, with eighty-five percent or more found to be abstinent in follow-up studies (Quinn, 1961: Bloomquist, 1958). Robins et al. (1974: 243) found that sixty-seven percent of soldiers who had been identified as "drug positive" before leaving Vietnam used no narcotics upon returning home, and ninety-two percent said they were not currently using opiates. Furthermore, although some soldiers who were addicted in Vietnam managed to escape official detection, stigmatization resulting from detection (compulsory treatment and an official record) had little effect in determining relapse (Robins et al., 1974b).

One explanation of continued deviance which is of special interest is that the option of conforming may not truly be available due to the difficulty of regaining acceptance by one who has been labelled an addict. In a study of seventeen subcultural addicts, Ray (1961) found that in some cases abstaining addicts had difficulty establishing a new identity because of the skepticism of nonaddicts around them. While Ray does not use the concept of secondary deviance, he was working in the same theoretical tradition, and his finding obviously fits the concept rather well. Even in Ray's analysis, however, it was the influence of addict friends which was deemed most important, and Ray did not attempt to assess the relative importance of psychopharmacological factors compared to the social. In my own data (McAuliffe, 1973: 129), pharmacological factors were highly important, and difficulties in gaining reacceptance were never mentioned when addicts were asked in an open-ended question why they relapsed, although there can be little doubt that barriers to reacceptance in such areas as employment exist (Ward, 1973). Waldorf (1970) found that relapse after long periods of abstinence (when pharmacological effects should be least important) seemed to be associated with psychological states such as unhappiness, depression, boredom, and so on. When the addicts were asked whether during abstinence people had continued to treat them as if they were addicts, seventy percent said no.

Whatever explanation we develop for the commitment to heroin of some users, to achieve parsimony we must at the same time be prepared to account for the fact that sooner or later many chronic addicts do stop for good (Robins and Murphy, 1967; Vaillant, 1973; Ball and Snarr, 1969; O'Donnell, 1969). Actually there are three paths an addict may follow in response to sanctions against drug use: (1) he or she may conform by giving up heroin use; (2) (s)he may develop some sort of holding pattern (sustaining the primary deviance without resorting to any secondary deviance) and (3) (s)he may resist and deviate in still other ways. Also, taking one of these options at a given point does not necessarily prevent switching later (Chambers, 1974: 131). In the remainder of this chapter, I shall present a theoretical framework for understanding the addict's choices between these various paths and movement from one path to another.

Bottoming Out

There is obviously nothing about many forms of deviance, especially the behavioral kinds, which makes them inherently either primary or secondary. That is determined by what the major antecedents of the act were. In some instances, heroin use could, in part, have been the result of one's having been labeled a "drug addict" for smoking marijuana, and smoking marijuana, in turn, might have resulted from being discovered and punished for sniffing glue. From a theoretical standpoint, the process seems to have almost no limit either backward or forward. Consequently, it follows that all deviance is secondary from one perspective or another, and without some sort of limiting mechanism, we would expect that every deviant act which has been detected should lead to ever more serious and varied forms of norm-violating acts. Neither of these is a particularly satisfying result, and, empirically, many addicts engage in only minor forms of secondary deviance in spite of being labelled repeatedly. For example, in our present sample of fifty-nine, two addicts said they had never been involved in crime. They have retained their primary deviance at a modest level and have refrained from undertaking risky forms of secondary deviance in support of it. We also just saw above that medical addicts–e.g., physician addicts (Winick, 1974)–react this way routinely.

For the rest of the sample, who have turned to crime, we may ask: what happens after secondary deviance? Shoplifting by an addict is only slightly tolerated than shoplifting by a nonaddict. Addicts may avoid punishment temporarily by promising to forsake their primary deviance by entering into treatment, but subsequent offenses or mere violation of probation conditions will exceed the court's patience. Then, upon release from prison, the individual is both an ex-addict and an ex-convict. Failure to get a job due to a criminal record may, of course, lead the addict to commit more crime, but he or she might also "bottom out" by continuing to use drugs but giving up the risky secondary deviance. For example, the addict may follow the pattern reported by eight of our respondents, who once committed crimes to get money for drugs but who now employ only legal means of obtaining money. Previously, we found for a different sample of addicts that ten of sixty-four claimed no illegal activities (McAuliffe and Gordon, 1974). Also, in the excerpt quoted above, O'Donnell (1969: 215) described this pattern for Kentucky addicts as well.

In general, whenever a deviant reaches a point in his or her career where (s)he "draws the line" and decides that (s)he will go no further or that (s)he has already gone too far and reverts to a less-extreme level, (s)he may be said to have "bottomed out." Of course, in many instances there is actually no conscious (or even unconscious) decision to this effect, and the precise point at which one bottomed out is determined only in retrospect. Bottoming out may occur along a number of conceptually distinct (although often empirically related) dimensions: frequency, seriousness, risk, extensiveness, and perhaps others. Addicts, for example, may forswear shoplifting except on occasion and in its place adopt legal activities such as begging or turn to low-risk hustles such as copping drugs for neophytes or fencing goods stolen or taken in burglaries by other addicts.

An area of special interest in which the bottoming out process is widely apparent is multiple drug use. As shown by the results of a study by Single et al. (1974: 346), the more serious use of a particular psychoactive drug, both legal and illegal, is perceived, the less likely it is to be used. For example, some persons bottom out at the experimental stage with marijuana, trying it only once or twice ever, and the largest percentage who tried only one drug ever were marijuana smokers. The drug tried by the smallest proportion (3 percent) was, of course, heroin. Certain proportions of those who experimented by taking heroin also go no further (Robins and Murphy, 1967; Robins et al., 1974a), and some individuals stop after a period of occasional use, as we saw in Schasre's (1966) study. Even confirmed addicts are known to bottom out of their careers by reverting to occasional use of heroin (Zinberg and Jacobson, n.d.) or by forsaking opiate use altogether in favor of less "serious" illicit drugs or heavy alcohol use (Robins and Murphy, 1967). Thus, remission from addiction may be viewed as a special case of bottoming out, and in the next section I shall illustrate the role of social forces in the bottoming out process by analyzing addict remission.

Social Bankruptcy

As exchange theorists have pointed out, social interaction will be sustained only when a certain degree of equity is achieved and the norm of reciprocity obeyed. Punishing or underrewarding egos soon have no alters with whom to interact, and failure to honor one's social debts leads to an erosion of social credit for future transactions. Continued daily use of illicitly obtained opiates is an expensive activity. It averaged $34 daily in the present sample and $40 in our other sample (McAuliffe and Gordon, 1974: 779), although smaller amounts, in the range of $20 a day, have been reported.[7] Even at first when the dollar amounts are still small, a young, lower-class male will quickly exhaust his *personal* resources (e.g., savings, belongings, income, and gifts from parents). At the same time, the ability to generate additional resources begins a long, but steady decline. Addiction to heroin is, in a majority of cases, not compatible with ordinary work routines, whether in Great Britain (Drug Abuse Council, Inc. 1973: 14; Glatt et al., 1967: 21) or in the United States (Meyer, 1952: 50-53; McAuliffe and Gordon, 1974; Winick, 1964: 272). At the time of the interview, eighteen of our respondents (thirty-one percent) were working full time and nine were working part time or occasionally. In twenty-eight cases, the addicts' longest-held job ended because of drug-related reasons (ranging from waking up sick and not able to work, needing a job near the copping site, being high on the job, getting arrested, not earning enough to support the habit, and being exposed as an addict).

When personal resources are gone and ability to produce new resources is reduced, the addict's desire for more drugs leads to drawing heavily upon *social* resources: one takes from one's family, borrows from one's friends, or begs from mere acquaintances. One frequently cheats, steals, or begs shots from other addicts. One becomes known as someone who cannot be trusted to fulfill interpersonal obligations and as an untrustworthy interaction partner. From the standpoint of persons who ordinarily interact with the addict on a face-to-face basis, not only does he or she possess an undesirable social identity (which they disapprove of but may be able to tolerate) but may also become for them an exploiting and punishing individual. Because an addict's needs are great and personal resources depleted, he or she engages in exchanges from which (s)he takes a great deal and gives little but pain in return. Interests are absorbed by the drug so the addict has little to share or hold in common with nonaddicts. Already socially offensive, he or she increasingly becomes interpersonally offensive as well.[8]

Many persons, especially the addict's family, are willing to tolerate these inequitable exchanges for long periods, but as our data showed, almost everyone reacts against the individual in one way or another. In the end, nonaddicts refuse to grant him or her the basic social credit granted to any "normal" member of society: (s)he may be barred from entering their store, or home, or social circle. Rightly or wrongly, the addict is feared, mistrusted, and avoided. This kind of *informal* social reaction adds to the pressure that the official controls which the network of agencies I described exert.

The *informal* process is illustrated by the following excerpt from one of our interviews:

I: When you first started using drugs, like heroin, was the effect on your social life good or bad?

R26: It was good at first. Then it started getting bad. When I first started, the people that didn't know that I used it, you know, I would still go down and we'd talk. . . . I could always go to them and talk, you know, and get something from them, even get money from them. But after a while, when people started finding out . . . some of them didn't want to talk to me, couldn't get no money out of some people, y'know. Then it got badder, because then I just didn't want to be with nobody but just the people that used drugs. And as a matter of fact, when I go around people that don't use it, I feel different, you know, I feel different from them.

Cast back almost completely onto the addict subculture, he or she finds that, after a brief period of closeness when drug use began, the group has become a collectivity of isolates. They may hang together on the same corner waiting for the local dealer and share needles when forced to, but there are no friends, only "associates." "Boosting" partnerships are unprofitable, and shooting together—once highly valued—is now done only if unavoidable.

As a consequence of the barrage of social sanctions, the addict slowly but surely becomes devoid of resources or social credit, and is eventually socially bankrupt. Getting a substantial shot with which to get high or even keep from being sick each day becomes ever more difficult. One complains of being tired, and the nonaddict life seems more and more attractive. Many bridges have been burned forever, but the most important ones are there if one will only stop taking drugs. The costs of continued drug use have caught up to the reinforcement, and any minor crisis is enough, especially among the less committed, to make going on no longer worth it (see Waldorf, 1973, who has reached similar conclusions). An excerpt from an interview reported by Tardola (1970: 60) illustrates the condition of the bankrupt addict:

> "[It was] the worst period of my life. I found myself wandering around the streets of New York filthy all the time. I had no place to stay. I slept on rooftops, in hallways, in damp cellars, any available place and always with one eye open. I felt that everyone was my enemy, and I thought everybody was a stoolie. I was really low then, not eating, using dirty 'works' and cold all the time." It was at this time that [he] got hepatitis and was finally taken to a hospital, where he made his decision to enter Daytop.

CONCLUSION

Thus, when we consider heroin addiction, we find that most secondary deviance stems from the public regulation of subcultural addicts by various agencies. A great deal of direct negative labelling of addicts is done officially by the agencies and informally by neighbors, friends, and family. However, official labelling occurs long after the onset of addiction in most cases, and the immediate effect of the informal labelling for producing crime or other deviance was not obvious. Indeed, to the extent that friends and family act as resources even after they find out, they inadvertently help the addict resist. But the long-term effects of labelling and informal social sanctions may be very different. As time passes, the addict's appetite for drugs outstrips his or her resources and social credits so that he or she becomes more desperate and his/her behavior and the stereotype increasingly coincide. The effect of society's reaction at this point is to place an unbearable amount of pressure on the addict to abstain for good, and sooner or later most do.

NOTES

1. The actual questions were: "Now, I'm going to ask you some questions about your experience with official agencies. I'm not going to check these agencies or anything like that, I just want to find out what *your* own experience has been.

(1.) At any place, or any time, have you ever been known to any agency (official, semi-official, public or private, including the police), *as an addict?*

(2.) (IF SO) What agencies?

(3.) (FOR EACH AGENCY) Did they record your name? What drugs were involved?

(4.) (IF NOT MENTIONED) How about the police? Have you ever come in contact with them *as an addict?* (IF YES) Did they record your name? What drugs were involved?

(5.) (IF NOT MENTIONED) How about hospitals or other medical agencies or programs? (IF YES) Did they record your name? What drugs were involved?"

2. See Nurco and Balter (1969: 89) for the actual recording form and their description of the activities of the police.

3. Nurco and Balter (1969: 22) asked members of the Baltimore City Police Department's Narcotic Unit to record for two years how they determined that an individual was a narcotic user. As in sanity hearings or court trials, the deviance (drug use) was inferred from symptoms (body marks, association) in twenty-seven percent of the 766 cases reported on, but it was determined in the rest of the cases from the addict's own admission. Most of those arrested also admitted to having been addicted for long periods of time, and therefore probably already conceived of themselves as addicts.

4. Although this type of admission is undoubtedly considerably less common today, in 1972 Maryland State Mental Hospitals still reported 718 addict contacts to the Maryland Narcotics Register (Maryland State Drug Abuse Administration, 1973).

5. Of course, street addicts such as the respondents in our study are probably the least likely of all addicts to pass successfully.

6. This is not to say that the same persons might not commit crimes and spend the resulting income on something else if it were not for their being addicted. But when they are addicted, the purpose of stealing is largely to buy drugs, and that is the point.

7. The median amounts for our samples were also smaller: $25 for the present sample and $35 for our other sample.

8. When a probation officer, I learned that one of my clients who was addicted visited his girlfriend to offer his condolences when one of her children was killed in an accident. On his way out, he stole her television.

REFERENCES

Anderson, Norman H.
1971 "Integration theory and attitude change." Psychological Review 78, 3: 171-206.

Asch, Solomon E.
1946 "Forming impressions of personality." Journal of Abnormal and Social Psychology 41, 3: 258-290.

Ball, John C. and Richard W. Snarr
1969 "A test of the maturation hypothesis with respect to opiate addiction." Bulletin on Narcotics 21, 4: 9-13.

Bentel, David J., D. Crim, and David E. Smith
1972 "Drug abuse in combat: the crisis of drugs and addiction among American troops in Vietnam." PP. 59-70 in David E. Smith and George R. Gay (eds.) "It's So Good Don't Even Try It Once." Heroin in Perspective. Englewood Cliffs, N.J.: Prentice-Hall.

Berk, Richard and Joseph M. Adams
1970 "Establishing rapport with deviant groups." Social Problems 18 (Summer): 102-117.

Bloomquist, Edward R.
1958 "The doctor, the nurse, and narcotic addiction." GP 18 (November): 124-129.

Bossart, Philip and Francis J. Di Vesta
1964 "Effects of context, frequency, and order of presentation of evaluative assertions on impression formation." Journal of Personality and Social Psychology 4, 5: 538-544.

Chambers, Carl D.
1974 "Narcotic addiction and crime: an empirical review." Pp. 125-142 in James A. Inciardi and Carl D. Chambers (eds.) Drugs and the Criminal Justice System. Beverly Hills, Calif.: Sage.

Chein, Isidor, Donald Gerard, Robert Lee, and Eva Rosenfeld
1964 The Road to H: Narcotics, Delinquency and Social Policy. New York: Basic Books.

Davis, A., B. B. Gardner, and M. R. Gardner
1941 Deep South: A Social Anthropological Study of Caste and Class. Chicago: University of Chicago Press.

Drug Abuse Council, Inc.
1973 Heroin Maintenance: The Issues, Washington, D.C.

Fishbein, Martin
1967 "Attitude and the prediction of behavior." Pp. 477-492 in Martin Fishbein (ed.) Readings in Attitude Theory and Measurement. New York: John Wiley.

Fishman, J. J., Donald P. Conwell, and Zili Ansel
1971 "New York City Narcotics Register: a brief history." International Journal of the Addictions 6, 3: 561-569.

Garfinkel, Harold
1972 "Conditions of successful degradation ceremonies." Pp. 53-60 in William J. Filstead (ed.) An Introduction to Deviance. Chicago: Rand McNally.

Gillespie, Duff
1969 "Drug abuse and social policy in Great Britain." Ph.D. dissertation. Washington University.

Glatt, Max M., David J. Pittman, Duff F. Gillespie and Donald R. Hill
1967 The Drug Scene in Great Britain. London: Arnold.

Goffman, Erving
1963 Stigma. Englewood Cliffs, N.J.: Prentice-Hall.

Gordon, Robert A.
1973 "An explicit estimation of the prevalence of commitment to a training school, to age 18, by race and by sex." Journal of the American Statistical Association 68 (September): 547-553.

--- and Leon Jay Gleser
1974 "The estimation of the prevalence of delinquency: two approaches and a

correction of the literature." Journal of Mathematical Sociology 3, 2: 275-291.

---, James F. Short, Desmond S. Cartwright, and Fred L. Strodtbeck
1963 "Values and gang delinquency: a study of street corner groups." American Journal of Sociology 69, 2: 109-128.

Gould, Leroy C.
1974 "Crime and the addict: beyond common sense." Pp. 57-75 in James A. Inciardi and Carl D. Chambers (eds.) Drugs and the Criminal Justice System. Beverly Hills, Calif.: Sage.

Gove, Walter
1970 "Societal reaction as an explanation of mental illness: an evaluation." American Sociological Review 35 (October): 873-884.

Hamblin, Robert L. and Carole R. Smith
1966 "Values, status, and professors." Sociometry 29, 3: 183-196.

Helmer, John and Thomas Vietorisz
1974 Drug Use, the Labor Market, and Class Conflict. Washington, D.C.: Drug Abuse Council, Inc.

Himmelfarb, Samuel and David J. Senn
1969 "Forming impressions of social class: two tests of an averaging model." Journal of Personality and Social Psychology 12, 1: 38-51.

Hughes, Patrick H., Gail A. Crawford, and Noel W. Barker
1971 "Developing an epidemiological field team for drug dependence." Archives of General Psychiatry 24 (May): 389-393.

Hughes, Patrick H. and Jerome H. Jaffe
1971 "The heroin copping area." Archives of General Psychiatry 24 (May): 394-400.

Hughes, Patrick H., Richard Parker, and Edward C. Senay
1974 "Addicts, police, and the neighborhood social system." American Journal of Orthopsychiatry 44, 1: 129-141.

Inciardi, James A. and Carl D. Chambers
1974 Drugs and the Criminal Justice System. Beverly Hills, Calif.: Sage.

King, Rufus
1974 " 'The American System': legal sanctions to repress drug abuse." Pp. 17-37 in James A. Inciardi and Carl D. Chambers (eds.) Drugs and the Criminal Justice System. Beverly Hills, Calif.: Sage.

Kramer, John C.
1972 "A brief history of heroin addiction in America." Pp. 32-44 in David E. Smith and George R. Gay (eds.) "It's So Good, Don't Even Try It Once": Heroin in Perspective. Englewood Cliffs, N.J.: Prentice-Hall.

Lemert, Edwin M.
1967 Human Deviance, Social Problems, and Social Control. Englewood Cliffs, N.J.: Prentice-Hall.

Leveson, Irving
1972 "Drug addiction: some evidence on prevention and deterrence." Urban Affairs Quarterly 8 (December): 131-160.

Lindesmith, Alfred L.
1965 The Addict and the Law. New York: Vintage.
1968 Addiction and Opiates. Chicago: Aldine.

McAuliffe, William E.
1973 "A test of Lindesmith's theory of opiate addiction." Ph.D. dissertation. Johns Hopkins University.

——— and Robert A. Gordon
1974 "A test of Lindesmith's theory of addiction: the frequency of euphoria among long-term addicts." American Journal of Sociology 79 (January): 795-840.
1975 "Issues in testing Lindesmith's theory (full version)." Catalog of Selected Documents in Psychology 5 (Winter): 196.

——— and Susan G. Doering
1974 "Seeking pleasure from heroin." Presented at the meetings of the Society for the Study of Social Problems, Montreal, Canada.

Mahon, Thomas A.
1974 "The 'eschewment of theory' theory of drug dependence." Drug Forum 3 (Summer): 311-319.

Manheimer, Dean I., Glen D. Mellinger, and Mitchell B. Balter
1969 "Use of marijuana among the urban cross-section of adults." Unpublished manuscript.

Maryland State Drug Abuse Administration
1973 "Summary of data reported to the Narcotics Addict Register for calender year 1972." Baltimore, Maryland.

Meyer, Alan S.
1952 "Social and psychological factors in opiate addiction." Bureau of Applied Social Research, Columbia University, New York, New York.

Musto, David F.
1973 The American Disease: Origins of Narcotic Control. New Haven, Conn.: Yale University Press.

Newman, Robert A., Sylvia Bashkow, and Margot Cotes
1974 "Applications received by the New York City Methadone Maintenance Treatment Program during its first two years of operation." Drug Forum 3 (Winter): 183-191.

Nurco, David and Mitchell B. Balter
1969 Drug Abuse Study–Maryland 1969. Maryland State Department of Mental Hygiene.

O'Donnell, John A.
1967 "The rise and decline of a subculture." Social Problems 15, 1: 73-84.
1969 Narcotics Addicts in Kentucky. Washington, D.C.: Government Printing Office, Public Health Service Publication 1881.

Orcutt, Ben A.
1964 "A study of anchoring effects in clinical judgment." Social Science Review 38, 4: 408-417.

Pascarelli, Emil
1972 "Alcoholism and drug addiction in the elderly." Geriatric Focus 11, 5: 1-5.

Quinn, W. F.
1961 "Narcotic addiction: medical and legal problems with physicians." California Medicine 94: 214-217.

Ray, Marsh B.
1961 "The cycle of abstinence and relapse among heroin addicts." Social Problems 9 (Fall): 132-140.

Robins, Lee N.
1973 The Vietnam Drug User Returns. Washington, D.C.: Government Printing Office.

——— and George E. Murphy
1967 "Drug use in a normal population of young Negro men." American Journal of Public Health 57, 4: 1580-1569.

Robins, Lee N., Darlene H. Davis, and Donald W. Goodwin
1974a "Drug use by U.S. Army enlisted men in Vietnam: a follow-up on their return home." American Journal of Epidemiology 99, 4: 235-249.

Robins, Lee N., Darlene H. Davis and David N. Nurco
1974b "How permanent was the Vietnam drug addiction?" American Journal of Public Health Supplement G4 (December): 38-43.

Rosnow, Ralph L. and Robert L. Arms
1968 "Adding versus averaging as a stimulus-combination rule in forming impressions of groups." Journal of Personality and Social Psychology 10, 4: 363-369.

Rubington, Earl
1968 "Two types of drug use." International Journal of the Addictions 3, 2: 301-318.

Schasre, Robert
1966 "Cessation patterns among neophyte heroin users." International Journal of the Addictions 1, 2: 23-32.

Scheff, T. J.
1974 "The labeling theory of mental illness." American Sociological Review 39 (June): 444-452.

Schur, Edwin M.
1964 "Drug addiction under British policy." Pp. 67-83 in Howard S. Becker (ed.) The Other Side: Perspectives on Deviance. New York: Free Press.
1965 Crimes Without Victims: Deviant Behavior and Public Policy. Englewood Cliffs, N.J.: Prentice-Hall.
1971 Labeling Deviant Behavior. New York: Harper & Row.

Shearn, Charles R. and David J. Fitzgibbons
1973 "Survey of reasons for illicit drug use in a population of youthful psychiatric in-patients." International Journal of the Addictions 8, 4: 623-633.

Single, Eric, Denise Kandel, and Richard Faust
1974 "Patterns of multiple drug use in high school." Journal of Health and Social Behavior 15 (December): 344-357.

Stevens, S. S.
1960 "The psychophysics of sensory function." American Scientist 48 (June): 226-253.

Stimson, G. V.
1973 Heroin and Behavior. New York: John Wiley.

Tardola, Harold
1970 "The needle scene." Pp. 48-63 in Glenn Jacobs (ed.) The Participant Observer: Encounters with Social Reality. New York: George Baziller.

Terry, Charles E. and Mildred Pellens
1970 The Opium Problem. Montclair, N.J.: Patterson Smith. (Originally published in 1928.)

Vaillant, George E.
1973 "A 20-year follow-up of New York narcotics addicts." Archives of General Psychiatry 29, 2: 237-241.

Waldorf, Dan
1970 "Life without heroin." Social Problems 18 (Fall): 228-243.
1973 Careers in Dope. Englewood Cliffs, N.J.: Prentice-Hall.
--- Martin Orlick, and Craig Arman
1974 Morphine Maintenance: The Shrevesport Clinic, 1919-1923. Washington, D.C.: Drug Abuse Council, Inc.
Ward, Hugh
1973 Employment and Addiction: Overview of Issues. Washington, D.C.: Drug Abuse Council, Inc.
Whitehead, Paul C., Reginald G. Smart, and Lucien Laforest
1972 "Multiple drug use among marijuana smokers in Eastern Canada." International Journal of the Addictions 7, 1: 179-190.
Willis, Richard
1960 Stimulus pooling and social perception." Journal of Abnormal and Social Psychology 60, 3: 365-373.
Winick, Charles
1962 "Maturing out of narcotic addiction." Bulletin on Narcotics 14, 1: 1-7.
1964 "Physician narcotic addicts." Social Problems 9 (Fall): 174-186.
1965 "Epidemiology of narcotics use." Pp. 3-18 in Daniel M. Wilner and Gene G. Kassebaum (eds.) Narcotics. New York: McGraw-Hill.
Zinberg, Norman E. and Richard C. Jacobson
n.d. "The natural history of chipping." Department of Psychiatry, Harvard Medical School, Cambridge Hospital, Cambridge, Massachusetts.

Chapter 9

SEXUAL DEVIANCE AND LABELLING PERSPECTIVES

EDWARD SAGARIN
and
ROBERT J. KELLY

In attempting to evaluate the applicability of the labelling perspective to sexual deviance, one is beset by several definitional and conceptual problems. The first is to determine what sexual acts are sufficiently disvalued by large enough numbers of people in American society to provoke hostile reactions and to be subsumable under the rubric of deviance and, further, to decide whether all or only some of these acts can profitably be studied in relation to a labelling orientation. The second problem is to decide just what the main contentions of that orientation are, and which of them lend themselves to the study of sexual deviance. In addition, in this paper we shall suggest two refinements derived from but not entirely consistent with the labelling position as heretofore set forth; in one instance, we shall suggest applicability in all areas of deviance, and in the other we shall restrict ourselves to certain forms of sexual behavior.

We should like to start with the definition of deviance offered by Schur (1971: 24):

> Human behavior is deviant to *the extent that* it comes to be viewed as involving a *personally* discreditable departure from a group's normative

EDITOR'S NOTE: In the original draft of this paper the authors concluded with a very interesting section dealing with certain existential attributes of self-labelling and role imprisonment. This section has been omitted in part due to space considerations, but primarily because it has relatively little bearing on the evaluation of labelling theory. Much of the material in that section can be found in Sagarin (1974, 1975).

> expectations, *and* it *elicits* interpersonal or collective reactions that serve to "isolate," "treat," "correct," or "punish" *individuals* engaged in such behavior [Note: Schur writes that "the most crucial phrases are italicized"].

If anyone wishes to object that such a definition does not make room for secret deviance, the definition can be extended by noting that it can include individuals who would be isolated, treated, corrected, or punished if it were known that they engaged in such behavior.

Using this definition, it would appear to us that, Ira Reiss (1970) notwithstanding, premarital or nonmarital consenting heterosexual relations cannot be considered deviant in 1974, and we doubt that it should have been so categorized in 1970 (see Sagarin, 1971). Deviant sexual behavior would include but not be limited to instances where force is used, where the partners are of the same sex, where one partner is far under the age of consent or cannot give consent because of mental incapacity or for some similar reason, where there is an exchange of money on a regular and promiscuous basis, where there is compulsivity and uncontrollability (particularly resulting in female promiscuity), and in a variety of other situations involving what has been termed the paraphilia. To this list, it might be interesting to add sexual conduct in which there is fraud and exploitation, where venereal disease is known by one of the parties to be present and in an infectious state, where there is group sex and orgiastic experience, where there is an age discrepancy but both parties are adults with the male far younger than the female, where there is an interracial relationship in strong violation of the norms, and several other situations. Deliberately omitted from this list are: adultery, whether with or without knowledge and consent of the spouse, for we see this as rather marginal, neither approved nor reacted to so strongly that it qualifies for the label of being deviant; and noncoital heterosexuality, such as oral-genital relations, which are by and large accepted as normal foreplay and alternative techniques. Along this line, it is valuable to keep in mind: (1) Schur's phrase "to the extent that," which emphasizes the degree of deviance rather than the either/or concept; (2) the frequent tension, especially in the area of sexuality, between the real culture and that which is merely a facade; and (3) the changing attitudes toward various forms of sexual behavior.

For purposes of this paper we should like to include for consideration only such sexual acts and behavior as constitute *a pattern* of experience for the participants, usually indulged in preferentially rather than *faute de mieux*, and arising because of what appears to the actor to be an inner need for precisely that type of experience. This need is characterized by continuity and chronicity, not for sexual outlet (tension release), but for the particular kind or type of outlet. Essentially, there are four important areas (important either because of the number of people involved, the social problems that their behavior or the reaction thereto creates, the publicity given to these areas, or for a combination of these reasons) that qualify for examination under the term sexual deviance. The areas are consensual adult homosexuality, pedophilia (heterosexual or homosexual), transvestism, and transsexualism. All four, it would appear, are areas populated disproportionately with genetic males; whether this is for biological or social reasons cannot be stated with certainty, but recent work by Money and Ehrhardt (1972) would suggest that the biological factor can hardly be excluded.

In choosing these areas for consideration, we are suggesting that rape is better conceptualized in terms of criminality, because of the force and violence involved; that it is, in fact, a special form of assault. Further, that prostitution is a "career" in the usual sense of that term, and not in special meaning that has been given to it by Becker (1963) and others, and is best interpreted as a socioeconomic phenomenon. Finally, that exhibitionism, voyeurism, necrophilia, coprophilia, and zoophilia probably involve relatively few people, and that there is a general agreement that they can best be analyzed within a psychological framework and best handled in a psychotherapeutic setting. However, for purposes of illustrating certain types of conduct, postures, and reactions, some references to rape, exhibitionism, and other forms of sexual and nonsexual deviance will be made from time to time in the pages that follow.

Many types of deviant sexuality are occasional (as forcible rape), or appear to be both voluntaristic and volitional, arrived at by decision and choice rather than because of conscious or unconscious libidinal urges. These would include prostitution, swinging, consensual adult incest, and to the extent that it is considered deviant, adultery. The four areas here mentioned (homosexuality, pedophilia, transvestism, and transsexualism) are in a category that lend themselves to study as one unit, whatever differences there are (and there are differences) in their etiology, the nature of the societal reaction, the outlook for alleviation of hostility, and the potential for personal and human fulfillment.

THE PLACING OF A LABEL: TWO MEANINGS AND THREE DIMENSIONS

Before entering into a consideration of some of the problems in the application of the labelling perspective to these types of sexual deviance, we should like to suggest that there has been confusion as to what is meant when sociologists speak of placing a label on someone, or tagging that person with a particular nomenclature. Essentially, two different meanings of this act of placing the label are used (and several minor meanings as well, which will not be examined here):

(1) *The act of identifying someone as a person who engages in a given type of behavior, and placing the label on that person as one who does that type of thing (or desires to do it, or even has a strong but repressed and latent potential for so doing).* This is the theme of an article by John Kitsuse (1962): the recognition by some others that an individual is homosexual; the removal of the secret by identification, from cues, gestures, statements, retrospective interpretations, and the like. This is known as reading an individual, a term widely used by transvestites when their mask (or dress) is recognized as impersonation. The extent to which others are aware of deviance has been described by Goffman (1963) under the simple term known-aboutness. When the known-aboutness is brought about against the wishes of the subject, this can be considered an instance of blowing the cover, a term generally confined to spies and informers; among the latter one may also speak of surfacing, which is usually a more voluntaristic action, and may be likened conceptually to what is termed in discussions of homosexuality as coming out.

Kitsuse (1962) identifies two factors, identification by another and differential (or negative) treatment, as being necessary in order that a person be labelled deviant:

> Forms of behavior *per se* do not differentiate deviants from nondeviants; it is the responses of the conventional and conforming members of the society who identify and interpret behavior as deviant which sociologically transforms persons into deviants. . . . If the subject observes an individual's behavior and defines it as deviant but does not accord him differential treatment as a consequence of that definition, the individual is not sociologically deviant.

(2) *The act of categorizing the type of behavior (not necessarily the individual) as bad, evil, sinful, antisocial: in short, of requiring some isolation, punishment, or treatment.* This is the meaning in the work of Becker (1963) on jazz musicians and marijuana users, in Gusfield (1967) on the Prohibition movement, and in Lindesmith (1965) on drugs, as well as others in the labelling tradition. This is captured in the oft-quoted statement of Becker that deviant behavior is behavior that people so label.

We suggest that it would be conceptually clarifying to separate these two meanings, and to specify, when one talks of placing a deviant label on a person and the consequences within some known category (the known-aboutness), or of using one's power in the society to give pejorative meaning to that category.

The Negative Label: A Third Meaning

Along this line, some writers speak of the rejection of the deviant label by the imputed deviant (Davis, 1961). What is usually meant here is not that the subject denies the status, condition, or behavior (although that may be true, as will presently be shown), but that he or she denies that it is a type that *ought* to bring forth negative response. This is nicely summarized by Becker (1963: 1-2):

> But the person labeled an outsider may have a different view of the matter. He may not accept the rule by which he is being judged and may not regard those who judge him as either competent or legitimately entitled to do so.

A highly simplified paradigm can be suggested, using the term "self-identification" to refer to how the subject defines him or herself and whether (s)he identifies him or herself as a member of the category of persons given a specific but not judgmental label (homosexual, pedophile, transvestite, or transsexual); "known-aboutness" to refer to whether (s)he has been identified and labelled by others as belonging to such a category; and "acceptance of verdict" to refer to the extent to which the subject accepts or rejects the hostile verdict of society. This is indicated in Table 9.1.

TABLE 9.1
THE INDIVIDUAL AND THE DEVIANCE

	Identification by Self	Known-aboutness	Acceptance of Verdict[a]
1.	+	+	+
2.	+	+	—
3.	+	—	—
4.	+	—	+
5.	—	+	+
6.	—	+	—
7.	—	—	—
8.	—	—	+

a. The (+) means that the hostile verdict of society is accepted by the subject; that is, the subject concurs in it. The (—) means that the hostile verdict is rejected by the subject. That the verdict of society is hostile is inherent in the definition of deviance. However, this hostility may be limited to a portion of the population or to specific subgroups within it, while others may be tolerant, accepting, or indifferent.

If sexual deviance is used as the example, and even more specifically, male homosexuality, it can be seen that each of the eight possible combinations (or cells) is filled with real people, in not inconsiderable numbers:

Group 1. The obvious: an individual cannot or does not conceal the sexual deviance from others or from himself, although he is unhappy with it; an example might be found in an effeminate male.

Group 2. The blatant: he accepts himself, makes an announcement to the world, and has what has come to be called "gay pride."

Group 3. The secretive: he rejects the rejectors, but will not subject himself to their slings and arrows.

Group 4. The secretive again: however, he accepts the verdict of the rejectors, feels himself trapped in a way of life that he does not like, and protects himself by concealment.

Group 5. The imputed: he is the talked about and rumored about individual, generally thought of by others as "one of them," a verdict he does not accept for himself. One might say that his hostility toward "them" may be a defense for the purposes of enhancing self-definition as straight; an example might be the hustler (male prostitute) who sees only his partner as "queer."

Group 6. Sympathizers of the gay movement: the people whom Goffman (1963) calls "the wise." They become suspect because of their activities in behalf of others, but although they do not accept the suspicion, their concern about their reputation is minimal. Several sociological researchers are in this category, although more frequently the "wise" or sympathetic researchers have made most explicit their self-identification as heterosexuals.

Group 7. That portion of the population regarded without ambivalence as straight, but who reject the social hostility.

Group 8. The traditional straight population consisting of people who accept the verdict of society.

All but the last two could be proper areas for the study of labelling and sexual deviants. We believe that, in sexuality particularly, but also in other areas of deviance in which secrecy and suspicion play a role, it would be helpful to distinguish between identification and verdict when one talks of labelling, and to investigate the effect of labelling as it differentially affects the first six categories. Thus far, to our knowledge, this has not been done.

Ambiguities in the Categorizations

The categories presented here are oversimplifications, because there may be an element of doubt in every situation. Each of the three vertical rows is distinct and should be separated from the others, but potentially each has a considerable amount of ambiguity that requires further investigation, elaboration, and clarification. Concepts like identification by self, known-aboutness, and acceptance of a verdict are not simple yes or no, plus or minus, categories. The ambiguities and alternate meanings that determine that one is in a given cell to a certain extent but not as fully, or not as slightly, as another, should be spelled out.

Some types of deviance, further, do not lend themselves to a distribution in all eight cells; in other words, whole areas would be closed by the logic of the situation. Narrowing this still further, some types of deviance, unlike homosexuality, can fit into only one cell. It would be helpful to try to use the distinctions suggested here as analytic tools, to determine under what conditions these various categories are open or closed, how an individual or an entire group might go from one category to another, and with what consequences.

Identification by Self. Identification by self constitutes the moment when one articulates to oneself that one belongs in and is part of a given grouping of people, and usually involves the acceptance of the word used to describe that type of person. However, self-identification may involve use of a more neutral and less pejorative term than that used by others, and this to some extent would be related to the third column, the degree of acceptance of the hostile verdict.

By self-identification is meant the act of making an inward confession, admission, or boast: "I am a . . ." followed by such a word as thief, rapist, or alcoholic, or whatever the category may be. This may be a matter of suspicion rather than admission; of sporadic and temporary admission rather than clear-cut acceptance; or of admission of the behavior without the term. A girl who indulges in sex for money, but with considerable discrimination, may reserve the words "prostitute" or "whore" for one who walks the street, has a pimp, or has no other job; but others who know that she makes herself available for the price may apply these terms to her.

In some instances, there may be a tendency for the individual to separate doing from being and in this way reject the concept of identity. A man who has been involved on a number of occasions with very young girls in sexual encounters may refuse to think of himself as a child molester, although admitting (at least to himself) that he has committed acts of touching, petting, and fondling children. Further, if the individual is steeped in Freudian vocabulary, his self-identification may revolve around problems of latency, sublimation, and repression, as he understands these concepts.

When a label is particularly pejorative, and there are no ideological supports to reinforce an ego that is in such a category, some individuals seek other and less hostile deviant groups for self-placement. Thus, the child molester stops short of using that term about himself, and claims intoxication; the exhibitionist takes refuge in the label of mental illness or emotional disorder. In the child molester instance, the problem arises (see McCaghy, 1968) that the claim of having been drunk, or even of being an alcoholic, may be deliberate subterfuge to mitigate guilt. One can say, in terms of the paradigm, that the self-identification was present, but that the known-aboutness was being manipulated. In the shift from a label of exhibitionism to one of emotional and mental illness, there is again mitigation, avoidance of a more unpleasant label for a less unpleasant one (not the same as the use of euphemism or the rejection of the synonymous slur), but the shift is of another nature. This is because the label of "drunkard" is meant to *negate* that of child molester; the label of "mentally ill" is meant, on the other hand, to *explain* the exhibitionist.

In the instance of rape, the self-identification is frequently avoided by other means (Gebhard et al., 1965), such as insisting that the female was a willing partner. Here, too, one cannot be certain as to whether the rejection of the self-identifying label is only a public stance of mitigation or punishment or for assistance in receiving a favorable image from others. However, there is always a strong possibility that continued denial of a label to others may influence the rejection of the label for oneself. Inasmuch as many male-female rapes between people who were not previously strangers to each other are in the borderline areas between the use of force by the male and the use of persuasion (Amir, 1971), the public denial may reinforce the private one.

Known-aboutness. Known-aboutness is not merely a matter of who knows, how many people, whether they are similarly situated (i.e., sharing the characteristic or trait), or belong to the world of others. It is also a matter of how certain these others are of what they presumably "know." Do they know, or do they think, suspect, and believe? In the area of sex deviance, this is expressed by the phrase, "I wonder whether he's one of them." There is a difference between the known-aboutness of the author who has made a public proclamation of homosexuality, and that of the prominent public official about whom there is widespread rumor without a word ever reaching the pages of a newspaper.

Then, complicating this question, there is suspicion, not of the deviance, but of the known-aboutness. The male with a (+) self-identification wonders if others know about him, and these others wonder if the subject suspects that he is suspected.

A further feature is the false known-aboutness of the pretended deviant. The latter may be a police informer, a sociologist, or a journalist. He or she is or may be known about, but the information known is wrong. Thus, it was known that X was a Communist, but X was not a Communist, only a police informer.

Finally, and this appears to exhaust this particular line of development, there can be a pretended pretender. One can make believe that one is making believe. An instance of this occurred in a New York criminal trial, when a man accused of attempted extortion claimed that he was only pretending to extort, while actually he was seeking to obtain material for a script. The jury rejected this defense; in other words, the jury claimed that he was pretending to be a pretender.

Acceptance of Verdict. By definition, deviance involves activity or status that is viewed negatively and reacted to with some hostility by the general public. The subject may well agree that the verdict is justified, or may reject it entirely. However, the subject (as well as many who do not share the trait) may reject the verdict in part, but not in its entirety; or the subject may see some parts of the verdict as not being an expression of hostility, while others are. Is the alcoholic sick? The alcoholic may well say that he or she is (as witness A.A., promulgating the thesis that alcoholism is a disease) and that the sufferer from it should be seen with the same compassion given to one afflicted with any other illness. Or the alcoholic may see the label "sick" as itself pejorative, giving society the legitimation for its hostile attitude.

Some persons contend that to place the label of "sick" on a deviant sexual category is to accept the hostile verdict, but others would disagree strongly with this judgment. Certainly, there is a difference between those who would imprison people for adult consensual homosexual acts, those who would decriminalize the act but argue strongly to educate the young in the direction of heterosexuality, and those who would accept and institutionalize homosexual behavior. There are many other shades of viewpoints that can be delineated.

A person may accept the hostile verdict at one time, but not at another; for some people in the category, but not for others; for all in the category, but not for oneself.

Categories Without Members

One problem that is of interest is to determine whether some of the three variables (self-identification, known-aboutness, and acceptance of verdict) would under certain conditions or with some types of deviants not be fillable, either in the plus or minus sections. There are six possible groups that might be blocked out, consisting of each of the three variables, multiplied by the two alternatives (+ or –).

The (+) category would be absent if there are types of deviants who are logically unable to identify themselves. Examples would be the severe retardate as well as the "unaware deviant" (the latter may be unaware that he or she is committing a given act, or unaware that the act is subject to hostile social reaction). Hallucinatory delusives would be unaware that theirs are hallucinations; for, if aware, they would not be in the category. However, they may have moments of awareness of themselves as suffering from delusions, and other moments (or long periods) of unawareness and delusion.

In the realm of sexual deviance, it is unlikely that there are any types of activity where the (+) category in the first vertical row would be blocked out and become logically impossible. A man might be attracted to adolescent girls and be guilty of statutory rape without knowing that the girls are under the age of consent; in such a case, persons of this sort would logically be found not to be able to fill the (+) cells for self-identification as rapist or child molester. But this merely means that there are some people who would be identified by others as child molesters or rapists, but who would refuse the label for themselves, similar to examples found when the eight categories were examined for homosexuality.

In the minus category of self-identification, one would place informers and impostors, who could not, by definition, have the trait in that they are, and must identify themselves to themselves as being, impostors.

When one moves to the second column, or known-aboutness, the pluses must be completely absent in cases of spying. The negatives, implying absence of known-aboutness, would not be filled in the case of proselytizers for a deviant cause, and in instances of extreme visibility, such as dwarfism and obesity, or easc of learing about a defect during interaction, such as stuttering.

In sexual deviance, it appears that known-aboutness can be either (+) or (–) for every category, but there are special factors at work. In the instance of child molestation, being known about makes the pursuit of the activity all the more hazardous; in transvestism it is highly gratifying to the subject while "dressed" to be admired as one who can pass (which means that one must be unable to be "read" but at the same time should be known about as one who does this); and in transsexualism, becoming known about to a circle of physicians and others is an essential stage in the transformation from male to female or in the legitimation and furthering of the attempt to make such a transformation.

On the question of the acceptance of the verdict, voluntary deviants (such as those who espouse unpopular political causes) would never show up in the plus rows of the third vertical column; and performers of activities in which there is a strong and near-universal condemnation would usually agree with that condemnation (i.e., the rapist would seldom argue that rape is "right" or "good"). Inasmuch as child molestation has the nearest to universal condemnation among the areas of sexual deviance here under consideration, there would be the fewest numbers who reject the hostile verdict (and this is borne out by studies).

If there are some categories of deviant people who can be found in all possible plus and minus combinations, there are others who could be found in only one. Returning to the eight rows, one finds:

(1) +++ Confessed and reported rapist.
(2) ++– Hare Krishna; political radical.
(3) +–– Pretended deviant; police agent.
(4) +–+ Undetected child molester.
(5) –++ Hallucinatory delusive person.
(6) –+– Friends of deviants.
(7) ––– Courtesy stigma recipient.
(8) ––+ The "straight" and hostile society.

The negative verdict of society is always rejected in instances of political deviance and other "chosen" or voluntary deviant activities and statuses; otherwise, if one agreed with the negative evaluation, apparently such an activity would not be chosen. On the other hand, the negative verdict is almost always accepted in the case of acts which, by common consent, are considered criminal and beyond the level of tolerance of a society, such as rape (except when sanctioned by a brutalizing war, nationalistic fury, or a dogma of racial inferiority). Even the participant agrees with the verdict, as Matza (1964) shows with regard to the juvenile delinquents; they are not self-righteous in their behavior because they do not believe that what they have done is right.

Again, for sexual deviance, most forms can carry either the acceptance or rejection of the negative verdict, but this is not necessarily the case. While people engaged in prostitution and homosexuality might be in either category, rapists would tend to accept the hostility of society as being justified and miscegenationists would tend to reject it.

Question Raised by Typology

The typology itself is an analytic tool, and it starts by specifying the rather strong and in fact almost self-evident (although hitherto largely overlooked) distinctions among the three uses of such expressions as "to label" or "to place a negative label" on someone. As such, it could serve to distinguish better the empirical testing of certain of the labelling contentions, particularly that labelling has an effect in fixing a person into an identity and producing new, secondary deviation; also that the label is applied selectively, according to who you are and what power you have. These questions and others must be tested and answered quite differently depending on the meaning of the word "labelling" in a given context.

For the moment, it appears that several variables are at work here, in determing whether an individual or a group is in one, more than one, or all of the possible categories; whether the individual has a choice; and how he or she makes that choice. The major variables that might be isolated, but that are highly interrelated with one another, appear to be: visibility, proselytization as a means of reaching a goal, voluntarism, secrecy as a path to a goal, degree of consensus to societal values, vulnerability (particularly the anticipated strength of the societal reaction), and power relationships. These are briefly discussed below.

Visibility. The major effect of the visibility variable is on known-aboutness; a highly visible type of deviant behavior is unable to be easily concealed. Further, some persons are visible even if their deviance is not, and should the deviant characteristic become known, it would be learned about because of the prominence of the individual. But visibility probably both affects self-identification and is affected by it, particularly when the self-identification is accompanied by rejection of the hostile verdict and by relatively low vulnerability. If visible to others, one is compelled to become visible to onself; one is almost forced to make an identification as the sort of person that others think one is. If a person makes this self-identification and if, accompanying it, he or she is firmly of the view that the social hostility is misplaced, (s)he may deliberately make him or herself visible, even if the characteristic did not force the visibility. However, a decision along such a line would to some extent be influenced by the anticipated reactions.

The decision not to make oneself visible is the decision to maintain secrecy, which for some types of deviance is easy and is highly rewarded. This has several implications, particularly as to whether this ignores (especially in the area of homosexuality) the crucial dimension of legal proscriptions. It is said that the legal proscriptions create the contours and territories of the homosexual's life, by defining a world of involvement and avoidance. In a sense, this is true of all illegal activities; and in the arena of sexual deviance, it would be much more true of child molestation than of homosexuality, and perhaps more true of prostitution than of adult consensual homosexual behavior as well. While it is indubitably true that illegal activities place a burden of secrecy and often of guilt and shame on the participants thereof, the major factor in the determination of secrecy for homosexually oriented persons seems to be the social stigma, the opprobrium, the anticipated disvaluation in the eyes of others, rather than the fear of arrest. The social life of homosexuality that centers around the bar scenes, the formal and informal associations (including civil rights-oriented groups), and the development of friendship groups and cliques, does not appear to be circumscribed so much by fear of the law as by anticipated rejection on a social level by others, causualness and relaxation with those like oneself, and such considerations as search for sexual partners and desire to engage in social protest activities. There is no evidence that, in those areas of the United States (as Illinois, for example) where legal proscriptions have changed, the pattern of concealment is in any way unlike its manifestation in most of the states.

Concealment and secrecy suggest that labels indeed have consequences in the way in which Lemert suggests. But one need not experience the labelling process to acquire first-hand knowledge of the consequences. In an important sense, the homosexual subculture's raison d'être is to provide not only insulation from the effects of being labelled homosexual, but also to equip its members with knowledge about the law, "safe" occupations and territories, and the like.. The subculture may be seen as a preemptive device enabling homosexuals to acquire the skills to negotiate their preferences with a minimum of risks.

Proselytization. Proselytization would be a major factor in determining the patterns of identification and attitudes of an individual or group. Rejection of social hostility would ordinarily be a predecessor of proselytization, and whereas it is not necessary to be self-identified as a member in order to espouse a cause, it is likely that that would assist recruiting and hence becoming known. In sex deviance, there is a minimum of proselytizing in the sense of seeking to convince others to join the ranks, as would be the case with political deviance. The little effort that may occur in the area of sexuality would be on a personal level and would be more akin to seduction than proselytization. However, most deviant sex collectivities (the child molesters excepted) are indulging in propaganda for acceptance of their way of life, and this might be easily confused with proselytizing for new members.

Voluntarism. A highly voluntaristic type of deviance is unlikely to have problems with the verdict of society; to the extent that the mode of behavior has been voluntarily espoused, it is to be expected that the individual and the group will reject social hostility. A voluntaristic trait would then also preclude denial of self-identification, but it would not preclude such denial to others, as this would involve goals, vulnerability, and other factors. Voluntarism is usually denied for the types of sexual deviance here under discussion; however, it would not be as easily deniable in the instance of prostitution.

Secrecy and goals. The problem of secrecy has already been discussed with regard to visibility; a highly visible trait is by its nature almost impossible to keep secret, but some traits are made visible by the actor. On the other hand, secrecy may be a means to a goal, and the spy and police informer have been cited as examples. In most criminal activities, secrecy is necessary; in sex deviance, this is most apparent in child molestation. If the child molester makes identification of this trait public, he almost automatically bars himself from success in the pursuit of the role. At the reverse end of the continuum is the transsexual: he wants to be known about in order to bring about a goal (sex reassignment), but once that has been brought about, he wants secrecy about his former life, to the extent that he would cease defining himself as a transsexual, and make a self-definition as a female, in accordance with the reassigned sex status.

Consensus on societal values. Although labelling partisans and sociologists of the conflict school are fond of underlining the dissensus in the society as opposed to the image of society as a social organism with a unified set of social values, it appears that there are many acts that meet well-nigh universal hostility. These would include child molestation and rape, among others. Persons committing these acts are unlikely to reject the hostility, unwilling to be known about, and often least willing to accept the self-identification.

Vulnerability. Vulnerability involves the likelihood of sanctions being imposed upon the individual if the negative trait is discovered, and the anticipated nature and strength of those sanctions. It operates both on the level of the individual and of the group having the trait; thus, the labelling perspective has emphasized that individuals of high social status and considerable influence can escape the sanctions that others would meet for the same or similar offenses that they can, almost and sometimes literally, get away with murder.

Highly vulnerable individuals and groups protect themselves from becoming known about, although they sometimes discover, as they do become known about, that the sanctions are not as severe as they had anticipated. When vulnerable individuals reject social hostility, they utilize the vulnerability to justify continued secrecy in light of the rejection of the verdict.

Power relationships. Power relationships are crucial to an understanding of the societal reaction. As Lemert suggests, they may appear to be the response of official agencies while in reality the agency merely transmits a point of view of a powerful, nonofficial segment of groups in the system. In New York, a controversy over homosexual employment in schools and in the Fire Department became a struggle between the Catholic archdiocese, the firefighter's union, and a loosely organized coalition of Gay Liberation activists and their allies. Even though the American Psychiatric Association had only a short time earlier removed homosexuality from its nosology of mental disorders, this had little or no effect on the City Council of New York. One might have anticipated that in matters involving emotional disturbance and sexual orientation, officials would defer to the psychiatrists rather than to the prelates and the firemen. But this was not the case.

The situation reflects the real and potential resources avilable to the competing factions: in this case, the power of the church versus an amorphous and for the large part inarticulate homosexual community. Clearly, the council members weighed this issue, not in terms of its constitutional merits and civil rights, nor of its scientific validity (and we are not so naive as to believe that any issues are ever weighed in those lights), but as a matter of pressure, votes, and power. What may have been at work here was a large sector of the public that was either undecided or indifferent (two categories that should be distinguished), and the politicians might have considered the "safer" route to be the one advocated by the church.

On the other hand, the abortion law struggle saw the Catholic Church opposed to a broad and powerful cross-section of society. Fewer people were indifferent, and the militant women's movement may have had more allies and fewer enemies than the corresponding homophile movement.

While not denying the significance of official agencies in power relationships, these official groups do not operate in a vacuum; they are sensitive to the opinions of various segments of the society, and they may in fact function as conduits for the transmission of policy emanating from various powerful nonofficial groups.

Power is, in short, a complex factor in determining the configuration of self-identification, known-aboutness, and attitude toward the hostility of society. Powerful groups may evoke agreement with such hostility in the individual deviant, but in a dialectic fashion they may bring into play the opposition to themselves, and thus be the cause of the deviant's exposure to counterpropaganda.

The Dimensions of the Label

We have sought to outline some of the ambiguities in the concept of labelling. Labels have many meanings and dimensions, and we should like to close this section of the chapter with a few remarks and questions:

(1) Labels (or mental constructs emanating from any number of sources) are utilized to sort out the focus of inquiry or action; they provide understanding of possible meaningful connections between the facts.

(2) To propose a label is to formulate a world. As Scheler (1961) so forcefully argued, we not only perceive but infuse sentiments, moral sentiments, into social reformers.

(3) Social objects have meanings conferred upon them by the labeler-observer, but these meanings do not necessarily coincide with those of the labelled, who is also a labeler and moreover a self-observer.

(4) Each label creates a perceptual whole within which observations make sense, but each label selectively directs attention to facts and provides an underlying logic for justifying the connection. Naming, labelling, and providing the limits of a concept all set some phenomena apart from the rest of the universe, while putting them together with objects that are like them in the named and defined respect.

(5) Labels construct phenomena: mere facts are made sensible as causes or consequences of a pattern of behavior. Labels initiate schemes of accounting for actions.

(6) The labeler, and particularly the social scientist, is always under an obligation to make explicit the criteria employed to justify and, more important, to delineate, the content of a label.

(7) According to Weber's formulation of the nature of historical explanation, there is a tendency toward selective attention: one cannot cope simultaneously with the range of facts which might under some conditions be considered relevant. The selection of antecedents lying behind the label should be carried out by imagining what might have happened if an antecedent were not present, and then attributing aspects of the phenomenon to the antecedent. One should try to imagine what the outcome of a particular process would be in the absence of an identified feature. As the next part of this paper will show, the identified feature for the labelling school has not been self-identification and probably not known-aboutness, but the existence of social hostility and the recognition of that as a social fact, whether one accepts or rejects the verdict of society.

PATHOLOGY, SUFFERING, AND THE HOSTILE VERDICT

There are many postulates that have been suggested by one or more influential thinkers in the labelling perspective. In another paper in this conference, Tittle has suggested what he regards as the two major labelling contentions; in another work (Sagarin, 1975), one of the authors offers several more that he finds running through most of the works by adherents of the labelling viewpoint. To attempt to determine whether the labelling perspective can be empirically validated, one must first decide just what this perspective includes. In our opinion, this would above all else involve the concept of secondary deviance, the subject of an important recent paper by Schur (1974).

Secondary deviance—or secondary deviation, as Lemert originally termed it (1951)—suggests that there is little that is intrinsically wrong, antisocial, or incompatible with social living in many types of behavior, but that the hostile social reaction creates new situations of self-hate, anger, suspicion, self-denigration, or conditions requiring the support of the illegal subculture, and that this new form of deviance is the result, not of the original behavior, but of the hostile reaction to it. The process has been called the amplification of deviance.

Lemert's dynamic sequelae in secondary deviation appear to move along the following scheme: (1) primary deviation (act) → (2) response (social penalties) → (3) further acts (defensive) → (4) stronger penalties (rejection) → (5) further deviation (hostility and resentment) → (6) community stigmatization (labelling) → (7) strengthening of deviation conduct (deviance) → (8) ultimate labelling by society of the subject as deviant → (9) ultimate acceptance by subject of deviant role and adjustment thereto.

Application to Four Areas

In the four areas of sex deviance here under consideration, there is a strong tendency to apply the thesis of secondary deviation to male homosexuality, to apply it somewhat less to transvestism and selectively to transsexualism and to avoid the problem in the instance of pedophilia. Since a perspective may be useful for one type of deviance and not another, and since it may have strong explanatory and analytic value in dealing with one manifestation of a phenomenon and not all others, it should be incumbent upon those supporting such a perspective to establish the boundaries for its applicability. It is not sufficient merely to ignore the basic tenets of labelling (or at least that single tenet of secondary deviation) in some instances, and then to embrace it in others, without establishing the conditions under which it would be called into play.

Further, we suggest that the ideological goals, not the evidence at hand, have determined the application of the secondary deviation concept to some but not other aspects of sexual deviance.

Looking at transsexualism, the subjects themselves seek to be certified as having an ailment, because such medical certification is necessary if they are going to be able to obtain the sex change surgery. Thus, they have no vested interest in denying mental anguish, distress, and the like: it is inherent in the condition. If societal reaction aggravates this, it is irrelevant. But it is not in the interests of the group (nor its champions) to make the societal reaction the culprit in the sense that it creates the secondary deviation (the distress). If the society is friendly to the transsexuals, this does not (in their view) alleviate the suffering, but merely makes it all the more likely that it will bring closer the day of surgery, making it less expensive, less hazardous, and less troublesome to attain. To validate the identity as transsexual, the subjects themselves must accept the verdict of "sick"but without the negative connotation generally imputed to this term when it is applied to deviance, particularly sexual. To use the distinction noted by Freidson (1966), leprosy would be sickness with stigma, pneumonia sickness without stigma. The transsexual would seek to be the "pneumonia patient" of sexual deviance; and only validation as sick would bring about the manifest goals (sex reassignment).

In the instance of adult-child sexuality, although social scientists and counselors sometimes suggest that the child should not be dragged into court and forced to go through traumatizing episodes—and for that reason that there should not be a public degradation of the offender—few people seriously suggest that the acts themselves be socially and legally accepted. So that, there being no important social movement toward the alleviation of hostility or even toward decriminalization, the humane thrust is in the direction of seeing the adult offender as "sick" (a term shunned for most other types of behavioral disorders). There seems to be no *interest* in establishing that there is secondary deviation or deviance amplification. No one has expressed an interest in determing whether and to what extent (if at all) the suffering is the result, rather than the cause, of the social reaction.

Transvestism, for the most part, has received only scant attention, except by the sensational media (it has received more than its share of time on TV, a coincidence when it is noted that the phenomemon is known in inner circle as TV, as distinguished from transsexualism, or TS). The transvestite has special problems that arise from the tension between the need for secrecy and the desire to be admired for one's ability to impersonate without being read—i.e., to pass (Kirkham and Sagarin, 1972). But the relatively small number of persons involved (or so it is believed), their secret activities, and their generally being considered either oddball or nuisance rather than a social threat have combined to make this behavior one in which the theme of secondary deviation has been seldom applied.

So that we come to homosexuality, particularly when it is chronic, when it exists as a pattern of behavior for an individual over a considerable period of time, when it is sought out and preferred. Here, there are two interlocking and difficult problems if the theme of secondary deviation is to be tested. The first is to determine whether there are aspects of the homosexual life that are less fulfilling to the participants than corresponding behavior among heterosexuals; and the second is to determine whether or not, and if so to what extent, these are manifestations of secondary deviation.

Ideological Bias and the Determination of Social Facts

Research on the question of homosexuality and secondary deviance is difficult; further, it has been strongly tainted by ideological bias and in other ways has been far from scientific. Partisans of the view that the social stigma should be lifted have not all been partisans of the perspective that homosexuality and heterosexuality are equally desirable modes of life, or that they would be if only hostility were overcome. Some have contended that injustice exists, that it must be fought, but that there is an underlying and primary pathology that would exist even without hostility (and it might, some would suggest, become worse because society would disappear as the convenient whipping boy on whom to blame one's distress). Most partisans of the cause of "gay liberation" have vacillated among three apparently irreconcilable positions, while a fourth position has not entirely been abandoned.

Before one can test labelling theory, it would appear to be necessary to make a choice among the following positions, or at least the first three, for the fourth is similar to the second, but claims primary and not secondary pathology:

(1) Homosexuality and heterosexuality are alike, they are two sides of a coin, and there is no more promiscuity, violence, lack of affection, fetishism, interest in youth, mental illness, and other symptoms of pathology in the homosexual than in the heterosexual world. Effeminacy, it is claimed, is no more characteristic of gay than of straight males. According to this argument, the public sees only the top (or the tip) of the iceberg. It learns about homosexuality from those who go to psychiatrists (by definition, the latter are allegedly disturbed, whether gay or straight), or by those who get arrested, who must be compulsives. If one were to examine the life of a cross-section of typical people in the gay world, according to partisans of this position, one would encounter psychologically normal persons, living rather normal and useful, well-functioning lives, not different from others except in the gender of their sex partner and except for such aspects of their lives as revolve around the need for secrecy and the management of a potentially damaging situation.

(2) There is a great deal of pathology in the homosexual life, but it is the result of stigmatization, scorn, rejection, enforced secrecy, and other facets of social hostility: in other words, it is a manifestation of secondary and not primary deviation. This would be the almost perfect model for the labelling perspective: that there is nothing inherently wrong with the behavior, but

that evil (in the form of ill-effects, of suffering) ensues from the manner in which the behavior is perceived and reacted to, not only by hostile others, but by the participants themselves. This position was articulated by Ruth Benedict (1934), is borrowed from the rich literature on race relations and the self-fulfilling prophecy (Merton, 1957), and is the theme of such works as that of Martin Hoffman (1968), as expressed in his title : *The Gay world: Male Homosexuality and the Social Creation of Evil,* and that of Thomas Szasz (1970), likewise expressed in the title: *The Manufacture of Madness: A Comparative Study of the Inquisition and the Mental Health Movement* (with homosexuality and drug use being the two major modern examples of madness being manufactured by an oppressive society).

(3) The homosexual and heterosexual life styles do differ, and the former does indeed manifest itself in promiscuity, a divorce of sex from affection, and other modes of behavior, but there is nothing inherently wrong or potentially unfulfilling therein. These may, in fact, be alternate patterns for living that do not mimic the heterosexual life but are better adapted to homosexuality; an example would consist of two persons of the same sex living together, sharing their housing, financial, and other interests, and professing not only affection but love for each other, while their sexual relations are exclusively with persons not in their household rather than with each other, and always with full knowledge and consent of the "lover" or "roommate."

(4) Against these three positions, there is a fourth, that the personal and social disorganization and distress noted by Hoffman and others is not due to the social hostility (or at least not to any great extent); that it is not secondary but primary deviation; that it inheres in a relationship between same-sex partners, regardless of social attitudes; and that it may precede and account for the homosexual pattern, rather than result from it, or from the societal reaction to it. It is interesting that this position is widely taken in works on pedophilia.

Now, it is crucial for the study of sex deviance and labelling to examine these four positons. It would require much more research data than are presently available to be able to come to definitive conclusions in making a choice from among these four perspectives. However, a few remarks may clarify some aspects of the problem. The four positions are largely incompatible with one another. Pathology cannot be denied and at the same time accounted for in terms of social hostility. If it is present in some homosexuals but not more frequently and to a greater degree than among heterosexuals, then it is not secondary deviation. Further, studies and the conclusions derived therefrom have for the most part been highly suspect. People seem to have begun with their conclusion, and then utilized that portion of the evidence at hand to fortify such a conclusion, rather than the reverse. Third, it is interesting that few people have attempted to apply the labelling model, which accounts for the distress in terms of secondary deviation, derived from societal reaction, to adult-child sexuality. If it is applicable to one form of sexual deviance and not another, the conditions for such applicability should be laid out, so that improper generalizations are not made to explain broader concepts than one can justify.

The Problem of Falsifiability

On the face of it, the contentions of the labelling school with regard to homosexuality and societal reaction are seductively appealing. People treated as if they were evil, sick, or sinners will show ill-effects from this treatment. The application of this thesis to interethnic relations only strengthens the case for labelling. The failure to apply it to *all* forms of sexual deviance may well be for ideological or public relations purposes, or because it has limitations in applicability which have not been spelled out in generalized or theoretical, conceptual terms; however, this does not negate the contention itself.

One of the problems with labelling and sexual deviance is that the adherents of the labelling position have not laid out the conditions, of a realizable nature, under which their perspective could be falsified. In social science, as in science itself, a theory cannot have standing if the conditions for its disconfirmation or falsifiability are not present. To disconfirm the concept of secondary deviation as applied to homosexuality, one would have to set forth the conditions that disprove: (1) that there is pathology, personal and social disorganization, distress and suffering, to a degree and in a greater portion of the deviant population than the normative; (2) that the degree and frequency are related to the extent to which some individuals were subject to hostile societal reactions; and (3) that the differences between the deviant and the normative populations would disappear if the homosexual way should be completely accepted as being on a par with heterosexuality, and not just tolerated and the legal sanctions removed.

If the first of these three contentions is rejected (as some spokesmen for the liberationist movement have done), then labelling is irrelevant and explains nothing. Labelling must be rejected because the hostile social reaction did not produce the effects that the labelling perspectives would have predicted. This would be an ironic end to the debate over labelling and sexual deviance, because the labelling people have espoused the cause of the deviant, they have taken their side; and yet their "clients"—in winning their case—would have annihilated the defenders.

Nonetheless, the evidence appears to be strongly against this position. Hoffman and Szasz, among those who strongly defend the "blame it all on societal reaction" position, and such psychiatrists as Hatterer (1970), Bieber (1962), Ellis (1965), and numerous others have delineated a world in which there is considerable disorganization. Hoffman's work in this respect is particularly important, because he left his practice in order to navigate in the social world of "normal" homosexuals that is, those who had not come for therapy—and he found the gay world replete with distress, instability, and other aspects of what might be considered a disorganized life style. Only Hooker (1957) is usually cited as finding the opposite, but a careful reading of her work discloses no such thing. She had a selected sample of people who had never been arrested, never been in therapy, and who were gainfully employed and in other ways living "ordinary" but homosexual lives, and she found that projective tests could not distinguish these people from a cross-section of heterosexuals. Although she found some manifestations of pathology in the homosexual sample over and above that in the heterosexual, her major finding was that homosexuals without pathology could be located. This is not the same as stating (which many of those who have paraphrased her have misrepresented her as finding) that a homosexual and a heterosexual population cannot be distinguished by projective techniques or by psychological study.

For the fullest elucidation of the pathology in the homosexual life, one should go to the liberationist literature. Parents are denounced for being "all screwed up themselves," or "for making us what we are." Promiscuity is defended as being good in and of itself; sadomasochism has its defenses, occasionally adult-child sexuality, and even coprophilia (an expression of the freedom and lack of inhibition that homsexuals achieve). A careful reading of the work of Paul Goodman (1972), Dave McReynolds (1969), Merle Miller (1971), and many others will disillusion those who deny pathology in the homosexual life (for specific examples, see Sagarin, 1970, 1973).

Thus labelling is saved; if only, like the cow being fattened, for future slaughter. There are still two other possibilities: that the degree of pathology differs with the degree of subjection to hostile societal reaction, and that, were this hostility absent, there would be no pathology. In the case of the first of these contentions, we believe that it has been almost never tested, and that the few tests (inadequate, it is admitted) appear to disconfirm the statement. The second has not only not been tested, it cannot be. This is the problem of taking a position incapable of disconfirmation.

Only a society in which homosexuality was accepted as being equally as good, as desirable, and as potentially fulfilling as heterosexuality would give conditions for testing the labelling thesis of secondary deviation. But such a society cannot be imagined, because the child would still be born into a home of a heterosexual couple, and would still be socialized with heterosexual role models.

By the nature of biosocial facts, there can be no anticipatory socialization into homosexuality, so that the lack of this socialization process will always make it impossible to test the labelling perspective. Even if there were no social sanctions but homosexually inclined persons were regarded as similar to the left-handed, such persons would still be in a milieu in which they have rejected identification with the same sex parent. It is true that some children might be brought up by two mothers or, less frequently, by two fathers; but aside from all the other difficulties of such a home, it starts as "broken" (although not necessarily loveless) in that children would learn that their parents (the biological ones) are separated, the children are removed from one of those parents, and their "foster" parents are in an important respect unlike the parents of others around them.

Labelling theorists must do more than guess or conjecture that pathology is caused by societal reaction; they must set up the conditions for testing and for invalidation of their hypothesis if it is to be given serious consideration as having explanatory value.

The Evidence for Primary Deviation

It is our belief, albeit a tentative one, that the contribution (if any) of hostile societal reaction to the pathology and to the suffering of the sex deviant points the way to a rejection of the labelling perspective. This conclusion is reached via two paths: (1) the failure of those most favorable to the labelling view to validate their hypotheses, and (2) the existence of an explanation in terms of primary pathology and not secondary deviation, as being more parsimonious in its theoretical value and more consistent with all other known facts and accepted viewpoints.

There have been only two efforts to empirically test the labelling hypothesis with regard to sex deviance, both efforts concerning themselves with homosexuality, and both being conducted by the same team (Williams and Weinberg, 1971; Weinberg and Williams, 1974). Bear in mind that both efforts were made by researchers with a pro-labelling bias, and both failed to validate the labelling contentions.

In their work on homosexuals in the military, or more exactly the lives of such persons after being discharged from the military, Williams and Weinberg (1971) failed to show that a more serious hostile societal reaction (in the form of a less than honorable discharge) had any major consequences on the life patterns of those labelled as compared to those whose deviation remained more secret. Their research expectation was, in brief, that regarding problems of self-acceptance, the officially labelled deviant would experience greater problems of self-acceptance than those whose deviance had not been brought to the attention of unsympathetic others. The secret deviant did not face the degrading confrontation of the officially labelled, but no significant difference was experienced in the post-military lives of the two cohorts under study.

It would be improper, however, to use this work as a scrious argument against the labelling perspective. Elsewhere, it has been severely criticized for its methodological deficiencies (Sagarin, 1973). Further, it is not at all certain that, at this point in American life, or a fcw years back when the study was undertaken, the nature of a military discharge was playing an important part in the adjustments of large numbers of males. Unlike the period immediately following World War II, every male is not being asked to account for the years of military eligibility and to show discharge papers to prospective employers and others. That a less than honorable discharge has disadvantages is indisputable, but that it should be a touchstone to determine whether greater social hostility produces secondary deviation is somewhat dubious.

A far more ambitious study of the labelling contentions, as applied to male homosexuality, was undertaken by Weinberg and Williams (1974). Rather than summarize the work ourselves, we are turning to a review of it (Beigel, 1974) which pinpoints the very issues with which this paper and this conference are concerned:

> [Weinberg and Williams] have compiled an appreciable amount of data on male homosexuality. Some of these summarize what they themselves or other sociological researchers have stated in previous publications, some of it is new and interesting *per se* or interesting in the setting of other data. The authors seem to have expected sensational findings by comparing two American cities, New York and San Francisco, with two countries other than the United States, namely the Netherlands and Denmark, both of which have become known for their far more liberal sexual attitude. Disregarding at the moment that Amsterdam is not the Netherlands and Copenhagen not Denmark, and that the tolerant attitude prevailing in these two cities is not necessarily shared in other places—disregarding this fact, the result is undoubtedly disappointing for all those who believed—or at least preached—that homosexual behavior and attitudes and problems are the result of only one factor, societies' intolerant reaction to them. For all the greater tolerance or freedom or acceptance in the two allegedly so much more liberal places, their laws and their law enforcement methods, there are—according to this study—practically no differences as regards the psychological problems of the homosexual male population here and there.
>
> And this is indeed a very important point even if the authors, who start the book with asserting as their creed and point of departure the "societal reaction theory," try to minimize the issue by a modification,

> namely that tolerance probably is not enough, that is to say, it is not the same as full acceptance. Thus, having followed the assiduous study through past and present experiences with the law and law enforcing agencies, the homophile organizations, political and bar activities, through the method of the study and the items of the questionnaires, the results of certain questions on self-acceptance and perceived appraisal of others, heterosexuals as well as homosexuals, the psychological correlates to the commitment to homosexuality, the authors' and their subjects' ideas about passing and being known, conclusions about bisexuality, age, occupation, living arrangements and many additional, sometimes rather interesting items, after all that this reader came to the conclusion that while indeed he was rather stimulated to read some passages over again and compare some tables with each other, the book was worthwhile and probably gave as much as a sociological investigation can give, but that just because of acceptance of the authors' findings their negative judgment of preceding approaches was unjustified. For if the environmental reaction is not the sole troublemaker—as this study against the authors' intention seems to confirm—it will be all the more important to know what are the reasons and causes for the disproportionate number of unhappy people in the "gay" population, the number of suicides, depression, loneliness and similar psychological or neurotic problems.

An examination of the work of Weinberg and Williams makes the Beigel conclusion indisputable. Inasmuch as this is the leading effort to empirically test the labelling contention with regard to homosexuality, and inasmuch as it was done by persons avowedly biased in favor of confirmation of that perspective, the findings of Weinberg and Williams constitute a devastating blow against the secondary deviation explanation. That the authors leave a way out, in concluding that tolerance may not be enough, but complete institutionalization may be necessary, must be discounted for the following reasons: (1) such a contention is conjectural and under present conditions not falsifiable; (2) the work fails to explain why lesser social hostility did not produce lesser psychological problems.

The evidence in favor of primary rather than secondary deviation is not based solely on the failure of the societal reaction theorists to prove their case, important as that would be. Ordinarily, the burden of proof is on those who make a contention, not on those who deny it; but this is hardly applicable in the case of primary and secondary deviance. For what exists here is that both sides are making a contention: one that pathology precedes hostile societal reaction and would exist independent of it; the other, the reverse.

The bulk of psychological and psychiatric literature appears to indicate the existence of pathological familial situations far more frequently among those who eventually embrace a homosexual life pattern than among others. In the sole report of multiple homosexual siblings, Dank (1971) describes a family where the personal and social disorganization can hardly be denied. In a society in which the parents are heterosexual, the mass media is projecting the ideal of heterosexuality, in which homosexuality is denigrated, and in which every effort is made to socialize the child into a heterosexual pattern, parsimony would demand that, in the absence of constitutional and biological factors, those who develop homosexually must have had severe problems adjusting to the cultural milieu. An exception to this would be to postulate a polymorphous perverse pre-pubertal and pubertal libido, that drifts into homosexuality because of ease of locating sexual outlet or nonsexual advantages, and adjusts to and learns the homosexual way of life. To accept this hypothesis, one would have to separate a homosexual population into those who "discovered" or "developed" early, and those who drifted, developed, or learned late, and determine whether major differences of psychological and psychosexual adjustment can be located.

It is not to be excluded that there is a diminishment rather than an aggrandizement of pathology following social hostility. The hostile societal reaction forces large numbers of deviants into a subcultural milieu of their own, where they give one another mutual support and an ideology that enhances the ego and the self-image. Along this line, it is interesting to compare the following two passages from Gagnon and Simon (1973: 232):

> Given that all forms of deviance may be seen as at least potential situations for the development of major psychopathology, one of the major functions of the culture of the prostitute is to reduce this potential by providing a system of supporting social figures who operate as a community. While there is a good deal of evidence for pathology among prostitutes, it is probably reduced by the existence of the culture of prostitution.

If, then, there is a probability of reduction of the pathology among prostitutes by the existence of the subculture, it is entirely possible that the same may be true of other sexually deviant groupings.

> These various kinds of [homosexual] social activity reinforce a feeling of identity and provide for the homosexual a way of institutionalizing the experience, wisdom, and mythology of collectivity. The cultural content of this community has been described in the past with irony, but more recently with a sense of affirmation, as the "gay life."
>
> For the individual homosexual, the community provides many functions . . . a source of social support . . . an environment in which one

> can socialize one's sexuality and find ways of deriving sexual gratification by being admired, envied, or desired, while not necessarily engaging in sexual behavior . . . the community includes a language and an ideology which provide each individual lesbian with already developed attitudes that help her resist the societal claim that she is diseased, depraved, or shameful [Gagnon and Simon, 1973: 194-195].

The thrust of the above quotations would appear to be that there are countervailing forces at work that reduce the primary pathology, in addition to the societal forces that appear to amplify it. This would be further evidence for the rejection of the labelling perspective.

Secondary Deviation: A Straw Man?

The thrust of our remarks has been to reject the concept of secondary deviation insofar as sexual deviation is concerned, although some lingering doubts must remain. However, it may well be contended that secondary deviation is not at all central to the labelling perspective, or is not even a necessary part of it, as Kitsuse (1974) maintains. It may well be that the perspective of Kitsuse can be validated, and that there will emerge a new orientation, called labelling or given some other name, rejecting secondary deviation but emphasizing the view of the other (the normative or normal) as the sine qua non of deviance. Inasmuch as Lemert and other theoretical leaders in the labelling perspective have emphasized secondary deviation, and inasmuch as it has been the primary concern of those in the labelling orientation who have turned their attention to sexual deviance (Hoffman, Szasz, Weinberg, Williams, and numerous others), we feel it sufficient and important to have examined this aspect of the societal reaction perspective.

REFERENCES

Amir, M.
1971 Patterns in Forcible Rape. Chicago: University of Chicago Press.
Becker, H. S.
1963 Outsiders: Studies in the Sociology of Deviance. New York: Free Press.
Beigel, H.
1974 "Review of Martin S. Weinberg and Colin J. Williams, Male Homosexuals: Their Problems and Adaptations." Journal of Sex Research 10: 339-340.
Benedict, R.
1934 Patterns of Culture. Boston: Houghton Mifflin.
Bieber, I.
1962 Homosexuality: A Psychoanalytic Study. New York: Basic Books.

Dank, B. M.
1971 "Six homosexual siblings." Archives of Sexual Behavior 1: 193-204.
Davis, F.
1961 "Deviance disavowal: the management of strained interaction by the visibly handicapped." American Journal of Sociology 9: 120-132.
Ellis, A.
1965 Homosexuality: Its Causes and Cure. New York: Lyle Stuart.
Freidson, E.
1966 "Disability as social deviance." In M. B. Sussman (ed.) Sociology and Rehabilitation. Washington, D.C.: American Sociological Association.
Gagnon, J. H. and W. Simon
1973 Sexual Conduct: The Social Sources of Human Sexuality. Chicago: Aldine.
Gebhard, P. H., J. H. Gagnon, W. B. Pomeroy, and C. V. Christensen
1965 Sex Offenders: An Analysis of Types. New York: Harper & Row.
Goffman, E.
1963 Stigma: Notes on the Management of Spoiled Identity. Englewood Cliffs, N.J.: Prentice-Hall.
Goodman, P.
1972 In J. A. McCaffrey, The Homosexual Delictic. Englewood Cliffs, N.J.: Prentice Hall.
Gusfield, J. R.
1967 "Moral passage: the symbolic process in public designations of deviance." Social Problems 15: 175-188.
Hatterer, L. J.
1970 Changing Homosexuality in the Male: Treatment for Men Troubled by Homosexuality. New York: McGraw-Hill.
Hoffman, M.
1968 The Gay World: Male Homosexuality and the Social Creation of Evil. New York: Basic Books.
Hooker, E.
1957 "The adjustment of the male overt homosexual." Journal of Projective Techniques 21: 18-31.
Kirkham, G. L. and E. Sagarin
1972 "Cross-dressing." Sexual Behavior (April): 53-59.
Kitsuse, J. I.
1962 "Societal reaction to deviant behavior: Problems of theory and method." Social Problems 9: 247-257.
1974 Private communication to Robert J. Kelly, December 24.
Lemert, E. M.
1951 Social Pathology: A Systematic Approach to the Theory of Sociopathic Behavior. New York: McGraw-Hill.
Lindesmith, A. R.
1965 The Addict and the Law. Bloomington, Ind.: Indiana University Press.
McCaghy, C.
1968 "Drinking and deviance disavowal: the case of child molesters." Social Problems 16: 43-49.
McReynolds, D.
1969 "Notes for a coherent article." Win 5 (November 15): 8-14.
Matza, D.
1964 Delinquency and Drift. New York: John Wiley.

Merton, R. K.
1957 Social Theory and Social Structure. New York: Free Press.
Miller, M.
1971 On Being Different: What It Means To Be a Homosexual. New York: Random House.
Money, J. and A. A. Ehrhardt
1972 Man & Woman, Boy & Girl: The Differentiation and Dimorphism of Gender Identity from Conception to Maturity. Baltimore: Johns Hopkins University Press.
Reiss, I. L.
1970 "Premarital sex as deviant behavior: An application of current approaches to deviance." American Sociological Review 35: 78-87.
Sagarin, E.
1970 "Behind the Gay Liberation Front." The Realist (May/June); reprinted "Sex raises its revolutionary head." In R. S. Denisoff and C. H. McCaghy (eds.) Deviance, Conflict, and Criminality. Chicago: Rand McNally, 1973.
1971 "Premarital sex as normative behavior." Presented to Eastern Sociological Society, New York, April.
1973 "The good guys, the bad guys, and the gay guys." Contemporary Sociology 2 (January): 3-13.
1974 "Homosexuality and the homosexual: an overview of the former and a denial of the reality of the latter." Presented to American Sociological Association and Society for Study of Social Problems, Montreal, August 29.
1975 Deviants and Deviance: An Introduction to the Study of Disvalued People and Behavior. New York: Praeger.
Scheler, M.
1961 Ressentiment. Glencoe, Ill.: Free Press. Reprinted, New York: Schocken Books, 1972.
Schur, E. M.
1971 Labeling Deviant Behavior: Its Sociological Implications. New York: Harper & Row.
1974 "The concept of secondary deviation: Its theoretical significance and empirical elusiveness." Presented at University of Massachusetts, Amherst, April 19.
Szasz, T. S.
1970 The Manufacture of Madness: A Comparative Study of the Inquisition and the Mental Health Movement. New York: Harper & Row.
Weinberg, M. S. and C. J. Williams
1974 Male Homosexuals: Their Problems and Adaptations. New York: Oxford University Press.
Williams, C. J. and M. S. Weinberg
1971 Homosexuals and the Military: A Study of Less Than Honorable Discharge. New York: Harper & Row.

Chapter 10

THE "NEW CONCEPTION OF DEVIANCE" AND ITS CRITICS

JOHN I. KITSUSE

For more than ten years now, criticisms, analyses, and commentaries about what Gibbs' (1966) called the "new conception" of deviance have accumulated in our journals. What is striking about this literature, as well as most of the rejoinders to the criticisms, is that they seem to plow over the same ground to come up with the same uninformative analyses. I have come to think that these investigations turn out the way they do because (1) the statements of this conception and their logical implications have not been closely examined and (2) the statements of the conception lend themselves to simplistic and often vulgar interpretations by proponents as well as critics.

In a sense, the fundamental proposition contained in the new conception appears so commonsensical that one wonders, with Hirschi, how it is that this conception has managed to command the attention of so many sociologists. Merton, for example, interprets Becker's (1963) formulation as stating that "behavior cannot be considered 'deviant' unless there are social norms from which that behavior departs" and he deduces the proposition that "no rule, no rule-violating behavior," which Merton finds "blatantly true and trivial" (1971: 827). But if it is all so trivial, is there anything to evaluate or discuss at a conference such as this? In view of the effort that has been expended to organize this series of meeting, it would seem that those who have gathered here think there is, that it is not as banal and trivial as Merton says it is. However that may be, I shall proceed on the assumption that where there is so much talk, there may be some substance to warrant an examination of the new conception of deviance.

Before moving to a discussion of the issues at hand, I should like to make a few prefatory comments on the contents of this book, directed to what I take to be the interpretation of the new conception that guides the various efforts to evaluate it. I shall be particularly concerned with how this interpretation tends focus the examination of the new conception on its implications for the analysis of deviants and their behavior rather than on the organizational features of deviance.

Second, with regard to the troublesome problem of what to call the object of examination, analysis, and evaluation, I confess to a self-consciousness with regard to this problem whenever I think, talk, or write about it. "Societal Reaction Theory" or "Labelling Theory" (with or without capitals) always strikes me as an inflation as well as loose usage of the term "theory."[1] I agree with Jack Gibbs that the formulation in question represents a "new conception" of deviance, and I shall refer to the perspective that shapes it, the approach to social phenomena it suggests, and the various formulations it generates, using these terms with or without the adjectives "societal reaction" or "labelling."

Finally, in view of Lemert's (1974) recent statements, in which he explicitly disassociates himself from the "labelling theorists" in particular, as well as from the ethnomethodologists, a comment on the relation of his work to the new conception of deviance seems in order. It is unfortunate that almost twenty-five years after the publication of *Social Pathology* Lemert finds those who honor him for his work both misread and misinterpret it. If he has found his association with the labelling perspective unwanted and onerous, he should be the first to recognize, as his own theory of sociopathic behavior would suggest, that the definitional and imputational process may be conditioned by a dynamic independent of the intent, statement, or action of the objects toward whom it is directed.

It should be noted, however, that as recently as 1972 Lemert clearly identified himself as a spokesperson for the new perspective on deviance. In the Preface to a collection of his papers he states:

> Despite the seeming diversity of the pieces, they have rendezvous points in theoretical issues crucial or central to sociology. Their common concern is with social control and its consequences for deviance. This is a large turn away from older sociology that tended to rest heavily on the idea that deviance leads to social control. I have come to believe that the reverse idea (i.e., social control leads to deviance) is equally tenable and the potentially richer premise for studying deviance in modern society [1972: ix].

This statement clearly reflects his continuing appreciation of the "societal reaction" processes as central to examination of deviant phenomena, and it is, of course, this concept, together with "secondary deviation" that has linked Lemert to the labelling perspective.

Lemert's protestations aside, I find it odd that his work has received so little systematic attention in this book. By contrast, the treatment given by Hirschi to the concepts of "tagging" and "the dramatization of evil" far exceeds Tannenbaum's contribution to the development of the societal reaction formulation. In noting this disproportion, I am not ignoring the discussion by participants here of the concept of "secondary deviation" and the propositions that are presumably derived from it. I find, however, that the several efforts to evaluate his theory have so fragmented Lemert's conception of "sociopathic behavior" as to make the negative conclusions less than convincing.

Proponents of the societal reaction perspective on deviance, and I count myself among them, might take it as a compliment that a conference is organized to assess the value of what they sponsor. However, it behooves us to be chary of positivists bearing evidence. It is important that we be clear about the issues to which the evidence is directed so that the evaluation can properly be audited. Having been a spectator of as well as participator in the development of the new conception of deviance, let me state at the outset that the literature has made us captives of the terms in which the debate has been cast. As a consequence, I think we have all been barking up the wrong tree—by which I mean, the questions and issues have been phrased in such ways as to deflect us from a consideration of the sense in which the new conception is distinctively new. The question we should be exploring ought not to be how the new conception can throw light on the traditional concerns in the sociology of deviance. Rather, we should ask how it directs us to investigate new and different aspects of deviance.

The persistence of the old questions is evident in the chapters preceding this one. The evaluations of the societal reaction formulation focus on two major issues. They may be stated as:

Proposition A: Deviant labels are applied without regard to (or independent of) the behaviors or acts of those labelled.

Proposition B: Labelling produces (stabilizes or amplifies) deviance and deviant behavior.

As the citations in this book indicate, there are statements in the works of labelling proponents that lend support to the derivation of these propositions. I will argue, in fact, that the early statements by Lemert and Becker were importantly shaped by the conceptions that they opposed, so that they attempted to address old questions and issues even as they sought to establish and delineate a new perspective on deviance. If their critics in this volume are less than appreciative of their efforts, it is in no small part a consequence of the ambiguities that are contained in them (Kitsuse and Spector, 1975).

As indicated above, I agree with Gibbs that the societal reaction/labelling perspective *does* represent a "new conception" that distinguishes it from the "old." I return to Gibbs' critical article because he went to the heart of the matter by identifying the treatment of "social norms" in the definition of deviance as the distinctive feature of the new conception. In his article, Gibbs raised a number of points pertinent to the evaluation of this conception—the logical problems inherent in Becker's typology of deviant behavior, the conceptual specification of "societal reaction" and so forth—but even more interesting to me is that he ended his trenchant critique as follows:

> As the tone of the above criticism suggests, this writer differs with Becker, et al., on the issue of identifying deviant behavior. My preference is to identify deviant acts by reference to norms, and treat reactions as a contingent property. However, *this preference reflects nothing more than opinion,* and the ultimate evaluation of the conception on this point must await an assessment of substantive theory generated by it. Accordingly, no claim is made that Becker, Erikson, and Kitsuse are "wrong." Rather, the criticism is that (1) they have not specified exactly what kind of reaction identifies behavior as deviant, and (2) they have failed to take a consistent stand on a particular conceptual issue [1966: 14; italics added].

I agree with the two criticisms Gibbs enumerates and his characterization of the norm-based definition of deviant as a preference and an opinion on his part. As I consider the previous chapters, my impression is that while the authors are one with Gibbs in his criticisms of the new conception, they would be less willing to describe their alternative definitions of deviant behavior as reflecting "nothing more than an opinion." I take Gibbs' statement seriously, and it suggests to me that we should be as judicious in our assessment of the "old conception" as we are of the new.

It is not at all clear to me that the problem posed by the societal reaction definition of deviance has been addressed by the critics, nor have they been clear about the alternative definitions, implicitly or explicitly invoked, against which the evaluations are being made. Let us be plain: The new conception of deviance requires that members of the society perceive, define, and treat acts and persons as deviant *before* the sociologist can claim them as subject matter for study. Gibbs rejects this requirement, stating his preference for a definition of deviance as a violation of norms. His preference, however, raises the question of how those norms are to be determined.[2] A consideration of this question reveals the ambiguities of the concept on which the conventional formulations of deviance rely so heavily.

How, then, is "a norm" to be identified, and when identified, how is it to be specified—i.e., what is it one must do, must not, may or may not do? If we refer to Blake and Davis' (1964) paper, "Norms, Values, and Sanctions," we are presented with the following opening paragraph. (p. 456):

> The meaning of "norm" in everyday usage is ambiguous. It often refers to a statistical regularity, as when we say one's temperature is "normal" or that a man who has been sick has resumed his "normal" activities. On the other hand, it may indicate an accepted standard or model, as in the phrase "set the norm" or "conform to ethical norms." In sociology the same ambiguity is found, although ostensibly, at least when a formal definition is given the second meaning is stipulated. Thus, the term is presumably employed, as is done in the present chapter, to designate any standard or rule that states what human beings should or should not think, say, or do under given circumstances.

Solutions to the problem of identifying the standards or rules that state the shoulds and should nots of behavior have been of two kinds. One directs the sociologist to ask members of the social systems in question, or otherwise elicit statements from them regarding what persons of particular social statuses should or should not do, think, say, etc., in particular situations. The other solution maintains that the sociologist can infer such standards or rules from our observations of how those members behave.

As a solution to the methodological problem of identifying social norms, each poses further problems. On the one hand, the verbal statements of members may be what they say but not what they do. The statements may not even be "normative" in the sense that they urge that persons *ought* to behave as their statements specify, but simply represent what is said when people are asked about conduct in certain circumstances, an expression of an ideal that prescribes no sanctions when the norm is violated, set aside, or otherwise ignored.

Inferring social norms from observations of behavior, on the other hand, presents the problem of determining which of a range of alternative inferences one might make with regard to the norm governing the observed behavior. The rules of inference must be constructed to allow the abstraction of norms from the observations, but how are these rules to be derived?

It is clear that when deviant behavior is defined "by reference to norms" as Gibbs prefers, the procedures by which such a definition is to be applied in empirical research are neither obvious nor simple. Indeed, such definitions require a greater degree of detailed specification (what conduct is prescribed or proscribed, by whom, for whom, in what situations, qualified by what circumstances, assuming what degree of social and mental competence, etc.?) than sociologists have been able to meet. In this circumstance, the common practice is for the sociologist to gloss over the methodological problems by relying, *as a member of the system being studying,* on his or her own implicit and tacitly held understanding of social norms.

This "solution" for the problem of specifying social norms presents further difficulties related to the fact that sociologists, as a consequence of their social background, training, political ideology, and other characteristics, are not likely to be the most representative members of the system. The significance they give to social norms in their theories makes them particularly attentive to their determinate effects on human conduct. Indeed, sociologists may perceive norms where members see nothing at all.[3] This being so, it would not be unusual or surprising if the sociologist's definition and characterization of norms differ from, even conflict with, those of the members whose conduct is asserted to be governed by those norms.

The question may then be raised: In the event of a conflict between the definitions of sociologist and member, what is the theoretical significance of that conflict? How would such conflicts become apparent to the sociologist? If we follow Gibbs' proposal that deviant acts be identified by reference to norms independent of the reactions to those acts, sociologists may find that members ignore, dismiss, and even applaud acts that sociologists classify as unambiguously clear violations of the norm. How are such phenomena to be interpreted—are the members in question blind, ignorant, incompetent, unsocialized, alienated? Or is it that sociologists have misperceived the behavior they have observed, or misconstrued its meaning, or referred it to an inappropriate norm? The possibilities are too numerous to specify, and the critics of the labelling view provide no bases for either enumerating those possibilities or for choosing an answer from among them.

In contrast, the logic of the new conception would hold that in any conflict between the sociologist's definitions and those of members, the latters' definitions must prevail, however "misinformed," "erroneous," or "misguided" they may appear to be from the sociologist's standpoint. The alternative of invoking the sociologist's definitions as the standards for assessing normative behavior is to face the problem of accounting, on the one hand, for the failure of members to negatively sanction behavior that is "obviously deviant," and on the other for the imposition of such sanctions in the absence of "norm-violating" behavior. In such instances, to credit the sociologist with "knowing" things that members do not know, and to assign greater theoretical significance to that knowledge than to the members' presumed state of ignorance is to raise the question of whether it is the sociologist's knowledge and actions or those of the members that constitute the subject matter of the study.

Critics of the new conception, however, are not persuaded by this analysis of the norms definition of deviance since it leads to the assertion that what and whom members define as deviant are not necessarily grounded in any behavior or acts that are independently observable by sociologists. If this is so, the phenomenon to be explained by the sociology of deviance cannot be the origins or the etiology of "deviant behavior." And, of course, Lemert and Becker, as well as Erikson (1962), Kitsuse (1962), Goode (1969), and others have explicitly proposed a shift of focus from questions about the etiology of "deviant behavior" to the processes by which behaviors and persons come to be perceived, defined, and treated as deviant. If these processes are indeed the concerns of the new conception, the proper perspective from which to identify the subject matter for the sociology of deviance is that of the members, guided by the principle that it is the actions of those members that produce the populations differentiated as deviants within the system. The logic of this view would support the assertion that the behavior which presumably is the occasion for the reactions of others to them as deviant is, if not theoretically irrelevant, certainly of secondary importance.

That any evaluation should begin with an examination of the definition of the subject matter would seem elementary, but I think this book does not as a whole properly appreciate the logic and implications of the labelling definition of deviance. I do not mean that Becker's well-known definition has not been cited and discussed, but rather that the context in which it was developed is generally ignored and the theoretical thrust of his statement is diffused. His proposal to shift the focus of analysis from the behavior of the putative deviant to the reactions of others to him was made on methodological as well as theoretical grounds. Becker argued that, since the process of labelling deviants may not be infallible, students of deviance "cannot assume that these people have actually committed a deviant act or broken some rule." Conversely, it cannot be assumed that "the category of those labeled deviant will contain all those who actually have broken a rule, for many offenders may escape apprehension and thus fail to be included in the population of 'deviants' " (1963: 9). That is, the reactions of others may be "in error," making it logically impossible to compare "deviants" with "non-deviants" in an etiological analysis.

If persons classified by others as deviants are not homogeneous with reference to the acts that define the category, what do they have in common? Becker (1963: 10) responds:

> At the least, they share the label and the experience of being labeled as outsiders. I will begin my analysis with this basic similarity and view deviance as the product of a transaction that takes place between some social group and one who is viewed by that group as a rule-breaker.

The logic of these statements seems clear enough, but they are ambiguous with regard to the emphasis intended. On the one hand, when he states that students of deviance cannot assume that those who are labelled "have actually committed a deviant act or broken some rule," there is the implication that the assumption might be tested. *Are* some persons labelled deviant in the absence of such acts? Conversely, do some persons commit such acts without being labelled? It is this implication that forms the basis of the interpretation that labelling proponents assert there is no relation between deviant acts and the labelling of deviants. This interpretation is expressed in the evaluation of Proposition A by Gove, Hirschi, Smith, Robins, and others, and they conclude that the evidence does not support the proposition.

On the other hand, Becker's statements direct us to a line of investigation based on the conception of deviance as a transaction between members of a social group and "one who is viewed by that group as a rule-breaker." Here the condition that differentiates deviant from nondeviant is that *the deviant is viewed* as a rule-breaker. The defining criterion is not the act of the putative deviant but the conceptions of others about the deviant. Thus, the contention is not that agents of control act without regard to the behavior of the one labelled, but that in labelling, rule-breaking behavior is imputed by others to the deviant. The proposition might be stated as follows: In each and every case of a labelled deviant, an imputation of rule-breaking behavior is made. So stated, the evidence appropriate for the examination of the labelling process is not whether the deviant has been "rightfully" labelled (i.e., is the imputation valid?) but whether those who label deviants without exception charge them with deviant acts.[4]

This interpretation of Becker's statements, then, directs us to investigate the imputation process and how those imputations activate a system of social control such that putative deviants are progressively differentiated through social exclusion and isolation. If it can be shown that no charges are made against those labelled, that individuals are randomly set apart, arrested, incarcerated, and committed to various institutions without imputations of offensive acts, then the most distinctive proposition of the societal reaction formulation would be challenged.

In short, what is at issue is the process by which the imputation of deviance is constructed and applied by members of social groups and agencies. In phrasing the matter in this way, there is no implication that the imputations are without basis in the behavior of the putative deviant. Indeed, we might assume that in the general case the actions of such members are conditioned by the behavior of the putative deviant—it is, as Becker says, a product of a transaction between them. So, evidence that demonstrates, for example, that "the child labelled delinquent is much more likely to deserve the label than this theory suggests" (Hirschi) or "that doctors tend to deny or ignore symptoms of alcoholism" (Robins) or that "prospective patients had been disturbed for some time prior to hospitalization" (Gove) does not negate this proposition of the labelling formulation.

There are, in fact, a number of studies that have followed this interpretation of the labelling perspective, but they have not been discussed in this book. For example, studies of the negotiations between the district attorney and public defender in the construction of offenses (Sudnow, 1965), the organizational differentiation of deviant careers in a high school (Cicourel and Kitsuse, 1963), the production of witches in Europe and England (Currie, 1968), how cases are assembled in juvenile courts (Emerson, 1969), the construction of moral careers among inmates of homes for unmarried mothers (Rains, 1971), how the interpretive and imputational activities of coroners produce judgments of suicide (Wilkins, 1970), the disposition of drunk cases by judges in municipal courts (Wiseman, 1970). In these studies, what the variously defined deviants have or have not done to warrant the attention of control agencies is not the issue. The focus is rather on how organizational features of those agencies typify cases, specify their deviant character, and routinize the classification and treatment of them.

The second major issue examined in this volume–Proposition B, the so-called self-fulfilling hypothesis–is regarded by many as the distinctive hypothesis of the societal reaction formulation. In so characterizing this proposition, reference is usually made to the concept of "secondary deviation." In the various statements of this proposition, however, the process of secondary deviation is simplified to the point of seriously distorting Lemert's formulation. A close reading of his discussion of secondary deviation will show that it is much more complex than implied by the "self-fulfilling prophecy."

Lemert (1951: 23) proposed as a postulate of his theory that:

> The deviant is one whose role, status, function, and self-definition are importantly shaped by how much deviation he engages in, by the degree of its social visibility, by the *particular* exposure he has to the societal reaction, and by the nature and strength of the societal reaction.

In differentiating primary from secondary deviation, Lemert (1951: 75-76) states:

> The deviant individuals must react symbolically to their own behavior aberrations and fix them in their sociopsychological patterns. The deviations remain primary deviations or symptomatic and situational as long as they are rationalized or otherwise dealt with as functions of a socially acceptable role.

> When a person begins to employ his deviant behavior or a role based upon it as a means of defense, attack, or adjustment to the overt and covert problems created by the consequent societal reaction to him, his deviation is secondary.

I find it difficult to comprehend how these statements can be reduced to the "self-fulfilling prophecy." Lemert is not reiterating Tannenbaum's simple proposition that "the person becomes the thing he is described as being." An evaluation of Lemert's formulation of secondary deviation processes requires a methodology that provides access to more than evidence of post-labelling deviance or indices of recidivism. Indeed, he states:

> Objective evidences of this change will be found in the symbolic appurtenances of the new role, in clothes, speech, posture, and mannerism, which in some cases heighten social visibility, and which in some cases serve as symbolic cues to professionalization [Lemert, 1951: 76].

Secondary deviation, then, is conceived as the putative deviant's responses to the societal reaction, but its significance for Lemert is in the "sociopsychological patterns" that organize the process of "sociopathic individuation." Thus, the appropriate formulation of the secondary deviation hypothesis is a proposition that investigates the contingent conditions specified in the postulate quoted above: the degree of the individual's deviation, its social visibility, the specific exposure to societal reactions with regard to kind and intensity. If this is so, clearly the evidence cited by Hirschi, Gove, Tittle, and Robins as bases for rejecting the "self-fulfilling prophecy" cannot be considered germane to an evaluation of the secondary deviation proposition.

In summary, my view of the matter is that the task of evaluating the societal reaction perspective is misconceived in the papers presented here. They are based on a narrow focus on some admittedly ambiguous passages in the writings of the major proponents of the perspective. The two propositions that organize the evaluative efforts ignore the central thrust of the new conception of deviance, forcing it into the mold of old conceptions.

The distinctive character of the societal reaction perspective is not that it presents a theory of deviant behavior in opposition to the "norms-based" theory, nor a theory of deviant behavior systems. Its distinctiveness leads away from these social-psychological issues to a consideration of how deviants come to be differentiated by imputations made about them by others, how these imputations activate systems of social control, and how those control activities become legitimated as institutional responses to deviance.

NOTES

1. In making this statement, I do not mean to discount Lemert's intent nor to detract from the substantial achievement represented by *Social Pathology.* Indeed, in my judgment, the specifically theoretical aspects of his work have not been fully appreciated by those who comment on his work at this conference and more generally in the literature on deviance.

2. In a revised and expanded version of his earlier paper published under the title "Issues in Defining Deviant Behavior" (in *Theoretical Perspectives on Deviance,* R. Scott and J. Douglas, eds., New York: Basic Books, 1972), Gibbs states (p. 56): "The critique of Becker, et al., and legal realism is obviously partisan, and it is admitted that the rejection of the reactive definition of deviation does not solve the problems associated with a normative definition. On the contrary, the problems are so vast that the proposed solution is to abandon the concept of norm and law." The reader is referred to Gibbs' interesting elaboration of this statement.

3. Lemert conceives of norms as refering to "limits of variation in behavior explicitly or implicitly held and recognized *in retrospect* by members of a group, community or society" (italics added). He goes on to note that "few people, unless they are professional social scientists, are conscious of the standards of behavior in their culture" (1951: 31).

4. Jack Katz (1972) goes further to propose that the concept of deviance should be distinguished from rule-breaking behavior. He conceives of the former as an imputation of ontological status, and, as such, he asserts that all deviance is "false accusation."

REFERENCES

Becker, Howard S.
1963 Outsiders: Studies in the Sociology of Deviance. New York: Free Press.

Blake, Judith and Kingsley Davis
1964 "Norms, values, and sanctions." Pp. 456-484 in R.E.L. Faris (ed.) Handbook of Sociology. Chicago: Rand McNally.

Cicourel, Aaron V. and John I. Kitsuse
1963 The Educational Decision-makers. Indianapolis: Bobbs-Merrill.

Currie, Elliott P.
1968 "Crimes without criminals: witchcraft and its control in Renaissance Europe." Law and Society Review 3: 7-32.

Emerson, Robert M.
1969 Judging Delinquents: Context and Process in Juvenile Court. Chicago: Aldine.

Erikson, Kai T.
1962 "Notes on the sociology of deviance." Social Problems 9: 307-314.

Gibbs, Jack
1966 "Conceptions of deviant behavior: the old and the new." Pacific Sociological Review 9: 9-14.
1972 "Issues in defining deviant behavior." In R. Scott and J. Douglas (eds.) Theoretical Perspectives on Deviance. New York: Basic Books.

Goode, Erich
1969 "Marihuana and the politics of reality." Journal of Health and Social Behavior 10.

Katz, Jack
1973 "Deviance, charisma, and rule-defined behavior." Social Problems 20: 186-202.
Kitsuse, John I.
1962 "Societal reaction to deviant behavior: problems of theory and method." Social Problems 9: 247-256.
--- and Malcolm Spector
1975 "Deviance and social problems: some parallel issues." Social Problems 23 (Fall): forthcoming.
Lemert, Edwin M.
1951 Social Pathology. New York: McGraw-Hill.
1972 Human Deviance, Social Problems, and Social Control. Englewood Cliffs, N.J.: Prentice-Hall.
1974 "Beyond Mead: the societal reaction to deviance." Social Problems 21: 457-468.
Merton, Robert K. and Robert Nisbet, eds.
1971 Contemporary Social Problems. New York: Harcourt, Brace & World.
Rains, Prudence M.
1971 Becoming an Unwed Mother. Chicago: Aldine.
Sudnow, David
1965 "Normal crimes: sociological features of the penal code." Social Problems 12: 255-276.
Wilkins, James L.
1970 "Producing suicide." American Behavioral Scientist 14: 185-201.
Wiseman, Jacqueline P.
1970 Stations of the Lost: The Treatment of Skid Row Alcoholics. Englewood Cliffs, N.J.: Prentice-Hall.

Chapter 11

COMMENTS

EDWIN M. SCHUR

At this stage in the proceedings, it seems unlikely that there are many relevant points which have not already been raised, one way or another.

I am not going to try here to spell out systematically all aspects of the way in which I would formulate a societal reaction perspective; those interested in further details of such formulation can consult my statements on this matter elsewhere (Schur, 1969, 1971, 1974). But I think it will be clear from my comments that my approach diverges substantially from that of some of the quantitatively oriented critics, and that it has at least some major themes in common with that adopted by Professor Kitsuse, in the previous chapter. What I would like to do now (and in this I believe my aim really is quite similar to Kitsuse's) is simply suggest some major dimensions of a broadly conceived reactions perspective that I feel the critics of "labelling" tend to neglect, and to use several statements made in a number of the conference papers as points of departure for that purpose.

Central to my reaction to some of the papers is the question of just how far the quantitative "checking out" procedure (as Kitsuse nicely labelled it) can take us in evaluating the pertinence of a societal reactions orientation. I too feel that such tests are largely unobjectionable (and, indeed, often quite valuable)–for certain (I would insist, limited) purposes. However, I do not believe that they do justice to the various dimensions and levels of societal reaction (Schur, 1971), and hence while they may indeed fill in some major gaps in our knowledge *about* certain aspects of societal reaction, at the same time they may unnecessarily have an inhibiting effect on your appreciation of the overall value of the central idea underlying this approach. In that sense–and not in terms merely of relative contribution (viewed quantitatively) to our understanding of the causation of individual deviating behavior—it will be apparent that what Professor Tittle calls the "stringent and more interesting form of the labelling proposition" I believe might better be termed an "unnecessarily narrow and somewhat less interesting form," and a version that in some ways approximates what he terms the "weak and essentially non-novel form" may in fact better be described as a "more general, or more basic form," one that is highly useful in its capacity to orient or re-orient analysis.

Now, this book contains an impressive array of evidence bearing on *some* of the propositions that might be adduced from a societal reaction perspective. Of course, various questions might be raised (and some already have been here) regarding the adequacy and meaning of some of these data. The authors themselves recognize that much of the evidence is weak or inconclusive. I would in addition like to stress the problematic element of meaning in these data, and in that connection it is perhaps worth reiterating the perplexing fact that often the very same findings cited by critics in support of arguments against a labelling analysis are taken by proponents of such an analysis to support rather than undermine their own position. Quite clearly, we find in such a situation very different conceptions of just what a reactions approach asserts or implies. Notwithstanding such considerations, however, it seems to me that at the very least the kinds of evidence that have been summarized here should impel a new cautiousness about making glib and extreme assertions concerning the labelling process (Professor Hirschi cited some examples of these more dogmatic kinds of assertions in his paper). In particular, we should be wary of statements implying inevitability, or exclusivity, or irreversibility, in labelling processes. (I would like to note, however, that the issue of irreversibility seems to me primarily to have been manufactured by the critics, who find it not difficult to refute such alleged claims; to my knowledge, few if any analysts working out of the reactions orientation have ever asserted that labelling effects are irreversible.) What I believe the kinds of findings presented here underscore is the desirability of thinking in terms of *variability of labelling processes*—a point to which I shall return shortly.

At the same time it might be pointed out that, somewhat paradoxically, these findings could be seen as indirectly supporting one of the major claims I would advance for the reactions perspective—namely, that it has served to redirect attention toward previously neglected aspects of deviance. Those very researches that may have been undertaken with an explicit interest in challenging or even in undermining the approach might never have been conducted at all but for the influence of the labelling argument. Indeed, what we have going on here may ultimately be seen as a good example of the process to which Professor Tittle refers, by which "sensitizing concepts become parts of genuine theories that serve the ends of science." Although I believe (as my remarks will continue to make clear) that for this to happen in any really meaningful way it will probably be necessary as well for the two "sides" in this debate to recognize that at least in some significant measure they are talking about *different aspects* of deviance situations (all of which deserve sociological attention), that they are quite simply addressing *different questions* germane to an understanding of deviance phenomena.

We are still left with the issue of what bearing, if any, such findings have on the overall usefulness of a societal reaction perspective. I would argue that while they seem to imply the need for qualification of the approach—or, I believe it would be more accurate to say, specification of it—any claim that the orientation should be rejected out of hand would be quite unwarranted. Furthermore, it may be precisely a feeling that somehow the approach must *either* be fully accepted *or* rejected which causes some critics to overlook its most valuable features. I myself believe quite strongly (and I have built this point rather crucially into this chapter—which is framed in just these terms) that, in fact, and notwithstanding disclaimers, this kind of all-or-nothing insistence has permeated much of the anti-labelling argument.

The either-or tendency in criticism of the societal reactions analysis is closely tied to an insistence that it satisfy the requirements of formal theory, and that it be submitted to quantitative validation procedures. Thus, Professor Tittle calls for specific testable hypotheses, and Professor Gibbs (writing elsewhere) has charged the approach with not having "empirical applicability" (Gibbs, 1972). Professor Gove, in Chapter 1, states, "If a perspective which presumes to explain a particular phenomenon cannot be operationalized and tested, then that perspective does not provide a sociologically valid explanation of that phenomenon."

In such calls for empirical testing, however, it is usually assumed that we are all agreed as to just what phenomenon we are seeking to explain. But the critics' focus rests almost entirely on the deviating individual's behavior. They require, in effect, that the reactions orientation should prove its worth *as a theory of deviance causation in the traditional sense.* Yet this is not at all its aim, which is instead to focus on the processes through which social *meanings* come to be attached to types of behavior (and to individuals), and the consequences of such attachment. The central focus, then, is on *characterizations of behavior* rather than on behavior itself.

Furthermore, since such characterizations of behavior occur at various levels of social interaction and organization, and have diverse kinds of ramifications, the unit of analysis cannot be simply (or always) the behavior of the individual deviator (which the critics, one must note, continue to concentrate on in much the same way as traditional deviance sociology always has done). I would suggest that we ought to be concerned much more fully with the impact of social definition and reaction (at various levels) in shaping *deviance situations,* some aspects of which I shall comment on in a moment. Admittedly, it is extremely difficult for purposes of empirical analysis to delineate the parameters of such an entity as a "deviance situation," but I feel we must adopt some broad conceptualization of this sort if we are to appreciate fully the potential contribution of a reactions outlook.

If we are to think in terms of the attachment of meanings, the process I have elsewhere called "deviantizing" (Schur 1974), and have as our focus "deviance situations" broadly conceived, then there is no question but that operationalizing and quantifying become extremely difficult. Yet, in a way, it has been the persisting focus on the individual, to which I've already referred, that has propelled this demand for quantitative testing of the labelling idea. (Certainly some labelling analysts themselves have contributed to this critical reaction by concentrating in their own work on analysis at the level of individuals.) At times, the critical effort at quantification seems to incorporate a premise or implication that I believe to be especially unwarranted—that a reactions perspective and alternative approaches must be viewed as mutally exclusive. Notwithstanding assertions by Professor Gove and others that they want to do no more than determine the relative strength of diverse "explanations," one has the strong impression that if their preferred lines of analysis appear to explain "more of the variance" (i.e., variance in the individual behavior *they* consider to pose the central explanatory issue), then they will not be prepared to view the reactions conception as having much if any real value in the sociology of deviance. Professor Gordon, after all, applied some rather harshly stigmatizing labels in describing the reactions orientation—referring to its "forms of pathology," to its "negativistic heuristic value," and asserting that it may be "destructive of the appraisal process."

If, as I believe to be the case, societal reaction (or, as I would also put it, social definition) is viewed most properly as neither more nor less than an absolutely basic social process, and therefore a central orienting concept in sociological analysis (presumably this formulation is an example of what Tittle would call the "non-novel" version of a labelling approach), then it seems questionable whether its illuminating value can be adequately depicted through the results of these quantitative procedures. And if this basic process is a complex multilevel phenomenon, then it seems particularly unlikely that we can adequately "measure" it by concerning ourselves only with the determinants of variance at the individual behavior level. By insisting that "labelling" be treated only as an explanatory or causal variable, critics can more easily discredit it, but I would suggest that they do so at the peril of casting aside its broader value as an orienting (or, if you will, sensitizing) perspective.

Related to the either-or spirit that pervades much of the criticism of societal reaction analysis is a failure to consider adequately a number of different kinds of variability in labelling processes. For example, while there have been efforts to take account of the standard "disadvantage variables" (such as socioeconomic status, race, age, etc.), these do not necessarily exhaust the possibly relevant factors affecting outcomes in particular types of labelling situations. They are indeed usually important ones, and they are perhaps the ones most amenable to incorporation in quantitative comparisons, but their salience may well vary when we analyze reaction situations involving diverse forms of deviation. With respect to some forms of behavior, other (less easily measured) characteristics or qualities may become more salient in influencing (and for our understanding of) labelling outcomes.

Another kind of variability is suggested by Hirschi's interesting comment that "since 'treatment' does not work . . . differential 'labelling' also and by definition has no effect." Intriguing as this argument is, the failure of this particular type of (intentional, positive) "labelling" hardly carries the more general implication that juveniles cannot be labelled at all. Indeed, these data could well be taken as support for the labelling analysts' argument that it is much easier (given current institutions and beliefs) to stigmatize than to destigmatize. Although Hirschi intimates that such juveniles may not usually be placed in so-called treatment as a consequence of "stigmatization," but more as a direct result of their own behavior, we would have to trace their careers quite a way back and in real depth–to consider perhaps initial "tagging" as a troublemaker in school, etc.–before concluding that negative reactions had not had an impact on them.

Also noteworthy in connection with the matter of variability is the assertion by Professors Sagarin and Kelly that homosexuality is "something that people *do* rather than what they *are*." (Incidentally, I find myself puzzled by their related argument that the labelling analyst needs to recognize an obligation to emphasize this point, because it seems to me that is precisely part of the thrust of a labelling interpretation. By stressing the processes of stereotyping and retrospective interpretation, by showing how deviant identity can take on a master status quality, a societal reactions approach is helping to highlight the way in which "that is what I do" often is [unwarrantedly] transformed into "that is what I am.") When the same authors go on to assert that "the deviant is imprisoned in the role to the extent that he or she accepts the definition of self by others and by him- or herself," they seem to gloss over important elements of variability. While consideration of the role of so-called "self-labelling" has contributed to a specification of the variety of factors involved in asserting or accepting any particular set of conceptions of self, it would be a mistake to consider such outcomes as reflecting nothing more than what the individuals in question "will" for themselves. Sagarin and Kelly do refer, in connection with transsexualism, to the significance of validation of identity (which process in turn requires consideration of the salience of resources of various kinds–psychological as well as social) but do not seem to find this pertinent in the case of homosexuality.

In this connection, I would emphasize that what a reactions perspective (according to my broad interpretation) implies about the possession of high (salient) resources is the following: (1) enhanced ability to avoid *unwanted* labels; (2) enhanced ability to *obtain wanted* labels (for example, recognition as a "healthy homosexual"; or *voluntary* admission to a mental hospital); and (3) enhanced ability to impose labels on others. (Of course, as the critics of this interpretation would be quick to note, if one begins to talk about obtaining "wanted" labels, then some question may arise about the appropriateness at the same time of considering those labels "deviant.") At any rate, I would emphasize that these processes are not either-or ones. (To believe that they are requires in effect that we assert simplistically clear-cut and unchanging distinctions between "deviant" and "nondeviant" categories, with respect to individuals or behaviors or both.) Susceptibility or resistance to negative reaction, and the outcomes of such labeling attempts, are not usually either totally nil or absolute. They vary greatly in degree and will be manifested in combination with a variety of other personal and situational elements.

If the will of the potential "deviant" can be exaggerated, so too can the aims of the control agents. Thus, Gove in his overview has suggested, "It would appear important to determine whether a particular reaction was inclusionary or exclusionary in intent." I am, again, somewhat perplexed by this assertion, because it seems to me one of the major values of the reactions perspective has been to contribute to a cutting-through of euphemism, in which we increasingly distinguish between the professed goals and actual consequences of reaction policies and procedures and increasingly recognize the crucial significance of the latter.

I would like now to turn to a matter I consider especially important, and which was just alluded to briefly in the discussion yesterday. One of the most significant reasons why the methodological critics–with their characteristic focus on individual behavior–fail to appreciate the broader value of a reactions perspective is that they see it as being concerned simply with the *application* of ("given" and presumably nonproblematic) "rules"; little attention is paid to the contribution the perspective makes by directing analysis to the question of how these rules emerge in the first place. Now, in one sense, a major implication of the reactions orientation is that we cannot always or easily distinguish between rule-creation and rule-application. When we examine social reaction processes in the context of situations of direct personal interaction, we have to recognize that in a way what is happening here is not just the application of pre-existing rules; at least in some degree the "rules" emerge out of that interaction itself. Likewise, labelling-oriented analysis is highlighting the fact that even with respect to more formal or highly institutionalized rules, our understanding of what the rule "consists of" cannot very meaningfully be developed without considering the ways in which the rule is used.

At the same time, there is a case for arguing that at least potentially (because, in fact, labelling analysts have not themselves developed the point much) a reactions perspective is centrally concerned with *rule-creation,* at various levels. After all, the frequently quoted statement by Becker, often presented as the epitome of the approach, begins, "social groups create deviance by making the rules." This dimension is particularly germane to analysis in the areas under consideration in this book–because in each of these, I would submit, the legal definitions of the behaviors in question represent a major factor shaping what I have called "the deviance situation." Yet the critics treat societal reaction as though it were nothing more than the "classification of persons" (to adopt a phrase of Tittle's). There is very little, if any, reference to the (in this case highly institutionalized) rules–the very existence of which in a sense constitutes a necessary condition of their "violation." Partly this may reflect the preoccupation with behavior or acts, because the critic probably is impressed that the behavior itself often will not disappear simply through a change in such rules. To eliminate the law defining larceny will not bring stealing to a halt, or so the argument goes (although note that Hirschi is prepared to admit that "toughness" is not really the same thing as "delinquency").

Yet beyond the possibility that such rules may directly affect self-conceptions and behavior, there is the important point that the indirect or snowballing ramifications of these rules for various aspects of deviance situations may be considerable. It is for this reason that I have suggested elsewhere (Schur, 1971, 1974) expanding the notion of secondary deviation somewhat beyond the meaning Lemert originally intended–so as to refer not only to deviance amplification at the level of individual social psychology, but also to various "secondary" aspects of overall deviance situations. Thus, to return to a point I made earlier–even if one were to employ "causal" or "explanatory" terminology, once one is interested in explaining, say, the current drug addiction *situation* rather than simply why individuals become addicted, then the rules simply cannot be ignored in framing such an "explanation."

As an example of the tendency to pass over this element, let me quote a passage from a recently published article by Professors McAuliffe and Gordon. In that article, they present fascinating evidence that clearly raises some question about at least parts of Lindesmith's theory of addiction causation.

However, they go on to write: "Addict criminality does not result primarily from a desperate need to relieve withdrawal symptoms, as a popular conception would have it, but rather from the desire for euphoria" (McAuliffe and Gordon, 1974: 820). Now what seems to be missing here is reference to the impact of criminalization on the growth of the illicit traffic—which some analysts attempt to play down, but which most consider to be very substantial indeed. It is neither the desire for euphoria nor the wish to avoid withdrawal that produces addict crime, but rather addiction (for either or both of these "reasons") *in combination with* the need to purchase large quantities of illegal drugs.

McAuliffe referred today to the Winick study of addicted physicians, although not on the issue of addict crime. The doctor-addict presumably is addicted for similar "reasons" (whichever they may be); the low criminality surely has something to do with a doctor's special resources for coping with the economic consequences of a drug habit's illegality. In all fairness, I should add that some of the interesting data McAuliffe's chapter contains could be interpreted as bearing on the emergence of "rules" out of direct interaction situations (his findings concerning knowledge of the addiction and reactions to it exhibited by various persons in the addict's immediate environment seem to suggest this line of analysis), but neglect of the broader context of formal illegality in the addiction situation would be a serious mistake.

It is similary interesting, given the major public controversy over anti-homosexuality laws, that Sagarin and Kelly make virtually no explicit reference to the impact of such laws when they consider whether a reactions perspective is useful or relevant in this area. Yet even such critics of labelling approach to homosexuality as Warren and Johnson (Warren and Johnson, 1972) have recognized that at the very least the homosexual's situation is colored by what they term "symbolic labelling" (at least in part as a consequence of knowledge that the behavior is in violation of the law).

Of course, it can be argued that we all know about the existence of these laws, and that therefore we should consider them as a "given" and get on with the (allegedly) more serious business of analyzing the other factors in the situation. This appears to me to be Professor Tittle's position, and I believe Professor Hirschi's as well. It's a position that I consider short-sighted. Hirschi makes interesting reference (I would assume not just facetiously) to the labelling approach's "insight" that "if the world did not exist as it does, the so-called causes of delinquency would not operate as they do." Formal rules constitute an important aspect of this "world as it does exist." Yet traditional sociologists of deviance did not just take such rules "for granted"; what they really did was ignore them altogether. And by treating such rules as "a given," they promoted inattention to the possible implications of rule-change. Here again, it is the reactions perspective (broadly conceived) that can direct our analysis to rule-creation and rule-change processes, as well as to the various ramifications of the existence and use of particular rules. In this connection, I believe we can look forward to a considerable development of what Mankoff has called "macro-labelling analysis" (Mankoff, 1971), even if recent proponents of the labelling approach have themselves tended to neglect such possibilities. The recent article by Lemert, entitled "Beyond Mead," (Lemert, 1974) points up some of the potential for such work, still under the general guidance of a reactions orientation.

By way of conclusion, let me refer to the statement by Professor Tittle, that the basic proposition of labelling analysis runs the risk of being "incontrovertible and thereby unscientific." I believe there is good reason to feel, on the contrary—and notwithstanding the basic scientific injunction of openness to refutation—that the central idea of the societal reaction perspective *is* incontrovertible, in the sense of being so well-established and so central to the sociological enterprise as to be (insofar as we can ever say it) undeniable, that is, true. *Specification* of the varieties of labelling processes, and the conditions under which various effects of labelling occur can only be applauded. But in attempting such specification, we should always keep in mind that a genuine reactions analysis must inevitably and centrally be concerned with social *definition* (at various levels) and not merely with specific control efforts taken *on the basis of those definitions.*

REFERENCES

Gibbs, Jack P.
1972 "Issues in defining deviant behavior." In Robert A. Scott and Jack D. Douglas (eds.) Theoretical Perspectives on Deviance. New York: Basic Books.

Lemert, Edwin M.
1974 "Beyond Mead: the societal reaction to deviance." Social Problems 21 (April): 457-468.

Mankoff, Milton
1971 "Societal reaction and career deviance: a critical analysis," Sociological Quarterly 12 (Spring): 204-218.

McAuliffe, William E. and Robert A. Gordon
1974 "A test of Lindesmith's theory of addiction: the frequency of euphoria among long-term addicts." American Journal of Sociology 79 (January): 795-840.

Schur, Edwin M.
1969 "Reactions to deviance: a critical assessment." American Journal of Sociology 75 (November): 309-322.

1971 Labeling Deviant Behavior: Its Sociological Implications. New York: Harper & Row.

1974 "The concept of secondary deviation: its theoretical significance and empirical elusiveness." Unpublished manuscript.

Warren, Carol A.B. and John M. Johnson

1972 "A critique of labeling theory from the phenomenological perspective." In Robert A. Scott and Jack D. Douglas (eds.) Theoretical Perspectives on Deviance. New York: Basic Books.

SUMMATION

WALTER R. GOVE

The substantive papers of this book have been primarily concerned with two questions. First, why is someone labelled a deviant? Second, what are the consequences for the individual of being labelled a deviant? In its stronger and more interesting form, it is the position of the labelling perspective that it is a person's marginal societal characteristics that play the prime role in being labelled a deviant and that being labelled a deviant is the major cause of the development of the deviant identities and life styles.

The substantive chapters in this book unanimously deny this formulation. The evidence reviewed consistently indicates that it is the behavior or condition of the person that is the critical factor in causing someone to be labelled a deviant. This is not to deny that the societal characteristics of the individual do not play a role; however, the limited role such characteristics play is often not the one posited by the labelling theorists. For example, with physical disability and mental illness, social resources appear to facilitate entrance into an official deviant status. Furthermore, the evidence reviewed consistently indicates that labelling is not the major cause of the development of stabilized deviant behavior. In fact, labelling often appears to have the opposite effect. For example, with mental illness and physical disability, labelling often appears to lead to effective treatment, while with crime and drug addiction labelling appears to have a deterrent effect. In the cases where labelling leads to effective treatment, or where it has a strong deterrent effect, labelling appears to minimize the degree of deviance.

These conclusions are consistently supported and would appear to require very drastic modifications of the labelling perspective. However, although the cumulative evidence is ample for a strong case against these propositions of the labelling perspective, the issue cannot be viewed as settled, for, as noted by the authors, in a number of areas of deviance the data are simply not good enough to permit a definitive conclusion.

As might be expected, in their comments, the two proponents of the labelling perspective, Kitsuse and Schur, are of the opinion that the book does not come to grips with the major contribution of the labelling perspective. They do not, however, attempt to deny the evidence reviewed, nor do they argue that contrary evidence has been overlooked. Instead, they argue that the two propositions that were focused on are not crucial to the labelling perspective. They indicate that the main contribution of the perspective has been to draw attention away from etiological issues and onto the social process involved in deviant identities and careers. Although I (and I think the other presenters) believe that Kitsuse and Schur are wrong in their denial of the critical nature of the propositions investigated, one can hardly disagree with what they advocate.

In all social interaction, symbols, norms, roles, identities, and status are important features of the interaction and are worthy of investigation. Because of the area's intrinsic interest and substantive importance, the investigation of social interaction is perhaps particularly warranted in the area of deviant behavior. As future researchers investigate this area, I hope they will be cognizant of the fact that the available evidence indicates that deviant labels are primarily a consequence of deviant behavior and that deviant labels are not the prime cause of deviant careers.

THE AUTHORS

ROBERT A. GORDON is Associate Professor of Social Relations at Johns Hopkins University. He received his Ph.D. from the University of Chicago in 1963. His major research interests are in the social psychology of deviant behavior, values, small group interaction, opiate addiction, sociology of intelligence, causes of crime and delinquency, sex identity, and socialization. He is the author of numerous articles and book reviews for professional journals.

WALTER R. GOVE is Professor in the Department of Sociology and Anthropology at Vanderbilt University. He received his Ph.D. in 1968 from the University of Washington, Seattle. His Present and future research activities are in the fields of density; sex, marital roles and mental health; labelling theory; statistics and methodology; crime and deterrence; race; and mental illness. He has authored or coauthored many articles in professional journals, has served as an Advisory Editor for *Social Forces,* and is now a Consulting Editor for the *American Journal of Sociology* and an Associate Editor for *Social Science Research.*

TRAVIS HIRSCHI received his Ph.D. in 1968 from the University of California (Berkeley). He is presently Robert A. Pinkerton Visiting Professor at the School of Criminal Justice at the State University of New York at Albany, on leave from the University of California (Davis). He is the author of *Causes of Delinquency* (1969, University of California Press), and coauthor with Hanan Selvin of Delinquency Research: An Appraisal of Analytic Methods (1967, Free Press).

ROBERT J. KELLY is presently a lecturer in the Department of Sociology and an academic counselor in the Department of Educational Services at Brooklyn College of the City University of New York, where he is presently a doctoral candidate. He has published articles in the areas of race relations, revolutionary and nationalist movements, social change, homosexual activities in prisons, and the sociology of knowledge.

JOHN I. KITSUSE is Professor of Sociology at the University of California, Santa Cruz. He received his Ph.D. in 1958 from the University of California (Los Angeles). He has published an abundance of articles in journals and edited the "people-Processing Institutions" special issue of the *American Behavioral Scientist* (1970). His books indude *Education in Urban Society* (with Lindley J. Stiles and B. J. Chandler; 1962, Dodd Mead) and *The Educational Decision Makers* (with Aaron V. Cicourel; 1963, Bobbs-Merrill).

WILLIAM E. McAULIFFE is Assistant Professor in the Department of City and Regional Planning and Department of Sociology, Harvard University. He received his Ph.D. in 1973 from Johns Hopkins University. His areas of professional interest include narcotics addiction, deviance, methodology and statistics, social psychology, social planning, and enviromental sociology. He is also a consultant with Contract Research Co. of Belmont, Massachusetts, working on the design and implementation of a survey of information needs of labor relations negotiators.

LEE N. ROBINS is presently affiliated with the Department of Psychiatry of the Washington University School of Medicine in St. Louis, Missouri. She received her Ph.D. in 1951 from Radcliffe College. Her article publications have been too numerous to detail. She is the author of *Deviant Children Grow Up: A Sociological and Psychiatric Study of Sociopathic Personality* (1966, Williams & Wilkins) and coeditor with M. Roff and M. Pollack of *Life History Research in Psychopathology,* Volume 2.

EDWARD SAGARIN received his Ph.D. in 1966 from New York University, and is presently Professor of Sociology at the City College of New York. He is the author of *Odd Man In: Societies of Deviants in America* and of *Deviants and Deviance: An Introduction to the Study of Disvalued People and Behavior.* He is a member of the Board of Editors of *Salmagundi,* an Associate Editor of the *Journal of Sex Research,* and a Consulting Editor for Criminology of the *Journal of Criminal Law and Criminology.*

EDWIN M. SCHUR is Professor and Chairman of the Department of Sociology at New York University. He received his Ph.D. in 1959 from the London School of Economics, after having earned an LL.B. from Yale Law School in 1955 and having been admitted to the Bar in Connecticut. His books include *Victimless Crimes: Two Sides of a Controversy* (with Hugo Bedau; 1974, Prentice-Hall), *Radical Nonintervention: Rethinking the Delinquency Problem* (1973, Prentice-Hall), *Labelling Deviant Behavior: Its Sociological Implications* (1971, Harper & Row), and many others.

RICHARD T. SMITH is Professor in the Department of Sociology at the University of Maryland, Baltimore, and Director of the Survey Research Unit of the Johns Hopkins Population Center. He is also Associate Professor in the Department of Social Relations at Johns Hopkins. He received his Ph.D. in 1960 from the University of Wisconsin. He has published numerous articles, and is currently working on a book entitled *Social Support Networks in Disability and Rehabilitation.*

CHARLES R. TITTLE is presently Professor of Sociology at Florida Atlantic University. He received his Ph.D. in 1965 at the University of Texas. He is the author of *Society of Subordinates: Inmate Organization in a Narcotic Hospital,* and has contributed many articles to professional journals. His current research is in the areas of sanctions and rule-breaking; arrest, crime and deterrence; and the empirical evaluation of labelling and crime.

SUBJECT INDEX*

*Compiled by Lisa Heinrich

AUTHOR INDEX*

*Compiled by Lisa Heinrich